First World War
and Army of Occupation
War Diary
France, Belgium and Germany

3 CAVALRY DIVISION
Divisional Troops
Royal Army Service Corps
Divisional Supply Column (73 Company A.S.C.)
3 October 1914 - 31 March 1919

WO95/1150/2

The Naval & Military Press Ltd
www.nmarchive.com
Published in association with The National Archives

Published by

The Naval & Military Press Ltd

Unit 10 Ridgewood Industrial Park,

Uckfield, East Sussex,

TN22 5QE England

Tel: +44 (0) 1825 749494

www.naval-military-press.com

www.nmarchive.com

This diary has been reprinted in facsimile from the original. Any imperfections are inevitably reproduced and the quality may fall short of modern type and cartographic standards.

© Crown Copyright
Images reproduced by permission of The National Archives, London, England, 2015.

Contents

Document type	Place/Title	Date From	Date To
Heading	WO95/1150/2		
Heading	3rd Cavalry Supply Column Oct 1914-Jun 1919		
Miscellaneous	Historical Record Of No 3 Cavalry Supply Column 73 (M.T.) Company		
Miscellaneous	Historical Record Of No 3 Cavalry Supply Column 73 (M.T.) Coy. A. S. C.		
Miscellaneous	Appendix "A"		
Miscellaneous	Appendix "B"		
Miscellaneous	Appendix "C" No 3 Cavalry Supply Column Casualties		
Miscellaneous	A.S.C. 2312	26/07/1917	26/07/1917
Miscellaneous	Historical Records.	03/06/1917	03/06/1917
Miscellaneous	Historical Record Of 3rd Cavalry Supply Column From Oct.-Dec. 1914	27/04/1917	27/04/1917
Miscellaneous	Special Order Of The Day By Major-General The Hon. J.H.G. Byng C.B. M.V.O. Commanding 3rd Cavalry Division.	23/11/1914	23/11/1914
War Diary	Woolwich	03/10/1914	04/10/1914
War Diary	Newbury.	05/10/1914	05/10/1914
War Diary	Avonmouth	05/10/1914	06/10/1914
War Diary	S.S Bord Tredegar.	07/10/1914	09/10/1914
War Diary	Ostend	09/10/1914	13/10/1914
War Diary	Roulers	13/10/1914	14/10/1914
War Diary	Dunkirk.	14/10/1914	16/10/1914
War Diary	Arneke	16/10/1914	18/10/1914
War Diary	Chestre	18/10/1914	19/10/1914
War Diary	Bailleul	20/10/1914	20/10/1914
War Diary	Chestre	24/10/1914	24/10/1914
War Diary	Zilliebeke	24/10/1914	24/10/1914
War Diary	Chestre	25/10/1914	25/10/1914
War Diary	Bailleul	20/10/1914	22/10/1914
War Diary	Poperinghe	22/10/1914	22/10/1914
War Diary	Ouderdom	22/10/1914	23/10/1914
War Diary	Chestre	23/10/1914	30/10/1914
War Diary	St Sylvestre	30/10/1914	06/11/1914
War Diary	Moorbecque	06/10/1914	06/10/1914
War Diary	Locre	07/11/1914	07/11/1914
War Diary	Moorbecque	07/11/1914	31/12/1914
Miscellaneous	Time & Mileage Record Appendix I		
Miscellaneous	Time & Mileage Record Appendix II		
Miscellaneous	Time & Mileage Record Appendix III		
Heading	War Diary Of O.C. 3rd Cavalry Supply Column From 1st January 1915 To 31st January 1915 Volume II		
War Diary	Moorbecque	01/01/1915	31/01/1915
Miscellaneous	Time & Mileage Record Appendix IV		
Heading	War Diary Of O.C. 3rd Cavalry Supply Column. From 1st February 1915 To 28th February 1915 Volume III		
War Diary	Moorbecque	01/02/1915	28/02/1915
Miscellaneous	3rd. Cav. Div. Sup. Col. Appendix V		
Heading	War Diary Of O.C. 3rd Cavalry Supply Column From 1st March 1915 To 31st March 1915 Volume IV		

War Diary	Moorbecque	01/03/1915	31/03/1915
Miscellaneous	3rd. Cav. Div. Sup. Col. Appendix VI		
Heading	War Diary Of O.C. 3rd Cavalry Supply Column From 1st April 1915 To 30th April 1915 Volume V		
War Diary	Moorbecque	01/04/1915	30/04/1915
Miscellaneous	Loading By Brigades Appendix VII	31/03/1915	31/03/1915
Miscellaneous	Loading By Units.		
Miscellaneous	War Establishments		
Miscellaneous	Appendix VII 3rd Cavalry Supply Column		
Heading	War Diary Of O.C. 3rd Cavalry Supply Column. From 1st May 1915 To 31st May 1915 Vol VI		
War Diary	Moorbecque	01/05/1915	31/05/1915
Miscellaneous	Appendix IX 3rd Cavalry Supply Column		
Heading	War Diary Of O.C. 3rd Cavalry Supply Column. From 1st June 1915 To 30th June 1915 Volume VII		
War Diary	Moorbecque	01/06/1915	30/06/1915
Miscellaneous	Appendix X 3rd Cavalry Supply Column.		
Miscellaneous			
Miscellaneous	To O i/c A.S.C. Records Woolwich	13/12/1917	13/12/1917
War Diary	Moorbecque	04/07/1915	31/07/1915
Miscellaneous	Appendix XI 3rd Cav Supply Column.		
Heading	War Diary Of O.C. 3rd Cavalry Supply Column. From 1st July 1915 To 31st July 1915 Volume VIII		
Heading	War Diary Of O.C. 3rd Cavalry Supply Column From 1st August 1915 To 31st August 1915 Vol IX		
War Diary	Moorbecque	01/08/1915	02/08/1915
War Diary	Blendecques	03/08/1915	08/08/1915
War Diary	Arques	09/08/1915	31/08/1915
Miscellaneous	O.C. 3rd Cavalry Supply Column Appendix XII		
Heading	War Diary Of O.C. 3rd Cavalry Supply Column. From. 1st September 1915 30th September 1915 Volume X		
War Diary	Arques	01/09/1915	23/09/1915
War Diary	Reveillon	23/09/1915	30/09/1915
Miscellaneous	O.C. 3rd Cavalry Supply Column Appendix XIII		
Heading	3rd Cav. Supply Column 1 To 31 Oct 1915 Vol XI		
Heading	War Diary Of O.C. 3rd Cavalry Supply Column From 1st October 1915 To 31st October 1915 Vol I		
War Diary	Reveillon	01/10/1915	03/10/1915
War Diary	Lillers.	04/10/1915	21/10/1915
War Diary	Lambres	21/10/1915	31/10/1915
Miscellaneous	O.C. 3rd Cavalry Supply Column Appendix XIV		
Heading	War Diary Of O.C. 3rd Cavalry Supply Column From 1st November 1915 To 30th November 1915 Volume XII		
War Diary	Lambres	01/11/1915	16/11/1915
War Diary	Beaurainville	16/11/1915	16/11/1915
War Diary	Lambres.	17/11/1915	17/11/1915
War Diary	Beaurainville	17/11/1915	30/11/1915
Miscellaneous	O.C. 3rd Cavarly Supply Column Appendix XV		
Heading	War Diary Of O.C. 3rd Cavalry Supply Column From 1st December 1915-31st Dec 15		
War Diary	Beaurainville	01/12/1915	05/12/1915
War Diary	Montreuil	05/12/1915	31/12/1915
Miscellaneous	O.C. 3rd Cav Sup. Coln. Appendix XVI		
War Diary	War Diary Of O.C. 3rd Cavalry Supply Column. From 1st January 1916 To 31st January 1916 Volume XIV		

Miscellaneous	O.C. 3rd Cav. Sup. Coln. Appendix XVI		
War Diary	Montreuil	01/01/1916	31/01/1916
Heading	War Diary Of O.C. 3rd Cavalry Supply Column. From 1st February 1916 To 29th February 1916 Vol XV		
War Diary	Montreuil	01/02/1916	29/02/1916
Miscellaneous	O.C. 3rd Cav. Sup. Coln. Appendix XVIII		
Heading	War Diary Of O.C. 3rd Cavalry Supply Column. From 1st March 1916 To 31st March 1916 Vol XVI		
War Diary	Montreuil	01/03/1916	22/03/1916
War Diary	Beaurainville	22/03/1916	31/03/1916
Miscellaneous	O.C. 3rd Cav. Sup. Coln. Appendix XIX		
War Diary	Fruges	01/04/1916	30/04/1916
War Diary	Beaurainville	01/05/1916	30/06/1916
War Diary	Road From Corby to Pont-Noyelles	01/07/1916	04/07/1916
War Diary	Longpre	05/07/1916	05/07/1916
War Diary	Arrainnes	06/07/1916	09/07/1916
War Diary	Corby-Pt Noyelles	10/07/1916	24/07/1916
War Diary	Beauranville	21/06/1916	30/07/1916
War Diary	Beauranville	26/07/1916	30/07/1916
War Diary	Beauranville	01/06/1916	08/07/1916
War Diary	Pt Noyelles R	26/07/1916	31/07/1916
Miscellaneous	War Diary		
War Diary	Hesdin	01/10/1916	22/01/1917
War Diary	Beaurainville	23/01/1917	08/04/1917
War Diary	Bouquemaison	08/04/1917	23/04/1917
War Diary	Beaurainville	23/04/1917	14/05/1917
War Diary	La Motte Brebiere	15/05/1917	18/05/1917
War Diary	Eterpigny	19/05/1917	21/05/1917
War Diary	Bussu	22/05/1917	31/05/1917
War Diary	Peronne J.19 Central Sheet 62c	01/06/1917	09/07/1917
War Diary	Bruay	10/07/1917	17/07/1917
War Diary	Aire	18/07/1917	22/10/1917
War Diary	Bernaville	22/10/1917	17/11/1917
War Diary	Harbonnieres	18/11/1917	19/11/1917
War Diary	Rancourt	20/11/1917	21/11/1917
War Diary	Acheux	23/11/1917	05/12/1917
War Diary	Corbie	06/12/1917	21/12/1917
War Diary	Halloy	22/12/1917	29/01/1918
War Diary	Estrees-En-Chaussee	30/01/1918	17/03/1918
War Diary	Mons-En-Chaussee	18/03/1918	21/03/1918
War Diary	Villers Carbonnel.	22/03/1918	22/03/1918
War Diary	Larbroye.	23/03/1918	30/04/1918
War Diary	Pernes.	01/05/1918	04/05/1918
War Diary	Domart-En-Ponthieu.	05/05/1918	31/05/1918
Miscellaneous	Ammunition Issued May 1918	03/06/1918	03/06/1918
Miscellaneous	Precis Of Work Carried Out In Workshops During Month Of May.		
Heading	War Diary 3rd Cavalry Division M. T. Coy. Vol 4 June 1918		
War Diary	Domart-En-Ponthieu.	01/06/1918	31/08/1918
Miscellaneous	Summary Of Work Carried Out In Workshops During August.		
Miscellaneous	Summary Of Work Carried Out By Workshops During August.		
Miscellaneous	Statement Of Ammunition Issued For Month Of August 1918		

Miscellaneous	Economy August 1918		
Miscellaneous	Mileage and Petrol.		
Miscellaneous	General Notes On The August Operations From A Mechanical Transport Point Of View		
War Diary	Averdoignt.	01/09/1918	05/09/1918
War Diary	Vacquerie	06/09/1918	25/09/1918
War Diary	Moislans.	26/09/1918	30/09/1918
Miscellaneous	Summary Of Work Carried Out During September 1918		
Miscellaneous	Economy September 1918		
War Diary	Feuilleres.	01/10/1918	08/10/1918
War Diary	Hamelet-Bernes Road	09/10/1918	14/10/1918
War Diary	Barastre	15/10/1918	31/10/1918
Miscellaneous	Ammunition Issued For Month Of October 1918		
Miscellaneous	Salvage During the Month.		
War Diary	Barrastre.	01/11/1918	11/11/1918
War Diary	Fives.	12/11/1918	17/11/1918
War Diary	Enghien.	18/11/1918	27/11/1918
War Diary	Gembloux.	28/11/1918	30/11/1918
Miscellaneous	Workshops Report For November.		
War Diary	Gembloux.	01/12/1918	14/12/1918
War Diary	Seraing.	15/12/1918	19/12/1918
War Diary	Engis.	20/12/1918	31/03/1919
Miscellaneous	3rd Cavalry Divl. M.T. Coy.	15/05/1919	15/05/1919
Miscellaneous	D.D.S.T. No. 4 Area		
War Diary	Engis.		

WO 95/11150/2

1914-1919
3RD CAVALRY DIVISION

3RD CAVALRY SUPPLY COLUMN
OCT 1914 - JUN 1919

(73 COY ASC)

Historical Record

OF

No 3 Cavalry Supply Column

73 (M.T.) Company

ARMY SERVICE CORPS.

6/France/8

— Appendices —
"A" Commanding Officers
"B" Column Moves & Dumps.
"C" Casualties

Notes, or Letters written.

1150

Formed 3rd Sept. 1914.

HISTORICAL RECORD

OF

NO. 3 CAVALRY SUPPLY COLUMN

73 (M.T.) COY. A.S.C.

Appendices.
"A" Commanding Officers.
"B" Company Moves.
"C" Casualties (Personnel.)

Recorded by
R. Victor Beveridge,
2/Lieut. A.S.C.,
Sept. 1917.

HISTORICAL RECORD

OF

NO. 3 CAVALRY SUPPLY COLUMN

73 (M.T.) COY. A.S.C.

1914.

This Company was formed on September 3rd 1914, a nucleus of the personnel being provided by a detachment of 100 N.C.Os. and men from Avonmouth and Aldershot, the remainder being provided during the next fortnight by drafts from Aldershot until the personnel was complete at WOOLWICH.

At this period 14 lorries were on the Strength of the Unit, 8 of which were being fitted as Workshops and Store vans.

On September 10th Major H.C.F. CUMBERLEDGE, who had been appointed to the Command, died, and Capt. G.K. ARCHIBALD was placed in Command.

As practically the whole of the personnel, with the exception of the Commanding Officer and a few N.C.Os. were specially enlisted, as much time as possible was given to drill and instruction; a great difficulty was also the provision of clothing and equipment in sufficient quantity.

1914.

The intention at first was that the Unit should become the Second Echelon of the 2nd Cavalry Divisional Supply Column and a detachment of what became 76 Company (Amm. Park 3rd Cavalry Division) but was then considered the Second Echelon of the 2nd Cavalry Divisional Ammunition Park, was included under the same Command.

On October 1st a party went to Bulford M.T. Depot and took over ninety 30-cwt. lorries: on the 2nd. a further fourteen, with drivers, arrived from Grove Park.

At 10 p.m. on November 3rd a wire was received from the WAR OFFICE ordering the Company to mobilize and proceed to Avonmouth at the earliest possible moment, at the same time altering the designation of the two Units to 3rd Cavalry Divisional Supply Column and Ammunition Park respectively.

This change necessitated the obtaining of more lorries to complete the new establishments and twenty five more, with drivers, were drawn from Grove Park on the morning of the 4th.

The Ammunition Park (76 Coy.) was taken over by Capt. BRANDER as a separate Command and at noon 73 Company marched by Sections to Avonmouth, billeting for the night at Newbury and completing the journey next day.

The embarkation of the vehicles and personnel was effected on the 6th on the S.Ss. "LORD TREDEGAR" and "ARTIST". Rations were drawn for a four days' journey.

1914.

the ships clearing port at 6 p.m. for an unknown destination.

Dover was reached at 2 p.m. on the 8th, where they remained off that port till the evening when they sailed in an easterly course, and anchored off Ostend at 4 a.m. on the following morning and docked at 10 a.m.

Arrangements were quickly made for disembarkation but as only 2 ton cranes were available it was only by the use of the ships' derricks that progress was made; by 2 p.m. 20 lorries of Section 2 were ashore.

These were immediately loaded with supplies from the Ostend Base Supply Depot and sent to Bruges to feed the Division which, composed of Cavalry, R.H.A. and Divisional Troops, had landed four days earlier at Bruges, Zeebrugge and Ostend and was then, with the 7th Infantry Division, attempting the relief of Antwerp.

The rations, however, were not required as the Divisional Staff had ordered a Supply Train to Bruges unloading direct to H.T. it not having been thought possible for motor lorries to arrive so soon. The lorries were sent, the following evening, to bring the rations back, delivering them in Bruges and Thourout Areas.

Whilst the lorries were being landed, enemy aeroplanes several times dropped bombs on the docks but without causing any casualties.

1914.

By the 11th of October Ostend was full of Belgian troops retreating from Liege and Antwerp and it soon became obvious that the town was to be evacuated. This was confirmed by the arrival of the remnants of the Naval Division who at once embarked on the two ships which had brought the Column to Ostend.

On the 12th, after both echelons of the Column had loaded, the Supply Depot was embarked and the ships cleared for Dunkirk. These supplies were delivered in Bruges and several other areas on the 12th and 13th. On that morning the Column received orders to evacuate the town and at once moved off. As one lorry had to be abandoned it was rendered useless before being left.

The Column marched to Roulers via Thourout and it is believed that the enemy entered the town as they moved out.

Roulers was reached about 3 p.m. and the Column parked in a lane about a mile out: about 6 p.m. Section 2 left to refill the Division which was in Oosroosebeke area returning about midnight.

Owing to the indefinite positions held by both Forces, great difficulty was experienced in selecting suitable dumps and it was afterwards found that the supplies for the R.H. Guards had actually been dumped at a point inside the German lines whence a strong escort was sent to fetch them with the regimental limbers.

On returning to Roulers and before they had time to park the lorries, a Staff Officer rode up and stated that the Column was nearly surrounded by the enemy. The whole

1 9 1 4.

Company was at once roused and the engines started up, but the road was in such a state through heavy rain and because of the danger of showing lights, it was 2 a.m. before the Column moved off in the direction of Dunkirk where the first lorry arrived at 9 a.m. and the last at midday.

During this journey the Column was frequently stopped by British and Belgian outposts who had barricaded the roads. German outposts were also passed but no attack was made; it was afterwards learnt from prisoners that the lorries were supposed to be full of troops and the enemy was not present in sufficient strength to warrant an attack.

A German Car also followed for a considerable time evidently thinking it was a German Convoy but on discovering its mistake turned and fled: it was only then it was found to be an enemy vehicle.

Two lorries which developed engine and back axle trouble on the march had to be abandoned but were rendered useless to the enemy. On the latter part of the run the lorries were filled with Belgian troops and refugees.

The Column remained at Dunkirk till the morning of the 16th loading from the R.N. Supply Depot and delivering to the Division in Zonnebeke and Menin.

On the 15th after delivering rations in the evening the lorries were ordered to rendezvous in the Square at

1914.

Ypres: five arrived there about 11 p.m. and the remainder during the night.   At that time the town was intact, the Germans retreating from the South, had passed through it the same day and the men of the Column were the first British soldiers seen by the inhabitants who greeted them in the morning with great enthusiasm.

The Column moved to Arneke on the 16th and from this Railhead loaded on the 16th and 17th, delivering to the Division still at Zonnebeke and Menin.   Caestre was Railhead for two days: on the 20th it moved to Strazeele, and for the 21st and 22nd was at Bailleul, the Column parking in the Square there.

On the 23rd the lorries loaded at Poperinghe and parked for that night at Ouderdom.   Railhead again changed to Caestre on the 24th, and the Column returned there, changing to Eblingham on the 29th (Column at St.Sylvestre), and to Hazebrouk on the 5th November when the Column moved to Morbecque, railhead. changing later to Steenbecque.

During the whole of this period the Division was in action, in what developed into the first battle of Ypres, rations being dumped in the village of Klein Zillebeke where they held positions;   in fact so close were the rations sometimes dumped that the lorry drivers were able to walk into the front positions.   This continued during the whole of the battle, the Column running from Morbecque 40 miles each way.

1914.

A great deal of night work, under very trying conditions was carried out at this stage, as, owing to the enemy shelling of Ypres and the surrounding roads, especially the Canal bridge by the Railway Station, the Column was often held up for hours with engines running, waiting a chance to get through the town. This, too, soon became a matter of driving skill, streets often becoming impassable, owing to houses falling in and blocking the way thus necessitating turning in a very confined space under shell fire.

It is notable that during one of these waits, the first shell was seen to hit the Cloth Hall bringing part of the central tower down.

On the 9th of November a man dressed as a Belgian Sergeant obtained particulars from some of the men as to the route followed, for whom supplies were carried etc. Later when the Column was actually passing through the town, heavy shells began to drop around; one actually exploded between two lorries putting both out of action temporarily, and killed two drivers wounding three others. The <u>soi disant</u> Belgian Sergeant was fortunately caught the following day and dealt with by the Authorities.

The roads in this area became increasingly bad at this time, the road consisting in most cases of a track of pavé stones in the centre and on either side of this a drop of sometimes nearly a foot into soft mud, so that "ditched" lorries were a frequent occurrence, owing to the Column often

1914.

meeting large bodies of French and British troops and Horse Transport. Insufficient traffic controls had been established and it soon became an accepted rule not to get off the pavé for anyone. On one occasion during this time, No.1 Section, consisting of 36 lorries, left the Park at Morbecque at 7 a.m., and after dumping rations at Klein-Zillebeke at 8 p.m. turned for home, but owing to the darkness and the thick fog, had every lorry in the convoy "ditched" in the first 6 miles, some of them more than once. They eventually returned to Park about 11 a.m. the following day. An alternative route through Steenvoorde & Poperinghe was sometimes used this being so the day the latter town was first shelled.

Whilst refilling the Division between Ypres and Zillebeke the lorries were standing close to a Park of 500 - 600 bicycles belonging to a French Chasseur Regiment, when some shells dropped in the middle of them blowing the whole lot of the machines to pieces, and at the same time another shell dropped near the ration dump, blowing the S.S.O. (Colonel - then Major Liddell) off his feet, but without doing any material damage to men or lorries.

During November a third Brigade was added to the Division and the Column was re-organized to meet its requirements, each Section (36 lorries) being sub divided into 4 Sub-Sections, i.e., 1 per Brigade and Div.Troops. Later in the month the Division was withdrawn from action and billeted

1 9 1 4.

in the Hazebrouk area, the Column feeding them from Morbecque with Railhead varying between Steenbecque, Hazebrouk & Eblinghem. At the end of this month 40 lorries (20 per Section) were added to the Column to carry hay to the Division. This was at first done separately from the ordinary rations but later was included with the usual loading and delivery.

On December 2nd the whole Division was reviewed by the King at LAMOTTE AU BOIS on His Majesty's first visit to the Front.

1 9 1 5.

From this stage nothing of import happened to the Column until April, 1915, the whole Division remaining in billets in the Hazebrouk area till the Germans began the second battle of Ypres, when the Division was called up in a hurry to the Ypres district. Rations were taken up the same night and delivered in Vlamertinghe. This was the day the enemy first employed poison gas, no respirators were of course available but no casualties occurred among the Column personnel, though the gas could be distinctly smelt. The Division remained in line for a few days and then returned to billets. It was again called up into action during the next phase of this battle during May, and refilling points were established at Reninghelst and Vlamertinghe and later at Watou, Proven and Oost Cappel. This continued for a fortnight and the

1 9 1 5.

Division then returned again to billets.

The Division then moved into billets in the Fauquembergues area on Aug. 2nd, 1915, the Column being located at Blendecques with Railhead at Arques; its Headquarters moved into Arques a week later. At this place it remained quietly until 2nd September; a detachment of 14 lorries then proceeded to a point near Aire (where Railhead was located) to feed the R.H.A. Batteries then called into action near Bethune. This party rejoined the Column on August 16th.

On the 22nd August, a detachment of 36 lorries proceeded to St. Sylvestre to feed the 7th Bde. (Railhead at Caestre) temporarily detached from the Division, while the remainder moved to Reviellon, railhead at Aire.

The Division (less 7th Bde.) moved up to positions in the Bois des Dames, and La Pugnoy on the 20th, where it remained hidden until the battle of Loos opened on the 23rd, rations being delivered there till the night 25/26th when it moved up to Vermelles and Mazingarbe, rations being delivered in the latter village, one and a half miles behind the front line just before daybreak on the morning of the 26th.

This was a point of considerable danger, as in daylight it was in full view of the enemy, but thanks to a mist, the lorries were got safely away. The Division afterwards moved into Loos and remained there for some days in the trenches: it was withdrawn on 3rd October into the Lillers area; the Column and Railhead was in the town and remained there till

1915.

22nd when it moved to Lambres with railhead at Aire. Here it remained till Nov. 16th when the Division moved South to the area between Fruges and Montreuil, railhead at the latter place; the Column was at Beaurainville.

On December 5th, the Column moved into Montreuil and the whole Division remained stationary till the end of June, 1916. The Column meantime moved back into Beaurainville in March, 1916, owing to G.H.Q. coming into Montreuil.

1916.

During January, 1916, however, a Dismounted Division was formed out of the 3 British Cavalry Divisions, each Supply Column furnishing a detachment of 36 lorries to feed the Brigade, found by its own Division; the combined Supply Column was commanded by Capt. A.H. Boswall Preston of this Unit. This Dismounted Division was disbanded on the 20th February, when the personnel rejoined their respective units.

On 20th April, Major G.K. Archibald was transferred to England and on 5th May, Major L.O. Dunphy took over the command, but was invalided to England on 8th May: the command was then taken by Capt. Preston till 2nd June when Major H.A. Gardner arrived.

On the 22nd June, the Division moved out of billets to the Somme area (4 days march) the Column feeding them from different railheads each day, the whole Division finally bivouacing together at La Neuville on the 26th, Railhead at Mericourt. On the 4th July, the whole Division moved back to

1916.

Hallencourt, railhead at Longpre, remaining there till the 8th when it again advanced to its former bivouac.

On August 1st the Division moved back to the Hesdin district, the Column and railhead both in the town, and remained there till Sept. 9th when it again moved up to near Corbie on the Somme (3 days march), Railhead being Frechincourt and Albert, Column Hd.Qrs. at Lamotte Brebiere.

With Albert as Railhead, loading had to be done at night, which led to much congestion in the station yard, 3 other Divisions trying to load at the same time, no lights being allowed and the enemy putting shells over occasionally. The only solution was to load in bulk and redistribute the loads next morning before delivering. No casualties were caused during this time, but some very narrow escapes were experienced.

On 21st inst. the two Sections rejoined Column Hd.Qrs. at Lamotte Brebiere and on the 22nd the whole Division, less Batteries, returned by a 4 day march to billets around Hesdin, Column and Railhead in the town as formerly. The Batteries remained in action above Albert and a dismounted party of Cavalry was also left behind working at Thiepval, 14 lorries being left with these parties.

On the Batteries rejoining the Division 3 weeks later, the whole of these lorries were withdrawn and the dismounted party fed by local Supply Columns. It was

1 9 1 6.

during one of these reliefs of this dismounted party that the longest run was done. One of the Brigades had moved to the coast district at Trepied and 12 lorries were detailed to convey a relief dismounted party to High Bluff near Thiepval.

For various reasons the direct route could not be taken and the total distance run during the day was 270 kilometres. This was done in 23 hours without a mechanical breakdown of any kind.

The Division remained in the Hesdin area, with one Brigade alternately in the coastal district and was fed by various ways, a detachment of lorries (20) being stationed at Wailly, Railhead at Montreuil, to feed the coast Brigade and Div. Troops. A Supply detachment was also kept at Montreuil Railhead, to tranship rations for part of the Brigade billeted in Fruges area, on to the Light Railway running to that place, and drawn from there by Horse Transport. The remainder of that Brigade drew rations direct from Hesdin Railhead, also by Horse Transport: the remaining Brigade was fed by a single echelon of lorries.

1 9 1 7.

This continued till 23rd January, 1917, when the Column and Railhead moved to Beaurainville; the Brigade formerly fed by lorry then drew from Railhead by Horse Transport and the other was fed in its turn by lorry.

The Wailly detachment for feeding Divisional Troops and coast Brigade rejoined the Column at this time, leaving only 4 lorries there for local work.

During January and February of 1917 very severe weather was experienced; in consequence of the sudden arrival of the frost, 17 Daimler cylinder heads were cracked.

1917.

The next occurrence of note was at the latter end of March, when 18 lorries were sent to Arras to load supplies at various Field Supply Depots and build a reserve dump of rations E. of Arras. The road to this dump was frequently under fire but no casualties were incurred and the lorries rejoined the Column on completion of the work on 2nd April.

On 4th April, the Division concentrated in the Hesdin area and the whole moved forward on the 5th inst. to bivouacs at Gouy-en-Artois (3 days march) the Column bivouacing near Railhead at Bouquemaison. On Easter Monday, April 9th, the Division moved to a point just E. of Arras and took part in the offensive then commencing.

During this action the Division subsisted on the "Gap Ration"*, but on the afternoon of the 11th, an urgent message was received to send 20 lorries with hay. This was done and the hay delivered at 3 a.m. the following morning. A further message was received at 7 p.m. to send up one complete day's rations. This was sent, but failed to reach the Division owing to various contradictory orders received en route, and, also partly owing to a very severe snowstorm which lasted practically all night.

It may here be mentioned that the weather during this time was very severe, continuous snow and rain storms with high winds and intense cold all the while. The roads, too, were in places in very bad condition and became almost impassable.

> * The "Gap Ration" is the Supply provision made by Cavalry in anticipation of breaking through a "gap" in the Enemy Lines. There is no regulation as to its constitution: it depends on the supplies available at the moment and, in some degree, on the country through which the Cavalry will operate.

1917.

This was due to the effect of the thaw on the chalk foundation of the roads after the hard frost, which had held for 5 weeks. This was naturally aggravated by the abnormal amount of traffic on them owing to the offensive; the repairs were being carried out as fast as possible. A large number of road springs were broken owing to this reason but beyond that no serious inconvenience was caused.

The Division remained E. of Arras holding Monchy till the afternoon of April 12th when they returned to bivouacs at Gouy-en-Artois: 12 lorries were sent up to bring back 150 Officers and Men of the 8th Bde. whose horses had been killed and they themselves cut off. These men had had no food for three days and hot food and tea were served to them before returning to bivouacs.

On 20th April, the Division returned to Hesdin area, Column and Railhead at Beaurainville, and remained there in billets till 13th May, when it moved forward to a point 5 miles E. of Peronne. From here 1 Brigade was alternately used as a dismounted Bde. holding a line of trench with the other Divisions of the Cavalry Corps, E. of Epehy.

These troops were fed by double echelon of lorries, 6 daily, and rations dumped at Villers Faucon; the remainder of the Division drew rations direct from Railhead by Horse Transport. Railhead was at Tincourt during this time, and the Column parked one and a half miles W. of it.

The Division stayed in this area 7 weeks and on an average, 30 lorries were provided daily by the Column for work

1 9 1 7.

under Cavalry Corps H.Q., carrying stone etc. for road building, as the roads in the area were in a ruinous state after the German retreat.

One complete Section (65 lorries with Workshop attached) was detached to 3rd Army and located at Candas to move an Ammunition dump. This lasted 16 days when it was ordered to Amiens, for work under the Town Commandant; there it stayed another 15 days and then rejoined the Column.

On 3rd July, the Division moved northward by 5 marches to Bruay District, being fed en route by double echelon of lorries. The Column arrived at Bruay on 8th July where Railhead remained till the 16th, when the Division moved to Busnes area, the Column and Railhead at Aire. Supplies were here delivered by double echelon of lorries for 7th Bde; the 6th Bde. and Div. Troops being supplied by single echelon of lorries, and the 8th Bde. drawing direct from Railhead by Horse Transport.

On 22nd August, a point of interest was reached by an order received to transfer 53 men immediately to the Base as Infantry Reinforcements, the men selected to consist of Class "A" men only. This was carried out, though it meant the loss of some of the best drivers, some of whom had been with the Column a period of two years. At the same time the Establishment was reduced from 25% to 15% spare drivers.

APPENDIX "A"

3rd September, 1914.
MAJOR H.C.F. CUMBERLEDGE,   O.C.

10th September, 1914.
CAPT. (NOW MAJOR) G.K. ARCHIBALD, O.C.

5th May, 1916.
MAJOR L.O. DUNPHY,   O.C.

2nd June, 1916.
MAJOR H.A. GARDNER,   O.C.

— Appendix "B" —

Date.	Railhead.	Hd.Qrs. at	Rations dumped at
9/10/14	Ostend Base Supply Depot	Ostend	Bruges and Thourout.
14/10/14	Dunkirk R.N. Sup.Depot.	Dunkirk	Ypres area.
16/10/14	Arneke	Arneke	" "
18/10/14	Caestre	Caestre	" "
20/10/14	Strazeele	Caestre	" "
21/10/14) 22/10/14)	Bailleul	Bailleul	" "
23/10/14	Poperinghe	Poperinghe	" "
24/10/14	Caestre	Caestre	" "
29/10/14	Eblinghem	St. Sylvestre	" "
5/11/14	Hazebrouck	Morbecque	" "
29/11/14	"	"	Hazebrouck area.
30/11/14) to) 2/8/15)	varying between Hazebrouck, Eblinghem & Steenbecque	"	" "
3/8/15	Arques	Blendecques	Fauquembergues area.
8/8/15	Arques	Arques	" "
22/9/15	Aire	Reveillon	Loos area.

Detachment of 7th Bde.

22/9/15) 22/10/15)	Caestre	St. Sylvestre	Steenvoorde area.
3/10/15	Lillers	Lillers	Lillers area.
22/10/15	Aire	Lambres	Aire area
16/11/15	Montreuil	Beaurainville	Montreuil - Fruges area.
5/12/15	"	Montreuil	" " "
23/3/16	Beaurainville	Beaurainville	" " "

Dismounted Division.

| 30/12/15) to) 22/2/16) | Chocques | Gonnehem | Bethune area. |
| 26/6/16 | Various | (On march to (Somme area | various. |

Continued. — Appendix "B" (contd.) —

Date	Railhead	Hd. Qrs. at	Rations dumped at
26/6/16 to 3/7/16	Mericourt	La Neuville	La Neuville.
4/7/16	Longpre	Airaines	Hallencourt area.
9/7/16	Mericourt	La Neuville	La Neuville.
1/8/16	Hesdin	Hesdin	Hesdin area.
12/9/16 to 21/9/16	Frechincourt & Albert	La Motte Brebiere	Corbie area.
22/9/16 to 25/9/16	Various	On march to Hesdin	Various.
26/9/16	Hesdin	Hesdin	Hesdin area.
23/1/17	Beaurainville	Beaurainville	Hesdin & Trepied areas.
5/4/17 to 7/4/17	Various	On march to Bouquemaison	Various.
8/4/17	Bouquemaison	Bouquemaison	Gouy-en-Artois & Arras.
20/4/17	Beaurainville	Beaurainville	Hesdin area.
13/5/17 to 20/5/17	Various	On march to Peronne.	Various.
21/5/17	Tincourt	Tincourt	Peronne area.
3/7/17 to 8/7/17	Various	On march to Bruay	Various.
15/8/17	Bruay	Bruay	Bruay area.
16/8/17	Aire	Aire	Busnes area.

APPENDIX "C"

No. 3 CAVALRY SUPPLY COLUMN.

C A S U A L T I E S
****

1914.

MEN - November 9th - Killed   2
                                                          Wounded 3

COPY.

1.

A.S.C.2312.

O. i/c A.S.C. Records,
 Woolwich Dockyard.

I would be much obliged if you would forward the War Diary (duplicate) of the 3rd Cavalry Divisional A.S.C., for reference and return to you.

It is now in your possession (vide your R/1299 dated 12/4/17) and it is required in connection with the anticipated visit of the A.S.C. Recording Officer.

I understand that you have the Historical Record of this unit compiled by Colonel SWABEY, lately in command of 3rd Cavalry Div. A.S.C. If at all possible, I should like to have this also.

(sgd) A.E. Cuming, Lt.Col.
26/7/17.   Comdg 3rd Cavalry Divl A.S.C.

CONFIDENTIAL.   2.

Officer Commanding,
 3rd Cavalry Divisional A.S.C.,
  BRITISH E.F. FRANCE.

1. Enclosed are:-

   (a) Duplicate War Diary from 4th September 1914 to 31st December 1916, which please return as soon as convenient. No duplicate Diaries have been received from your Unit since that date.

   (b) Typed copy of the early records of No. 81 Coy., which you may retain.

2. I shall be grateful if you will kindly bring up to/date the history of your Unit. The copy now enclosed is all that has been received up to the present, and I am anxious to secure a complete history.

Woolwich Dockyard, S.E.18.
 4th August 1917.

Colonel,
 i/c A.S.C. Records.

D.D.S.& T. 3rd Army. C/55.

COPY.

Subject - <u>Historical Records.</u>

Colonel F. Horniblow,
   A.S.C. Records,
     Woolwich.

    The enclosed Historical Records regarding the exploits of Nos 73 and 81 Companies, Army Service Corps in this country during the early part of the campaign, and which may be of use for record purposes, are forwarded to you.

                        (sgd) W.S. Swabey,
Headquarters   Colonel,
Third Army.   D.D.S. & T. 3rd Army.
3/6/17.

2.

D.D.S.& T.,
   Third Army H.Q.
      British E.F. France.

          Received, with many thanks.

                        (sgd) F. Horniblow,
                              Colonel,
                        i/c A.S.C. Records.

81 Coy detached & indexed separately. 5/France/1

HISTORICAL RECORD
of
3rd CAVALRY SUPPLY COLUMN from OCT. - DEC. 1914.

Oct. 3rd. 1914. After training on Woolwich Common from Sept. 4th, at 10.0 p.m. on 3/10/14 orders were received from the War Office for the 3rd. Cavalry Supply Column to proceed overseas, and preparations for this move were carried out during the night.

Oct. 4th. At 12.30 p.m. No: 1 Section, followed at ½ hour intervals by No: 2 Section and Hd. Qrs. left Woolwich for NEWBURY via LONDON, BRENTFORD, HOUNSLOW and READING, the first lorry arriving at 8.30 p.m. the men being billetted in the Town Hall for the night.

The Column was made up to Establishment by the arrival at NEWBURY of 2/Lieut. Preston and 11 lorries.

Oct. 5th. No: 2 Section followed by No: 1 Section and Hd. Qrs. Section at ½ hour intervals left NEWBURY at 8.45 a.m. for AVONMOUTH via BRISTOL, the head of the column arriving at 6 p.m.

Oct. 6th. After consultation with the M.L.O. at AVONMOUTH it was decided that the column should be sent overseas on the "LORD TREDEGAR" and "ARTIST", Capt. Archibald being in charge of the former and 2/Lieut. Bell of the latter. Loading was started on the "LORD TREDEGAR" at 7 a.m. but owing to lack of cranes, work did not commence on the "ARTIST" till 11 a.m. The "LORD TREDEGAR" sailed at 3 p.m. and the "ARTIST" at 11 p.m.

The "ARTIST" carried 5 Officers, 46 lorries, 3 motor cars and 250 other ranks, the remainder of the column having sailed on the "LORD TREDEGAR"

The exact establishment is not known, but the following was somewhere near the exact figure.

Captain Archibald in Command.
2/Lieut. Teulon) Workshops
2/Lieut. Fowlis)

Oct. 6th. continued.	2/Lieut. Price, Hd. Qrs. 2/Lieut. Smith, Interpreter, (Joined at Ostend). 2/Lieut. Bell) 2/Lieut. Thorp) No: 1 2/Lieut. Preston) Section. 2/Lieut. Farrer (Supply) 2/Lieut. Swan) 2/Lieut. Cumberlege) No: 2 2/Lieut. Whitelark) Section. 2/Lieut. Farran (Supply)) 5 Motor Cars) 12 Motor Cycles) Approx. only. 100 Lorries) 450 Other Ranks.) The 3rd Cavalry Amn: Park under Capt. Brander parted company with the Supply Col: for the first time to-day, as they were not to load till Oct. 7th on a separate ship.
Oct. 7th.	At sea all day.
Oct. 8th.	H.T. "ARTIST" joined up with the "LORD TREDEGAR" off DOVER at 3.45 p.m. and reported by signal to Capt. Archibald. The two ships sailed for OSTEND at 11 p.m.
Oct. 9th.	From and including this date, this record only deals with the movements of No: 1 Section. Anchored off OSTEND at 7 a.m., came alongside station jetty about noon, unloaded 8 lorries and then moved into inner harbour. Went over to report to Capt. Archibald who was on the "LORD TREDEGAR".
Oct. 10th.	Finished unloading from the "ARTIST" and as lorries became available, loaded supplies from A.S.C. Depot. No: 1 Section left for BRUGES at 4.15 p.m. Lack of maps made work exceedingly difficult for the next few days. Tried every Stationers shop we came across for maps, but found them all sold out.
Oct. 11th.	Returned from BRUGES at 3 a.m.. Loaded supplies from A.S.C. Depot, OSTEND, at 4 p.m.
Oct. 12th.	Moved off to ROULERS via BRUGES at 11.45 a.m.
Oct. 13th.	Returned to OSTEND at 5.0 a.m. Left again empty in somewhat of a hurry at 10.30 a.m. after having saved General Byngs Mess Stores from the Station. Arrived ROULERS at 1 p.m. At 11.35 p.m. Major AIREY dashed up in a car to parking

Oct. 13th continued.	parking ground at ROULERS and ordered retreat on DUNKIRK forthwith.
Oct. 14th.	Got away from ROULERS at 12.45 a.m. and arrived at DUNKIRK at 11.30 a.m.

The 7th Div. Supply Column were just ahead all this journey and judging by the material they abandoned they must have been suffering from "nerves".

However the 3rd. Cav. Supply Column became the possessors of a good selection of spares which had long been needed. Started loading lorries from DUNKIRK Docks at 12.30 p.m. and at 6 p.m. left for YPRES.

Oct. 15th.	Returned from YPRES at 11.45 a.m. and at 3 p.m. again loaded supplies at DUNKIRK Docks.
Oct. 16th.	Left DUNKIRK at 9 a.m. for ARNECKE. Arrived at 1 p.m. and was ordered by Major AIREY to deliver my supplies to 7th Div. I refused pending written orders from my own Division or 4th Corps. These orders never came. No: 1 Section left for POPERINGHE at 2 p.m.
Oct. 17th.	Left POPERINGHE loaded, at 10.30 a.m. for YPRES and returned empty at 11.45 p.m.
Oct. 18th.	Moved to and loaded at CAESTRE, but as train was short loaded drew remainder of supplies at STRAZEELE.
Oct. 19th.	Left for YPRES at 5.50 p.m.
Oct. 20th.	Reached BAILLEUL at 3 a.m. and waited for 3rd. Cav. Supply Column to join up. Loaded at BAILLEUL in the afternoon. It was here that the Officers of No: 1 Section took their clothes off for the first time since landing at OSTEND. The whole Section enjoyed a well earned rest.
Oct. 21st.	Left BAILLEUL at 10.30 a.m for YPRES.
Oct. 22nd.	Returned from YPRES at 2 a.m. Left at 10 a.m. for POPERINGHE loaded supplies there and proceeded to OUDERDOM.
Oct. 23rd.	Left at 8.45 a.m. for YPRES and returned to CAESTRE at 11.55 p.m.
Oct. 24th.	Loaded supplies at CAESTRE.
Oct. 25th.	Left at 10.30 a.m. for YPRES and returned at 10 p.m.
Oct. 26th.	Loaded supplies at CAESTRE.

Oct. 27th.   Left for YPRES at 10.30 a.m. Back again at 9.30 p.m.; one of the most satisfactory runs the section had to date.

Oct. 28th.   Loaded at CAESTRE and then went by car to BILLIBECKE to report to XXX D.A.A.Q.M.G. of Division for special orders.

Oct. 29th.   Left for YPRES at 10.30 a.m.

Oct. 30th.   Arrived back at CAESTRE from YPRES at 2.30 a.m. Loaded at EBBLINGHAM and parked up at St. SYLVESTRE.

Oct. 31st.   Left at 10 a.m. for BAILLEUL; waited there for orders from S.S.O. and then proceeded to YPRES.

NOV. 1st.   Arrived back from YPRES at 3 a.m. and loaded at EBBLINGHAM.

NOV. 2nd.   Left for YPRES at 10.30 a.m. and returned to St. SYLVESTRE at 11 p.m.

NOV. 3rd.   Loaded at EBBLINGHAM.

NOV. 4th.   Left at 10.30 a.m. for YPRES and returned at 11.30 p.m.

NOV. 5th.   Loaded supplies at STRAZEELE and returned to St. SYLVESTRE.

NOV. 6th.   Left for YPRES at 9.30 a.m.; under continual shell fire at rendezvous and at YPRES.

NOV. 7th.   Returned from YPRES at 1 p.m.; after being on road all night men suffered a good deal and many fell asleep driving, with the result that many lorries were badly ditched.
On arrival at St. SYLVESTRE found that the Column had gone to MORBECQUE. Loaded at HAZEBROUCK and then parked up at MORBECQUE.

NOV. 8th.   Left at 9.30 a.m. for YPRES.

NOV. 9th.   Returned at 1 a.m. to MORBECQUE, after coming through fairly heavy shell fire in YPRES. Loaded at HAZEBROUCK.

NOV. 10th.   Left at 9.30 a.m. for YPRES. Heard that No: 2 Section had casualties coming through YPRES on the 9th.
Returned at 11 p.m.

NOV. 11th.   Loaded supplies at HAZEBROUCK.

NOV. 12th.   Left for YPRES at 9.30 a.m.

NOV. 13th.   Arrived from YPRES at 2 a.m. Loaded at HAZEBROUCK.

NOV. 14th.   Left for YPRES at 10 a.m.
Up to this date lorries had been loaded for dumping to Brigades, but for the first time lorries are now loaded for

NOV. 14th continued. loaded for Regiments, and Regimental Dumps are to be made in future.

Like all new schemes, the men do not like the change and a little more forethought would have made an instant success instead of which that degree was not reached for some days.

NOV. 15th. Arrived from YPRES at 1.15 a.m. Loaded at HAZEBROUCK.

NOV. 16th. Left for YPRES at 10 a.m.; back at 11.30 p.m.

NOV. 17th. Loaded at HAZEBROUCK.

NOV. 18th. Left for YPRES at 9.0 a.m.

Owing to the fact that one of the Brigade Supply Officers did not turn up at the rendezvous, and later in the day took his X8 Brigade lorries to an unknown dumping ground, a good deal of confusion was caused, one lorry was left under shell fire for many hours, but the drivers received a "Mention" in the next list of honours.

NOV. 19th. Arrived back at 12.30 a.m.; Loaded at HAZEBROUCK.

A good deal of blockage round railhead owing to new M.P's on duty who have not yet got used to lorries.

NOV. 20th. Left for YPRES with 7th Brigade lorries at 9.0 a.m.; very heavy shell fire, worst day since we ran to YPRES. Arrived back at 9.0 p.m.

6th Brigade on way down to rest.

From Nov. 21st. to March, the Division being in rest there was nothing of interest to report.

No: 1 Section loaded and delivered on alternate days.

Railheads were HAZEBROUCK till about Dec. 15th then STEENBECQUE except during the last 4 days of 1914, when the Division drew from EBBLINGHAM and then returned to STEENBECQUE Railhead.

The New Year brought in a new scheme of Squadron loading and delivery on the suggestion of the G.O.C., 7th Brigade.

On December 2nd. the whole Division was inspected by His Majesty the King on the road between HAZEBROUCK and LA MOTTE. The training of the Supply Column men for this inspection could be more appropriately dealt with in a music hall sketch

sketch than in an Historical Record, but fortunately it was decided to "Slope" and not "Present" at the supreme moment of that eventful day.

A copy of General BYNG'S Special Order of the Day " Nov. 23rd 1914 is attached.

                                                                                       C. F. Bell.   Major, A.S.C.,
                                                  Commanding "J" Corps Amm: Park,
27/4/1917.   attached XIVth Corps.

SPECIAL ORDER OF THE DAY

-- by --

Major-General the Hon. J.H.G. BYNG, C.B., M.V.O.

Commanding 3rd Cavalry Division.

In circulating this short diary of the operations in which the Division has taken part, I wish to take the opportunity of conveying to all ranks my gratitude and admiration for their conduct. With little or no experience of trench work, exposed to every vagary of weather, and under a persistent and concentrated shelling, the regimental officers, N.C.Os, and men have undertaken this most arduous and demoralising work with a keenness and courage which I place on record with the greatest pride.

With the exception of October 30th, when the ZANDVOORDE trenches held by the Household Cavalry Brigade and the CHATEAU of HOLLEBEKE held by a Squadron of Royal Dragoons were attacked by a German Corps, no trench has been lost and no ground evacuated.

On eight occasions Brigades were sent in support of the line which had been partially penetrated, and on nearly or every occasion either I or one of the Brigadiers have received the thanks and congratulations of the Commander of that zone of defence for the gallant behaviour of our troops.

The 6th Cavalry Brigade may well be proud of their action at ST. PIETER on October 19th. KRUISEUK, Oct.26th. CHATEAU DE HOLLEBEKE, Oct.30th. HOOGE WOODS, Oct.31st. and the ZILLEBEKE trenches on Nov.17th; while the actions of the 7th Cavalry Brigade at OOSTNIEUWKERKE Oct.16th, MOORSLEDE, Oct.19th. ZONNEBEKE, Oct.21st. ZANDVOORDE, Oct.26th. ZANVOORDE trenches, Oct.30th. VELDDHOEK, Nov.2nd, KLEIN ZILLEBEKE, Novr.6th, have been the subject of official recognition and well-merited praise.

Each Regiment, Battery, R.E. and Signal Squadron and Administrative and Medical Service has more than maintained its historic reputation, and during the last six weeks has added to the renown of the British Soldier as a magnificent fighter, and it is with the utmost confidence in their steadfast courage that I contemplate a continuance of the campaign until our enemy receives his final overthrow.

(Signed). J. BYNG. Major-General,

Commanding 3rd Cavalry Division.

November 23rd, 1914.

Army Form C. 2118.
Page I.

WAR DIARY
3rd Cavalry Supply Column
INTELLIGENCE SUMMARY.
(Erase heading not required.)

Instructions regarding War Diaries and Intelligence Summaries are contained in F.S. Regs., Part II. and the Staff Manual respectively. Title pages will be prepared in manuscript.

Hour, Date, Place	Summary of Events and Information	Remarks and references to Appendices
Woolwich. 3/10/14. 4.30 AM	Sixty lorries arrived from BULFORD. One lorry badly damaged.	} G.H.
10.0 AM	One steam Central - one Pak shaft broken - one crank case broken. Visited by C.I.S.T. who gave orders re to	
7.0 PM	Complete 73 + 76 Coys except 11 light. Detailed to send 6.30 PM	
10.0 PM	Capt. M.S. Brandon arrived as O.C. 76 Coy. Orders from W.O. to move 4/10/14 + reach AVONMOUTH 5/10/14.	
4/10/14 12.10 AM	Towed all possible others for more of two Conferences.	} G.H.
5 AM	Sent 2 badly damaged lorries + 13 men to GROVE PARK.	
9.30 AM	1 lorry under 2/Lt Cambridge with drivers to travel via	
10.0 AM	BULFORD + pick up 11 lorries to complete establishment. Handed over Camp. equipt. etc. to N° 2 Co. A.S.C.	
12.0 Noon	76 Coy left - } Route via HYDE PARK CORNER, HOUNSLOW + READING.	
12.30 PM	73 Coy left —	
NEWBURY 3.0 PM	arrived NEWBURY 7.30 PM } 8.30 - 10.30 PM	
10.30 PM	2/Lt Cambridge arrived	
11.0 PM	All fixed up. Men in Corn Exchange + Lorries in Wharves + Square.	
5/10/14 8.0 AM	76 Coy left } Route via MARLBORO' - BATH ROAD - BRISTOL	} G.H.
8.20 AM	73 Coy	
9.15 AM		

Army Form C. 2118.
Page 2

WAR DIARY 3rd Water Supply Column
INTELLIGENCE SUMMARY.
(Erase heading not required.)

Hour, Date, Place	Summary of Events and Information	Remarks and references to Appendices
AVONMOUTH 5/10/14 12.30 PM	Reported to O.C.M.T. Depot, who allotted us a bunk & gave orders to follow at 3.0 PM	
2.30 PM	4 days rations	
3.45 PM – 6.0 PM	7 & 8 Coy arrived	
	7 & 3 Coy arrived except Halfpenny which came in late & in very bad order. Defects I man drunk — I horse cherstic — I sleeve burst already.	
	Motored 3/10/14.	
6.0 PM	Orders to start embarkation on 6/10/14 at 6.0PM at Tilbury with ½ Coy.	
6/10/14 9.0 AM	2nd Section a Turkey nearly. Embarkation started 9.15 PM	
9.0 AM	Reported to O.C. M.T. Depot. Workstations received shift. Handed over Hereford lorry as too bad to embark	
11.30 PM	Embarkation for embarkation & all shift. M.T. Section	
6.0 PM	All lorries ready to embark. Lunged work done & workshop lorries during day to fit them up, but still incomplete.	
7.15 PM	S.S. LORD TREDEGAR sailed with 5 motorcycles 2 motorcars & Morris 7 seater 2 youths	
10.0 PM	S.S. ARTIST	
	TOTAL	

```
            1   —   3   —   45   —   8   —  240  —
           10   —   5   —   94   —  12   —  490  —
```

1 Officer one W.E. due to written W.O. authority increased of 30%.
8 other ranks under W.E. due to Avonmore Sub etc from WOOLWICH
2 lorries — W.E. due to 2 lorries not attached to Govt Park
4/10/14 & 1 handed to O.C.M.T. Depot Avonmouth 6/10/14 which is a non-
accounted for against 12 supplied from BULFORD 4/10/14 instead of 11

Army Form C. 2118.

Page 3

WAR DIARY 3rd (Cavalry Supply Column
or
INTELLIGENCE SUMMARY.
(Erase heading not required.)

Hour, Date, Place	Summary of Events and Information	Remarks and references to Appendices
S.S. LORD TREDEGAR 7/10/14 9.0 AM	Roll call & service parade. General cleaning up.	J.R.
3.0 PM	Rifle & revolver inspection, cleaning & examination	
8/10/14 10.0 AM	General parade & lectures.	J.R.
1.45 PM	M Dove P.	
3.45 PM	S.S. ARTIST joined up.	
9/10/14 3.30 AM	Anchored about 5 miles off OSTEND. S.S. ARTIST joined up at 7.0 AM	J.R.
1.0 NOON		
OSTEND 3.30 PM	Moved into Docks.	
10.0 PM	Started disembarkation. Very slow — Cranes & electric current too weak.	
11.0 PM	12 Lorries ready	
—	Started working at S. Depot. Delays due to Railway transit difficulties. Being continually checked.	
10/10/14 12.45 AM	Finished loading. Ration & Lubricating Lorries, Rum — Biscuit motorcar,	Mem Brakes
1.45 PM	Lorries left for BRUGES where supplies were dumped.	6" Can. Pate. 1152
10.0 PM	No wind. One wounded civilian.	7 " " 1240
11.30 PM	Order for B.H. O.M.E. 3rd C.S. Column to back by Belin on days supplies from	1848
12.0 NOON	S. Depot, also 200 of ab rations & about all vice.	Sur Pangs 921
4.15 PM	No 1 Section started loading. Took Horses, Grist, tinned & dry[?] kimmer[?]	800
	— left for R.V.: GRAND PLACE BRUGES. Picked up last when enroute & all used up previous day for return	J.R.

Army Form C. 2118.

Page 4.

WAR DIARY
3rd Cavalry Supply Column
or
INTELLIGENCE SUMMARY.
(Erase heading not required.)

Hour, Date, Place	Summary of Events and Information	Remarks and references to Appendices
OSTEND. 10/10/14. 5.0 PM	No.2 Section started loading, took little lorries.	
— 11/10/14 3.30 AM	No.1 — returned. Lorry badly damaged, recovered frame & engine free.	JSH
2.0 PM	Started to see I.G.C. about move of R.V. for loaded section. Met A.Q.M.G. 3rd Cav. Div., who ordered section to move at once to R.V. Croonrode 5 miles N.N.E. of THOROUT on BRUGES—THOROUT road. Found out Lieut. I.G.C. had had R.V. for 2.0 P.M. Lt. Arrers night but had not informed me.	JSH
	No.2 left R.V. at 7.0 P.M.	
3.0 PM	No.1 Section started to reload took 3 hours.	
4.0 PM	Started on day for Headquarters. No.2. 3rd Cav. Div. Reinforcements collected all spare lorries into headquarters. Found it impossible to get M.T. spares as utilized parts of badly damaged lorry which returned with No.1 Section to make good all three lorries reported damaged 5/10/14 & reloaded 10/10/14. 2nd Lt. J.G. Smith joined as Interpreter.	
— 12/10/14 3.10 AM	No.2 returned.	
7.0 AM	Arranged for No.1 to load. Started 7.45 AM finished 10.30 AM	
8.0 PM	Received verbal message three offrs. Lorries from I.G.C. for R.V. at 2.30 P.M. road junction 3 miles W. of THOROUT of ROULERS—THOROUT rd. road. from H.Q.G.L.S.D. (Later changed by I.G.C. to 5 miles N. of ROULERS) No.1 Mt. loaded.	JSH

WAR DIARY or INTELLIGENCE SUMMARY.

Army Form C. 2118.

3rd Cavalry Supply Column

Page 5

Hour, Date, Place	Summary of Events and Information	Remarks and references to Appendices
OSTEND 12/10/14 11.0 AM	No 3 started loading - finished & parked 2.30 P.M.	
12.5 PM	Received message to R.V. at 1 P.M. from I.G.C. published 1.25 A.M.	
6.0 PM	Received verbal orders from I.G.C. for R.V. for 13th. =	
	(1) Rout junction on OSTEND - THOROUT road about 2 miles NW of THOROUT (1) Head quarter & all other lorries to pick up remaining S.	J.H.
13/10/14 3.30 AM	Schot to proceed to R.V. closing OSTEND between 10 & 11.0 AM by Regiments.	
6.0 PM	Loaded all possible lorries additional to those already on night.	
9.30 PM	No 2 left loaded, followed by remainder. Well clear by 10.45 P.M. Abandoned damaged lorries already partially stripped of their money all fitted useful spare parts.	
10.45 PM	Orders from 2nd Bn. G.S. & 4th Bn. to divide of I.G.C. to push loaded lorries on to ROULERS (GRAND PLACE). Remainder of lorries to move to Place Neu Rail head. Loaded section parked. Orders from IV Corps A.S. to Parks & Refill.	
ROULERS 1.0 PM	all parked. Sent N.P.M. & IV Corps to camp of our lorries next day for Rats to DONKIRK. Sent 6C, 7th & S. Col. to arrange for accordingly.	
11.35 PM	Received personal orders to send G. IV Corps to more at once to DONKIRK.	J.H.
14/10/14 12.35 AM	T. not lorries left today due to heavy rain have made roads but workshop lorries best heavy sliding of blocky roads.	
1.40 AM	All away except subsection still out refilling & arrived at 2.0 PM delayed 1½ hours blocked roads. Two lorries stuck in trouble back wheels would not revolve owing to difficulties being augured up. Three hours spent on them, but of no use, so they were abandoned	Jh.A.

(9 29 6) W 4141—463 100,000 9/14 H W V Forms/C. 2118/10

WAR DIARY or INTELLIGENCE SUMMARY.

Army Form C. 2118.

3rd Cavalry Supply Column

Page 6

(Erase heading not required.)

Hour, Date, Place	Summary of Events and Information	Remarks and references to Appendices
DUNKIRK 14/10/14 8.0AM	First lorries arrived all in by 11.30 A.M. Personnel very tired	
10.0 AM	Rptd. I.G.C. (1) Rendez-vous 3.30 PM at WESTVLETEREN today supplies + 2 tons oats. (ii) the lorries supplied from OSTEND to S.Dept	
12.15 PM	Started loading. Impossible before + personnel required a meal. Lorries also had to be filled up with petrol, oil etc + greased round. Note the used up all reserve petrol which was carried on 3 spare lorries from OSTEND had been largely used during night to get lorries away from REULERS where no by supply was available.	
5.30 PM	Loading finished. Great delay owing to oats being shipped under hay — incident of wheat.	
6.0 PM	No. 1 left for R.V.	
6.30 PM	No. 2 to load oats — delay in removing hay from top of oats in hold.	J.H.
11.0 PM	— finished & rptd.	
---15/10/14 3.15 AM	Went to I.G.C. Orders (1) Leave here at 10.0 am loaded with 100 galls petrol, some lubricating oil + company oats. respective. (2) R.V. OOSTVLETEREN via FURNES + YPRES road.	
10.40 AM	No. 2 left followed close to lorry — a wheel was out. Working same number.	
11.15 AM	No. 1 returned + 11 extra lorries. Oats refused by Division. All number. 1 section 11 lorries had gone 4 miles S.W. of YPRES = waste of 14 hours	
5.0 PM	own affair. I.G.C. Orders (1) Take oats only 16 F. (2) Spare lorries to take return for S.A.C. & F. Coln. (3) R.V. ROUSBRUGGE = from	
8.0 PM	Arranged with O.C. 7th Div. S. Col. for self to take special motor station.	J.H.
	also 34 Tons Oats	

H W V

WAR DIARY
3rd Cavalry Supply Column
INTELLIGENCE SUMMARY
(Erase heading not required.)

Army Form C. 2118.
Page 7

Hour, Date, Place	Summary of Events and Information	Remarks and references to Appendices
DUNKIRK 15/10/14 11.30 PM	Went to I.G.C. Telephone message from DAQMG IV Corps for 15,000 rations meat & salt, 18,000 sugar, 17 tons to G to be at above R.V. at 3.0 PM 16/10/14. Also Railhead to move 16/10/14 to ARNEKE	J.R.
— 16/10/14 9.15 AM to 11.30 AM	Lorries left except 17 with 2 ft Swann.	
ARNEKE — 1.0 PM	Arrived. Saw S.A.O. & IV Corps DADS. OWE to load 1 day ration filled & more off at once under orders of S.S.S.O. (ii) No 1 to load 1 day rations as soon as No 2 finished & to be started PÖPERINGHE by 12 noon 17 R.	
2.30 PM	No 2 Started loading. Very awkward yard.	
6.0 PM	— Left.	
7.45 PM	No 1 Started loading — finished.	
9.30 PM		
— 17/10/14 5.0 AM	Message from O.C. IV Corps for altering R.V. to YPRES.	J.W.
10.30 AM	No 1 left Railhead. No 2 back empty & stands by uphill.	
3.0 PM	No 2 lorries below due to contamination of train.	
11.30 PM	Telephoned to SLOP & G (2) D.C. Corps. Orders (1) Railhead 18th CAESTRE (2) R.V. 3.0 PM 3½ miles S.W. YPRES on BAILLEUL–YPRES road.	J.W.
— 18/10/14 5.30 AM 5.30 AM to 9.30 AM	Lorries left. No 2 loaded in front.	
CAESTRE — 11.0 AM	Arrived — went to R.V. No lorries at CAESTRE. Arranged R.V.V. went to late fruit. Found at STRAZEELE 2.0 PM	J.R.

WAR DIARY 3rd Cavalry Supply Column

Army Form C. 2118.
Page 8.

INTELLIGENCE SUMMARY
(Erase heading not required.)

Hour, Date, Place	Summary of Events and Information	Remarks and references to Appendices
CAESTRE 18/10/14 3:15 PM	No 1 loading at STRAZEELE. Finished, took & parked 5·30 PM. Delayed p.a.	
— 19/10/14 1·45 PM	My blanks a narrow roads.	
	Mia took a fit.	
7·30 AM	Received my first copy of Routine Orders. No supply Railway Train.	
8·45 AM	Arrived at STRAZEELE 8·45 AM	
1·00 PM	No 2 left Strazeele. Took 2 hrs 10 minutes to load.	
1·30 PM	— Took & parked.	
3·15 PM	As no orders for loaded section went to YPRES. Saw A.Q.M.G. IV Corps who said RV was as for 18th at 1·0 PM. This was at 5·0 PM. On returning saw S.S.O	
6·0 PM	No 1 left RV at 6·0 PM.	
7·0 PM	Headqrs. R.T.O. of Staff Train L of C. Parked 2·6/7 lorries BAILLEUL Together with	
12·45 PM	2 F Pack returned instructive information as RV etc for P. attempt ARMENTIERES. [signed]	
BAILLEUL 20/10/14 5·0 PM	No 1 took empty	
10·30 AM	No 2 arrived full staff to RV. A.Q.M.G. a Workshops pushed.	
10·45 AM	Orders by BHQ M.C. IV Corps. (1) 2 lorries to be detached unit to info 2 other stations (2) O.C.'s Car to go to RV; remainder about roads (3) Orderly Officer applies with this (R.O.C.'S Car to go to RV; remainder). (4) Getting news of Ry before 6·0 PM, and send to H.Qrs.	
12·0 Noon	left to RV. arrived 10·45 AM 3½ miles Sw of YPRES on BAILLEUL-YPRES road.	
	Saw S.S.O.& O.C. Sec 2.	
2·10 PM	Back. No news of train at Staten.	
3·0 PM	Lorries attached to load.	
4·0 PM	No 1 started loading. Took 1 hour 5 minutes. Entrance bad to station	
	yard. Was 2 lorries to the Corps troops	

WAR DIARY 3rd Cavalry Supply Column

or

INTELLIGENCE SUMMARY

Army Form C. 2118.

Page 10.

(Erase heading not required.)

Instructions regarding War Diaries and Intelligence Summaries are contained in F. S. Regs., Part II. and the Staff Manual respectively. Title pages will be prepared in manuscript.

Hour, Date, Place	Summary of Events and Information	Remarks and references to Appendices

CAESTRE 24/10/14 4.15 P.M. No 1 Troubling test 2 hours. awkward gait.

4.0 P.M. Self at HQrs. Obtained RV rate as for 23rd. Also news to evacuate wounded. f. A.

6.30 P.M. Billing points. Guerathes & wounded returned to CAESTRE.

ZILLEBEKE 24/10/14 10.0 A.M. No 2 back. Noticed formation.

CAESTRE 24/10/14 10.30 A.M. No 1 left for RV. took 2 hours.

4.30 P.M. No 2 loaded. took 2 hours.

9.0 P.M. Manage Railhead. RV etc as were an 24th.

10.0 P.M. No 1 back.

Refueled lorries & blue horses told of. T. (now at OSTEND two or more from POPERINGHE) f. A.

— " — 26/10/14 10.0 A.M. No. 2 left loaded for RV. Lony went at RV.

3.0 P.M. Left to HQ & to ZILLEBEKE. Refilling point & .... S.O. .... a
9.0 P.M. Beek, message. Railhead. HAZEBROUCK .... guns.
No 1 took 2½ hours to load. then down by 7th and 5 Gds

11.30 P.M. No 2 back.

— " — 27/10/14 8.0 A.M. message ...... in charge A Railhead RV.

10.30 " No 1 Railhead.

2.30 P.M. No 2 back. took 1 hour & 5 minutes. good yard. HAZEBRUCK.

4.0 P.M. West of YPRES—ZILLEBEKE. Refilling point. Seftin left also a shot time
            at RM. R.E. Orbus Railhead. Quite rate as for 24th

9.30 P.M. Back with No 1 Section

— " — 10.30 A.M. No 2 left.

1.0 P.M. No news ... in .... General Lock .... HAZEBROUCK
1.45 P.M. .... No 1 left. cracked loading 3.0 P.M. took 1 hr. 10 mins.

WAR DIARY 3rd Cavalry Supply Column

INTELLIGENCE SUMMARY

Army Form C. 2118.
Page 9.

(Erase heading not required.)

Instructions regarding War Diaries and Intelligence Summaries are contained in F.S. Regs, Part II. and the Staff Manual respectively. Title pages will be prepared in manuscript.

Hour, Date, Place	Summary of Events and Information	Remarks and references to Appendices
BAILLEUL. 20/10/14 9.0 PM	Went to HQrs at POPERINGHE & rec'd orders re R.V. 21st etc.	
— 21/10/14 2.0 AM	No. 2 truck empty	
9.0 AM	3 lorries left to be attached to IV Corps Troops.	
10.30 AM	No. 1 left loaded.	
12.35 PM	No. 2 started (empty) took 1 hr + 10 minutes.	
	Issued various stationery orders for Column, M.T. & Supply Officers	R.A.
3.0 PM	Message to IV Corps. Railhead R.V. etc same as 20th acknowledged.	
7.0 PM	Informed same "Mayor had left sealed message Railhead POPERINGHE	
— 22/10/14	arriving accordingly"	
	No. 2 M.T. loaded J.R.V. 10 PM 3/4 mile SW of YPRES on BAILLEUL-YPRES road.	
10.0 AM	No. 1 at station. HQrs etc also well up. Kept unity 6 3/4 hours to load. E.O.	
11.0 AM	6.15 PM finished. 7.30 PM	
7.30 PM	HQrs + workshops failed. Informed all of my position.	
9.0 PM	Rec'd message that HQ & MT & IV Corps. Railhead CAESTRE R.V. etc as for 21st	
11.0 PM	Went & started HQrs &	
	Issued march orders for Column	
— 23/10/14 3.0 AM	No. 2 truck empty	
CAESTRE 11.0 AM	— Nearly to load. Workshops & HQrs failed. Issued various orders for Column.	
2.10 PM	— Lorry took 3 hours outward journey.	
9.15 PM	Left for HQrs. Met No. 1 Journey. Message Railhead same as Sunday	
	R.V. 3/4 mile W of YPRES on POPERINGHE-YPRES road. Rec'd via STEENWOORDE	
— 24/10/14 12.0 midnight 12.0 PM	Arrived with No. 1 Section	
8.0 AM	No. 2 left loaded. Also left lorries with lorry for full officers, HQrs M.T. Base	
2.8 PM	after 5 etc but no more till 9.0 PM	

WAR DIARY or INTELLIGENCE SUMMARY

Army Form C. 2118.

3rd Cavalry Suffly Column

Page 1

Instructions regarding War Diaries and Intelligence Summaries are contained in F. S. Regs, Part II. and the Staff Manual respectively. Title pages will be prepared in manuscript.

(Erase heading not required.)

Hour, Date, Place	Summary of Events and Information	Remarks and references to Appendices
CAESTRE 28/10/14	Informed next part of Cavalry Cyks instead of 4th Cyks	
5am	Cut off St Bell to report to HQ 2nd Cav Bde. No change except	
	RV at BAILLEUL-YPRES road. Railhead STRAZEELE	
29/10/14 10.30am	No 2 Cyk to load STRAZEELE. Took 2 hours.	
10.40am	No 2 left there	
10.30am	No 1 left [illegible]	
11.15pm	Left Orders to R.V. Saw St QMG. Informed Railhead is BAILLEUL	
6.30pm	Roads Informed orders to move Headquarters from CAESTRE	
30/10/14	No 1 back	
	Battle Gate for Parts	
ST SYLVESTRE 7.0 pm	No 2 left Workshop for Parts. No. 1 to Station. Very awkward yard to	
1.0am	Rt Guard Workshop parked. No. 1 to Station. Very awkward yard to get to. 3 Collisions. Level Crossing Continually shut, or motion road	
11.30pm	to box, inside yard before opening out. Roads very bad & approach to station	
	Locally took 5½ hours. Impossible to do 3 C/L at once.	
	Names of Railhead R.V. etc.	
	Handed over Workshop complete to 5 section S.C/L	
31/10/14 4.0am	No 2 back. Sent off M Cyclist with orders Railhead not changed.	
	Sent off an order to find next Rendezvous & Place at RV, Orchard Sev. tried	
	to BAILLEUL left at 10.0am. No 2 to GF ready to load.	
10pm	at EBBLINGHEM. Not allowed to draw the 1·45pm on account of congestion took	
	5 hours. Went to RV. Road BAILLEUL to YPRES blocked shrunk.	
	No 1 at 5.45 pm. A full P's each & Bde left in 15 minutes, was allowed to	
10.45pm	HQ me told us RV. etc same for RV as today. Left section	
	very heavy division	

Army Form C. 2118.

WAR DIARY
or
INTELLIGENCE SUMMARY
(Erase heading not required.)

3rd Cavalry Supply Column

Page 12.

Hour, Date, Place	Summary of Events and Information	Remarks and references to Appendices
ST. SYLVESTRE 3.0 AM 1/11/14	No. 1 Back.	
10.15 AM	No. 2 left loaded. Message that we were required to load.	
12.30 PM	No. 1 arrived at EBBLINGHEM 7.30 AM. Had to wait two hours before starts. Took 2 hours to load. Sent 10 previous correspondence to A.G. Base. Rolls etc received 78.103'.	J.R.
2/11/14 2.10 AM	No. 2 Back.	
10.30 AM	No. 1 left loaded. Same R.V.	
1.0 PM	Visited EBBLINGHEM. Loading took 1½ hours. Refreshments 1½ hours. Visited No. 1 in Station Yard YPRES. Walked about 4.45 P.M. Went on to R.V. Found No. 1. Refilled P.G. R.V. etc as usual for 2nd. before moving off to Refill P.G. second trip to A&M.T. depot. Sent off 2nd Rendis second Trip to A&M.T. depot.	J.R.
11.0 PM	No. 1 back.	
3/11/14 9.45 AM	Informed to load at 12.30 PM from R.S.O. EBBLINGHEM.	
10.45 PM	No. 2 left loaded. Went to R.V. Roadscarpentel.	
1.30 PM	Visited Ruillied. Loaded in 1 hour. Was ordered to take back slaughter. Rou't about R.V. etc same as usual. was moved off by Colonel on Staff with ambulance in tow from R.Q. to BAILLEUL. Lorries moved off by Colonel on Staff with ambulance in tow from R.Q.	J.R.
4/11/14 2.0 AM	No. 2 Back.	
10.30 AM	No. 1 left for R.V.	
2.10 PM	visited Ruillied. Took 1 hour 15 minutes. EBBLINGHEM	
4.30 PM	Sgt. A. Priest to M.G.o 7th about stout skirt Car Reft Jerry 6 FQM. No definite news of his return	
11.30 PM	No. 1 Back. Ruilliad 5th STRAZEELE. R'ete as before.	J.R.

WAR DIARY or INTELLIGENCE SUMMARY

Army Form C. 2118.

3rd Army Suffk
Collection
Page 13

Instructions regarding War Diaries and Intelligence Summaries are contained in F. S. Regs., Part II. and the Staff Manual respectively. Title pages will be prepared in manuscript.

(Erase heading not required.)

Hour, Date, Place	Summary of Events and Information	Remarks and references to Appendices
ST SYLVESTRE CAPPEL 10 XI/14 12.0 Mn	No 2 W/Meaded	
	Railhead STRAZEELE Visited. Located w 2 hours. On to R.V. but on account of blocked roads met No 2. Convoy turned back before P.	
7.30 PM	No 2 tack. Learnt Railhead moved to STEENBECQUE.	
— 6/11/14. 4.30 AM	No 1. left for R.V. Self to select a Park.	R.M.
10.30 AM MOORBECQUE	No 2 arrived & went to Railhead. Started in 1½ hours. No 1 not whole/had arrived. Started. Went on to R.V. Road from BAILLEUL thickest with transports & 197 E Div's 66½ South. Rain very heavy, caught No 1. Foggy bivouac for lorry & rather ditched one or even two hours. Broke off here 3—3 inches. Very hard on tyres. Took from 11.0 AM to 8.30 AM BAILLEUL to R.V. very heavy work for all personnel. R.V. & YPRES under heavy shell fire. Saw B.A.Q.M.G. who gave permission to use any road back.	
LOCRE 7/11/14 1.0 AM	Bivouacked by adm from G.H.Q. taken via POPERINGHE, STEENVOORDE	
9.0 AM MOORBECQUE	No 2 left. bivouac to R.V.	
1.30 PM	No 1. h. in return. Arrived at 3.0 PM. Took 1½ hours STEENBECQUE	R.M.
11.30 PM	No 2 tack.	
— 7/11/14 6.30 AM	No 1. left for R.V.	
11.0 PM	No 2 doubled. Took 1¾ hours	
8.30 PM	At R.V. with No 1. Left on base before moving off to Refill No 2. Pce. Joined up with 9 Lorries carrying 156 nm reinforcements	R.M.

WAR DIARY or INTELLIGENCE SUMMARY

Army Form C. 2118.

3rd Cavalry Supply Column.

Page 14.

(Erase heading not required.)

Hour, Date, Place	Summary of Events and Information	Remarks and references to Appendices
NOORBEECKE 9/11/14 10.5AM	No 1 returned -	
9.30 AM	No 2 left Sadul	
12.0 Noon	No 1 lorries took 13¾ hours water to Brit HQrs. On return found Lt Teale who met badly wounded man Pte Lockyer. Pte Anger & Cpl. Flower volunteered to go back to Stratasgunne at YPRES to retrieve abandoned lorry with Lt Teale, Smith & self. Done. On joining up with Number of lorries found 3 more men wounded. 1 more died — admission to hospital. Two lorries damaged, driving hut by shrapnel.	Jr. 9
10/11/14 11.30 PM	No 2 back.	
9.30 AM	No 1 left for R.V.	
10.30 AM	No 2 to load took 2 hours. Visited Ruckhead & on to Hopre Sir. On 4 Refilling Points & back. Arranged to load & enter Can. Regt.	B.9.
11.0 PM	No 1 Back.	
11/11/14 4.15 PM	No 2 left. Went to G.H.Q. Sent in for 12 lorries which joined later.	
12.15 PM	Sgt BART secured with 2 lorries short unexpectedly. Battalion & now 160 lorries which supposed to be added strength to Army.	
2.30 PM	Went to BERGUES & supplied 2 Bde 27th. The men thankful. Bulk load p't	
	train 2 hours. HAZEBROUCK.	
12/11/14 2.30 AM	No 2 back.	
9.30 AM	No 1 left to unload.	
12.30 PM	No 2 to unload took 2¾ hours owing to having from 3 sections of train.	
	HAZEBROUCK.	
	Discussed system of loading systematically with S.S.O. for a three Bde train. Would take 40 loaded during the day, with spare for section.	J.S.A.

WAR DIARY or INTELLIGENCE SUMMARY

Army Form C. 2118.

3rd G.H.Q. Supply Column

Page 5.

Hour, Date, Place	Summary of Events and Information	Remarks and references to Appendices
MOORSEELE 13/11/14 7am	No.1 Park	
9am	No.2 left Park	
	Sent to tyre press BERGUETTE. Saw DADT. (M.T.) & arranged with personnel etc required to be provided.	
	Pulled HAZEBROUCK. Took 12 hours to obtain bulks. Ordnance issued to load Rfg. in bulk. Personnel too tired to work. To leave early 14th	
11am	No.2 back	
14/11/14 6am	All just loads up immediately. No lorries available for B2 a HQrs a very few armoured with infantry & Number of HQrs own class in workshops.	
10am	No.1 left for RV.	
	Wrote to OC of C. Ammn to be carried. No.1 Sec. Rfg HQ Rfg 2, 6th Bde.	
	Took 25 hours obtained buffs as arranged in previous road by Staff	
	Return ? 2 lorries of tender all extra Refgts P.E.	
	Loading HAZEBROUCK. Kept working 7 hours. Took 4 hours. Some delay due to failure of guering trucks.	
15/11/14 11:15am	No.1 back. 2 lorries 4 stores 4/8 which owing to bad return roads spilled.	
9am	No.2 left	
11:30am	Convoy took 3¾ hours	
	Received 4 lorries from GHQ	
	Must go No.2 back. Remainder much later. Waiting for reload of units	
11:30pm	Whichever turns up.	
16/11/14 noon	No.1 left. Ralm at Refilly. Route & officials 1½ – 2 hours	
	Ist Cav Div. Took 3 hours. 11:30pm No.2 back.	

Army Form C. 2118.

Page 16.

WAR DIARY
or
INTELLIGENCE SUMMARY

3rd Cavalry Supply Column.

(Erase heading not required.)

Hour, Date, Place	Summary of Events and Information	Remarks and references to Appendices
MOORSEECQUE 17/11/14 9:30AM	No 2 left the R.V.	
10 AM	No 1. Nothing. HAZEBROUCK took 2½ hours. Only 40 gals. num or turn.	
11:15 PM	3 vehs of No 2 broke. Everything went to No 2 Coy. Referenced with Mulby Whel Spirit. Result Lance broken, after which about lost its authority, infort not safe. So decided to wait till all vehicles etc enough of which had to be ½ unloaded & thereafter turn off petrol etc. shut hin further trainset.	[initials]
18/11/14 5:15 PM	Improved receptacle for water. Reminder No 2 Coy.	
9:0 AM	No 1. left.	
1:0 PM	No 2 totaled took 2 3/4 hours. Bacon all but MOV equivalent. Afelor to S.S.O. Also that full loaded. Full ration As num Aprilic twice a week. Observed only ½ ration.	
10:0 PM	Tell Just just no to No 1 back. Visited gun till 9:30 of refill. Promise of Belns etc except 70 vehs which was changed by S.O. without warning.	[initials]
19/11/14 9:15 AM	No 2 left the R.V. Back at 11.15 PM.	
1:0 PM	No 1 took HAZEBROUCK took 2 hours. Been but equivalent loaded to some Rum.	
	Visited R.C. Com. BEASE. Untanked in R.V. MOORSEECQUE 8:45 at 7:0 PM	[initials]
20/11/14 9:0 AM	1:0 PM Enclosed to 7:45 late as for today.	
	No1 boris diff full.	
4:30 PM	Reminder No 1 left. Menu & from * Col B did not come down with not fill on body	
	CAN info with S.O. who would not leave units of additional lorries full at 7:0 PM.	[initials]

1247 W 3209 200,000 (E) 8/14 J.B.C. & A. Forms/C. 2118/11.

WAR DIARY or INTELLIGENCE SUMMARY

Army Form C. 2118.

3rd Cavalry Supply Column

Page 17

Hour, Date, Place	Summary of Events and Information	Remarks and references to Appendices
MOORBEEQUE. 20/11/14. 4.46pm	No 2 loading HAZEBROUCK. Kept waiting 2½ hours & then fixed to load in —	J.H.
21/11/14 7.0am	Wait by Bebo to allow train to leave. Took 1½ hours. No 2 largest loads regrettably. Took it hours. No 1 six troops Left, Rest delivered. Took 4½ hours.	
10.30pm	Remainder No 1 loading to lay until our Troop lorries returned. Finished 3.0pm	
11.0 pm	No 2 off loaded. R.V. for 7a B24 CAESTRE.	
5.0 pm	VISITED CAESTRE with S.S.O and half trucks known. Eventually modelled them out.	
9.0 pm	All lorries back.	J.H.
22/11/14	Last trip deep, loading weather very bad. Snow sleet rain & frost. All small lots against have transport movements. Took 4 hours HAZEBROUCK Onboard small siding. No 2 to load. No 1 left to Refill C. Points.	
10.0 am		
1.15 pm		
6.15 pm	Visited various Regt Refill C. Points. Arranged to deliver about 30 tons hay daily known by using alterable lorries served Supp. by the Half of Supply Rear	
	Left Railhead early. Red 7 Numbers from G.H.Q. To and back 8 Napiers.	J.H.
23/11/14 9.0am	No 2 skewing over lorries that loads. Took 2½ hours. When they left.	
9.30 am	No 1 W to load as request R.S.O. Wasn't allowed to start for Beach 5½ hrs owing to shunting. Eventually when loading 3rd supplies dumped to allow train to run, but train did not move off till 45 minutes after loading	
7.15 pm	finished, all lorries back	J.H.
	Every day sent in 7 Napiers to ST OMER. Supervised delivery of hay.	

WAR DIARY or INTELLIGENCE SUMMARY

Army Form C. 2118.

3rd Cavalry Supply Column

Hour, Date, Place	Summary of Events and Information	Remarks and references to Appendices
MORBECQUE 24/11/14 1:10 AM	No.1 Coy offloaded. Back 6.30 PM	
2:30 PM	Load'g No.2 took 3½ hours. STEENBECQUE	F.S.
	Visited Railhead twice. Been told inadequate supply platform	
25/11/14 9 AM	No.1 left to load. Took 3½ hours.	
11 AM	No.2 unloaded. Back at 6.0 PM	
	Visited Sir W. Asc. HQrs & Railhead. Been told No. 1 coy & Asc. Hrs, Hazebrouck, F.S.	
26/11/14 9 AM	No.2 to load. Took 3¾ hours.	
11 AM	No.1 left loaded. Back at 5:45 PM	
	Visited McGui & Railhead. Report of hemp delivered satisfactory. Insufficient	
	Sent SOS Return per STORES. Pay & Billiting's Beaucher-Ribecourt	
	First precaution results. Furniture necessary when starting to prevent	
	Steerers crushing owing to back jolt. II Radiator Tubes are light to freeze at	
	below warm without sufficient [?]. III. Impossible to fully drain cylinder heads	
	Cartwright-Daimlers liable to crack. IV water/pet carburettor have to	
	be wrapped & the Rollwertzs V Small tubes of antnrila liable to	
	choked by continually falling cloud with any water to hand; try this	
	keep in water & filter back with funnel. Issued further orders to	
	clerical staff.	F.S.
27/11/14 11:0 AM	No.2 left loaded. Back 6.0 PM	
3:30 PM	No.1 loaded after 2 hours wait. Took 3¼ hours	
6.0 PM	News to shift Collonne Off Main HAZEBROUCK-AIRE road. Gone in ½ hour.	
	Reconnaissance party to look for water supply & road	
	Started in from Costelaar — Steenbecque	F.S.

Army Form C. 2118.

Page 19.

WAR DIARY
or
INTELLIGENCE SUMMARY

3rd Cavalry Supply Column

(Erase heading not required.)

Instructions regarding War Diaries and Intelligence Summaries are contained in F.S. Regs., Part II. and the Staff Manual respectively. Title pages will be prepared in manuscript.

Hour, Date, Place	Summary of Events and Information	Remarks and references to Appendices
MOOR 28/11/14 11.0AM	No.1 left barracks at 5.30 P.M.	
12.15PM	No.2 barracks. Finished 6.0 P.M. Owing to awkward placing of trucks.	J.H.
29/11/14 11.0AM	No.2 left barracks at 5.30 PM	J.H.
6.30PM	No.1 started loading. Kept 4½ hours waiting owing to train being left outside station & not shunted in. Took 3 hours.	Appendix II. Time envelope sheet for month.
30/11/14 11.0AM	No.1 left barracks at 5.15 PM	
2.15PM	No.2 loading. Took 2¾ hours.	
1/12/14 11.0AM	No.2 left barracks. Back at 3.45PM.	
1.0PM	No.1 loading. Took 2½ hours.	J.H.
3.15PM	Two hours practice parade for H.M. The King	
2/12/14 7.30AM	Parade.	
9.0PM	En festive. Inspection by H.M. The King	
2.0PM	No.1 left loaded, back at 5.45 PM.	
2.30PM	No.2 loading. Took 2¾ hours.	J.H.
3/12/14 11.0AM	No.2 left loaded. Back at 3.45 PM	
2.0PM	No.1 loading. Took 4 hours	
	Worked out Provisional New Box Establishment. 8 Truck Hay Lorries for ST OMER.	J.H.
4/12/14 11.0AM	No.1 left loaded. Back 3.45 PM	
12.0Noon	No.2 to load. Took 2½ hours.	
	Finished. Remarks etc on New W.E.	
	10 New Hay Lorries from ST OMER.	J.H.

Army Form C. 2118.

3rd Cavalry Supply Column.

Page 20

WAR DIARY
or
INTELLIGENCE SUMMARY

(Erase heading not required.)

Instructions regarding War Diaries and Intelligence Summaries are contained in F. S. Regs., Part II. and the Staff Manual respectively. Title pages will be prepared in manuscript.

Hour, Date, Place	Summary of Events and Information	Remarks and references to Appendices
MORBECQUE 6/12/14. 11.0 am	No 1 left full. Back 3.15 PM	
3.30 PM	No 2 lorry took 2½ hours - Refuse waiting 1½ hours owing to breakdown engine. Visited Hdqrs. Arranged for allotted annexes lorries to Sections.	J.A.
— 7/12/14 11.0 AM	No 2 left. Back at 3.15 PM	
2.50 PM	No. 1 lorry. Took 1hr 35 mins. HAZEBROUCK post yard. Visited Railhead. & L.G.O.C's from ST OMER.	J.A.
— 8/12/14 1.00 PM	No 1 left. Backed except 7th Bn which left behind in ambulette. Back 3.30 PM	
3.30 PM	No 2 lorry after today. Left 1½ hours while Gunbay shunted. Took 2½ hours. Visited Railhead HAZEBROUCK	
— 9/12/14 10.0 AM	No 2 left. Back 4.15 PM. Today due to delivering to Squadrons.	
3.20 PM	No 1 lorry after 1½ hours Gunl. Took 2½ hours. HAZEBROUCK	
6.30 PM	DTOMG ordered No 1 Afta park tack for 7 hours. To allow of movements of FRENCH.	J.A.
— 10/12/14 11.45 PM	No 1 left loaded delay- moving- to after lorry's left. Back at 4.30 PM	
	O.C. Section refused tackle to squadrons	J.A.
4.15 PM	No 2 loaded. Went 2 hours. loaded in 2 hours	
	Received 6 Xmas lorries for ST OMER.	
— 11/12/14 10.0 AM	No 2 left. Back at 3.0 PM	
3.15 PM	— 1 loaded. HAZEBROUCK. Took 2½ hours. Visited valve on oil 7th Bn arrived out of pet. Arranged towards Essex Yeomanry. Had worried 2 pts by Hdqrs to accelerate MT stores urgently required ammunition.	J.A.
— 12/12/14 10.00 AM	No 1 left. Back at 2.45 PM	
3.45 PM	No 2 to load HAZEBROUCK. Waited 1¾ hrs for train. M2 willing empty. Took 2½ hours further fit. Transferred 8 Clerks + 4 butchers to R.S.O	J.A.

1247 W 3299 200,000 (E) 8/14 J.B.C.& A. Forms/C. 2118/11.

WAR DIARY or INTELLIGENCE SUMMARY

Army Form C. 2118.

3rd Cavalry Supply Column — Page 21

Hour, Date, Place	Summary of Events and Information	Remarks and references to Appendices
MORBECQUE 13/12/14 10·0AM	No. 3 Offloaded. Back in TSPM today due to delivery to Regt. & Fire. Possible for MT. officer to wait will, so 15 minutes start in delivery to Squadrons.	
3·40 PM	No. 1 leaving HAZEBROUCK West 1¾ hours took 2¾ hours	A.H.
9·0 AM	Visited O.C. Asc. Railhead HAZEBROUCK	
14/12/14 12·45 PM	No. 1 left for R.V. short of BAILLEUL on CAESTRE–BAILLEUL road.	
2·45 PM	" at R.V. Back at 7·0 PM	
3·30 PM	No. 2 started loading STEENBECQUE took 2¾ hours	
	Self visited G.H.Q. at R.V. & Railhead. Orderd No. 2 to be at today's R.V. at 1·10 PM as no news.	R.N.
15/12/14 8·50 AM	Wire for RV as above at 12·0 Noon.	
10·0 AM	No. 2 left after lying N.covered. R.V. 12·35 P.M. Back 6·30 P.M.	
3·45 PM	No. 1 trouble after wait 1¾ hours. This delayed 20 minutes by sentry, lost out trailers from centre of train. took 3 hours.	
6·0 PM	Visited H.Q.S. HQ return. Investigate supply of newspapers at Railhead	A.H.
9·0 PM	Recd wire some. Railhead to-day	
	—— O.C. Asc. R.V. 10 PM MOORSLEDE Lorry in old billet.	
16/12/14 1·0 PM	No. 1 left loaded back at 5·0 PM	
2·15 PM	No. 2 loading STEENBECQUE took 2¼ hours.	
	Visited Railhead & inspected all horses of Cav. & good. Saw rifles very old. Some Service issues.	A.H.
17/12/14 10·0 AM	No. 2 left Back 4·0 PM.	
2·45 PM	No. 1 loading STEENBECQUE took 2¼ hours. Only enough Troops meat etc., do so 1/4.1 Belu etc Bit.	A.H.

Army Form C. 2118.

Page 22.

WAR DIARY
or
INTELLIGENCE SUMMARY

3rd Cavalry Supply Column

(Erase heading not required.)

Hour, Date, Place	Summary of Events and Information	Remarks and references to Appendices
MARBECQUE 18/12/14 10:0AM	No 1 left loaded. Back 3:15PM	
3:0PM	No 2 loading STEENBECQUE. Took 3 hours	
19/12/4 10:0AM	No 2 left loaded. Back 3:15PM	R.A.
3:0PM	No 1 loading STEENBECQUE Took 3½ hours. Delay due to badly packed train & slow working by Railway staff.	
	Visited No 9 & No 3 G.H.Q. Railhead	
20/12/14 10:0PM	No 1 left loaded. Back 3:0PM	R.A.
2:30PM	No 2 loading STEENBECQUE. Took 3 hours. Slow loading by Railway staff	R.A.
21/12/14 10:0AM	No 2 left loaded. Back 3:0PM	
3:15PM	No 1 loading STEENBECQUE. Train well loaded, but was rather slow 3 hours	
	Visited H.Q. Pks & Railhead. Paraffin supply very short referred to S.S.O.	R.A.
22/12/14 11:40PM	No 1 left delayed by Bus Convoy. Back 4:0PM	
3:20PM	No 2 loading STEENBECQUE. Took 3 hr 10 minutes	Sd.H
23/12/14 10:0PM	No 2 left loaded. Back 3:0PM	
3:30PM	No 1 loading STEENBECQUE Took 2½ hours. S.S.O. arranged lowering Plum Pudding.	
	Report to take Plum full wagons unless checked over arranged beforehand.	R.A.
24/12/14 10:0PM	No 1 left loaded. Back 3:30PM arrived with 550 about HR.H. PM's gift. THIENNES STN reported	
	fit to load from 25th	
2:30PM	No 2 to load STEENBECQUE. Took 3 hours	R.A.
	Left rail affected THIENNES was cancelled	
25/12/14 10:0AM	No 2 left loaded, back at 2:45PM	
2:45PM	No 1 loading STEENBECQUE. Took 3 hours. PM's gift taken round	
	A. Schmidt Lance Corporal down in stable for men. Ramsbrie's regrettable	
	Had sit down dinner in stables for men. Plum-pudding etc, Enemy Concert in evening	

WAR DIARY or INTELLIGENCE SUMMARY

Army Form C. 2118.

3rd Cavalry Supply Column

Page 23.

Hour, Date, Place	Summary of Events and Information	Remarks and references to Appendices
MOORSEELE 26/12/14 10 PM	No 1 left today. Back about 2.30 P.M.	J.A.
2.30 PM	No 2 leaving STEENBECQUE. Took 3½ hours. Delay in having confirmn. Checked stacks in several places before trucks took hill.	
	Visited G.H.Q. NOEUX W.[?] out. Also Div'n HdQrs Westland.	
27/12/14 10 AM	No 2 left. Arrived Back 2.30 P.M.	
2.30 PM	No 1 leaving STEENBECQUE. Took 3½ hours. Arranged system of loading chits with R.S.O. Each command on observer of each train a columm. Column endeavour that of units work amongst a given truck is clubbed. Too much to unload. Spent chit for lorry after wells as amount of troop meat, bread etc varies daily, & that some can not be worked out satisfactorily overcome.	J.A.
	Visited A.S.C. HdQrs ? Rouelhends & A.S.C. are to run about where we puts day a rather a lift yet ensuring most satisfactory	
	4 Cy lorries had a crash by Forest. Class material for relief from H.Q. B 4 Wall etc. Not yet set up in full & several demands were ? except small insufficient quantity of provende	A.S.
28/12/14 10 AM	No 1 left loaded. Back 2.30 PM	
2.45 AM	No 2 leaving STEENBECQUE. Took 2½ hours. Informed leaving arrangement made yesterday satisfactory of pinch. Still mad.	A.S.
29/12/14 10 DAM	About 3rd nature began heart at Bruest.	
2 PM	No 2 left loaded. Back 2 30 PM	
	No 1 leaving STEEN BECQUE. Took 2¾ hours.	
	Visited train HdQ. HdQrs	V.A.

Army Form C. 2118.

WAR DIARY
or
INTELLIGENCE SUMMARY

(Erase heading not required.)

3rd Cavalry Supply Column

Page 24.

Hour, Date, Place	Summary of Events and Information	Remarks and references to Appendices
MOORSEQUE 30/10/14 11:00AM	No. 1 left to railhead back 3.0 PM	
3.0 PM	No. 2 loading STEENBECQUE. Took 2½ hours	
	Visited the HQ or Railway. 3/t D.G. Small Petupile left for ENGLAND. Investigated and put in supply substitution of newspapers.	Rot
31/10/14 10.0 AM	No. 2 left to railhead. Back 2.30 PM	
2.0 PM	No. 1 ready to load ESSBLIN & HEM. No train in sight to entrain to full strength. Two to 4 1/2 trains in queue, of fm which one train was not allowed to until for from Sickly STOMER.	
7.30 PM	Loading started. Took 2½ hours. Went 9 5½ hours in cold wind rain & sleet. Finished work 11.0 PM	Appendix III. Time & mileage sheet for month. F.A.

J. Mitchell
Major
OC 3rd Cav. S. Col.

Time & Mileage Record

Appendix I.
3rd Cavalry Supply Column

1914 October	No. I Section		No. II Section	
	Miles	No. of Hours on road*	Miles	No. of Hours on road*
3rd	80	16	80	16
4th	75	17	75	17
5th	70	14	70	14
6th	5	16	5	14
7th	0	0	0	0
8th	0	0	0	0
9th	0	6	5	8
10th	25	16	55	15
11th	30	9	25	13
12th	25	15	30	10
13th	50	12	35	15
14th	64	24	44	23
15th	29	18	34	14
16th	20	13	57	24
17th	29	15	22	15
18th	48	12	32	17
19th	22	14	31	10
20th	20	11	18	15
21st	21	15	20	9
22nd	37	14	23	15
23rd	35	14	30	19
24th	5	6	23	17
25th	46	14	28	10
26th	5	7	44	15
27th	47	13	16	8
28th	16	8	48	13
29th	23	15	11	7
30th	50	12	23	14
31st	26	14	27	8
	903	360	911	375
27 working days	33 4/9 miles per day 334/9	13 1/3 hrs per day 13 1/3	33 20/27 per day mean	13 8/9 hrs per day 13 8/9

* Includes normal time required to fill up with petrol oil etc.

J. Hulmbutton Capt. ASC

Time & Mileage Record

Appendix III
3rd Cavalry Supply Column

1914 November	No. I Section		No. II Section	
	Miles	No. of Hours on road*	Miles	No. of Hours on road*
1st	52	12	28	14
2nd	54	13	53	10
3rd	26	7	27	14
4th	55	15	52	9
5th	18	9	50	12
6th	27	16	12	8
7th	42	15	64	16
8th	33	16	6	7
9th	40	9	66	16
10th	65	15	8	7
11th	10	8	33	15
12th	34	15	42	11
13th	42	10	62	15
14th	32	16	10	10
15th	40	11	62	15
16th	64	14	12	10
17th	12	9	60	14
18th	62	16	11	10
19th	12	10	62	15
20th	27	12	12	9
21st	25	11	15	13
22nd	16	9	12	10
23rd	12	13	15	12
24th	15	10	6	9
25th	6	9	15	10
26th	15	9	6	8
27th	6	11	15	10
28th	16	10	6	9
29th	6	12	15	9
30th	15	9	6	9
	879	351	843	336
average	29 3/10 miles	11 7/10 hrs	28 1/10 miles	11 1/5 hrs

* Includes normal time for filling up with petrol, oil etc.

J. Auchinbeck
Capt. ASC.

Time & Mileage Record Appendix III
3rd Cavalry Supply Column

1914 December	No. I Section		No. II Section	
	Miles	No. of Hours on road*	Miles	No. of Hours on road*
1st	6	10	15	11
2nd	15	13	6	11
3rd	6	10	15	9
4th	15	9	6	9
5th	6	9	15	9
6th	17	10	8	10
7th	12	11	15	10
8th	15	9	12	10
9th	12	11	15	10
10th	16	10	12	10
11th	12	9	15	9
12th	15	9	12	9
13th	12	10	16	11
14th	4.5	12	6	10
15th	6	9	4.5	12
16th	16	11	6	9
17th	6	10	15	11
18th	15	10	6	10
19th	6	11	15	9
20th	15	9	6	10
21st	6	10	15	10
22nd	15	10	6	9
23rd	6	9	15	9
24th	15	9	6	9
25th	8	9	15	8
26th	15	9	6	10
27th	6	10	15	9
28th	15	9	6	9
29th	6	9	15	9
30th	15	9	6	9
31st	22	15	15	10
Total	407	310	381	300
Average	13 4/31 miles	10 hrs	12 15/31	9 21/31

*Includes normal time to fill up with petrol oil etc. &c.

*Included no normal time to fill up with petrol oil etc. &c.

Ex Ambulance Cap & Axle

121/4331

Contibuted:

War Diary

of

O.C. 3rd Cavalry Supply Column

Lt Colonel Wingate

from 1st January 1915 to 31st January 1915

(Volume II)

Army Form C. 2118

3rd Lorry Supply Column

Page 25

WAR DIARY
INTELLIGENCE SUMMARY
(Erase heading not required.)

Hour, Date, Place	Summary of Events and Information	Remarks and references to Appendices
MORBECQUE 1/1/15 10.0 AM	No 1 left loaded. Back at 2.30 PM.	
1.30 PM	No 2 at EBBLINGHEM station ready, kept waiting 2¾ hours, altogether as lorry & other lorries ¾ hour before engine arrived, on her shunting. Took 2½ hours to load.	
3.30 PM	No 2 back & parked. Returned surplus FIAT car & drivers borrowed from Commandant BOULOGNE, with Hupmobile car belongs T/MTCF Bell ASC to GHQ under escort from Cmr. Corps.	H.H.
2/1/15 10.00 AM	No 2 left loaded. Back 2.45 PM.	
2.0 PM	No 1 ready to load EBBLINGHEM. Kept 3½ hours waiting. Took 2½ hours to load. Refuelled the supplies lorries to O.C. A.S.C.	
3.30 PM	No 1 back & parked.	
ditto	Visited C.H.Q. Received twice of Sn. H.Q. Cn. Instructions from D.A.Q.M.G. to as to distribute unnamed gifts for 3rd Lr. Cn.	R.P.
3/1/15 10.0 AM	No 2 left loaded back at 3.0 PM	
2.0 PM	No 2 ready to load EBBLINGHEM as requested. Delayed 2¼ hours. Took 2 hrs 5 minutes.	J.H.
5.0 PM	No 2 back & parked.	
4/1/15 10.0 AM	No 2 left loaded. Back 2.45 PM.	
2.0 PM	No 1 ready at EBBLINGHEM, delayed 2½ hours. Took 2½ hours.	
5.0 PM	Back & parked.	J.A.

WAR DIARY or INTELLIGENCE SUMMARY

Army Form C. 2118

3rd Wester Supply Column

Page 27.

Hour, Date, Place	Summary of Events and Information	Remarks and references to Appendices
MOORBECQUE 10/1/15 10:00AM	No 2 left loaded. Back 2.15PM	
3.45PM	No 1 loading STEENBECQUE. Took 2 hours.	
	2/Lt R. Pugh detained M.I.O Station took STOMER 9/1/15 returned. 53 men inoculated	F.A.
11/1/15 10:00AM	No 1 left. Back 2.30PM	
3.45PM	No 3 loading STEENBECQUE. Took 1¾ hours	F.A.
	Inspection by A.D.M.G. Gun Corps.	
12/1/15 10:00AM	No 2 left loaded. Back 2.15PM	
2.45PM	No 1 loading STEENBECQUE. Took 3½ hours	
	Returned 3 - 3 Ton lorries G.H.Q. vice Light 5 Squire. With Column	F.A.
	Now 5 Car. 10 M. Cycles. 152 lorries (includes 6 new units) 55 men inoculated.	
13/1/15 10:00AM	No 1 left loaded. Back 2.15PM	
4.30PM	No 2 loading STEENBECQUE. Took 2½ hours. No engine till 4.10 PM	F.A.
	Visited first time H.Q. for Sect in afternoon stay. Second application for engine oil costed of ZEIT.	
14/1/15 10:00AM	No 2 left loaded. Back 2.36PM	
3.0PM	No 1 loading STEENBECQUE. Took 2 hrs	F.A.
	Inspected by A.D.M.S. Gun Corps. 57 men inoculated	
15/1/15 10:00AM	No 1 left loaded. Back 2.30 PM	
3.0PM	No 2 loading STEENBECQUE. Took 2 hours	F.A.
	Started system of receipt books for newspaper gifts	

WAR DIARY or INTELLIGENCE SUMMARY

Army Form C. 2118

3rd Cavalry Supply Column

Page 20

(Erase heading not required.)

Hour, Date, Place	Summary of Events and Information	Remarks and references to Appendices
MOURBECQUE 16/1/15. 10.0AM 3.15PM	No 2 left loaded. Back 2.30 PM. No 1 loading STEENBECQUE. Took 2½ hours. Visited G.H.Q. Received instructions for keeping main road clear for French troops. 17 I.O.M. & 15th Cuirassiers with S.S.O. + O.C. Amn. 43 inoculated.	J.A.
— 17/1/15 7.0PM 11.0PM	Cleared road of both Sections. Took 1 hour. No.1 left loaded. Back 3.15 P.M. No 2 loading STEENBECQUE. Took 2½ hours. Remain on these absolutely constant after wars. First time for several weeks, probably owing to rain previous days partly into clerk. Third application for oil. Exchanged 1 L.G.O.C. for 1 Dennis lorry.	J.H.
— 18/1/15 10.0AM 11.0PM	No 2 left loaded. Back 2.30 P.M. No 1 loaded STEENBECQUE. Took 2½ hours. Visited Sen. Sec. #2 Q.M.G. Refunded stock of lunch to D. of T. G.H.Q. 40 men inoculated. Lieut Johnson Tait attached as M.O.	J.H.
— 19/1/15 10.0AM 11.0PM	No 1 left loaded. Back 2.15PM. No 2 loading STEENBECQUE. Took 2½ hours. Informed S. Col to return cars of Lieusan Officers.	J.H.
— 20/1/15 10.0AM 10.45AM	No 2 left loaded. Back 2.15 PM. No 1 loading STEENBECQUE. Took 2¼ hours. Sent away one clerk who came from Records. Forwarded request for no more to be sent over this O.S.A.C. 54 men inoculated	J.H.

WAR DIARY or INTELLIGENCE SUMMARY

Army Form C. 2118

3rd Cavalry Supply Column.

Page 29.

Hour, Date, Place	Summary of Events and Information	Remarks and references to Appendices
MOORBECQUE 21/1/15 10.0 am 10.45 am	No 1 left loaded. Back 2.30 PM. No 2 loading STEENBECQUE. Took 2 hours. Sent two manuches to S.S.O. for engine oil asked for 5/1/15 not yet received. Sent infant in HAZEBROUCK Stn.	J.R.H.
—"— 22/1/15 10.0 pm 11.0 am	No 2 left loaded. Back 2.30 PM. No 1 loading STEENBECQUE. Took 2½ hours. Man inoculated. Supplied S.S.O. with an/his Noel supplies & required explanation why actual only enough for two days not enough to obtain locally. None but possible tomorrow a little.	J.R.H.
—"— 23/1/15 10.0 am 10.45 am	No 1 left loaded. Back 2.30 PM. No 2 loading STEENBECQUE. Took 2½ hours. Visited B.H.Q. Sub R.D. of S. who informed me petrol would arrive 24/1/15. Obtained 100 gals locally. Had to use ZE740d on a lorry. Served up to 10 minutes 3 sleeves broken. 53 inoculated.	J.R.H.
—"— 24/1/15 10.0 AM 10.45 AM	No 2 left loaded. Back 2.15 PM. No 1 loading STEENBECQUE. Took 2½ hours. Proper oil arrived in Railway supply train. Visited Divl A.S.C. H.Q. gm Train.	J.R.H.
—"— 25/1/15 10.0 AM 10.45 AM	No 1 left loaded. Back 2.30 PM. No 2 loading STEENBECQUE. Took 2½ hours. Visited Div HQRS. Handed in Oct Nov Dec '14. Also A.O. to Gen	J.R.H.

WAR DIARY
or
INTELLIGENCE SUMMARY

3rd Cavalry Supply Column

Army Form C. 2118

Page 30

Instructions regarding War Diaries and Intelligence Summaries are contained in F.S. Regs., Part II. and the Staff Manual respectively. Title pages will be prepared in manuscript.

Hour, Date, Place	Summary of Events and Information	Remarks and references to Appendices
MORBECQUE 26/1/15 10.0AM	No 2 left loaded. Back 2.30 PM.	
11.0 AM	No 1 loading STEENBECQUE. Took 2½ hours.	
3.0 PM	New instruction 27th by C in C. Two hours practice parades.	
11.0 PM	Received alia for above	
27/1/15 11.30 AM / 12.0 Noon	No 2 loading STEENBECQUE. Took 1¾ hours. Inspection by C in C.	F.A.
2.30 PM	No 1 left loaded. Back 6.15 PM.	
— 28/1/15 10.0 AM	No 2 left loaded. Back 3.30 PM. New billets.	F.A.
11.0 AM	No 1 loading STEENBECQUE. Took 2 hours. Fished wheel oil for BAILLEUL.	
— 29/1/15 10.0 AM	No 1 left loaded. Back 2.45 PM.	
10.45 AM	No 2 loading STEENBECQUE. Took 1¾. Visited A.A. + M.C. M.O. Pns.	F.A.
— 30/1/15 10.0 AM	No 2 left loaded. Back 3.0 PM. Rendezvous left by new route.	F.A.
10.45 AM	No 1 loading STEENBECQUE. Took 2 hours. Furnished map grounds now used to serve. Visited G.H.Q.	
— 31/1/15 10.0 AM	No 1 left loaded. Back 2.45 PM.	Appendix IV Summary of miles + hours on road.
11.0 AM	No 2 loading STEENBECQUE. Took 2½ hours. Received 4 CB Saunder lorries & 1 Maker from ST OMER which was visited O.C. Ale A.S.S.O. for number of units. Grocery drivers left behind beach on accomplishing	F.A. R. A. Lubbett Major A.S.C.

Time & Mileage Record

Appendix IV
3rd Cavalry Supply Column

1915: January	No 1 Section		No 2 Section	
	Miles	No. of Hours on road	Miles	No. of Hours on road
1st	15	9	22	13
2nd	22	13	15	9
3rd	15	10	22	12
4th	22	11	15	9
5th	15	9	22	12
6th	22	14	15	9
7th	16	9	22	12
8th	6	9	15	9
9th	15	9	6	10
10th	6	9	15	9
11th	15	9	6	9
12th	6	9	15	9
13th	15	9	6	9
14th	6	9	15	9
15th	15	9	6	9
16th	6	10	15	9
17th	18	11	9	11
18th	8	10	18	10
19th	18	10	8	9
20th	7	9	15	9
21st	15	9	6	9
22nd	6	9	15	9
23rd	15	9	6	9
24th	6	9	15	9
25th	15	9	6	9
26th	6	9	17	10
27th	17	11	8	10
28th	6	9	16	12
29th	16	10	6	10
30th	6	9	16	9
31st	16	9	6	9
TOTAL 31	392	292	392	302
Daily average approx.	12 2/3	9 2/3	13	10

*: Includes normal time for filling up water, petrol etc.

Confidential.

War Diary
of
O.C. 3rd Cavalry Supply Column.

From 1st February 1915.

Volume III

121/4530

to 20th February 1915.

WAR DIARY 3rd Cavalry Supply Column

INTELLIGENCE SUMMARY

Army Form C. 2118.

Page 31

Hour, Date, Place	Summary of Events and Information	Remarks and references to Appendices
MORBECQUE 1/2/15 10:30 AM	No 2 left Morbecque. Back 2:15 PM.	
11 AM	No 1 North. STEENBECQUE. Took 2½ hours. No train.	
	Visited DAPM G. Informed RFC Pk 3rd Fd Amb. POPERINGHE at 10 AM.	
	Handed over 11 Corner lorries to 2nd Divn S.C. (1-4) 1 A.G.O.5 to	
	7th Ammn Park. Work from M.T. Base about magnets & coil leads	
	trouble. Sent each - On enquiry heard of an attack although lettuce	
6:0 PM	There have been a demand for several weeks.	
	So that 3 lorries (one per Bde) with additional rations for Armoured Horse	
	Transport, motor ambce S.S.O. Supplies from Railhead	f.q.
	Figures for D.H. Bde as follows promised for 8.30 PM. Arrived in time.	
—2/2/15 1:00 PM	No 1 left Morbll. Back 2:30 PM.	
10 AM	No 2 loaded STEENBECQUE. Took 2¾ hours. Extra time	
	due to lorries (four units in billets & trenches). No train.	
	Handed over into DAPM G for Jan. Estimate to 2 ADOS.	
	Exchanged 2 LGOC's for 2 3-ton lorries H.Q. ret'd fr 7th Ann Ch Pk Bde.	f.q.
—3/2/15 6:0 AM	No 2 left. R.V. POPERINGHE. Arrived 9:15 AM. Back 2:0 PM. Food for trenches	
10:0 AM	Remainder No 2 left. Took foot for billets. Back 2:15 PM.	
3:0 PM	No 1 loaded. STEENBECQUE. Took 2¾ hours. No train.	
	Visited Railhead, R.V. ADS & T. R.V. in future POPERINGHE 2.0 PM.	f.q.

WAR DIARY *or* **INTELLIGENCE SUMMARY**

Army Form C. 2118

3rd Cavalry Supply Column

Page 32.

Hour, Date, Place	Summary of Events and Information	Remarks and references to Appendices
MORBECQUE H.Qrs. 9:0 pm	Part No 1 left with food for men in trenches. R.V. POPERINGHE. Convoi 1.15 P.M. Back 8.45 P.M. Only 2500 lbs straw required in future.	
10:0 A.M.	Remainder No 1 left. Back 2.15 P.M.	
10:15 P	No 2 loading STEENBECQUE. Took 2½ hrs. Motor New Prov. W.E.'s arrived. Visited Railhead & HQ 5th T. Cav Corps	f.a.
5/2/15 9:0 pm	Part No 2 left with food for men in trenches. R.V. POPERINGHE. Arrived 1.20 P.M. Back 6.30 P.M. Trouble in H.Q. car - damaged en route with Field Wks. Convoyed to nearest similar. Remainder No 2 left. Back 2.15 P.M.	f.a.
10:0 A.M.	No 1 loading STEENBE C.Q.U.E. Took 2½ hours Motor. Visited R.V. Rutkins for Gen Bee spent due to No given by S.O. for stuck suffering along colored slow trains	
6/2/15 9:30 am	Part No 1 left with bread for R.V. POPERINGHE. Arrived 2.0 P.M. Road for 6 miles W. of POPERINGHE very bad. Pavé given way only room for one line of traffic. Surface very greasy. Back at 6.45 P.M.	f.a.
10:0 A.M.	Remainder No 1 left. Back 2.15 P.M.	
10.30 A.M.	No 2 loading STEENBEC.Q.UE. Took 2¾ hours. Been arrived. Men stowing 160 hrs a Loria	

Army Form C. 2118.

WAR DIARY or INTELLIGENCE SUMMARY

O.C. 3rd Cavalry Supply Column

Page 33

(Erase heading not required.)

Hour, Date, Place	Summary of Events and Information	Remarks and references to Appendices
MORBECQUE 7/2/15 9.30am 9.0 am 10.30 am	Part No 2 left for R.V. as yesterday. Arrived 1.30 PM. Back 6.0 PM. Part No 2 left train. Back 2.45 PM. Took 2 hrs. No 2 lorry STEENBECQUE :	J.A.
— 8/2/15 9.0 am 10.0 am 10.30 am	Visited R.V. C.M.O. S&T. Cav Corps. Part No 1 left for R.V. as before. Arrived 1.0 PM. Back 5.45 PM. Roads + bridges for French M.T. Part No 1 difficulties. Back 9.15 PM. No 2 lorry STEENBECQUE. Took 2½ hours. Received 1 motorcar + 5 lorries = Cav Corps Reserve not to be	J.A.
— 9/2/15 9.30 am 10.0 am 10.45 am	used. Visited Railhead & R.V. Part No 2 left for R.V. as before. Arrived 1.30 PM. Back 6.45 PM. Part No 2 Ambulances Park 2.45 PM No 1 lorry STEENBECQUE. Took 2 hours. Visited Railhead & R.V.	J.A.
— 10/2/15 9.30 am 10.0 am 10.30 am	No 1 Part left for R.V. as before. Arrived 1.30 PM. Back 6.0 PM. Part No 1 left horsed. Arrived 2.20 PM No 2 lorry STEENBECQUE. Took 2 hours. Exchanged 3 1.G.O. Co for 3 lorries at G.H.Q. Visited Railhead + Pn HQrs Capt G. R. Sumner left for P.H.& S. Arranged details New premises + siding at Railhead	J.A.

Army Form C. 2118.

WAR DIARY
or
INTELLIGENCE SUMMARY

(Erase heading not required.)

O.S. 3rd Cavalry Supply Column

Page 34

Instructions regarding War Diaries and Intelligence Summaries are contained in F. S. Regs., Part II. and the Staff Manual respectively. Title pages will be prepared in manuscript.

Hour, Date, Place		Summary of Events and Information	Remarks and references to Appendices
MOORBECQUE	11/2/15 9.0 AM	Part No 2 left for R.V. St Jans-ter-Biezen. Arrived 1.0 PM Back 5.0 PM	
	10.0 AM	Part No 1 " Back 2.15 PM	
	11.0 AM	No 4 loading STEENBECQUE. Took 2 hours.	
		Visited Div. HQrs & R.V.	J.H.
— " —	12/2/15 9.0 AM	Part No 1 left R.V. as for 11th. Arrived 12.30 PM due to troops on road. Back 4.0 PM. Received R.V. due to having to clear STEENWOORDE by 3.45 PM.	
	10.0 AM	Remainder No 1 left. Back 2.14 PM.	
	11.0 AM	No 2 loading STEENBECQUE. Took 2 hours.	
		Visited HQ 3rd S.& T. Corn Cafe. Saw A.S.C. H.Q. B.S. Arranged re hauling over of reinforcements by R.& D. Corn Bat. Sent 4 lorries ST OMER one of reinforcement lorries recalled. Xmas postal lorries recalled.	J.H.
— " —	13/2/15 10.0 AM	No 2 left. Back at 2.30 PM. Visited billets	
	10.30 AM	No 1 loading STEENBECQUE. Took 2½ hours	
		Visited A.D. of S.& T. Corn Cafe & visited HQrs.	J.H.
— " —	14/2/15 10.0 AM	No 1 left. Back 5.30 PM. Visited billets	
	10.30 AM	No 2 loading STEENBECQUE. Took 2½ hours	J.H.
— " —	15/2/15 10.0 AM	No 2 left loaded. Back 5.30 PM.	
	10.30 AM	No 1 loading STEENBECQUE. Took 2½ hours	J.H.

WAR DIARY or INTELLIGENCE SUMMARY

Army Form C. 2118.

O.C. 3rd Cavalry Supply Column

Page 35

Hour, Date, Place	Summary of Events and Information	Remarks and references to Appendices
MOORBECQUE 16/2/15. 10:0 AM	No. 1 left loaded. Back 2.15 PM	Fr. A.
10:45 PM	No. 2 started loading STEENBECQUE. Took 2 hours. Started system of fetching newspapers early & delivering same day.	
17/2/15. 10:10 AM	No. 2 left loaded. Back 2.15 PM	Fr. A.
10:45 PM	No. 1 loading STEENBECQUE. Took 2 hours.	
18/2/15. 10:04 PM	No. 1 left loaded. Back 2.15 PM	Fr. A.
10:30 AM	No. 2 loading STEENBECQUE. Took 2 hours. Very few newspapers	
	Off Pte C.C.H. King A.S.C. joined	
19/2/15. 10:0 AM	No. 2 left loaded. Back 2.30 PM	Fr. A.
10:30 AM	No. 1 loading STEENBECQUE. Took 2½ hours. V. few newspapers	
20/2/15. 10:0 AM	No. 1 left loaded. Back 2.30 PM	Fr. A.
10:45 PM	No. 2 loading STEENBECQUE. Took 2¼ hours. V. few newspapers	
21/2/15. 10:0 AM	No. 2 left loaded. Back 2.15 PM	Fr. A.
10:15 AM	No. 1 loading STEENBECQUE. Took 2 hours. V. few newspapers	
22/2/15. 10:0 AM	No. 1 left loaded. Back 2.30 PM	Fr. A.
10:15 AM	No. 2 loading STEENBECQUE. Took 2 hours. V. few newspapers	
23/2/15. 10:0 AM	No. 2 left loaded. Back 2.20 PM	Fr. A.
10:15 AM	No. 1 loading STEENBECQUE. Took 2 hours. V. few newspapers	

WAR DIARY
or
INTELLIGENCE SUMMARY

(Erase heading not required.)

Army Form C. 2118.

O.C. 3rd Cavalry Supply Column

Page 36

Hour, Date, Place	Summary of Events and Information	Remarks and references to Appendices
NOORBECQUE 24/2/15. 10·0 AM 10·30 AM	No 1 left loaded. Back 2·15 PM No 2 loading STEENBECQUE Took 2 hours. V few vehicles 10 Issues sent to Base instead of 10 lorries arrived previous day Status Transferred 2 wheelers + 2 clerks	Fitt. Fitt.
25/2/15 1·0 AM 10·15 AM	No 2 left loaded. Back 2·15 PM No 1 loading STEENBECQUE. Took 2 hours. V few vehicles 17 Sacks Roads salt handed available for S.S.O. Carried out various experiments with horseshoe studs.	Fitt.
26/2/15 10·0 AM 10·30 AM 7·0 PM	No 1 left loaded Back 2·15 PM No 2 loading STEENBECQUE Took 2 hrs. V few vehicles Lecture Stretcher NCO's	Fitt.
27/2/15 10·0 AM 10·30 AM	No 2 left loaded. Back 2·30 PM No 1 loading STEENBECQUE. Took 2 hrs. few before. Fitt. Too much work, salt last few days.	Fitt.
28/2/15 10·0 AM 10·30 AM 7·0 PM	No 1 left loaded. Back 2·15 PM No 2 loading STEENBECQUE. Took 2 hrs. few before Lecture organization Officers + NCO's	Appendix V

R.M.Wilson Capt
O.C. 3rd Cav Supply Column

fire mileage + horses shoes

3rd. Cav. Div. Sup. Col., Appendix V
Third Cavalry Supply Column

SECTION 1' SECTION 2'

February 15.	Miles	No. of Hours on Road	Remarks.	February 15.	Miles	No. of Hours on Road.	Remarks.
1	6	9		1	15	10	
2	15	9		2	6	9	
3	6	10		3	27	12	
4	27	11		4	7	9	
5	7	9		5	27	12	
6	27	11		6	7	9	
7	7	9		7	27	11	
8	27	12		8	7	9	
9	7	9		9	27	12	
10	27	11		10	7	9	
11	7	9		11	30	12	
12	31	12		12	7	9	
13	7	10		13	15	10	
14	15	10		14	6	9	
15	6	9		15	15	9	
16	15	9		16	6	10	
17	6	9		17	15	10	
18	15	10		18	6	9	
19	6	9		19	15	9	
20	15	9		20	6	9	
21	6	10		21	15	10	
22	15	10		22	6	10	
23	6	10		23	15	9	
24	15	10		24	6	10	
25	6	9		25	15	10	
26	15	9		26	6	9	
27	6	9		27	15	9	
28	15	9		28	6	9	
TOTAL	363	272			362	274	
Daily Average	10.3	9.75			10.3	9.75	

121/485

Confidential

War Diary
of
O.C. 3rd Cavalry Supply Column.

From 1st March 1915 To 31st March 1915

Volume IV

J H Whitham Major

Army Form C. 2118.

WAR DIARY
or
INTELLIGENCE SUMMARY

(Erase heading not required.)

O.C. 3rd Cavalry Supply Column. Page 3.

Instructions regarding War Diaries and Intelligence Summaries are contained in F.S. Regs, Part II. and the Staff Manual respectively. Title pages will be prepared in manuscript.

Hour, Date, Place	Summary of Events and Information	Remarks and references to Appendices
MOORSEELE 1/3/15. 1.06pm	No 2 left loaded. Back 2.15 PM.	
10.30 PM	No 1 loaded STEENBECQUE. Took 2 hours. Good supply Newspapers. No work Sat.	J.H.
2/3/15. 7.00 AM	No 1 left loaded. Back 2.30 PM	J.H.
10.45 PM	No 2 loading STEENBECQUE. Took 2 hours	
3/3/15. 10.0 AM	No 2 left loaded. Back 2.30 PM	J.H.
10.45 PM	No 1 loading STEENBECQUE. Took 2 hours.	
4/3/15. 10.10 AM	No 1 left loaded. Back 2.15 PM	
10.45 PM	No 2 Lorry STEENBECQUE. Took 2½ hours. 3 lorries went to FLETRE for kits & machine gun section 3 Regts.	J.H.
5/3/15 10.0 AM	No 2 left loaded. Back 2.30 PM.	
10.30 PM	No 1 loading STEENBECQUE. Took 2½ hours. Frozen meat truck duty meat about 3000 over may be bad. 3 lorries to METEREN for kits.	J.H.
6/3/15 8.0 AM	No 1 left loaded. Back 2.30 PM	
10.30 PM	No 2 loading STEENBECQUE. Took 2 hours	J.H.

Army Form C. 2118.

WAR DIARY
or
INTELLIGENCE SUMMARY

(Erase heading not required.)

O.C. 3rd Cavalry Supply Column p. 38

Instructions regarding War Diaries and Intelligence Summaries are contained in F.S. Regs, Part II. and the Staff Manual respectively. Title pages will be prepared in manuscript.

Hour, Date, Place		Summary of Events and Information	Remarks and references to Appendices
MORBECQUE	7/3/15 10.0 AM	No 2 Coy left loaded. Back 2.15 PM	
	10.45 PM	No 1 loading STEENBECQUE. Took 2 hours	J.A.
—	8/3/15 10.0 AM	No 1 Coy left loaded. Back 2.30 PM	
	10.45 PM	No 2 loading STEENBECQUE. Took 2 hours	J.A.
		Sent S.S.O's car to Base refuse depot	
—	9/3/15 10.0 AM	No 2 left loaded. Back 2.30 PM	
	10.20 AM	No 1 loading STEENBECQUE — Took 2 hours	J.A.
		Field out Sections with spare rations, petrol, etc. Stir	
—	11/3/15 10.0 AM	No 1 Coy left loaded. Back 2.30 PM	
	10.30 AM	No 2 loading STEEN BECQUE. Took 2 hours	J.A.
		Filed out Sections with spare rations, petrol etc. Stir	
		Standing by. Refers to 6 Hd Qr Cars	
—	11/3/15 9.0 AM	Rendezvous at 10.0 AM cancelled. Loaded section to charge.	
	10.30 AM	No 1 loading STEENBECQUE Took 2½ hours	
	5.6 PM	Order rec'd. Refill. Pt 6th Bde Xroads just short of MERVILLE — 7.5 PM	
		Minute just beyond LES LAURIERS. — 8th Bde between HAZEBROUCK, ARMENTIERES	
		Rly HAZEBROUCK — LA MOTTE road. — Div Troops as before + Artillery	
		S of MORBECQUE. At Refilling Pt by 7.0 PM. Back 11.45 PM	

WAR DIARY
or
INTELLIGENCE SUMMARY

(Erase heading not required.)

Army Form C. 2118.

O.C. 3rd Cavalry Supply Column   Page 39

Instructions regarding War Diaries and Intelligence Summaries are contained in F.S. Regs., Part II. and the Staff Manual respectively. Title pages will be prepared in manuscript.

Hour, Date, Place	Summary of Events and Information	Remarks and references to Appendices
MORBECQUE 11/3/15.	Delay due to defaulters returns for "B" Echelon transport, must not exceed 1 return.	
12/3/15. 10.45Pm	No 2 loaded STEENBECQUE. Took 3½ hours delay due to loading. "B" Echelon separately. No 1 adjusted accordingly.	
1.30Pm	Orders No 1 to move at 1.15Pm. Ready lorries as yesterday. Left 1.45Pm. Back 6.30Pm. Refilled to Regt. 13 Echelon present up.	
13/3/15 - 10.30Am	No 1 loading STEENBECQUE. Took 2½ hours.	
10.45Pm	Manage to hang on till 4.0Pm before orders out loaded section for Div Loaded section could start at once. Refill'g place Yesterday. 3.0Pm No 2 left loaded.	
1.0Pm	Turned round by SO's reminded when to return to new billets. Confirmed 3.45Pm. 6th & 7th Echelons stopped 4.0Pm went to old billets. 8th Regt hung on till the same except R+G who did not. Sent out horses/pushed them up & delivered old billets. RA units carried their own supplies. All lorries back 9.0Pm	f.A
14/3/15. 10.30Am	No 2 loading as usual STEENBECQUE. Took 2 hours.	
4.0Pm	No 1 left loaded to refill old billets. Back 8.0Pm.	f.A

WAR DIARY
or
INTELLIGENCE SUMMARY

(Erase heading not required.)

Army Form C. 2118.

O.C. 3rd Cavalry Suppl'r Column   Page 40

Hour, Date, Place	Summary of Events and Information	Remarks and references to Appendices
MOOR BECQUE 15/3/15 10.0 AM	News batteries sent to Cavalry Hd. Ammn Col'n. Arranged Refille Pt between STEELY and ESTAIRES at 6.20 PM	
10.20 AM	No 1 tending STEENBECQUE. Took 2 hours. Arranged with Railway supply officer about loading chits signatures.	Sgt.
3.30 PM	No 2 RA lorries left. Back 11.0 PM	
4.0 PM	Rest No 2 left loaded. Back 8.15 PM	
16/3/15 1.30 PM	No 2 tending STEENBECQUE. Took 2 hours	
3.30 PM	No 1 RA lorries left. Rendezvous as for 15th. Back 9.15 PM	Sgt.
4.0 PM	No 1 ammunition left. Back 8.15 PM	
17/3/15 10.0 AM	No 2 left loaded. Back 2.0 PM. Batteries broken up	
	Lullus & Delivery much uphiuown	
10.30 AM	No 1 loading. Took 2½ hours. Delay due to R.S.O.'s staff not complying to arrangements made 15th. Saw R.S.O.	Sgt.
	Arranged again. Arranged that my S.O. should always tally load to make up deficiencies in fresh met. Trucks confused to wrong bills.	
18/3/15 10.0 AM	No 1 left loaded. Back 9.15 PM	
10.30 AM	No 2 loading STEENBECQUE. Took 2 hours	Sgt.

Army Form C. 2118.

WAR DIARY
or
INTELLIGENCE SUMMARY

(Erase heading not required.)

O.C. 3rd Cavalry Supply Column

Page 41

Hour, Date, Place	Summary of Events and Information	Remarks and references to Appendices
MOORBECQUE 19/3/15 10.0 AM	No 2 left loaded. Back 2.0 PM	R.N.
10.30 PM	No 1 loaded STEENBECQUE. Took 2½ hours	
20/3/15 10.0 AM	No 1 left loaded. Back 2.15 PM	
10.30 PM	No 2 loading STEENBECQUE. Took 2¼ hours. Frozen hard, wiring offensible	J.C.M.
21/3/15 10.0 AM	Shaft/way filled weight hole two weeks. Hay badly baled	
	No 2 left loaded. Back 2.30 PM	
10.30 PM	No 1 loading STEENBECQUE. Took 2½ hours	J.A.
22/3/15 10.0 AM	No 1 left loaded except Batteries. Back 2.15 PM	
10.30 PM	No 2 loading STEENBECQUE. Took 2½ hours	
4.0 PM	R.A. lorries left. R.V. CASSEL-BAILLEUL road ½ mile W.Z.	
	BAILLEUL 6.0 PM. R.F.M.G. Pts ST JANS CAPPEL area. Back 10.0 PM	J.H.
23/3/15 10.0 AM	No 2 left loaded except R.A. Back 2.15 PM	
10.30 AM	No 1 loading STEENBECQUE. Took 2 hours	
12.15 PM	R.A. lorries left. R.V. 22nd R.F.S. Batteries LOCRE. Ammn Col	J.H.
	ST JANS CAPPEL. Back 7.0 PM	
24/3/15 10.0 AM	No 1 except R.A. left. Back 2.15 PM	
10.30 AM	No 2 loading STEENBECQUE. Took 2 hours	
12.15 PM	R.A. lorries left. Same R.V. R.P. Back 6.45 PM	J.H.

Army Form C. 2118.

WAR DIARY
or
INTELLIGENCE SUMMARY

O.C. 3rd Cavalry Supply Column

Page 42

(Erase heading not required.)

Instructions regarding War Diaries and Intelligence Summaries are contained in F. S. Regs., Part II. and the Staff Manual respectively. Title pages will be prepared in manuscript.

Hour, Date, Place	Summary of Events and Information	Remarks and references to Appendices
MOORSEQUE 25/3/15 10.0 AM	N=2 except R.H. left. Back 2.30 PM	J.A.
10.30 AM	N=1 loaded STEENBECQUE. Took 2½ hours	
12.15 PM	R.A. lorries left adjust. Back 6.30 PM	
— 26/3/15 10.0 AM	N=1 except R.H. left. Back 2.10 PM	J.A.
10.30 AM	N=2 loaded STEENBECQUE. Took 2½ hours	
12.0 Noon	R.H. lorries left as before. Back 6.30 PM	
— 27/3/15 10.0 AM	N=2 except R.H. left & loaded. Back 2.15 PM	J.A.
10.30 AM	N=1 loaded STEENBECQUE. Took 2 hours	
12.0 Noon	R.A. lorries left as listed. Back 6.15 PM	
— 28/3/15 10.10 AM	N=1 except R.H. left & loaded. Back 2.15 PM	J.A.
10.30 AM	N=2 loaded STEENBECQUE. Took 2 hours	
12.0 Noon	R.A. lorries left. Back 6.15 PM	
— 29/3/15 10.0 AM	N=2 except R.H. left & loaded. Back 2.15 PM	J.A.
10.30 AM	N=1 loaded STEENBECQUE. Took 2 hours	
12.0 Noon	R.A. lorries left. Back 6.15 PM	

Army Form C. 2118.

WAR DIARY
or
INTELLIGENCE SUMMARY

(Erase heading not required.)

Oc. 3rd Cavalry Supply Column Page 4/3

Hour, Date, Place	Summary of Events and Information	Remarks and references to Appendices
MORBECQUE 30/3/15	No 1 except R.A. lorries left loaded. Back at 9.15PM	
10.0AM	No 2 loaded STEENBECQUE. Took 2 hours	
10.30AM	No 1	
12.0 Noon	RA lorries left loaded. Back at 6.15 PM	
" 31/3/15		
10.0 AM	No 2 loaded left loaded except R.H. Back at 2.30 PM	
11.30 AM	No 1 loaded STEENBECQUE. Took 2½ hours	
12.0 Noon	No 2 RA left loaded. Back 6.30 PM	

J.A. Mitchell Major
OC. 3rd Cav. S.Co.

J. Mackie Lt.
Mileage & Stores Lt.

OC. 3rd Cav. S.Co. Lt.

3rd. Cav.Div. Sup. Col.,

Appendix VI
3rd Aviation Supply Col⁻

March 15.	SECTION 1.			SECTION 2.		
	Miles	No. of Hours on Road	Remarks	Miles	No. of Hours on Road	Remarks
1*	6	9		15	9	
2	15	9		6	9	
3	6	9		15	9	
4	16	9		8	9	
5	8	9		16	9	
6	15	9		6	9	
7	6	9		15	9	
8	15	9		6	9	
9	6	9		15	9	
10	15	9		6	9	
11	6	9		33	16	
12	30	12		6	10	
13	6	10		38	14	
14	15	10		6	9	
15	6	9		18	11	
16	18	10		6	9	
17	6	9		15	10	
18	15	9		6	9	
19	6	9		15	9	
20	15	9		6	9	
21	6	9		15	9	
22	18	11		6	9	
23	6	9		18	11	
24	18	11		6	9	
25	6	9		18	11	
26	18	11		6	9	
27	6	9		18	11	
28	18	11		6	9	
29	6	9		18	11	
30	18	11		6	9	
31	6	9		18	11	
Total	357	295		392	305	
Daily	11.5	9.5		12.6	9.85	

CONFIDENTIAL.

War Diary.

O.C. 3rd Cavalry Supply Column

from 1st April 1915. to 30th April 1915.

(Volume V)

J. Archibald Major

121/5/61

Eng 96

WAR DIARY
or
INTELLIGENCE SUMMARY

Army Form C. 2118.

O.C. 2nd Cavalry Supply Column. Page 44

(Erase heading not required.)

Hour, Date, Place	Summary of Events and Information	Remarks and references to Appendices
MORBECQUE 1/4/15 10.0 AM	No 1 left loaded except RA. Back 2.30 PM.	
10.30 AM	No 2 loading STEENBECQUE. Took 2½ hours	for A.
12.0 Noon	RA lorries left loaded. Back 6.18 PM	
2/4/15 10.0 AM	No 2 left loaded except RA. Back 2.15 PM	
10.30 AM	No 1 loading STEENBECQUE. Took 2 hours	for A.
12.0 Noon	RA lorries left loaded. Back 6.15 PM	
3/4/15 10.10 AM	No 1 left loaded except RA. Back 2.15 PM.	
10.45 AM	No 2 loading STEENBECQUE. Took 2 hours. Back 6.15 PM	for A.
12.0 Noon	RA lorries left loaded. Infantry by GADGET M.T.	
4/4/15 10.0 AM	No 2 left loaded except RA. Back 2.30 PM	
10.45 AM	No 1 loading STEENBECQUE. Took 2½ hours	for A.
12.0 Noon	Half DADGT M.T. in exchange of lorries. No 2 RA lorries left loaded before. Back 6.15 PM. Finished loading Abbé	vide Appendix VII
5/4/15 10.0 AM	No 1 left loaded except RA. Back 2.30 PM	
10.30 PM	No 2 loading STEENBECQUE. Took 2¼ hours	for A.
12.0 Noon	RA lorries left. Back 6.15 PM	

Pro S. Sgt A/Sup MH Borton. Lieut Col Commission as 2nd Lieut ASC. temporary 23/3/15 9 posted to 3rd Cav S Colr.

Army Form C. 2118.

WAR DIARY
or
INTELLIGENCE SUMMARY O.C. 3rd Cavalry Supply Column
Page 45
(Erase heading not required.)

Hour, Date, Place		Summary of Events and Information	Remarks and references to Appendices
MORBECQUE 6/4/15	10.0 AM	No 3 Left Hondenecq for R.H. Back 2.15 P.M.	
	10.30 AM	No 1 loading STEENBECQUE Took 2 hours	
	12.0 Noon	Rallway lorries left. Back 6.30 P.M.	
		Visited ADQ, S.T/CC arranged for interchange of lorries	
7/4/15	10.0 AM	No 1 left for all except Batteries. Back 2.30 P.M.	
	10.30 AM	No 2 loading SAINT GEORGE Took 2 hours	
	12.0 Noon	R.H. lorries No 1 left Hondeul. Back 6.30 P.M.	Pt.
		Fetched Batteries from G.H.Q. R.H. & G.o.C. 4 Command lorries	
		Halford. Total N. Sec I. 8 4/6 Spinka de Saunton Sec I=	
		1st Car Sec for Supply Column	
		Two Stores S.T/CC re files orle etc spent daily now returning	
8/4/15	10.0 AM	No 2 left for all except R.H. Back 2.30 P.M.	Pt.
	10.30 AM	No 1 loading STEENBECQUE Took 2½ hours	
	12.0 Noon	R.H. lorries left. Back 6.30 P.M.	
		Received 3 Common lorries from O.C. Troops S. Col = Brantly Of Pts lamb	
		Tarpaulin of Umbrellas + loading Platform. Sec I C.B. Saunders	
		4 1st Car S Col =	
9/4/15	10.0 AM	No 1 Left Houdeul. Back 2.30 P.M.	
	10.30 AM	No 2 loading STEENBECQUE Took 2½ hours	
	12.0 Noon	R.H. Col= No 1 left. Back 6.15 P.M. Sec 2 Tr. Allbones 1 3 Tr. Halley to G.H.Q.	
		Sec I B Stu Daunders 2 2 Tr Allbones	

Army Form C. 2118.

WAR DIARY
or
INTELLIGENCE SUMMARY
(Erase heading not required.)

O.C. 3rd Cavalry Supply Column
Page 46

Hour, Date, Place	Summary of Events and Information	Remarks and references to Appendices
MORBECQUE 9/4/15.	Received orders tonight to cart the S.A.A. Convoy on with two cars.	J.H.
10/4/15 11.0 AM	No 2. left loaded for G.H.Q. Back 2.30 P.M.	
11.30 AM	No 1 convoy STEENBECQUE took 2½ hours	
12.0 Noon	No 2. R.A. convoy left. Back 1.15 P.M.	
11/4/15 10.0 AM	No 1 left loaded for Bethune. Back 2.30 P.M.	J.H.
10.30 PM	No 2 convoy STEENBECQUE took 2½ hours	
12.0 NOON	No 1. R.A. left. Back 6.15 P.M.	J.H.
12/4/15 10.0 AM	No 2 left loaded. Back 2.45 P.M.	
10.30 AM	No 1 today STEENBECQUE took 2½ hours	
12.0 Noon	No 2. R.A. convoy left. Back 6.15 P.M.	J.H.
	Sect 3. M.O.E. lorries left G.H.Q. 6.15	
13/4/15 10.0 AM	No 1 left loaded. Back 2.30 P.M.	
10.30 AM	No convoy STEENBECQUE took 2½ hours	
12.0 Noon	No 1 R.A. lorries left. Back 6.15 P.M.	J.H.
	One I.C.O.C. returned from re Aire Scolre	

WAR DIARY
INTELLIGENCE SUMMARY
(Erase heading not required.)

Army Form C. 2118.

Instructions regarding War Diaries and Intelligence Summaries are contained in F.S. Regs., Part II. and the Staff Manual respectively. Title pages will be prepared in manuscript.

O.C. 3rd Cavalry Suffolk Yeomanry

Hour, Date, Place	Summary of Events and Information	Remarks and references to Appendices
MORBECQUE 10.0am 14/4/15	No 2 left tented. Back 2.30 P.M.	
10.30am	No 1 today STEENBECQUE Took 2½ hours.	
12.0 Noon	Battn. horses left. Back 6.15 P.M.	
	79 Loads of Pachers found unarmed.	
	Received 1 Common Lorry from GHQ Broken down on way.	J.M.
15/4/15 10.0am	No 1 left tented. Back 2.30 P.M.	
10.30am	No 2 today STEENBECQUE Took 2½ hours.	
12.0 Noon	Battn. horses left. Back 6.15 P.M.	
	Sgt. T.S.O. & shell late F.C.P.L. & Col.	
	Exchanged 2 Common inventoried 9 W&W/EC) in 2.40 P.M.	
	J Bonnier 1st Sheets. 4 W.O. S&T/EC	
	Sgt. Jt. 2/F HT man ordered to duty Night ordnary	
	to Pub. Commn Transfer to Plater ustz of F HG SGT/SC.	
16/4/15 10.0am	No 2 left tented. Back 2.30 P.M.	
10.30am	No 1 today STEENBECQUE Took 2 hours.	
	Battn. horses left. Back 6.10 P.M.	
	Exchanged 3 CD Steenbeeque 2 Vehicles and 10 Billheads with F.R.A.Co. SGT = Exchange Transfers and tents Cav. SGT = OC = Forts Col.	

WAR DIARY
or
INTELLIGENCE SUMMARY

O.C., 3rd Cavalry Supply Column

Army Form C. 2118.

Page 48

Hour, Date, Place	Summary of Events and Information	Remarks and references to Appendices
MORBECQUE 17/1/15 1.00 PM	No 1 left Ordrel Back 2:30 PM	
11.15 AM	No 2 lorry STEENBECQUE. Took 2¼ hours	
12.0 Noon	R.A. lorries left. Back 5.45 PM	
	Received 6 Commers 3 Dennis from 2nd Kd Cav. S. Coln	
	3 — — 1 — — from 2nd Kd Cav. S. Coln to —	
	Gave 10 Staff Dennis 1 Coln to — " —	
	Several Commers rultisted other Engine bearings by axles shackles brakes Dennis short of one tub wheel trash, waterfront funnel/cover/lid	J.S.A.
	Back brake shoes off, but furnished, shortof toggles etc	
18/1/15 10:10 PM	No 2 left Back 2.30 PM	
10:30 AM	No 1 lorry STEENBECQUE Took 2½ hours. Meat slowing 2 pm	
	of hot weather. Returned to DAD S.of T.	
12.0 Noon	Batten lorries left. Back 6. 30 P.M.	
	Inspection by DDT's superintendent	
	Took over 5 Commers to Hallfords from 1st Kd Cav. Front spring broke	
	Hosier Hallfords, Commer brakes, engine knocks shackles. One axle badly bent.	J.S.A.
	2 Lt Whitlock left for 1st Cav.tn M.T.C.	

WAR DIARY or INTELLIGENCE SUMMARY 3rd Cavalry Supply Column

Army Form C. 2118.

Page 49

(Erase heading not required.)

Hour, Date, Place	Summary of Events and Information	Remarks and references to Appendices
MOORBECQUE 19/9/15 10:00 AM	No 1 left loaded. Back 2:15 PM.	
10:30 AM	No 2 loaded STEENBECQUE. Took 2½ hours.	
12:10 Noon	R.A. lorries left. Back 6:15 PM.	J.F.A.
	Inspection carried out, finished	
20/9/15 10:00 AM	No 2 left loaded. Back 2:15 PM.	
10:30 AM	No 1 loaded STEENBECQUE. Took 2½ hours.	
12:10 Noon	No 2 R.A. lorries left. Back 6:15 PM.	J.F.
	Sent to 6 Hq. 13 offs Saddles, 1 Bernie, 1 Holdfast & SS equin.	
	42 September.	
21/9/15 10:00 AM	No 1 left loaded. Back 2:15 PM.	
10:20 AM	No 2 loaded STEENBECQUE. Took 2½ hours.	J.F.A.
12:10 Noon	No 1 Battery lorries left. Back 6:30 PM.	
22/9/15 10:00 AM	No 2 left loaded. Back 2:15 PM.	
10:45 AM	No 1 loaded STEENBECQUE. Took 2½ hours.	
12:10 Noon	No 2 R.A. lorries left. Back 6:30 PM.	J.F.A.
23/9/15 1:00 PM	No 1 left loaded.	
10:20 AM	Mens Service attended by Only 6th Bde chaplain at Battle chef egin.	
10:30 AM	No 2 loaded STEENBECQUE. Took 2½ hours.	
12:10 Noon	R.A. lorries left. Back 6:0 PM.	
3,4,5 PM	No 1 left via LA BRIARDE – CAESTRE to GODEWAERSVELDE as family lorr.	

WAR DIARY or INTELLIGENCE SUMMARY

Army Form C. 2118.

O.C. 3rd Cavalry Supply Column Page 50

Hour, Date, Place	Summary of Events and Information	Remarks and references to Appendices
MOORBEQUE 23/4/15	Arrived 6.0 pm & at a standstill because of messages from cars. Cars to follow if the troops felt attacks. Refilled ABEELE — GODEWAERSVELDE & EECKE.	
— 24/4/15 3.0 pm	No. 1 Back.	
8.30 am	Sent Waggons & Horses. Sent out R. Soldiers Rations between them & No. 2 &	
10.35 am	No. 1 Moved. STEENBECQUE. Took 2½ hours.	J.A.
11.0 am	Message RV. GODEWAERSVELDE at 9.0 pm	
12.0 Noon	Rest Horses left Back 6.15 pm.	
12.45 pm	No. 2 left Arrived RV. 2.55 pm.	
— 25/4/15 1.0 am	No. 2 left RV. Refilled BOESCHEPE, WESTOUTRE & RENINGHELST.	
9.30 pm	— Back.	J.A.
10.45 am	balc. STEENBECQUE. Took 2¾ hours.	
12.0 Noon	R Horses left Back 6.0 pm.	
2.30 pm	Message RV. as before	
3.15 pm	Horses left Sent Sketch by Head Columns.	
6.0 pm	S.S.O. arrived with cultivation of RV. to STEENVOORDE. Sent Officer to acquaint Sections.	
9.15 pm	R.H. Gallery Horses picked up & ordered return to Echelon	J.A.
— 26/4/15 5.0 am Bitsten	No. 1 South end of B. Sent ADS+T/o who issued orders for Artl/ supplies landed as follows Bechelen — Rest of 43 Mess 125 men, Rest of horses & 125 Mess all depots	

WAR DIARY
or
INTELLIGENCE SUMMARY

O.C. 3rd Cavalry Supply Column

Army Form C. 2118.

Page 57

Hour, Date, Place	Summary of Events and Information	Remarks and references to Appendices
MOORBECQUE 26/4/15	Issued instructions & arranged Echelon ration lorries to be loaded next as to issue hotter supplies for demounted men & to be delivered at Bde points early every morning. Lorries return again into next A Column.	
10.45am	No.1 loading STEENBECQUE – Took 3 hours	
2.0 PM	Orders R.V. STEENVOORDE at 3.0 PM & 6 follow, to Cav. S. Col=	
2.45 PM	Section left. Arrived R.V. 4.15 PM.	
6.0 PM	Near Battalion Sta. at LOCRE. Despatched same. Back midnight	
9.30 PM	Orders to move on main road to within 1 Mile of POPERINGHE – S.S.O informed me Aechelon transport lorries with demounted men, Staff car etc. start 40 minutes over to transferry horse ration also sector forth arrived at MAEELE. Onward at about R.V. full alteration of [?] orders, further delay of 35 minutes Horse & grooms rations to [?] & demounted lorries back 6.0 PM. Units arranged about 200 for Regt. left with horses & no issue was given by AOS & Cav Corps. No exact figure available so settled with & P Q M G 3 CD & S.S.O. to load to haversacks for 150 to 1 Echelon with demounted men, & 200 mens rations per regt. for those holding lines.	J.H.
27/4/15 12.0 midnight		
1.15 AM	Dismounted men's lorries left, Refilled VLAMERTINGHE. Back 7.30 AM.	J.H.

WAR DIARY
or
INTELLIGENCE SUMMARY

(Erase heading not required.)

Army Form C. 2118.

O.C. 3rd Cavalry Supply Column

Page 52

Hour, Date, Place	Summary of Events and Information	Remarks and references to Appendices
MORBECQUE 22/4/15		
9.0 AM	2/Lt N. Coates joined for duty. 2 Halford lorries joined 26th from 1st Divl Sup S. Col.	
9.30 AM	2 echelon left Back 11.30 AM. Totals adjusted to new figures	
11.0 AM	New R.M. ao yesterday	
11.15 AM	N°2 loading finished 2.0 PM STEENBECQUE	
2.20 PM	N°1 left for R.V. May due to load adjustment. Returned O.C. to have Rations at Sylvestre with early call extra to R.V.	
6.30 PM	O to go to LOCRE	
	N°1 M.R.V. in fills as yesterday — Boltire R.V. - B-8.45 PM	
11.30 PM	Boltires Back	
23/4/15. 3.30 AM	N°1 Back	
6.0 AM	N°2 & 3 echelon left (truck w.T. M./S AM)	
11.15 AM	N°1 load 1 ST COMBE C JOE Total 2½ lorries	
11.30 AM	Ration orders for RV ao yesterday	
2.0 PM	N°2 left arrived R.V. 3.15 PM. Rations by FORSYNESTRE	
7.15 AM	N°3 lorries sent to LOCRE Back 14.45 PM	
9.30 PM	Rum dro left tonight	
24/4/15 3.30 AM	N°2 Back	
8.30 AM	N°1 & 3 lorries left. Back Dinner	
11.0 AM	R.V. today. S.I.E.E NBECQUE Today 2 pm. Men ao yesterday	
12.30 PM	NBE CQUE Total 2 pm. Men ao yesterday Stores half killing at HAZEBROUCK closed at 4.15 PM	

Army Form C. 2118.

O.C. 3rd Cavalry Supply Column

Page 53

WAR DIARY
or
INTELLIGENCE SUMMARY

(Erase heading not required.)

Instructions regarding War Diaries and Intelligence Summaries are contained in F.S. Regs., Part II. and the Staff Manual respectively. Title pages will be prepared in manuscript.

Hour, Date, Place	Summary of Events and Information	Remarks and references to Appendices
MOORBECQUE 29/11/15 5.0 PM to 7.0 PM	No 1 left R.A. office at SYLVESTRE CAPPEL R.V. 6.30 PM. Coll O.S. Lorries left R.V. Batteries back 11.30 PM.	J.A.
30/11/15 12 AM	No 1 Back.	
8.30 AM	B Section left.	
11.0 AM	No 1 lorries took 2½ hours STEENBECQUE	
12.15 PM	Despatched lorry with rations for 3 & 4 Field Squadrons. Open 2 hrs S.W.	
1.30 PM	Lorries No 2 to draw Ry at HAZEBROUCK. 3 & 4 RWF R.V. STE ENYOORDE 4.40 PM. Left 6.30 PM Back midnight	J.A.
8.10 PM	No 2 left Council R.V.	Appendices VIII Mileage Summary

Loading by Brigades

	Hay Ration 10 lbs	Lorries	Average Load	Hay Ration 8 lb	Lorries	Average Load
6th Brigade	47,812	15	3187	44,164	13	3397
7th do	49,066	15	3271	45,292	13	3484
8th do	49,272	15	3285	45,484	13	3499
Div Troops	41,980	13	3229	38,928	13	3000
Total Div.	188,130	58	3244	173,868	52	3344

Notes.

Figures are pounds except columns for men, horses and lorries.

Ration reckoned as 4 lbs. per man.

Ration of Oats per horse reckoned at 12 lbs.

31st March 1915.

Appendix VII

J. Archibald

OC 3rd Div S Col

Loading of Mules.

Unit	Men	Horses	Rations	Oats	Hay & Ollo.	Mails	Total	Number of Loonies	Average Load	Hay & Ollo.	Total.	Number of Loonies	Average Load
6th Bgde H.Qrs	185	128	740	1536	1280	80	3636	1	3636	1024	3380	1	3380
1st R.D.	551	602	2204	7224	6020	120	15568	5	3114	4816	14364	4	3898
3rd D.G.s.	532	583	2208	6996	5830	120	15154	5	3031	4664	13968	4	3494
N.S.I.Y.	523	511	2092	6132	5110	120	13454	4	3364	4088	12432	4	3108
Total Bgde	1811	1824	7244	21888	18240	440	47812	15	3187	14592	44164	13	3397
7th Bgde H.Qrs	188	125	732	1500	1250	80	3082	1	3082	1000	3332	1	3332
1st L.G.	535	620	2220	7440	6200	120	15980	5	3196	4960	14740	4	3685
2nd L.G.	520	585	2080	7020	5850	120	15070	5	3014	4680	13900	4	3475
L.Z.Y.	515	557	2060	6684	5570	120	14434	4	3609	4416	13320	4	3330
Total Bgde	1778	1887	7112	22644	18870	440	49066	15	3271	15096	45292	13	3484
8th Bgde H.Qrs	196	127	784	1524	1270	80	3658	1	3658	1016	3404	1	3404
10th Hussars	556	613	2224	7336	6130	120	15810	5	3196	4904	14584	4	3646
R.H.G.	533	595	2132	7140	5950	120	15342	5	3068	4760	14152	4	3538
Essex I.Y.	511	559	2044	6708	5590	120	14462	4	3616	4472	13344	4	3336
Total Bgde	1796	1894	7184	22708	18940	440	49242	15	3283	15152	45484	13	3499
Amn. Coln	336	432	1344	5184	4320	120	10968	3	3656	3456	10104	3	3368
C. Battery	240	276	960	3312	2760	80	7412	2	3556	2208	6560	2	3280
G. —"—	202	223	808	2676	2230	80	5794	2	2697	1784	5348	2	2674
K. —"—	215	232	860	2784	2320	80	6044	2	3022	1856	5580	2	2790
Div. Trfd.	599	363	2396	4356	3630	280	13062 *	4	3016	2904	11336 *	4	2834
Total Div. Trfd.	1592	1526	6368	18312	15260	640	41980	13	3229	12208	38928	13	3000
Recapitulation													
6th Brigade	1811	1824	7244	21888	18240	440	47812	15	3187	14592	44164	13	3397
7th —do.—	1778	1887	7112	22644	18870	440	49066	15	3271	15096	45292	13	3484
8th —do.—	1796	1894	7184	22708	18940	440	49272 *	15	3285	15152	45484 *	13	3499
Div. Troops	1592	1526	6368	18312	15260	640	41980	13	3229	12208	38928	13	3000
Total Div.	6977	7131	27908	85552	71310	1960	188130	58	3244	57048	173868	52	3344

* Includes 900 lb petrol 500 lb oil (winfunkel do)

War Establishments

		30 cwt. lorries
For each Brigade. 10 lorries.		
Total 3 Brigades.		30.
For Divisional Troops.		6.
For Postal.		2.
For Hay.		20. ᵃ
	Total	58

ᵃ Includes no Spares.
If 25% spare for hay. Total is. 54.

Required by Division Hay Ration. 10 lbs. Including Mails. 58
— do — — do — 8 lb. — do — 52

Hay.// Total for Division 71310. lbs. Lorries 22. Ration 10 lbs.

Total for Division 57048 lbs. Lorries. 17. Ration. 8 lb.
W.E. allows 16 lorries plus 4 as 25% spare

Appendix VIII — 3rd Cavalry Supply Column

	SECTION 1.			SECTION 2.		
April 15	Miles	No. of Hours on Road	April 15	Miles	No. of Hours on Road	Remarks
1	18	11	1	6	9	
2	6	9	2	18	11	
3	18	11	3	6	9	
4	6	9	4	18	11	
5	18	11	5	6	9	
6	6	9	6	18	11	
7	18	11	7	6	9	
8	6	9	8	18	11	
9	18	11	9	6	9	
10	6	9	10	18	11	
11	18	11	11	6	9	
12	6	9	12	19	11	
13	19	11	13	6	9	
14	6	9	14	19	11	
15	19	11	15	6	9	
16	6	9	16	19	11	
17	19	11	17	6	9	
18	6	9	18	19	11	
19	19	11	19	6	9	
20	6	9	20	19	11	
21	19	11	21	6	9	
22	6	9	22	19	11	
23	53	16	23	6	9	
24	6	12	24	65	14	
25	45	15	25	6	14	
26	6	12	26	50	15	
27	50	15	27	6	14	
28	6	11	28	42	15	
29	42	15	29	6	11	
30	6	9	30	42	15	
31	—	—	31			
Total	483	325	Total	493	327	
Daily Av.	16.1	11		16.4	11	

3rd Cavalry Division
Confidential

War Diary
of
O.C. 3rd Cavalry Supply Column.

From 1st May 1915 to 31st May 1915.

(Vol. VI)

137/5526

Copy
No 6

J. Archibald Major.

WAR DIARY
or
INTELLIGENCE SUMMARY

(Erase heading not required.)

Army Form C. 2118.

O.C. 3rd Cavalry Supply Column
Page 574.

Hour, Date, Place	Summary of Events and Information	Remarks and references to Appendices
MOORBECQUE 1/5/15 8 am	"B" Echelon Convoy left. Back 10.45 AM	
10.45 AM	No 2 Convoy STEENBECQUE Took 2¾ hours	
12.15 PM	News RV. STEENVOORDE	
10.45 PM	Lorry to 3rd ACC Squadron Left to form 2nd Echelon HAZEBROUCK 6.20 PM	
1.15 PM	Wet Puff RV. 3.15 PM. Back 10.30 PM	
	Received 1 Sergeant, 1 Halford, 2 Gunners — Sentry the 5 cats	J.P.
	Sent 1 Gunner to Corps Reserve Supply	
2/5/15 8.30 AM	"B" Echelon Left. Back 11.30 AM.	
10.45 AM	No 1 Convoy STEENBECQUE took 2¾ hours	
12.30 PM	Battery supply lorries left returning around	
1.15 PM	No 5 RV. Reg[?] Saturday 3.30 PM. F.W. Squadron as yesterday. No 2 unused	
	R.P. 3.45 PM. Left to HQ 5.15 PM Back 10.15 PM	J.P.
3/5/15 8.30 AM	Sgt J & G.O.C.'s to 2nd Cav. S. Col.	
	"B" Echelon Left Back 10.30 AM.	
10.45 AM	No 2 Convoy STEENBECQUE took 2 hours.	
12.30 PM	Batteries left delivering as usual	
2.0 PM	Order RV at WATOU at 6.30 PM. HQ Squadron at BOESCHEPE.	
3.00 PM	Nil GFA	
3.20 PM	Sgt M'Grath Heath of O.C. New RV at STEENVOORDE as each afternoon	
5.0 PM	Moved off + at 6.0 bi[?] Started 5.45 PM	
6.0 PM	Moved via WATOU ST JANSTER BIEZEN POPERINGHE to VLAMERTINGHE	
	Large amount Transport on road at Watou	J.P.

Army Form C. 2118.

WAR DIARY
or
INTELLIGENCE SUMMARY O.C. 3rd Cavalry Supply Column
(Erase heading not required.)   Page 53

Instructions regarding War Diaries and Intelligence Summaries are contained in F. S. Regs., Part II. and the Staff Manual respectively. Title pages will be prepared in manuscript.

Hour, Date, Place	Summary of Events and Information	Remarks and references to Appendices
MOORBECQUE 4/5/15 1.0 PM	Started dumpy. A.C. echelons safeguard near VLAMERTINGHE.	
2.30 AM	Collected (?) Return Back 6.30 AM.	
9.30 AM	B Echelon left. Back 11.20 AM. B Echelon staying on.	
10.40 AM	No 1 lorry STEENBECQUE. Took 2¼ hours	
2.15 PM	Orders R.V. WATOU at 4.0 PM. 7ld Sqdn BOESCHEPE 4.5 PM.	
2.40 PM	All No 1 left M.N. Arrived 4.0 PM. Back 9.45 PM.	
12.30 PM	B Battery lorries left returned as usual.	
5/5/15 8.30 AM	B Echelon left Back at 11.45 AM	J.B.
10.40 AM	No 2 lorry STEENBECQUE. Took 2½ hours	
10.45 AM	Men Run yesterday as each as possible. 3rd 7ld Squadron 4.0 PM	
11.15 PM	No 3 left. Back 6.45 PM	
12.15 PM	Butter lorries left Back 6.10 PM.	
6/5/15 8.30 AM	B Echelon left. Back 10.45 AM	J.B.
10.30 AM	No 1 lorry STEENBECQUE. Took 2½ hours.	
11.0 AM	News R.V. WATOU at 2.0 PM. 7ld Squadron as yesterday.	
12 Noon	No 2 left. Back 6.30 PM	
12.30 PM	Butter lorries left Back 6.15 PM	
7/5/15 8.30 AM	B Echelon left. Back 10.45 AM	J.B.
10.30 AM	No 2 lorry STEENBECQUE. Took 2½ hours. 7ld Squadron as yesterday. bye-cept 7ld Squadron from Corps lorries start	

1247 W 3299 200,000 (E) 8/14 J.B.C. & A. Forms/C. 2118/11.

WAR DIARY
or
INTELLIGENCE SUMMARY

(Erase heading not required.)

Army Form C. 2118.

O.C. 3rd Cavalry Supply Column

Page 50

Hour, Date, Place		Summary of Events and Information	Remarks and references to Appendices
MOORBECQUE	7/5/15 12:30PM	Bullion lorries left. Back 6:15PM	
	3:0PM	5th Bde lorries left. Back 3:15PM	
	9:0PM	Remainder left. Back at 12:0 midnight. Arranged for R.V. in future at 10:0PM	J.H.
	8/5/15 10:0AM	No 2 Lift loaded. Back 2:30PM	
	10:40AM	No 1 lorry STEENBECQUE. Took 2¼ hours	
	12:30PM	R.H. lorries left. Back at 6:15PM	J.H.
	9/5/15 10:0AM	News of change of direction	
	10:47AM	No 2 loaded STEENBECQUE. Took 2½ hours.	
	12:30PM 1:30PM	Batten inside Bttn's B.side 6:15PM	
		Supper hr Bttn's Back 6:30PM	
	3:30PM	B.f.C. Echelon left. Back 6:30PM	
	4:0PM	R.V. 9:0PM at STEENVOORDE for A Echelon.	
	4:0PM	(No 1 delivered Acetelin near VLAMMERTINGHE)	J.H.
		Helped army for A.S.C. HQ reported	
	10/5/15 10:50AM	No 1 lorry STEEN BECQUE Took 3¼ hours	
	12:15PM	to Echelon Left Back 3:45PM	
	12:30PM	Batteries left. Back 6:15PM	
	5:0PM	No 2 Echelon left for R.V. as yesterday 6:30PM. Back 11:45PM	J.H.
		Sgt Clemow to E.S.Q. in place of Mulford. see of sent	
	11/5/15 9:0AM	B Echelon left. Back 11:30 PM	
	11:0AM	No 2 lorry STEEN BROQUE. Delay due to frequent changes in new area

Army Form C. 2118.

WAR DIARY
or
INTELLIGENCE SUMMARY

(Erase heading not required.)

Hq. 3rd Cavalry Supply Column
Page 57

Instructions regarding War Diaries and Intelligence Summaries are contained in F. S. Regs., Part II. and the Staff Manual respectively. Title pages will be prepared in manuscript.

Hour, Date, Place	Summary of Events and Information	Remarks and references to Appendices
MOORBEQUE 11/5/15 12.30pm	Battans left back 6.20 P.m.	
2.15 P.m	New RV. at Behela as before earliest possible	
4.0 P.m	No 1 Lechelm at RV. moved onto R.P's an before Back 10.30 P.m	G.St.
12/5/15 6.0 AM	B Echelons left. Back 8.15 A.m.	
9.15 A.m	A Echelon left No 2 RV. STEENVOORDE at 11.0 A.m. R.P's an	
	before Back 6.0 P.m.	
10.45 A.m	No 1 Lorries ST EAUBECQUE Took 2½ hours	G.St.
12.30 P.m	R.A. lorries left Back 6.15 P.m	
13/5/15 6.0 A.m	B Echelons left. Back 8.15 A.m	
9.15 A.m	A Echelons left as yesterday Back 5.0 P.m	
10.45 A.m	No 2 lorries STEENVOORDE. Took 2½ hours	
12.30 P.m	R.A. lorries left Back 6.15 P.m	G.A.
14/5/15 6.0 A.m	B Echelon left. Back 8.15 A.m	
9.15 A.m	A —— as yesterday. Back 5.15 P.m	
10.55 A.m	No 1 lorries STEENBECQUE. Took 2 hours	
12.45 P.m	Batty lorries left Back 6.20 P.m	
	1S-Spare lorried returned to 1 Hallfour front axle badly bent due to collision with passing lorry	G.A.

Army Form C. 2118.

WAR DIARY
or
INTELLIGENCE SUMMARY O.C. 3rd Cavalry Supply Column
Page 3-5.
(Erase heading not required.)

Instructions regarding War Diaries and Intelligence Summaries are contained in F. S. Regs, Part II. and the Staff Manual respectively. Title pages will be prepared in manuscript.

Hour, Date, Place	Summary of Events and Information	Remarks and references to Appendices
POPERINGHE 15/5/15 - 6.0 AM	C echelons left. Back 8.15 PM	
9.15 PM	A echelons left as before. Left R.V. 2 PM. Back 8.0 PM	
10.25 PM	No 2 Lorry STEENBECQUE. Took 24 hours	
12.30 AM	Battery returns left. Back 6.15 PM	
6.30 PM	Sent 3 lorries to B echelon 6.2 Bde to pick up & convey to Achelon	
	Various kit & equpt. Hulford build attached, had to be left for 2nd lorry	Spt
	on T 16A	
- 16/5/15 - 6.0 AM	B echelons left. Back 8.15 PM	
9.15 AM	H echelons left as before. Back 6.0 PM	
10.0 AM	No 1 Lorry STEENBECQUE. Took 24 hours	Spt
12.30 PM	Battery lorries left. Back 6.15 PM	
- 17/5/15 6.0 AM	B echelons left. Back 8.15 PM	
9.15 AM	A echelons left as before. Back 5.30 PM	
10.0 AM	No 2 Lorry STEENBECQUE. Took 24 hours	
12.30 PM	R.A. Lorries left. Back 6.15 PM	
1.0 PM	Sent 6 No. 1 lorries with straw for A echelons. Back 8.45 PM	Spt
- 18/5/15 6.0 AM	B echelons left. Back 8.15 PM	
9.15 AM	A echelons left - ", - 5.15 PM	
10.0 AM	No 1 Lorry STEENBECQUE. Took 24 hours	
	R.A. Lorries left. Back 6.15 PM. Left for MERVILLE 4.0 PM. Left Staff	
9.0 PM	Lt S.S.O. 4 lorries for potatoes queried. Left for MERVILLE 4.0 PM. Left Staff	
	HAZEBROUCK Back 11.30 PM	

Army Form C. 2118.

WAR DIARY
or
INTELLIGENCE SUMMARY

O.C. 3rd Cavalry Supply Column

Page 60.

(Erase heading not required.)

Instructions regarding War Diaries and Intelligence Summaries are contained in F. S. Regs, Part II. and the Staff Manual respectively. Title pages will be prepared in manuscript.

Hour, Date, Place		Summary of Events and Information	Remarks and references to Appendices
MOORBECQUE	19/5/15 6.0 AM	"B" echelons left. Back 8.15 AM.	
	9.15 AM	A — — — — 5.30 PM. R.V. & R PT as before.	
	10.0 AM	No 2 lorry STEENBECQUE Took 2¼ hours	J.H.
	12.30 PM	R.A. lorries left. Back 6.15 PM.	
—	20/5/15 6.0 AM	Haystacks shot at Rieubiens. Drew oats in afternoon from WARDECQUES, harvested hay from ARNEKE. Dark	
	9.0 AM	"B" Echelons left. Back 8.15 AM.	
	9.15 AM	2 lorries to hay to ARNEKE.	
		A Ecelon lorries left. Back 5.30 PM. as before.	
	10.0 AM	No 1 lorry STEENBECQUE Took 2¼ hours	J.H.
	12.30 PM	Battery lorries left. Back 6.15 PM.	
—	21/5/15 6.0 AM	"B" echelon lorries left. Back 8.15 AM	
	10 AM	A — — — — ordered to hang on.	
	10.15 AM	No B lorry STEENBECQUE Took 2¼ hours.	
	12.30 PM	Battery lorries left. Back 6.15 PM	
	2.30 PM	New Division returns	old billets. Fell squadron to remain up	Jak
		Hqrs to start at 4am. Remainder left 4.30 PM Back 6.30 PM	
—	22/5/15 10.45 AM	No 1 lorry STEENBECQUE took 2 hours	
	12.30 PM	R.A. lorries left. Back 6.15 PM	
	3.0 PM	Remainder No 2 left. Back 4.30 PM. Fell squadron 4.30 PM	J.H.

WAR DIARY or INTELLIGENCE SUMMARY

Army Form C. 2118

O.C. 3rd Cavalry Supply Column
Page 61

Hour, Date, Place	Summary of Events and Information	Remarks and references to Appendices
MORBECQUE 23/5/15 8.30AM	Reliance 4th H.Q. Squadron left. Back 3.0 PM	
10.0 AM	No 2 loading STEENBECQUE. Took 2 hours	
2.0 PM	Remainder left. Back 4.30 PM	
24/5/15 8.30 AM	R.A. & F.A. Squadron left. Back 3.0 PM	J.A.
10.0 AM	No 1 loading STEENBECQUE. Took 2 hours	
3.0 PM	Remainder left. Back 4.45 PM	
25/5/15 8.30 AM	R.A. & F.A. Squadron left. Back 3.0 PM	J.A.
10.0 AM	No 2 loading STEENBECQUE. Took 2½ hours	
2.0 PM	Remainder left. Back 4.45 PM	
26/5/15 8.30 AM	R.A. & F.A. Squadron left. Back 3.0 PM	J.A.
10.0 AM	No 1 loading STEENBECQUE. Took 2½	
3.0 PM	Remainder left. Back 4.45 PM	
27/5/15 8.30 AM	R.A. & F.A. Squadron left. Back 2.45 PM	J.A.
10.0 AM	No 2 loading STEENBECQUE. Took 2 hours	
3.0 PM	Remainder left. Back 4.45 PM	

WAR DIARY or INTELLIGENCE SUMMARY

Army Form C. 2118.

O.C. 3rd Cavalry Supply Column

Page 62

Hour, Date, Place	Summary of Events and Information	Remarks and references to Appendices
MOORBECQUE 29/5/15 6.15 AM	The Squadron Headqtrs horse left. Back 2.45 PM	
10.15 AM	No 1 loading STEENBECQUE. Took 2 hours.	
2.0 PM	Remainder left. Back 6.0 PM. 9th Bn & New Wells Attd to Arcques. No definite number available, no arranged supplies to go to Ry Coy. as before 4 units to eat up train own & 40 extra.	JRS
29/5/15 6.0 PM	Numbers to be in for lunch 89 = by 10.0 PM	
3.0 PM	No 1 left to bivvy. Back 10.0 AM where when returns	
10.30 PM	Ration lorrie left. Back 2.30 PM	
	No 2 lorry at station STEENBECQUE to be seen to put in late + Report citerne	
2.30 AM	R.V. A echelon arranged 6.0 PM Je To W. of VLAMERTINGHE lorries left at once Arrived R.V. 6.0 PM Back 9.45 PM	Put
30/5/15 6.0 AM	B echelon left. Back 2.30 PM	
10.0 AM	No 1 load of STEENBECQUE. Took 2½ hours	
11.0 AM	A echelon left R.V. W of VLAMERTINGHE R.P.F as yesterday	
4.0 PM	Back 6.0 PM	Put
	Rations letters before	
	Sent lectr Army Sup letr with Rn.	

Army Form C. 2118.

WAR DIARY
or
INTELLIGENCE SUMMARY

(Erase heading not required.)

O.C. 3rd Cavalry Supply Column

Hour, Date, Place	Summary of Events and Information	Remarks and references to Appendices
MOROSECQUE 31/5/15 6:15am B. Schutau Left Bark 9.30 AM		
8:00am RA convoy left Bark 3.15 PM		
10.30pm No 2 convoy STEENBECQUE Took 2½ hours		
11.30pm A echelon left Bark 6.15 PM		

Aubdullinger
OC 3rd Cav S Col

Appendix IX 3rd Cavalry Supply Column

	SECTION 1.			SECTION 2.		
May 19 15	Miles	No. of Hours on Road	May 19 15	Miles	No. of Hours on Road	Remarks
1	42	13	1	6	9	
2	6	9	2	42	13	
3	40	15	3	6	9	
4	34	14	4	40	12	
5	40	12	5	6	10	
6	6	9	6	42	12	
7	25	12	7	6	9	
8	6	9	8	18	9	
9	27	12	9	6	9	
10	6	11	10	28	12	
11	28	10	11	6	9	
12	6	9	12	30	13	
13	30	12	13	6	9	
14	6	9	14	30	12	
15	32	15	15	6	9	
16	6	9	16	32	13	
17	35	14	17	6	9	
18	6	9	18	38	15	
19	35	13	19	10	10	
20	6	9	20	36	14	
21	18	11	21	6	9	
22	6	9	22	18	9	
23	18	9	23	6	9	
24	6	9	24	18	9	
25	10	9	25	6	9	
26	6	9	26	18	9	
27	18	9	27	6	9	
28	6	9	28	24	10	
29	38	16	29	6	9	
30	6	9	30	38	13	
31	38	13	31	6	9	
Total	600	337	Total	552	321	
	19.7	10.9		17.8	10.4	

3rd Cav. Division

CONFIDENTIAL

12/5870

WAR DIARY.

of

O.C. 3rd Cavalry Supply Column.

From 1st June 1915 to 30th June 1915.

(Volume VII)

J.A. Alebury Mjr
OC 3rd Can S.C.

WAR DIARY O.C. 3rd Can. Supply Col Army Form C. 2118.

or

INTELLIGENCE SUMMARY.

(Erase heading not required.)

Page 64.

Hour, Date, Place	Summary of Events and Information	Remarks and references to Appendices
MOORBECQUE 1/6/15 6am	B echelon left. Back 9.45 AM	
8.30am	R.A. Lorries left. Back 2.45 PM	
10 AM	No 1 Lorry STEENDECQUE. Took 2½ hours	
10.30 AM	Ammunition A wheeler left VIEUX BERQUIN Back 6.15 PM	fine
2/6/15 6 AM	B echelon left. Back 9.45 AM	
8.30 AM	R.A. Lorries left. Back 2.30 PM	
10.15 AM	Mo. 9 Lorry STEENBECQUE. Took 2½ hours	
—	A echelon left. Back 6.15 PM	
—	Received 6 Halford Lorries 2nd Ind Can S.C.	fine
3/6/15 6 AM	B echelon left. Back 9.45 AM	
10.0 AM	No 1 Lorry STEENBECQUE Took 2½ hours	
10.20 AM	A echelon left. Back 6.30 P.M.	
2.0 PM	R.A. Lorries left for billets with Batteries	fine
—	Sent 5 Lorries to 2nd Can S.C.	
4/6/15 6 AM	B echelon left. Back 9.45 AM + Batteries	
10.0 AM	No. 2 Lorry STEENBECQUE Took 2½ hours	
10.15 AM	A echelon left. Back 6.10 PM	
10.30 AM	Am. Col. left Sent 2 Lorries to 2nd Can S.Col.	fine

Army Form C. 2118.

O.C. 3rd Cavalry Supply Column
Page 65

WAR DIARY
or
INTELLIGENCE SUMMARY.
(Erase heading not required.)

Instructions regarding War Diaries and Intelligence Summaries are contained in F.S. Regs., Part II. and the Staff Manual respectively. Title pages will be prepared in manuscript.

Hour, Date, Place		Summary of Events and Information	Remarks and references to Appendices
MORBECQUE	5/6/15 6.0 AM	Bechelins lifted before. Back 9.30 AM	
	10.10 AM	No 1 loading STEENBECQUE Took 2 hours	
	10.20 AM	Achelins left. Back 6.20 PM.	
	12.30 PM	Nevers 3rd Fld Squadron Athletic to REMESCURE & rechb returns also back.	
	6.15 PM	Newsrunner for Armd C/T = 3 AA returned from A to F to L next from Cal 2	J.A.
"	6/6/15	12th Siraim Artillery billeted in neighbourhood. Roads turned up 6.10 PM	
	10.15 AM	No 2 loading STEENBECQUE Took 2 hours	
	4.0 PM	B9A returns to billets Buses cleared at 3.55 PM. Back 8.30 PM.	
		12th Siraim cleared by 2.0 PM roads turned like the —	J.A.
"	7/6/15 9.45 AM	No 1 loading STEENBECQUE Took 2½ hours	
	2.0 PM	No 2 left Back 6.15 PM	J.A.
"	8/6/15 10.0 AM	No 3 loading STEENBECQUE Took 2 hours	
	2.0 PM	No 1 left. Back 6.10 PM	J.A.
		Rendezvous altered to 10.0 AM.	
"	9/6/15 10.0 AM	No 1 loading STEENBECQUE Took 1¾ hours	
		No 2 left toM.W. Back 2.15 PM	J.A.

Army Form C. 2118.

WAR DIARY
or
INTELLIGENCE SUMMARY.
(Erase heading not required.)

O.C. 3rd Cavalry Supply Column

Page 66

Hour, Date, Place		Summary of Events and Information	Remarks and references to Appendices
MORBECQUE. 10/6/15	10.0 AM	No 2 loading STEENBECQUE. Took 1¾ hours.	J.H.
	---	No 1 left Enfill. Back 2.15 PM.	
11/6/15	10.0 AM	No 1 loading STEENBECQUE. Took 2 hours.	J.H.
	---	No 2 left. Back 2.15 PM.	
12/6/15	10.0 AM	No 2 loading STEENBECQUE. Took 2½ hours	J.H.
	---	No 1 left. Back 2.30 PM	
13/6/15	10.0 AM	No 1 loading STEENBECQUE. Took 2¼ hours	J.H.
	---	No 2 left. Back 2.0 PM	
		Inspected No 1 S.O's Books etc.	
14/6/15	10.0 AM	No 2 loading STEENBECQUE. Took 2½ hours	J.H.
	---	No 1 left touched. Back 2.15 PM	
	4.0 PM	Practice parade for G.O.C's inspection. Inspected No 2 Section S.O's Bottles	
15/6/15	10.0 AM	No 2 left loaded. Back 2.30 PM. Met few Ind Cars as usuals which were not blocked	J.H.
	10.15 AM	No 1 loading STEENBECQUE. Took 2½ hours	
		Inspected Cookhouse. Workshop, records, diary, stock books, Servants etc.	J.H.

WAR DIARY
or
INTELLIGENCE SUMMARY.

(Erase heading not required.)

Army Form C. 2118.

O.C. 3rd Cavalry Supply Column
Page 67

Hour, Date, Place	Summary of Events and Information	Remarks and references to Appendices
MOORBECQUE 16/6/15 10.0 AM	No.1 left to refill. Back 2.20 PM.	
	No.2 loading STEENBECQUE. Took 2½ hours	
	3.0 Ill SSgt. G.H. Dawson despatched to Matron 11th Stationary with letter explaining their tools. Note of obligation. Inspected garage arrangements. Drove Lieut. Scott King to hospital.	
17/6/15 10.00 AM	Movements of HQ "Coy" as in diary	
	No.2 left to refill. Back 2.15 PM.	
	No.1 loading STEENBECQUE. Took 2 hours.	
—	Visit by G.O.C. Gen. also Mulhead	
	Collected 5 dennies for G.HQ. 1 Daimler at 2 AA Bdes fr. 3rd Cav. Sent 2 L60Cs to 2nd Cav & 2 Singers fr. B.	
	2 hubwheel fr. Car Corps.	
	2 Cases of Marrel at G.HQ	
18/6/15 10.0 AM	No.2 loading STEENBECQUE Took 2 hours	
11.30 AM	90 men inspected by C. in C.	
2.0 PM	No.1 left to refill. Back 6.15 PM	
	Sec. 2 Lt Coates for Paris with 3 Crossley Cars for repair	
19/6/15 10.0 AM	No.1 loading STEENBECQUE. Took 2 hours.	
	No.2 refilling. Back 2.0 PM.	
	Inspected Workshops, Stores fire Botha	

Army Form C. 2118.

O.C. 3rd Cavalry Supply Column   Page 68.

WAR DIARY
or
INTELLIGENCE SUMMARY.
(Erase heading not required.)

Hour, Date, Place	Summary of Events and Information	Remarks and references to Appendices
MOORBECQUE 20/6/15. 10.0 AM " 10.0 "	No 2 loading STEENBECQUE. Took 2 hours. No 1. Refilling. Took 2 hrs. Back 2.0 P.M. Inspected Tyres, loading & marking of all Sections.	J.R.
— 21/6/15. 10.0 P.M. —	No 1 loading STEENBECQUE. Took 2 hours. No 2 Refilling. Back 2.0 PM Visited by Major Hutchison Adviser to work for uniformity in appearance of lorries kits etc. ½ Lieut P.G.S. Clarke joined from G.H.Q. (13/5/15)	J.R.
— 22/6/15. 10.0 AM —	No 2 loading STEENBECQUE. Took 2 hours. No 1. Refilling. Back 2.0 P.M. Sent forward requests for hastening A.O.D & M.T. spares & material Verify all units.	J.R.
— 23/6/15. 10.0 AM —	No 1 loading STEENBECQUE. Took 2¼ hours No 2. refilling. Back 2.0 PM. Inspected bodies of empty lorries No 2 Section. Clean. No rubbish other than manure & three surplus lorries returned from units.	J.R.
— 24/6/15. 10.0 AM —	No 2 loading STEENBECQUE. Took 2¼ hours. No 1 Refilling. Back 2.0 PM. Inspected bodies of No 1 Section. All clean. No returns of rubbish manure etc. Received 1 Dennis from B.H.Q. Sect 1 Armour'd Car S section.	J.R.

Army Form C. 2118.

O.C. 3rd Cavalry Supply Column
Page 69.

WAR DIARY
or
INTELLIGENCE SUMMARY.
(Erase heading not required.)

Instructions regarding War Diaries and Intelligence Summaries are contained in F.S. Regs., Part II. and the Staff Manual respectively. Title pages will be prepared in manuscript.

Hour, Date, Place		Summary of Events and Information	Remarks and references to Appendices
MORBECQUE 25/5/15 10 am		Nº 2 loading STEENBECQUE Took 2½ hours	
		Nº 2 refilling Back 2.0 P.M.	
		Arranged standardization of lorries as far as possible to carry 9 of each petrol, oil, water, paraffin etc. Arranged fresh issue of S.T. Column disarmament except 1 carbine or rifle per lorry.	fit.
26/5/15 10 am		Nº 2 loading STEENBECQUE Took 2¾ hours.	
		Nº 1 refilling Back 2.15 P.M.	
		Visited ADfsrr. Arranged further lorry exchanges. Visited Div H.Q. Arranged lorries for R.E. work very urgent.	fit.
27/5/15 10.0 am		Nº 1 loading STEENBECQUE Took 2¾ hours.	
		Nº 2 refilling Back 2.15 P.M.	
		Sent 9 lorries for R.E. work all day. Past Ord to dig trenches. DADOS discovered mistake only 1 drawn a ½ day to be withOUT rifle, recommended 25 inst. Arranged linings of petrol in smaller lorries.	fit.

WAR DIARY
or
INTELLIGENCE SUMMARY

Army Form C. 2118.

O.C. 3rd Cavalry Supply Column
Page 70

Hour, Date, Place		Summary of Events and Information	Remarks and references to Appendices
MOORBEQUE 28/6/15	9 am	No 2 loading STEENBECQUE. Took 2½ hours. No 1 refilling. Back 2.15 PM. Received 8 Dennis lorries from G.H.Q. Sent 5 Crossleys to 2nd Car S Col=	J.H.
29/6/15	9 AM 10 am	No 2 refilling. Back 1.15 PM. No 1 loading STEENBEEQUE. Took 2½ hours. Went to Div HQrs re Motor mules. Class GHQ publishing exchanges	J.H.
30/6/15	5.g.0 am 9.30 AM 10.0 PM	Lorry left to truck digging party. Back 1.30 PM. No 1 left refilling. Back 1.45 PM. No 2 loading STEENBECQUE. Took 2½ hours. Motor GHQrs lorry exchanges. Also O.C. side.	J.H. Appendix X. Mileage & hours.

[Signature] O.C. 3rd Cav S Col=

Appendix X 3rd Cavalry Supply Column

	SECTION 1.			SECTION 2.		
June 15	Miles	No. of Hours on Road	June 15	Miles	No. of Hours on Road	Remarks
1	6	9	1	45	13	
2	45	13	2	6	9	
3	6	9	3	45	13	
4	45	13	4	6	9	
5	6	9	5	45	13	
6	22	12	6	6	9	
7	6	9	7	22	11	
8	22	10	8	6	9	
9	6	9	9	22	9	
10	22	9	10	6	9	
11	6	9	11	22	9	
12	22	9	12	6	9	
13	6	9	13	22	9	
14	22	9	14	6	9	
15	6	9	15	22	10	
16	22	9	16	6	9	
17	6	9	17	22	9	
18	25	10	18	6	10	
19	6	9	19	22	9	
20	22	9	20	6	9	
21	6	9	21	22	9	
22	22	9	22	6	9	
23	6	9	23	22	9	
24	22	9	24	6	9	
25	6	9	25	22	9	
26	22	9	26	6	9	
27	10	10	27	26	10	
28	22	9	28	6	9	
29	6	9	29	22	9	
30	24	10	30	6	9	
31	—		31	—		
Total	475	285	Total	493	287	
Daily av:	15.8	9.5		16.4	9.6	

2

Capt. Atkinson
Historical Section
Committee of Imperial Defence
(Military Branch)
Public Record Office
Chancery Lane, W.C.2.

Duplicate Diaries of the IC VII Corps from February to June 1917 inclusive, received with very many thanks.

Original Diaries of 3rd Cavalry Supply Column returned herewith. Extracts have been taken to serve as a duplicate.

W. Aylward Capt.
/Colonel.
i/c A.S.C. Records.

WOOLWICH DOCKYARD
A.S.C. RECORDS
21 DEC 1917

To O i/c
A.S.C. Records
Woolwich

S.M.T.O. VII Corps
　　　Herewith War diaries of above for Feby. March. April. May. June 1917. These are duplicates

38 Ammunition Sub-Park
　　　We have none of these diaries.

3rd Cavalry Supply Column.
　　　Herewith diary for period 1.7.1915 — 31.1.1916. This is an original so could you return it at your convenience

　　　　　WPS for Capt Atkinson

HISTORICAL SECTION,
COMMITTEE OF IMPERIAL DEFENCE
(MILITARY BRANCH),
PUBLIC RECORD OFFICE,
CHANCERY LANE,

13.12.1917　P.76　　　W.C.2

Army Form C. 2118.

WAR DIARY
or
INTELLIGENCE SUMMARY.
(Erase heading not required.)

O.C. 3rd Cavalry Supply Column
Page 72

Instructions regarding War Diaries and Intelligence Summaries are contained in F.S. Regs., Part II. and the Staff Manual respectively. Title pages will be prepared in manuscript.

Place	Hour, Date	Summary of Events and Information	Remarks and references to Appendices
MOORBECQUE	1/1/15 2.0 Pm	Trench returns left. Back 2.0 Pm	
	11/15 Pm	No 1 left loaded. Back 1.45 Pm	
	1.0 Pm	No 2 Lorry STEEN BECQUE. Took 2 hours	
		Inspection by ADMS. Arrangements satisfactory	
	5/1/15 2.0 Pm	Trench party returns off. Back 2.0 Pm	J.R.
	9.30 Pm	Remounts. No 2 left. Back 1.40 Pm	
	9.45 Pm	No 1 Lorry STEENBECQUE. Took 2 hours	
		Lecture by ADMS. Killed all latrines & billets.	J.R.
	6/1/15 8.0 Pm	Trench returns left. Back 2.0 Pm	
	9.30 Pm	Rations No 1 left. Back 1.45 Pm	
	9.50 Pm	No 2 Lorry STEENBECQUE. Took 2 hours	
		Inspected & said Mass Arros & church. Painting of harness & cleaning	J.R.
	7/1/15 2.0 Pm	Trench party left. Back 2.0 Pm	
	9.40 Pm	No 2 left. No 1 fell. Back 1.45 Pm	
	10.0 Pm	No 1 Lorry STEENBECQUE. Took 2 Lorries. Oats for 1 Reg Field	
		Received issue to make up for 2 w.s.g.lb. from WAZENCOURT.	
		Tested Down the car & cleaned a top spring.	J.R.

Army Form C. 2118.

WAR DIARY
or
INTELLIGENCE SUMMARY.
(Erase heading not required.)

O.C. 3rd Cavalry Supply Column.

Page 73

Instructions regarding War Diaries and Intelligence Summaries are contained in F.S. Regs., Part II. and the Staff Manual respectively. Title pages will be prepared in manuscript.

Hour, Date, Place	Summary of Events and Information	Remarks and references to Appendices
MORBECQUE 8/7/15 8.0 AM	French ration left. Back 1.45 P.M.	
9.30 AM	No 1 left to refill. Back 1.45 P.M. Oct 6:30 & Ges made up.	
10.0 AM	No 2 lorry STEEMBECQUE. Took 2½ hours.	
2.15 PM	Rations for Leicesters. Beyond THEROUANNE's left. Back 8.0 P.M.	
	Arranged for re-issuing fresh rifles + equipt. All 2 now 1 rifle	
	& Carbine per man except motor cyclist, car + lorry drivers	J.R.
9/7/15 8.0 AM	French ration left. Back 1.45 PM	
9.30 AM	No 2 to refill. Back 1.45 P.M.	
--	No 1 lorry STEEMBECQUE. Took 2½ hours.	
	Issued arms + equipt to Nos 1 + 2 Section	J.R.
10/7/15 8.0 AM	French ration left. Back 1.45 P.M.	
9.30 AM	No 1 left to refill. Back 1.30 P.M.	
--	No 2 lorry STEEMBECQUE. Took 2 hours.	
	Issued arms to H.Qrs + Workshops. Tested clutch stop	
	spring on twinder cars	J.R.
11/7/15 8.0 AM	French ration left. Back 1.45 P.M.	
9.30 AM	No 2 left to refill. Back 1.30 P.M.	
	No 1 lorry STEEMBECQUE. Took 2 hours. Took Gen CdC to SAILLY-ON-LYS. Sent rations to 2nd Cav Bde Inspected No 2 Section	J.R.

(9 29 6) W 4141—463 100,000 9/14 H W V Forms/C.2118/10

Army Form C. 2118.

WAR DIARY
or
INTELLIGENCE SUMMARY.
(Erase heading not required.)

O.C. 3rd Cavalry Supply Column

Page 74

Instructions regarding War Diaries and Intelligence Summaries are contained in F.S. Regs., Part II. and the Staff Manual respectively. Title pages will be prepared in manuscript.

Hour, Date, Place	Summary of Events and Information	Remarks and references to Appendices
MOORBECQUE 12/7/15 8.0 AM	Trench parties lorries left. Back 2.0 PM.	
9.30 AM	No 1 left to refill. Back 1.30 PM.	
	No 2 lorries STEENBECQUE. Took 2 1/4 hours.	J.A.
13/7/15 8.0 AM	Inspected No 2 section. Returned as with Leander car. Clutch stop spring.	
	Trench parties lorries left. Back 2.0 PM.	
9.30 AM	No 2 left to refill. Back 1.30 PM.	J.A.
14/7/15 8.0 AM	No 1 lorries STEENBECQUE. Took 2 1/4 hours. Inspected all billets, armoy HdQrs. Cookhouse & latrines.	
	Trench lorries left. Back 2.0 PM.	J.A.
9.30 AM	No 2 left to refill. Back 2 1/4 hours. No 1 left loaded STEENBECQUE. Took 2 1/4 hours. Back 1.30 PM. receipt for truck.	
2.30 PM	Truck 2.30 PM ordered to change all bullets. Checked lorries of Headquarters wheel antlock. All HOD except me.	
15/7/15 8.0 AM	Trench lorries left. Back 2.0 PM.	
9.30 PM	No 2 left loaded. Back 1.30 PM.	
5.0 PM	Receipt for 11,000 pm Back Lorries used as rectus stand, rehid normal for all units.	
	No 1 left today STEENBECQUE. Took 2 1/4 hours. Checked lorries of No 1 section.	J.A.

Forms/C. 2118/10

Army Form C. 2118.

WAR DIARY
or
INTELLIGENCE SUMMARY.
(Erase heading not required.)

O.C. 3rd Cavalry Supply Column
Page 75.

Instructions regarding War Diaries and Intelligence Summaries are contained in F.S. Regs., Part II. and the Staff Manual respectively. Title pages will be prepared in manuscript.

Hour, Date, Place		Summary of Events and Information	Remarks and references to Appendices
MORBECQUE	16/7/15	8.0 AM	Train pulled in SAILLY & NEUVE EGLISE. Left. Back 2.45 PM.	
		9.30 AM	No 2 lorry STEENBECQUE. Took 2 1/2 hours.	
		—	No 1 left horsed. Back 2.30 P.M. Our troops 5.0 P.M.	
			Rode round PILHEM, GRAND & PETIT BOIS, very narrow & bad.	
			Inspected No 2 section, & took numbers of horses etc for census.	J.A.
	17/7/15	8.0 AM	Train parties left as before. Back 2.45 P.M.	
		9.30 AM	No 2 MT lorry. Back 2.30 P.M. to 5.0 P.M.	
		9.45 PM	No 1 lorry STEENBECQUE. Took 2 1/2 hours.	J.A.
			Took census of Head Quarters Cav & Arty lorries, inspected same.	
	18/7/15	8.0 AM	Train parties left as before. Notified SAILLY ration not required.	
			Men at 9.0 AM. Set out on bicycle to ... Back 2.45 P.M. Rations transferred to Regtl lorries for distribution tomorrow.	
		9.30 AM	No 1 left horsefield. Back 2.30 – 5 · 6 P.M.	
			Refused out requirements to ADSuppt. commenced census	
			9.45 PM. Commenced census of motor lorries & horse & harness.	J.A.
			No 2 lorry STEENBECQ vre. Took 2 1/2 hours.	

WAR DIARY or INTELLIGENCE SUMMARY

Army Form C. 2118.

O.C. 3rd Cavalry Supply Column
Page 76.

(Erase heading not required.)

Instructions regarding War Diaries and Intelligence Summaries are contained in F.S. Regs., Part II. and the Staff Manual respectively. Title pages will be prepared in manuscript.

Place	Hour, Date	Summary of Events and Information	Remarks and references to Appendices
MOORBECQUE	19/7/15 6.0 am	NEUVE EGLISE returning 6/c. Back 2.30 p.m.	
	9.30 am	No 1 lorry STEENBECQUE. Took 2½ hours.	
	9.15 am	No 2 left to refill. Back 2.30 – 5. 6 p.m. D/S visited Column. Expanded chains for lorry tops to be of service. Circular pulleys with channel rim frames. Lorries to have forward covers. Handles of pistol carriers for oil & water to be across middle. Filled cans, to distinguish, in dusk. Visited G.H.Q. 3.58 Coy unable to carry out as above. Nearly completed census.	
	20/7/15 6.0 am	No 1 left to refill sent to allow of ELVERDINGHE Rendezvous taken in return with them in bruise. Back 12. Noon to 2.30 p.m.	
	8.0 am	French troops as before. M.T. Back 9.45 p.m.	
	9.45 am	No 2 leaving STEENBECQUE. Took 2½ hours. Figures for new Truck lorry not all ready. Those for Field Squadron in at 6.0 p.m. Also made out that for Completed Census & sent to O.C.A.S.C. Pool vehicles. Inspected Mob. Section. A few which not crashed up too. Gill Burdon allowed running to destruction skipper leaves G.H.Q.	

Army Form C. 2118.

WAR DIARY
or
INTELLIGENCE SUMMARY.
(Erase heading not required.)

O.C. 3rd Cavalry Supply Column
Page 47

Hour, Date, Place		Summary of Events and Information	Remarks and references to Appendices
MORBECQUE 21/7/15.	8.0AM	NEUVE EGLISE trench party returns left. Back 2.30 PM.	
	9.30 AM	No 2 left Refill. Back 2.30 - 5.0 PM.	
	9.45 AM	No 1 lorries STEENBECQUE. Took 2 1/4 hours.	
	1.0 PM	Trench party returns to ELVERDINGHE left. Hr. R.V. Buckfells on STEENVOORDE - POPERINGHE Road just short of POPERINGHE.	J.A.
		Also took Harry W.A. wood & tentatoes Thimblets attached to 3rd Field Squadron to cluster for a few days by Div. orders. Back 8.0 PM.	
22/7/15.	8.0 AM	NEUVE EGLISE returns left Back 2.30 PM.	
	9.30 AM	No 1 left to refill. Back 2.30 - 5.0 PM.	
	9.45 AM	No 2 lorries STEENBECQUE. Took 2 1/4 hours.	J.A.
	1.0 PM	ELVERDINGHE rations left. Back 6.30 PM.	
23/7/15.	8.0 AM	N.E.GLISE returns left. Back 2.30 PM.	
		No 2 left to refill. Back from to 1.30 PM 2.30 PM.	
	9.30 AM	No 1 Refilling at STEENBECQUE. Took 2 1/4 hours.	J.A.
	1.0 PM	Second Trench party left. Back 6.30 PM.	
		Dennis Lorry lent to 3rd Fld Squadron returned. Pvt. H. Lester reported for duty.	

Army Form C. 2118.

O.C. 3rd Cavalry Supply Col'n
Page 70?

WAR DIARY
or
INTELLIGENCE SUMMARY.
(Erase heading not required.)

Hour, Date, Place		Summary of Events and Information	Remarks and references to Appendices
MOORBECQUE 24/7/15			
	6.0AM	No1 refilling Back 11.15 - 1.30 PM	
	9.30AM	No 2 lorries STEENBECQUE. Took 2¼ hours	
		Visited ADSN. Hopeful meeting situation easy	
		Manufactured Otto pitted tops	
		Smoky end curls run	
	7.0 PM	SILVERDINGHE lorries left. Back 6-2.8PM	
25/7/15.	8.0AM	NEUVE EGLISE rations left. Back 2.30PM	
	9.30AM	No1 lorries STEENBECQUE. Took 2¼ hours	Lt.
	9.45AM	No 2 left to refill. Back 2.30PM - 5.0PM	
	1.0PM	ELVERDINGHE lorries left. Back 6.15AM	
		Visited AIRE as a possible new Railhead & Column Pick	Lt.
26/7/15.	8.0AM	NEUVE EGLISE rations left. Back 9.30PM	
	9.30AM	No 2 lorries STEENBECQUE. Took 2¼ hours	
		No1 refilling Back 2.30PM - 5.0PM	
	1.0PM	ELVERDINGHE rations left. Back 2.30PM - 5.0PM.	
		Visited various Railheads etc with ADST.	
		T/Lieut J. STEVENSON left for England	Lt.

Army Form C. 2118.

WAR DIARY or INTELLIGENCE SUMMARY.

O.C. 3rd Cavalry Supply Col^n
Page 709

(Erase heading not required.)

Hour, Date, Place	Summary of Events and Information	Remarks and references to Appendices
MORBECQUE 27/4/15	2.0 AM. NEUVE EGLISE fruit. left Park 2.20 PM.	
	6.30 AM No 2 left to refill Park 2.15 – 4.45 PM	
	Meinselfelij STEENBECQUE Took 2/4 horses.	
	ELVERDINGHE horses left Park 6.30 PM. Present numbers to	
	10 PM be retained at Erquinghem necessitates two lorries which work	
	that to NEUVE EGLISE (via a total of 3 extra lorries daily	
	out of place which were formerly very scarce. In addition	
	transport has to be provided to carry vegetables + wood to these	
	parties. This handicaps us to column vehicles & will	
	also so several of further demands are made. ...under	
	system of Regimental lorries, the distribution of rations for	
	these parties from regiments does not allow of	
	economising any lorry to partially equalize	
	Visited WISERNE to transfer new Sergeant	JRH

Army Form C. 2118.

WAR DIARY
or
INTELLIGENCE SUMMARY.
(Erase heading not required.)

O.C. 2nd Cavalry Supply Column.

Page №

Instructions regarding War Diaries and Intelligence Summaries are contained in F.S. Regs., Part II. and the Staff Manual respectively. Title pages will be prepared in manuscript.

Hour, Date, Place	Summary of Events and Information	Remarks and references to Appendices
MOERBECQUE 28/7/15 9.30am 9.45am 10 PM	No.1 left to refill. Back 2.30 - 4.30 PM. No.2 loading STEENBECQUE. Took 2 hours. French ration left pack 6.30 PM. Wire from division Railhead 3rd para at ARQUES. Inspected No.2 Section lorries.	
29/7/15 9.30am 9.45am 1 PM	No.2 left to refill. Back 2.10 - 4.30 PM. No.1 loading at STEENBECQUE. Took 2 hours. French ration left. Back 6.30 PM. Inspected Belts Lubricator Gearbox house. Inspected No.1 Section lorries. Went to BLENDECQUES to look for new parking ground. Unable to billet, fair with Webster's but to not fill up with scattered. Our troops. Very scattered.	
30/7/15 9.30am 9.45am 10 PM	No.1 left to refill. Back 2.30 - 4.0 PM No.2 loading STEENBECQUE. Took 2 hours. French rations left. Back 6.15 PM. Inspected No.2a + No.2b lorries.	

Army Form C. 2118.

WAR DIARY
or
INTELLIGENCE SUMMARY.
O.C. 3rd Cavalry Suppl. Column

(Erase heading not required.)

Page 84

Instructions regarding War Diaries and Intelligence Summaries are contained in F. S. Regs., Part II. and the Staff Manual respectively. Title pages will be prepared in manuscript.

Hour, Date, Place	Summary of Events and Information	Remarks and references to Appendices
M○9 R B○ CQ○= 31/1/15 9.30am	N○9 left to refill, Back 2.30 – 4.30 P.M. N○1 refilling. Took 2 downs Third push as before Saw AD/S+T & met him in GHQ at 2.30 PM. Went him to GHQ & wrote staff stories not in "messages" left upwith necessary billets in BLENDECQUES on their of ground roughly allotted.	P.T. Appendix XI Miles Known.

Ja Walsingham S. Col=
O.C. 3rd Can. S. Col=

Appendix VI. 3rd Cav. Supply Column

	SECTION 1			SECTION 2		Remarks
July 15	Miles	No of Hours on Road	July 15	Miles	No of Hours on Road.	
1	6	9	1	24	10	
2	24	10	2	6	9	
3	6	9	3	24	10	
4	24	9	4	6	9	
5	6	9	5	24	9	
6	24	9	6	6	9	
7	6	9	7	24	9	
8	30	11	8	6	9	
9	6	9	9	28	10	
10	28	10	10	6	9	
11	6	9	11	28	10	
12	28	10	12	6	9	
13	6	9	13	28	10	
14	32	10	14	6	9	
15	6	9	15	32	11	
16	32	10	16	6	9	
17	6	9	17	32	10	
18	32	10	18	6	9	
19	6	9	19	32	10	
20	32	10	20	6	9	
21	6	9	21	33	9	
22	33	9	22	6	9	
23	6	9	23	34	10	
24	34	9	24	6	9	
25	6	9	25	34	10	
26	34	10	26	6	9	
27	34 6	9	27	34	10	
28	34	10	28	6	9	
29	6	9	29	34	10	
30	34	10	30	6	9	
31	6	9	31	34	10	
Total	551	279	Total	569	293	
Daily Av	17.74	9.38	Daily Av	18.35	9.45	

CONFIDENTIAL

3rd Cavalry Division

WAR DIARY

OF

O.C. 3rd Cavalry Supply Column.

From 1st July 1915 — To 31st July 1915.

Volume VIII

121/6401

3rd Cavalry Division

CONFIDENTIAL.

WAR DIARY

OF

O.C. 3rd Cavalry Supply Column.

From 1st August 1915 to 31st August 1915

(Vol. IX)

J. Archibald, major RAC

WAR DIARY
or
INTELLIGENCE SUMMARY.

(Erase heading not required.)

Army Form C. 2118.

O.C. 3rd Cavalry Supply Column Coy. "B"

Hour, Date, Place	Summary of Events and Information	Remarks and references to Appendices
MOORBECQUE 1/8/15. 6.30am	No 1 refilling. Go before Back 2.30 — 4.15 P.M.	
9.45 am	No 2 loading STEENBECQUE took 1¾ hours	
1. P.M.	EVERDINGHE returns left with wool & vegetables. Back 6.30 P.M.	
	Visited BLENDECQUES & GHQ Troops staff & called on billets at GHQ Troops base 8.30 am and Back 9.0 P.M. received orders	Pte A. M.A. Toomey joined as Workshop Officer
	to move. Bakehouse & adequate in morning. No 1 after loading	
	in afternoon No 2 thought to new park after refill	
	Arrived fully workshop left	
— 2/8/15. 6.0 am	No 1 loading STEEN BECQUE took @ 1.5 hours	
9.45 am	No 2 left to refill. B & 6th Back 12-0 Noon. Workshop to convoy	
—	Headquarters arrived. Arranged — No BLENDECQUES 2. 30 P.M.	
12.15 P.M.	Workshop left arrived BLENDECQUES 2.45 P.M.	
1.0 P.M.	Headquarters & Cooks etc left 3.30 P.M.	
	arrived & remain night in MOORBECQUE w.o. 6. AOD	
	Orders to No 1 Section — Remain night in MOORBECQUE w.o. Officers & GTO	
	Lorries & 3 Pool vehicles Arranged	
3.0 P.M.	Self at BLENDECQUES. Workshop in place 6.0 P.M. Officers & GTO	
	etc ready 8.0 P.M. Spares No 1 Section returned to MOORBECQUE	
	Workshop billets to Workshop Headquarters & No 2 Section Personnel	
	in old Mill. Found in very unsanitary state Has been used	
	as stables. ELDER DINGTE 24 tons		J.H.

Army Form C. 2118.

WAR DIARY
or
INTELLIGENCE SUMMARY.
(Erase heading not required.)

O.C. 3rd Cavalry Supply Column
Page 83

Hour, Date, Place	Summary of Events and Information	Remarks and references to Appendices
BLENDECQUES 3/8/15. 8.0 AM	No 2 loading ARQUES. Took 1½ hours. Good yard.	
9.30 AM	Attended R.V. at MOERBECQUE for No 1 Section. Left toneful at 10.0 AM	
	Alfred 4.0 PM. Two tents in new billeting area. Parked in meare	
	road just N. of & parallel to Railway. Staff Capt. GHQ Troops	
	forbade the afternoon. No 2 Parked at side road with rest room	
	for heavy traffic. Billet No 1 Section in new Paper mill outbuildings	
	Visited OC HSC. R.V. for 4th in BIENBECQUES - THEROUANNE road	
	road direction post. W.D. 1st E in ECQUES at 9.30 AM	
	T.O.3 Lt & later left for DI Sun Ammn Sub. Park.	
— 4/8/15. 7.45 AM	No 1 loading ARQUES took 1½ hours.	
—	No 2 left for R.V. Thus at 9.30 AM Back 3.0 PM	
9.15 AM	E WEROINGHE & Bechelm RAMC return left Back 7.30 PM	
	Visited OC HSC w/ furkes of Pile Majr GHQ Troops in new suitable	
	except in reservoir south & Staff ditto.	
	R.V. for 5th as today. No rations in ELIRDINGHE after today.	
	No 2 parked as before. No 1 in memorial ARQUES - WIZERNE. Arr	
— 5/8/15 7.0 AM	Arranged AOD lorry park at ARQUES.	
9.30 AM	No 1 left for R.V. at 9.30 AM Back & parked on side road with Anti Aircraft	
	6 6.0 PM. No 2 loading ARQUES. Took 1½ hours. Parked 12.20 PM	

Army Form C. 2118.

WAR DIARY
or
INTELLIGENCE SUMMARY.
(Erase heading not required.)

Of 3rd Cavalry Supply Column
Page 84.

Hour, Date, Place	Summary of Events and Information	Remarks and references to Appendices
BLENDECQUES 6/8/15	Post Corporal to Report. Patrol with handcarts hurried off men's neat posted as HQ + OHQ Troops Staff RV for 6A to leave at 2.0 P.M.	J.A.
6/8/15 9.15AM	No 1 loading ARQUES Took 1½ hrs. Returned 1.30 P.M. to lunch.	
	Due to bad hilton narrow road.	
12.0 Noon	No 2 left for R.V. Then at 2.0 P.M. Moved off 2.30 P.M. All units R.V. in their new billet. Back 6.0 P.M.	
4.0 P.M.	Sent one lorry to BERTHEN for details. Back midnight. Staff (Capt.) G.HQ informed us between now & middle to ARQUES & site & best divisional Car Corps would be notified	J.A.
7/8/15 8.30AM	Details from BERTHEN left. Lorry back 2.0 P.M.	
8.45AM	No 3 left to load ARQUES. Took 1½ hour.	
9.30AM	Visited Ruitheut & on to ARQUES to see their billets formed all arranged by G.HQ. On to ADSvT. Back 1.30 P.M. On return found note from G.HQ ordering move to ARQUES at 8 P.M. west.	
12 Noon	No 1 left to R.V. as yesterday. Back 6-8 P.M.	
2.30 P.M.	Arranged various details of field-milage & economic records	
3.30 P.M.	for Section Dr. To O.C.A.S.C. Back with him to ARQUES to see OP.H.Q.P.M.E. not there. Thence to Office. More approved. Drive out to was thro' THEROUANNE now 3rd Car Divisional area. Extreme difficulty caused over fuel very hilly roads with transport extra weary or vehicles. Miles 31.0 with. Petrol 50 gallons heat.	J.A.

Forms/C. 2118/10.

Army Form C. 2118.

WAR DIARY
or
INTELLIGENCE SUMMARY.

(Erase heading not required.)

O.C. 3rd Cavalry Supply Column
Page 85.

Instructions regarding War Diaries and Intelligence Summaries are contained in F.S. Regs, Part II. and the Staff Manual respectively. Title pages will be prepared in manuscript.

Hour, Date, Place		Summary of Events and Information	Remarks and references to Appendices
BLENDECQUES 7/10/15		After a little time in bad weather also some of more roads would be impassible.	
	9.0 PM	Park received orders for move. No 1 to load at ARQUES also No 2 to go to new park. No 2 to refill & then come to new park. HQrs to move at 7.30 AM. Workshops to remain until 9 AM.	
— 8/9/15 5.10 AM		No 2 left to refill. 6th & 9th Bdes as before. Sn troops & 7 Bde.	
	9.15 AM	At 7.0 AM at FAUQUEMBERGES. Back 5.0 PM. No 1 refilling ARQUES, took 1½ hours.	
	10.0 AM	Headquarters at ARQUES. Billets & Offices allotted in Mairie Schools. Yardused as Cookhouse Park & Rec. on HQ & Sqn. All billets useful out of doors. Old Town remained. Workshop crew cleaned out. Headquarter moved to workshop billets tonight. Notified Capo Stevenson of new office	JSR
ARQUES 9/8/15	7.45 AM	No 1 left for R.V.'s as yesterday. Back 4.30 PM.	
	9.30 AM	No 2 loading ARQUES took 1½ hours. Understand a Train of am. For last two days supplies of this had to be fetched from BORDEAUX	
	1.45 PM	Workshops arrived. Ready for work 7 PM. Went out road material to get better roads to & Hqs of Bde lorries. New case of via THEROUANNE. Sent officer to HQM GHQ to ascertain rules of GHQ am.	JSR

Forms/C. 2118/10

Army Form C. 2118.

O.C. 3rd Cavalry Supply Column
Page 56

WAR DIARY
or
INTELLIGENCE SUMMARY.
(Erase heading not required.)

Instructions regarding War Diaries and Intelligence Summaries are contained in F.S. Regs., Part II. and the Staff Manual respectively. Title pages will be prepared in manuscript.

Hour, Date, Place	Summary of Events and Information	Remarks and references to Appendices
ARQUES 10/5/15. 7.45AM	No.2 left for RV's as before. Back 4 – 5.0 PM.	
9.15 AM	No.1 towing ST ARQUE'S took 1½ hours.	
	Pay day + exchange of Gold	J.S.
— 11/5/15. 5.30 AM	Sent out returns for advance party digging Trenches + Enquiries	
	MINES at 7.0 AM.	
7.45 AM	No.1 left for RV's as before. Back 3.45 – 4.30 PM	
9.45 AM	No.2 loading. Took 1¾ hours.	
	Visited DCASC & Field Cashier. Delayed by defects on AOD lorry which was in an accident with a Ford car owned by Fred Sinclair.	
	Sent one lorry to STOMER to get vegetables to bench party + sent one lorry to others to load up potatoes required en route to ARMENTIERES lorry at 5.0 AM 12th inst.	J.S.
— 12/5/15. 8.0 AM	No.2 left to refill as before. Back 3.45 – 4.45 PM	
8.15 AM	Truck Lines left St Lucy due 10 late arrival A.S.O. Arrived ARMENTIERES	
2.0 PM.	Back 10.0 PM	
9.30 AM	No.1 loading ARQUES. Took 1¾ hours	
	Held court of Enquiry on injuries of Pte Bello G. Wrote report on earlier mishap of Ford used by accident. This is to be noted on return.	J.S.

Army Form C. 2118.

WAR DIARY
or
INTELLIGENCE SUMMARY.
(Erase heading not required.)

O.C. 31st Divl Supply Column

Instructions regarding War Diaries and Intelligence Summaries are contained in F.S. Regs., Part II. and the Staff Manual respectively. Title pages will be prepared in manuscript.

Hour, Date, Place		Summary of Events and Information	Remarks and references to Appendices
ARQUES 13/8/15	3.45am – 4.30am	No 1 left to refill so as to allow tinned rations taken out of the ambulances. Too early to collect most of newspapers. Back 1.30 P.M.	
	9.45am	No 2 lorry ARQUES. Took 13¾ hours today due to lack of correct numbers.	
	11.0 am	Sent off 2 lorries to be stationed at ARMENTIERES to feed such units by fetching rations from Lt GORGE station.	
		General Company inspection of arms & equipt worthwhile.	JL
— " — 14/8/15	4.0 am – 4.45 am	No 2 left to refill as yesterday. Back 1.30 P.M. Sent 2 lorries out with No 2's meals & supplements.	
	9.30 am	No 1 lorry ARQUES. Took 11½ hours test. Visited Abel (S.&T.) Twice. Various pickets & sections. Inspected by S.&T. Supervisor as workshops & stables of horses etc.	
	3.0 PM	J.S.S.O. informed me returns for two Bdes would be out tonight on account of alterations in Divisions left 5.45 P.M. Back 10.15 A.M. 15.8. (No 1 Sect)	JL
— " — 15/8/15	5.0 am	Reveille. No 1 left to refill. Back 12.30 P.M.	
	9.30 am	No 2 lorry ARQUES. Took 1½ hours. Started new system of mails, newspapers to Brigades Q in ARMENTIERES. Traction of all units by something arranged	JL

Forms/C. 2118/10

Army Form C. 2118.

WAR DIARY
or
INTELLIGENCE SUMMARY.

O.C. 2nd Cavalry Supply Column
Page 38

(Erase heading not required.)

Instructions regarding War Diaries and Intelligence Summaries are contained in F.S. Regs., Part II. and the Staff Manual respectively. Title pages will be prepared in manuscript.

Hour, Date, Place	Summary of Events and Information	Remarks and references to Appendices
ARQUES 16/8/15 — 6.0 am	No.3 left to refill watering. Back 2.30 PM.	
9.30 am	No.1 Loading. ARQUES took 1½ hours	Jno
— 17/8/15 6.0 am	Inspected various parts of Post Office, H.Q.Pr whole etc. Visited ox ASC. Two lorries for reinforcements.	
9.30 am	No.1 left to refill as before. Back 2.30 PM. No.2 Loading ARQUES Took 1½ hours.	Jno
— 18/8/15. 6.0 am	Inspected Books of No.1 Section. Visited ox ASC.	Jno
9.30 am	No.2 left to refill as before. Back 2.30 PM. No.1 Loading ARQUES Took 1½ hours. Inspected Books of No.2 Section. Also A.O.D. lorries. Visited AM4PAG. Sent 2 lorries with water to ARMENTIERES.	Jno
— 19/8/15 6.0 am	No.1 left to refill. Back 2.15 PM. No.2 Loading ARQUES Took 1½ hours. Sent 1 lorry to be attached at ARMENTIERES for wood supply. Held court of enquiry. Inspected No.1 Section lorries.	Jno
— 20/8/15 5.0 am	6th Bde No.2 left to refill Back 11.0 am. Rec'd to be observed for supply.	
6.0 am	Armentieres —	
9.30 am	No.1 Loading ARQUES Took 1½ hours. Back 2.30 pm. Visited lorries at ARMENTIERES. Pay Day.	Jno

Army Form C. 2118.

WAR DIARY
or
INTELLIGENCE SUMMARY.

(Erase heading not required.)

O.C. 3rd Cavalry Supply Column

Page 59

Hour, Date, Place	Summary of Events and Information	Remarks and references to Appendices
ARQUES. 21/8/15 6.0 P.M.	No. 1 left to refill. Back 2.15 PM	
9.30 PM	No. 2 Battery Arques took 1½ hours. Detailed 3 lorries for division for reinforcement. Visited officers	
22/8/15 6.0 AM	A.D.S. & T. Worked out today. Talked etc. Anew.	
9.30 PM	No. 2 left to refill. Back 2.15 PM. No. 1 loaded ARQUES. Took 1½ hours. Inspected Workshop & all killed on leave without Trouble to ABBEVILLE for M.T. spares.	J.A.
23/8/15 8.0 AM	No. 1 left to refill. Back 2.15 PM. No. 2 loaded ARQUES. Took 1½ hours. Visited WARDRECQUES & arranged drawing	
9.30 PM	Saw O.C. H.C. Visited WARDRECQUES & arranged drawing hay, petrol etc from them.	J.A.
24/8/15 6.0 AM	No. 2 left to refill. Back 2.30 PM. No. 1 loading ARQUES. Took 1½ hours.	
9.30 AM		
3.0 PM	No. 2 — Hay etc at WARDRECQUES. Back 5.0 PM. Visited Wardrecques & G.H.Q. n Workshop Tools etc	J.A.

WAR DIARY
or
INTELLIGENCE SUMMARY. O.C. 3rd Cavalry Supply Column.

Army Form C. 2118.

Page 9

(Erase heading not required.)

Hour, Date, Place	Summary of Events and Information	Remarks and references to Appendices
ARQUES. 25/9/15 6.0am	No 1 left to refill. Back 1.30 — 2.30 PM.	
9.30am	No 2 loading ARQUES. Took 1½ hours.	
3.0 PM	We 1 left to hand pay etc WARDRECQUES. Back 4.30 PM. Inspected motorcycles & R/o. Visits SADJT GHQP At new workshop Lorries & machine tools.	F.A.
26/9/15 6.0am	No 2 left to refill. Back 1.15 — 3.15 PM	
9.30am	No 1 loading ARQUES. Took 1½ hours.	
3.15 PM	No 2 left to load hay etc WARDRECQUES. Back 4.0 PM. Inspected AOD lorries, & No 1 Section footchill	J.A.
27/9/15 6.0am	No 1 left to refill. Back 1.15 — 2.15 PM	
9.30 am	No 2 loading ARQUES. Took 1½ hours.	
1.45 PM	No 1 load hay etc WARDRECQUES. Back 4.0 PM. Visited WARDRECQUES & GHQ.	J.A.
28/9/15 6.0am	No 2 left to refill. Back 1.15 — 2.15 PM	
9.30am	No 1 loading ARQUES. Took 1½ hours.	
1.45 PM	No 2 loaded WARDRECQUES. Back 4.0 PM. Visited HQ of S + T, Inspected No 2 Section Lorries.	D.T.

Army Form C. 2118.

WAR DIARY
or
INTELLIGENCE SUMMARY.
(Erase heading not required.)

O.C. 3rd Cavalry Supply Column
Page 91

Hour, Date, Place	Summary of Events and Information	Remarks and references to Appendices
ARQUES. 29/10/15 6am	No 1 refilling. Back 1-2.0 PM.	
9.30am	No 2 loading ARQUES. Took 1¼ hours.	
1.45 PM	No 1 loading WARDRECQUES. Back 4.0 PM. Inspected various petrol dumps at Rapho. All satisfactory. Visited OC A1C.	
30/10/15 6am	No 2 refilling. Back 1-2.0 PM.	
9.30am	No 1 loading ARQUES. Took 1¼ hours.	
1.45 PM	No 2 loading WARDRECQUES. Back 4.0 PM. Visited APM. AO S&T & GHQ.	
31/10/15 6.0 am	No 1 refilling. Back 1-2.0 PM.	
9.30 am	No 2 loading ARQUES. Took 1¼ hours.	
1.45 PM	No 1 loading Hay etc. WARDRECQUES. Back 4.0 PM. Received 1 Halford lorry from G.HQ to replace small Dennis.	Appendix XII List of miles covered etc.

J. Archibald
Major ASC

Appendix XII OC 3rd Cavalry Supply Column

August 15	SECTION 1 Miles	No. of Hours on Road	August 15	SECTION 2 Miles	No. Of Hours on Road	Remarks
1	34	10	1	6	9	
2	12	10	2	40	11	
3	38	10	3	8	9	
4	8	9	4	40	11	Rough.
5	40	11	5	8	9	Average
6	8	9	6	42	10	Mttisfer
7	42	10	7	8	9	Salt & petrol
8	12	10	8	45	11	5.5.
9	42	10	9	6	9	
10	6	9	10	42	10	
11	42	10	11	6	9	
12	6	9	12	44	11	
13	44	11	13	6	9	M.P.G. = 6.
14	28	14	14	44	11	
15	24	10	15	6	9	
16	6	9	16	44	11	
17	44	10	17	6	9	
18	8	10	18	46	11	
19	44	10	19	6	9	M.P.G.
20	6	9	20	44	10	= 6.5.
21	44	10	21	6	9	
22	6	9	22	44	10	
23	44	10	23	6	9	
24	6	9	24	49	11	
25	49	10	25	6	9	
26	6	9	26	49	10	M.P.G.
27	49	10	27	6	9	= 6.8.
28	6	9	28	49	10	
29	49	10	29	6	9	
30	6	9	30	49	10	
31	49	10	31	6	9	
Total	805	305	Total	773	302	
Daily Av	26	9.8	Daily Av.	25	9.7	

3rd Cavalry Division
CONFIDENTIAL

121/6950

WAR DIARY
of
OC. 3rd Cavalry Supply Column

From 1st September 1915 — 30th September 1915.

Volume X

Army Form C. 2118

WAR DIARY
or
INTELLIGENCE SUMMARY.
(Erase heading not required.)

O.C. 3rd Cavalry Supply Column
Page 92

Hour, Date, Place	Summary of Events and Information	Remarks and references to Appendices
ARQUES 1/9/15. 6.0am 9.30am Jr. 4.8pm	No 2 Left hour fill Back @ 1-2.0 pm No 1 separately ARQUES Took 1½ hours No 2 — Hay etc WARDRECQUES. Back 4.0 pm. Returned small jemmis to G.H.Q. Detailed following for Car Corps R.H.A. park. Lt FARRER as Supply Officer with a Pool car Sgt CLARKE as Tpt. Offr. 3rd Can S.C. Lorries 16 lorries & 65 other ranks supply 2 M.T. Arranged to reserve petrol, rations Cooks etc for park Car 1252 TM 8th Can Bde damaged (referred to O.C. A.C. on 31 ult) sent into 360 Car Resve. G Battery supplies transferred to T to entrain at LOZINGHEM N.a.m	S.M. S.M.
— 3/9/15. 6.0 am 9.30 am 3. 45 pm	No 1 Left hour full Back 1-2.0 Pm No 2 Groceries MFQ u ES Took 1½ hours No 1 — Hay etc WARDRECQUES, Back 4. 8 Pm G. Bty rations R.V. at LOZINGHEM, lorries returned to S Quentin +	
2.0 PM	Hutchison took CLARKE left with T to Diese for St QUENTIN.	

Army Form C. 2118.

WAR DIARY or INTELLIGENCE SUMMARY.

O.C. 3rd Cavalry Supply Column
Page 93

(Erase heading not required.)

Instructions regarding War Diaries and Intelligence Summaries are contained in F.S. Regs., Part II. and the Staff Manual respectively. Title pages will be prepared in manuscript.

Hour, Date, Place	Summary of Events and Information	Remarks and references to Appendices
ARQUES. 2/9/15. 1.30 PM	Sent 2/Lt BORLACE with 6 lorries to HAVERSKERQUE to fetch hood for RHA. All lorries clear of at St QUENTIN. 2 lorries proceeded on to 2 Pt CLARKE to complete him to 14.	
	Name returned. 8.0 PM.	
	Visited St QUENTIN. Arranged billets, funk, cookhouse etc. for 3rd Cav Sup Col. Det.	
3/9/15 6.0 AM	No 2 refilling. Park. 1 - 2.0 PM	
9.30 AM	No 1 loaded at ARQUES. Foot 1½ loads. Hay on train already.	
	loaded for WARDRECQUES. Remainder dry. Arranged for No 2 Section to remove after refilling until adjusted by army.	
	Stopped one lorry on train.	
	Provided 2 lorries for requirements. Asked D.H.A. Q.M.G. to arrange about reinforcements for R.H.A. now detached.	
	Supplies for R.H.A. & H.Q. & H.Q. 6th accomp. put into delivery from St QUENTIN at refilling point.	
	Received wire that ARMENTIERES lorry would return on 4th	J.A.

Forms/C. 2118/10

Army Form C. 2118.

O.C. 3rd Cavalry Supply Column
Page 94

WAR DIARY
or
INTELLIGENCE SUMMARY.
(Erase heading not required.)

Instructions regarding War Diaries and Intelligence Summaries are contained in F.S. Regs, Part II. and the Staff Manual respectively. Title pages will be prepared in manuscript.

Hour, Date, Place	Summary of Events and Information	Remarks and references to Appendices
ARQUES 4/9/15 6.0 AM 9.30 AM	No 1 Refilling Back 1-2.0 PM No 2 infested ARQUES. Took 1½ hours. No 1 lorry slung from station Visited ADS & T.CC. Supply Officers Can No 1 Sup⁺ Sent 80 to Can Bde week order & ADE. Major Hutchinson inspected lorries etc from D.F.T. Suggested tops of canopies of aniline rolls. Proofs for tarpaulins all tops proofs to be kept on site. No sleeves to be used. 3 lorries cleared at ARMENTIERES returned. No 9 refilling Back 1-2.0 PM. No 1 lorry ARQUES took 1¼ hours.	
5/9/15 9.0 PM 8.0 AM 9.30 PM	Visited S⁺ QUENTIN. Various reports etc sent in	O.A.
6/9/15 6.0 AM 8.30 AM 9.30 AM 1.45 PM	No 1 refilling Back 1-2.0 PM. Sent 2 lorries extra to S⁺ QUENTIN for wood. No 2 Refilling ARQUES. Took 1¼ hours. Hay etc WITHDR & COVER. Back 4 PM. No 1 Visited G.H.Q. Index for 2 lorries to proceed S⁺ Quentin 3 days to wood. Infield Modificatic lorries the need repairs received in workshop too	R.A. J.H.

(9 29 6) W 4141—463 100,000 9/14 H W V Forms/C. 2118/10

Army Form C. 2118.

WAR DIARY
or
INTELLIGENCE SUMMARY.
(Erase heading not required.)

O.C. 3rd Cavalry Supply Column Page 55

Hour, Date, Place	Summary of Events and Information	Remarks and references to Appendices
ARQUES 7/9/15. 6.0 am 9.30 am 1.45 pm	Nos 2 & Nightly Back 10.45 – 1.45 P.M. No 1 Loading ARQUES. Took 1½ hours. No 1 — to Harvest WARDRECQUES. Back 10.0 P.M. Inspected M.T. lorries, lamp-boxes, wind-locks, also lining of bodycoverings. Indulge of lubin incorrect too little. no allowance except for distances as can fluctuates at Headquarters enquflts S.E.O. ARMENTIERES. Also to do — No stores of Invicta Knight Daunters Engines. Demands Considered excessive. Not one in Stock 4 stone Engines Inquiry enquflts S.E.O.	P.T.O.
— 8/9/15. 6.0 am 9.30 am 1.45 pm	No 1 Nightly Back 12.30 – 1.30 PM. No 2 Loading ARQUES. Took 1½ hours. No 2 — "— they sat WARDRECQUES. Back 4.0 P.M. Visited M.D.S.+T. nearby. Demns lorries to base for Repairs. Bent Team shafts etc. No available shares except own repair. On to ST QUENTIN Detachmt of Gestures there in food order. Inspected books of Sanitary section found complete Infantry lorry of	G.H.

Army Form C. 2118.

O.C. 3rd Cavalry Supply Column
Page 96

WAR DIARY
or
INTELLIGENCE SUMMARY.
(Erase heading not required.)

Hour, Date, Place		Summary of Events and Information	Remarks and references to Appendices
14/9/15 ARQUES	6.0am 9.30am 1.45pm	No 2 refilling. Back 12.15 - 1.15 PM. At lorries ARQUES. Took 1¼ hours. No 2 — hay at WARDRECQUES. Back 4.0 PM. Visited HQ 9ST N Dennis lorry to Base transport repair. Steam etc. Visited huts at ST QUENTIN. Examined all No 4 new supply group. Sent 1 Headquarter lorry spare to RITASE.	
19/9/15	6.0am 9.30am 1.45pm	No 1 refilling. Back 12.15 - 1.15 PM. At lorries ARQUES. Took 1½ hours. No 2 — hay at WARDRECQUES. Back 4.0 PM. Inspected 100 lorries & books of Sect 2. Received 1 halftoed lorry from GHQ in lieu of Dennis to go to Base. Surprise inspection of light trucks. 95% burnt well. Arranged re War-Skids.	Fng
19/9/15	6.0am 9.30am 1.45pm	No 2 refilling. Back 12.15 - 1.15 PM. At lorries ARQUES. Took 1½ hours. No 1 — hay at WARDRECQUES. Back 4.0pm. No 2 — visited HQ of ST QUENTIN + O.C. the following which cannot be mentioned which sent receipts etc, hay etc Inspected R.E. lorry. Rations refilled. Engine	Fing

Army Form C. 2118.

WAR DIARY
or
INTELLIGENCE SUMMARY.
(Erase heading not required.)

O.C. 3rd Cavalry Supply Column
Page 9 (?)

Instructions regarding War Diaries and Intelligence Summaries are contained in F.S. Regs., Part II. and the Staff Manual respectively. Title pages will be prepared in manuscript.

Hour, Date, Place	Summary of Events and Information	Remarks and references to Appendices
ARQUES. 10/9/15. 6.0 AM 9.30 AM 1.45 PM	No. 1 refilling. Back 12.15 - 1.15 PM. No. 2 loading ARQUES. Took 1½ hours. No. 2 — Hay etc. WARDRECQUES. Back 4.0 PM. Inspected Foot vehicles. Visited O.C. A.C. & 2 A.M.T.S.A.A B.H.Q. Issued billet etc inspection.	
— 13/9/15. 6.0 AM 9.0 AM 1.45 PM	No. 2 refilling. Back 12.15 - 1.15 PM. No. 1 loading ARQUES. Took 1½ hours. No. 2 — Hay etc WARDRECQUES. Back 4.0 PM. Visited WARDRECQUES. Inspected M.O. lorries.	T.A.
— 14/9/15. 6.0 AM 9.30 AM 1.45 PM	No. 1 refilling. Back 12.15 - 1.15 PM. 8th Bde left 12.45 PM Back 6.30 PM No. 2 loading ARQUES. Took 1½ hours. No. 1 — Hay etc WARDRECQUES. Back 4.0 PM. Visited S. & O.A.T. & H.Q. Stores. Section Weekly Parades.	S.A.
— 15/9/15. 6.0 AM 9.30 AM 1.45 PM	No. 2 refilling. Back 12.15 - 1.15 PM. No. 1 loading ARQUES. Took 1½ hours. No. 2 — Hay etc WARDRECQUES. Back 4.0 PM. Visited H.Q. & T's inspection. S.O. A.C. HQ or Workshop lorries allthose under repair. A.C. lorries rather dirty	

WAR DIARY or INTELLIGENCE SUMMARY

Army Form C. 2118.

O.C. 3rd Cavalry Supply Column
Page 98

Hour, Date, Place		Summary of Events and Information	Remarks and references to Appendices
ARQUES 16/9/15	6.0 am	N°1 refilling. Back 12.15 – 1.15 pm	
	9.30 am	N°2 loading ARQUES. Took 1½ hours	
	1.15 pm	N°1 two etc WIRROAECQUES. Back 4 pm.	
		Vehicle inspection continued. Finished N°1 workshop vehicles.	
		Comm to repair the half N°2 section. Satisfactory.	
		Went with O.H.P. Turner up to S.M.T.	
17/9/15	6.0 am	N°2 refilling. Back 12.15 – 1.45 pm	
	9.30 am	N°1 loading ARQUES. Took 1½ hours	
	9.45 pm	N°2 fatigue party etc to etc WITDRELCQUES. Back 4 pm	
		Inspection started to engineers & Dragoons. Inspection not continued afterwards detailed rules.	
		M.D.J.T. also O.C. H.Q. Imperial Bus M.T. & my 2 cars.	
		Inspected N°1 section lorries. Very clean & well looked	
		after. One pair of cylinders from a bed. New wind two	
		treacle spring influence tore.	
18/9/15	7.0 pm	SEQUEN TIP lorries to R.H.A. all returned	
	6.0 am	N°1 refilling. Back 12.15 – 1.15 pm	
	9.30 am	N°2 loading ARQUES. Took 1½ hours	
	1.15 pm	N°1 two etc WITROREEQUES. Back 4.0 pm. Fatigue party for	
		two Inspected N°3 section. Lorries very clean. Well cared for two men absent unknown.	

WAR DIARY
or
INTELLIGENCE SUMMARY

Army Form C. 2118.

O.C. 3rd Cavalry Supply Column

(Erase heading not required.)

Hour, Date, Place		Summary of Events and Information	Remarks and references to Appendices
ARQUES 18/9/15	5.15 PM	7th B de convoys Lft to N.R.H. Back 10.0 PM	
19/9/15	6.0 AM	No. 2 Section nothing. Also J's Rte. Back 12.15 – 11.15 PM	
	9.30 AM	No. 1 Loading ARQUES. Took 18 hours	
	5.0 PM	" WATTRELOS	
	10.0 PM	No. 2 — " Inc. rations 3 blankets 3 days	JR
	11.15 PM	No. 2 — " — Aug the. Back 4.0 PM	
		Supplied future push for 2nd & 3rd Cavalry Bde. Posted Letter	
20/9/15	6.0 AM	No. 1 section refilled. Back 12.15 – 1.15 PM	
	9.30 AM	No. 2 loading ARQUES. Took 1½ hours	
	10.15 PM	No. 1 " " WATTRELOS. Back 4.0 PM	
	11.0 PM	No. 2 section left with 6th Bde rations + No.1 section water carts non-specified	JR
		rations. Refilled LAPUGNOY.	
21/9/15	8.0 AM	Exchanged Section for Peerless Workshop tour complete with C.H.Q.	
		Sir Tho DS Bde No.2 refilled with 6th Sta B Schedule. Back 1.30 PM	
	9.30 AM	RHG refilled supplies direction to near FERME PALFART Back 6.0 PM	
	3.0 PM	No. 1 loading ARQUES. Took 1½ hours	
	11.30 PM	No. 2 Sect. 7th Bde refilled aux CHATEAU NIEPPE. Back 6.0 PM	
	9.0 PM	+ lorries returned.	
	11.0 PM	Visited or rec. of Dragoons & settled recon J rd. to HQ Bde.	JR
		No. 1. A detachment of 2nd Sqd. & Tr. The left with special Coys near	
		rations for the in No. 2. 6th Bde. lorries LAPUGNOY	
		1.30 PM – 5 PM. Loaded Hay, & WATTREQUES v LA BUISSIÈRE	

Army Form C. 2118.

WAR DIARY or INTELLIGENCE SUMMARY.

(Erase heading not required.)

O.C. 3rd Cavalry Supply Column
Page 100

Hour, Date, Place		Summary of Events and Information	Remarks and references to Appendices
ARQUES. 22/9/15.	6.0 P.M.	No. 1 A. echelon for 6th Sta. filled Noshaft. Refilled WESTREHEM. Back 10.15 P.M. No. 1, 7th Pale refilled CHATEAU MIEPPE. Back 9.0 P.M. Loaded special 2 days rations, delivered + returned 2.0 P.M.	
	9.30 A.M.	No. 2 lorry ARQUES. Took 1½ hours. No. 1 Cp. lorries back	
	3.0 P.M.	Settles in new column park intrees CITO QUES & LILLERS. Detached Lt Prestor + 2 Lt Clarke with 36 supply lorries, 141 all ranks as Supply Column for 7th Cav. Bde to push at ST SYLVESTRE'S Corner. 1 Section went full + one empty.	
	3.30 P.M.	No. 1 Section + H.Q. Pre. left arrived REVEILLON 6.30 P.M.	
	4.30 P.M.	Whistler ——— 7.45 P.M.	
	10.0 P.M.	No. 2. A. echelon for 6th S. Jd. D.T. left as yesterday. Pvt Avery Fears transferred to Cl. Sup. Col. Set as Bennetts Bevan unit cracked back axle casing. Received from G.H.Q. 2 Bennies, 1 Hallford, 1 Little van and 5 mile brake steering faulted. Also an Sunbeam car to complete establ. Left 6 A.O.D. lorries at ARQUES.	

WAR DIARY or INTELLIGENCE SUMMARY

Army Form C. 2118.

O.C. 3rd Cavalry Supply Column
Page 101

Hour, Date, Place		Summary of Events and Information	Remarks and references to Appendices
ARQUES 23/9/15	1 am	No 2. B. Echelon left as yesterday. Returned REVEILLON W. 5.0 P.M.	
REVEILLON	5.30 AM	No 2. ※ Train.	
	8.30 AM	No 1. B. Echelon lorries & A. 6th Bde proceeded AIRE to load	
	11.0 AM	Part surplus off fresh & part off Bosie. Took 2¾ hrs. B. Echelon strength 76 & delivered Back 7.45 P.M. Ammunition back 3.30 P.M.	
	10.0 AM	Visited 7th Bde S. Col- detached & sent them off. 1 Whof & 1 Store lorry went extra is artificier	J.H.
	1.30 PM	5th Bde A. lorries & Sup Col- + 1 Amm Pk loading Cheques Took 1¼ hours Received 1 Halford from G.H.Q. in lieu of deficience	J.M.
— 24/9/15	8.30 AM	Out yesterday Casualty spread 2 ordinary & 2 vin rations others 3&4 7.4 Sqdron No 2 to load at AIRE Taken. Delayed 2¾ hours. B. echelons	
	10.15 PM	rations delivered on 23rd et No 1. A echelon left to fetch Back 6.15 P.M.	
	1.45 PM	No 2. 8th Bde & loading Cheques as yesterday Exchanged 1 De Dion lorry with G.S.O. Brig- for box MARRACY Car	
	4.45 PM	Sent out special lorry for men were to sixteen	J.M.

Army Form C. 2118.

O.C. 3rd Cavalry Supply Column
Page 102

WAR DIARY
or
INTELLIGENCE SUMMARY.
(Erase heading not required.)

Instructions regarding War Diaries and Intelligence Summaries are contained in F.S. Regs., Part II. and the Staff Manual respectively. Title pages will be prepared in manuscript.

Hour, Date, Place	Summary of Events and Information	Remarks and references to Appendices
REVEILLON 25/9/15. 9am. 1.45 pm	Nº 1 to load AIRE x CHILBON BEEBUL as yesterday. Nº 1 --- CHOQUES 8th Bde Sent 1 Dr Dvr & 1 Bearey by road to Paris Plage: now arrvd. Impossible to start work to keep accounts or even approx. record of mileage, horses etc worked in bulk, only to mention of lorries wishing in detached parties supervised nightly CR. Arranged collection of Supp. M.T. stores etc from ARQUES. Accommodation at this place very bad. 2 rooms & no other. Conv. to whole column. Third field workshops at side of road. Lorries on full, bad for tires & springs when man-handled & conveyed inside lorry, necessity for rubber tires on lorry axle to be authorised, or issue of two ton Ford car. Sick & evacuation no means. Received mechanical unit necessity for ambulance motor to convey in any death to Cav. Sgt. Two lorries off work thereof notion to detached parties. S.S.r. informed me, Nº 2 would not deliver to Hechelvin.	

G. of M

Army Form C. 2118.

WAR DIARY
or
INTELLIGENCE SUMMARY.
(Erase heading not required.)

O.C. 3rd Cavalry Supply Column
Page 10 ?

Instructions regarding War Diaries and Intelligence Summaries are contained in F.S. Regs., Part II. and the Staff Manual respectively. Title pages will be prepared in manuscript.

Hour, Date, Place		Summary of Events and Information	Remarks and references to Appendices
REVEILLON 26/9/15	2.15 AM	S.S.O. arrived with return for N°2 to deliver at once to Hechelen at L.II.C. Sheet 36.B.	
	3.0 AM	N°2 left. Buck 5.10 AM	
	9.15 AM	Left AIRE to load as yesterday. Also 3 lorries	
	1.45 PM	N°1 with 3 days meat for "B" echelon nw at RINQUE.	
	7.10 PM	N°2 left to load CHOQUES as yesterday	
		Received orders for N°1 to stand at once to NOEUX-LES-MINES RY.STN	
	7.30 PM	Arrived 10.30 AM. Took 1½ hours off loading station yard	
		emptied. Back 2.15 AM. News now of CHOQUES Railhead to NOEUX-LES-MINES. R.H.
27/9/15	9.30 AM	N°1 section & afairs up to 53 lorries proceed to ROBECQ to carry 53rd Inf	
		Bde. to BETHUNE. Thence followed AIRE & NOEUX-LES-MINES.	
	1.15 PM	Left ROBECQ & offloaded one mile beyond BOEUVRY Bk.	
	7.30 PM	6th Bn. detached BETHUNE to load. Latter Back 10.30 PM total	
		Remainder loaded AIRE	L.H.
	10.0 PM	Turnage N°2 to R.V. at NORM. SAILLY-LA-BOURSE. Then 11.45 PM	
28/9/15	3.0 AM	N°1 AIRE loading issue truck	
	4.4 AM	N°2 truck empty	
	9.0 AM	— left for AIRE to load (1st & 5th) "B" echelon stores + deliveries	
		then Bechelen. Back 4.0 PM	
	11.45 PM	N°2 left for NOEUX-LES-MINES to load 3/15 12 M. Hechelen at Back 5.0 PM	

(9 29 6) W 4141—463 100,000 9/14 HWV Forms/C. 2118/10

Army Form C. 2118

WAR DIARY
or
INTELLIGENCE SUMMARY. OC. 3rd Divl'y Supply Column
(Erase heading not required.)   Page 104

Instructions regarding War Diaries and Intelligence
Summaries are contained in F. S. Regs., Part II.
and the Staff Manual respectively. Title pages
will be prepared in manuscript.

Hour, Date, Place	Summary of Events and Information	Remarks and references to Appendices
REVEILLON 28/9/15. 7.0 PM	Orders to No 1 to move RV at 9.30 PM as yesterday. Off 9.20 PM	
— 29/9/15 12.0	Arrived NOYELLES 11.0 PM. Road very congested with horse transport	
Midnight	Orders to dump in J4 BUISSIERE clobered. Turned lorries	Apps.
9.0 AM	3.15 PM dumped. Back 6.30 PM.	
12.30 PM	No 1 to load at HIRE as before. Back 5.0 PM.	
1.30 PM	— — NOEUX-LES-MINES as yesterday. Back 5.30 PM.	
	No 3 to fill area LABUISSIERE. Off 2.15 PM returning 2.30 PM	Apps.
	Back 6.30 PM. Supplied extra lorries for Rum, AOD, & M/c Gun parties	
— 30/9/15 12.30 PM	No 2 to load at NEURLESS-MINES. Rail yard much traffic. Back 6.30 PM.	
12.45 PM	No 1 refilling ROSNAY. Bull des Dames etc. back 5.30 PM.	
2.30 PM	Sort lorries ESTREE BLANCHE to pick up quantities 8 & 9 Ser. Bth. (a) (b) (c)	
	— 4 — FRUGES	
	— 1 — NOYELLES	
	— 25 — Mr S... Dth Essex y/Bn (b) (c)	
	Back (a) 10.30 PM. (b) 1.30 AM 1st Oct. (c) 6.45 PM.	
	Slight firing on German lorry from Lucky Strike Fort. Few days from CRE.	
	Damage Tenfahtin scrapped. 24 for ammunition issued.	
	Many tires very bad. Very difficult to get wheels retyred. No	At Reveillon XIII
	Halford Solid tyres in country.	At Bruloge tower Reticulet
	A. A. Lulball major	
	OC 3rd Divl. Sup. Colm	

Appendix XIII

	SECTION 1			SECTION 2			
September 15	Miles	No of Hours on Road	September 15	Miles	No of Hours on Road.	Remarks
1	6	9	1	49	10	
2	57	11	2	9	10	Petrol
3	6	9	3	47	10	
4	47	10	4	6	9	Rough
5	6	9	5	44	10	Average
6	47	12	6	6	9	M.P.G. = 6.9
7	6	9	7	49	10	
8	49	10	8	6	9	
9	6	9	9	49	10	
10	49	10	10	6	9	
11	6	9	11	49	10	M.P.G = 8.3
12	49	10	12	6	9	
13	6	9	13	49	10	
14	49	10	14	6	9	
15	6	9	15	49	10	
16	49	10	16	6	9	
17	6	9	17	49	10	M.P.G = 8.0
18	49	10	18	21	11	
19	6	9	19	40	10	
20	69	15	20	26	15	
21	30	14	21	65	20	
22	32	15	22	42	18	
23	25	12	23	6	9	
24	25	12	24	27	12	
25	27	12	25	4	10	M.P.G
26	30	12	26	58	16	= 6.5
27	84	17	27	27	14	
28	36	13	28	28	12	
29	28	16	29	20	11	
30	20	14	30	28	12	
31	—	—	31	—	—	
Total	911	333	Total	877	333	
Daily Av	30.3	11.1	Daily Av	29.2	11.1	

3rd Cavalry Division

121/7437.

3rd Cav. Supply Column

1 to 31 Dec. 1915

Vol XI

CONFIDENTIAL.

WAR DIARY.

OF

O.C. 3rd Cavalry Supply Column.

From 1st October 1915 to 31st October 1915 —

(Vol. 1)

Army Form C. 2118.

WAR DIARY
or
INTELLIGENCE SUMMARY.
(Erase heading not required.)

O.C. 3rd Cavalry Supply Column
Page 105.

Instructions regarding War Diaries and Intelligence Summaries are contained in F.S. Regs., Part II. and the Staff Manual respectively. Title pages will be prepared in manuscript.

Hour, Date, Place		Summary of Events and Information	Remarks and references to Appendices
REVEILLON 1/10/15	12.30 PM	No 2 left to refill GOSNAY – BOIS DES DAMES etc. Back 5.30 PM	
	1 PM	No 1 to load LILLERS. Good station. Took 1½ hours. Back 5.0 PM	
2/10/15		Visited HQ division & LILLERS. Trip for Halford lorries – impossible to obtain. Sent 2 lorries to H.O.D.	
	12.30 PM	No 1 refilling LABOURIERE etc. Back 5.0 PM	
	1 PM	No 2 loading LILLERS. Took 1½ hours. Back 4.45 PM	
		Visited DDST & asked for better supply Halford tyres. LILLERS found fresh Hd qr'e 3CD who phoned 1st Gunn & gave orders to move	G.H.
		Col — LILLERS tomorrow. Sent 2 lorries to H.O.S.	
3/10/15	9.0 AM	Headquarters etc left with No 1 Section to its new area above	
		Aubedets. On to station. Train not in.	
	1.30 AM	Wokestoffs left allied LILLERS. 1.0 PM	
	11.45 AM	No 1 Started loading LILLERS. Delay of train. Finished about 2.30 PM	
	7.30 PM	3 lorries No 1 w/ 8th Cav Bde in chargé clothing with Dvr Stroh FRUGES	G.H.
	3.0 PM	No 2. 2nd & 4th Bn Troops left their hqr LILLERS. Back 7.0 PM	
	3.30 PM		7.15 PM
LILLERS 4/10/15	10.30 AM	No 2 Section left for factory for trade. Back 12.30 PM	
	1.30 PM	No 1 refill as yesterday. Back 5.15 PM	J.M.
		2 lorries for mails. Still acting as Reserve M.T. Amts.	

Army Form C. 2118.

WAR DIARY
or
INTELLIGENCE SUMMARY.

O.C. 3rd Cavalry Supply Column Page 106.

(Erase heading not required.)

Hour, Date, Place	Summary of Events and Information	Remarks and references to Appendices
LILLERS 5/10/15 — 10·0AM 1·30PM	No 1 loading LILLERS. Took 1¾ hours. No 2 refilling as yesterday. Back 5·0 PM Sent 2 lorries to HQRE for meat etc. v 2 for hay for HQE.	F.A. F.A.
— 6/10/15 10·0AM 1·30PM	No 2 loading LILLERS. Took 1½ hours No 1 refilling. Back 5·0 PM Sent one lorry to Div.l reinforcements	F.A.
— 7/10/15 10·0AM 1·30PM 10·30AM	No 1 loading LILLERS. Took 1½ hours. No 2 refilling. Back 5·0 PM 2 lorries reinforcement LILLERS to Rouville. Sent 2 lorries for mails AIRE, & 1 to Q case to Eye.	F.A.
— 8/10/15 10·0AM 1·30PM	No 2 loading LILLERS. Took 1½ hours No 1 refilling. Back 5·0PM Supplies for 1st echelons 6th Bde to unit, & 5th Bde at HORIONVILLE Don 7th Bn still at RINGOT & drew rations & flour from LILLERS	F.A.
— 9/10/15 10·0AM 1·30PM	withdrawn down 2 lorries AIRE for fifth DMI. Parts No 1 loading LILLERS. Took 1½ hours No 2 refilling. Back 5·0 PM. SSO for coal. Sections workshops Sent 1 lorry inspected	F.A.

WAR DIARY
or
INTELLIGENCE SUMMARY.

(Erase heading not required.)

Army Form C. 2118.

O.C. 3rd Cavalry Supply Column

Page 107

Hour, Date, Place	Summary of Events and Information	Remarks and references to Appendices
LILLERS. 10/10/15. 10AM 1.30 PM	No 2 loading LILLERS. Took 1½ hours. No 1 refilling. Back 5.0 PM. Sent a lorrie MOD to Clay, one lorry RHGs to FROGESCHOL very GHQ to Lyres.	
" 11/10/15 10.0 AM 1.30 PM	No 1 loading LILLERS. Took 1½ hours. No 2 refilling. Back 5.0 PM. One lorry to HIRE to deliver extra rations 'B' echelon to bring them into line with rest of division. 2 ft CB rain transferred to 7th Cav Bde Supt-as S.O.	J.D.
" 12/10/15 10.15 AM 1.30 PM	No 2 loading LILLERS. Back 1.50 PM. No 1 refilling. Back 5.30 PM. Dvr Troops less F20 Spln went BOURECQ to Army Col. ST HILAIRE. M.T. spares bad delivery strenuous weekends due to being attached to 1st ARMY. Telephoned all WSt railheads v. tried to remedy by informing school M.T. depot of movements of sections. D Supply Train.	J.D.
" 13/10/15 8.30 AM 1.30 PM	No 1 loading LILLERS started 9.45 AM. Took 1½ hours. No 2 refilling. Back 5.0 PM. Dysentry of Halford & Jennings Tyler still very acute such as Preston Knight Gudgeon becks Huffnell unstable. 3 CC Beamtree hung up for spares hno mosquito grinding post especially	

WAR DIARY or INTELLIGENCE SUMMARY

Army Form C. 2118.

O.C. 3rd Cavalry Supply Column

Page 108

Hour, Date, Place	Summary of Events and Information	Remarks and references to Appendices
LILLERS 14/10/15 – 8.0PM 1.30PM	No. 2 to load LILLERS. Took 1½ hours No. 1 refilling. Back 5.0PM. 10 R.H at ECQUE DECQUES. Sent 2 lorries ARE M.T. workshops.	JM
— 15/10/15 – 8.30AM 1.30PM	No. 1 to load LILLERS. Took 1½ hours. No. 2 refilling Back 5.0PM. Sent lorries to load to S.S.O. & further supplies for BETHUNE	JM
— 16/10/15 10.30AM	No. 2 to load LILLERS. Started 12.30PM finished 1.35PM Sent 10 lorries on to BETHUNE to complete convoy.	
1.30PM	No. 1 refilling. Back 5.0PM. One lorrie back en route broke busy half time. Twelve 4 pin. allowing broke blocks to hold spare lorry housed by S of T's inspector in nearby had 4 cases. Lorry No shows saw 30 lorries. Remarks: steam & willobahid often out in all direction. Badly need front back wheel probably both needs. Sent to be sorrid fun. 2 lorries to RoD	J.D.
— 17/10/15 10.20AM	No. 1 to load LILLERS. Took 1½ hours. 12 lorries to complete load Augusta BETHUME No. 2 refilling. Back 5.0PM. 4 Bob RHA + 2nd Cav: MATHING HEM	JM
1.30PM	2 lorries ARE MT hubs etc. 2 lorries No. D.3 lorries to Reinforcements. Handed Bourrie to to PARIS for release.	

Army Form C. 2118.

WAR DIARY
or
INTELLIGENCE SUMMARY. O.C. 3rd Cavalry Supply Column

(Erase heading not required.)   Page 109

Hour, Date, Place	Summary of Events and Information	Remarks and references to Appendices
LILLERS. 10/10/15. 9.0AM	No.1 refilling as before Beuvry. 12.30.PM.	
10.15AM	No 2 loading LILLERS. Took 1 3/4 hours. Loaded & delivered 1 day's rations for Sqdn 10th R Hussars. No M.T. required so sent back.	
2.0PM	No 1 loading LILLERS 2 days rations return B. echelon BETHUNE 2 days & 1 lb extra ration 1 day with Hdqrs. Retd further 10.30AM this spreads 2 days complete rations for division who concern them received 2 days iron rations @ ordinary scale outs. Informed division men to new billets. no delivery of H.Q. after 6.0PM.	
3.0PM	Informed division semany from billets till 21st except our troops.	
5.0PM	Saw Bde S.O. & obtained new areas. O.C. Bdes informed.	
9.0PM	S.S.O. arrived & said orders were for whole Divn to move to temporary new billets. Rodehead at 31st A.I.R.E. Lieut I Francis A.S.C. & one for mails. No M.T. or M.T. men even for Sup Col!	J.9

Army Form C. 2118.

O.C. 3rd Cavalry Supply Column
Page 110

WAR DIARY
or
INTELLIGENCE SUMMARY.
(Erase heading not required.)

Hour, Date, Place	Summary of Events and Information	Remarks and references to Appendices
LILLERS 9/10/15 9.0 A.M.	Bde S.O.S ammunition to temporary cream. Arranged R.V's for all at 3 P.M. between B'de AUCHY-AU-BOIS. Remainder units of Regt PALFART.	
1.0 P.M.	W.2. Left for R.V. Left R.V. 3.50 P.M. Par/for FRUGES Arq - FAUCHEM BURGES B.E. - FRUGES LAIRES 6.E. - Back 9.15 P.M. Visited A.D.S.C. who said allotment of khaki flannel with Division. Requested 1st Arm. Leave to park at LAMBRES. Visited LIERES, RELY & AUCHY AU BOIS as possibly places to fall back on. X Divi Hqrs. Relay Bicycles extra ammunition lorries or Motycycling also left on hart No 21 with No 2. Sent 1 lorry Spare parts A.R.E. 1 G.M.O to fetch motorcycles. Visited Q first army & obtained leave to park LAMBRES. Informed Q 3rd Cav Divn.	R.A.

WAR DIARY or INTELLIGENCE SUMMARY

Army Form C. 2118.

O.C. 3rd Cavalry Supply Column Page 111

Hour, Date, Place	Summary of Events and Information	Remarks and references to Appendices
LILLERS 20-10-15 9.0 PM	No. 2 left to load WAR STORES rations for issue after 22nd, with war & other rations abandoned. Back 1.30 pm.	
1.0 PM	No. 1 left with Res. 4 Res. rations as yesterday. Change tyres & also outfits echelon complete return. Remainder of rations now held in A.R.R.E.C. Twice tarped lub & spunk. (Some Batts. 7.6 pm.) Also 40 tons lump coal. Infused 9 tons old Scots rations & 21 cwt Repair brushing on 21 st. Hay stocks: Also complete rations Beketom. Remainder 2 delays own rations to be consumed afterwards. All wan rations of division normal. Issued orders for move of cols. to LILLERS about 9 at AIRE. R.f.	
9.30 AM	Headquarters & first Sec 2 lorries left. Workshops 7/4 km later.	
10.30 AM	No. 1 left for load AIRE 10.30 AM. Finished 12.50 PM. 9/4 hours stay. Easy to chunks of train.	
1.0 PM	No. 2 left to refill to Govnmt. bullets Back 8.0 PM except 4 R.H.f.A & 10th R. Hussars. Back 2.0 PM next day. 4 lorries Sec. 2 at AIRE S/D conducted dumps of 102 hf.f. & Govnmt.	

Army Form C. 2118.

WAR DIARY
or
INTELLIGENCE SUMMARY.
(Erase heading not required.)

O.C. 3rd Cavalry Supply Column

Page 1/2

Hour, Date, Place	Summary of Events and Information	Remarks and references to Appendices

LUMBRES 21/10/15 5.0 AM — All settled into new billets. Proceeded apart for workshops & parking.

Several No. 2 motor lorries moved.

5th Bde detachment rejoined. Capt Preston, 2/Lts Clarke & Price. 150 OR — 31 Workshop, 1 store lorry, 2, 3 Ton 4.30 — 30 curtains. Part refilled, loaded with M.G at A.R.E. Part refilled 7th billet. FAUCHEMBERGUES.

2/Lt C.B. Price temp attached with S.O. 7th Can Bde & replaced by Lieut Riley.

Note: Force Reg to increased by drafts of 102 men bringing the unit up to about 1500 own War Est. Also today, loaded up for ...

9.10 AM — H.T. Coy about 100 mn + 164 horses, also not allowed (by W.E.). This means additional 2 3 cwt lorries required clearly each section. Also telephone communication this Bn Coy Ruchard + cyclists.

Visited S.C.A.T.C of B.A.G. M.G. F arranged for lorries to leave parties No. 1 & 4 Bde. Squadrons left RV at 11.0 AM. Back 2 PM & 3.30 PM.
Bri Troops lorries used to convey pts of 9th Bde from aerodrome at FROGES to billets. Left RV at 10.15 AM. Back 12.30 PM.

9.30 AM — No. 1 & No. 2 left to load A.R.E. tot 1/2 hours.

No. 2 left to load A.R.E. tot 1/2 hours

Arranged with R.E. post officer & O.C. R.E. Fylers to collect fm newhead mechanical units same day. Mails delivered Polycarp dump. Will R.T.O. to collect reinforcement 61 bitter fm 10.30 AM shortly

WAR DIARY or INTELLIGENCE SUMMARY

Army Form C. 2118.

O.C. 3rd Cavalry Supply Column
Page 113

Hour, Date, Place	Summary of Events and Information	Remarks and references to Appendices
LA M BRES 23/10/15 8.0AM	No. 2 Section left to refill as follows: R.V. 6th Bde at 10.15 AM Auchy-Au-Bois — 7th Bde Fauchembergues. — 8th Bde between Cuhem & at 11.0 AM Fleurelle at 10.30 AM — sent 7 wagons at 11.30 AM. Heavily	
	Back 1.45 PM Liégarde 5.30 PM dismantled. Could 10 lorry loads of kit from Bde store to units. Hence delay.	
10.30 PM	No. 1 load A.T.R.E. took 1½ hours. Visited A.D. S+T, Cav. Corps + discussed scheme for feeding Cav. Who acting as Infantry. Sent 2 lorries for reinforcements + officers to met same 10 AM Some extra lorries not obtained by 7.0 PM.	
9.0 PM	Wir "24 E – 29 E" load HIRE 8.30 PM. A++ lorries with the main road LATMBRES – AIRE before 10.30 AM. Arranged sun with both sections. Informed Rin, PR & AD Remte S.So. repairs lorry to go on Major Turis? to SEMPY with returns 3.5.M. 3.S.H. for 1st + 3rd T.10 Squadrons. Arranged to am to draw reinforcements.	

10.30 PM

Army Form C. 2118.

WAR DIARY
or
INTELLIGENCE SUMMARY.

O.C. 3rd Cavalry Supply Column
Page 114

(Erase heading not required.)

Instructions regarding War Diaries and Intelligence Summaries are contained in F.S. Regs., Part II. and the Staff Manual respectively. Title pages will be prepared in manuscript.

Hour, Date, Place	Summary of Events and Information	Remarks and references to Appendices
LAMBRES 24/10/15 3.AM 7.45AM	No 1. Left to refill. Back 1.30PM & 5.0PM. No 2. Left to load A.R.E. No Train. 10.0AM loaded from 3rd Can. Train. Finished 11.30AM. – 3rd Can. Train arrived 10.45PM with newspapers, which so could not catch No 1. Good stock of tyres now at ISBERGUES. Sent 4 lorries to Cyclist 2 lorries AOD	Copy
" 25/10/15 7.45AM 9.0AM	No 1 left to load A.R.E. Took 1½ hours. Back 11.30AM. No 2 left to refill. Back 1.0 – 6.0PM. Lorry for SEMPY took 8.0PM. Visited AOQS+T. Also applied 4 new lorries to feed Area H.T. bay & make up for 102 entrusted to 6 Can. Ry. Co. Applied for authority to mount water carts & lorry wheels & obtain necessary spare parts from Base thro ADMS Sent 2 lorries AOD. One broke down VINCLY. Arranged tow here overnight. Tomorrow ther.	P.R.
" 26/10/15 7.45AM 9.0AM	No 2 left to about A.R.E. Took 1½ hours. Back 11.30AM. No 1 left to refill. Back 1.0 to 5.0PM. Visited novels of 6th Cav Bde will move to Aumerval	

(9 29 6) W 4141—463 100,000 9/14 H.W.V. Forms/C. 2118/10

WAR DIARY
or
INTELLIGENCE SUMMARY.

Army Form C. 2118.

OC. 3rd Cavalry Supply Column.

115

Hour, Date, Place	Summary of Events and Information	Remarks and references to Appendices
LOMBRES. 26/10/15	Parade by Squadrons as ordered by AA & QMG. Mostly fresh goat at present. Visited OC ASC & requested if possible return for SEMPY to be sent in by Div. HQ. lorry from FRUGES. Held Committee meeting to form a Mess Room, Coffee bar, small Canteen. Sent lorry APD.	J.H.
— 27/10/15 7.45am 8.0pm	No 1 to load ARE. Took 1½ hours. Back 11.30am. No 2 left to refill. A 6th Cav Bde. Took entire hour. Drew glycerine for radiators of 3 cwt vehicles. Arranged for applications for winter clothing, gumboots, Coalwood nature etc. Instructed Section officers to have horse chambers cleaned out — Radiator tubes of Daimler lorries — ditto — & Timsken improved. Sent lorry to APD.	J.H.
— 28/10/15 7.45am 8.0pm	No 2 to load ARE. Took 1½ hours. Back 11.45am. No 1 left to refill. Back 1.30 – 5.0pm. Sent 1 lorry APD. Further arrangements for winter clothing. Further arrangements of children & clothing for winter.	J.H.

Army Form C. 2118

WAR DIARY
or
INTELLIGENCE SUMMARY. O.E. 3rd Cavalry Suppty Col/2
(Erase heading not required.) Page 116

Instructions regarding War Diaries and Intelligence Summaries are contained in F. S. Regs., Part II. and the Staff Manual respectively. Title pages will be prepared in manuscript.

Place	Date	Hour	Summary of Events and Information	Remarks and references to Appendices
LAMBRES	29/10/15	7.45am	No 1 R left to load AMRE. Took 1½ hours. Back 11.45am	JS
		2 pm	No 2 left to refill. Back 1.30 – 4.30 pm	
			Out on tour ABD.	
			Met reinforcement for front – 1 horse –	
			Rifle inspection for return of types	
"	3/11/15	8 am	No 1 left to load. Back 11.30 – 4.30 P.M.	J.A.
		6.30 am	No 2 left to load AMRE. Took 1¾ hours.	
			Visited by new OC. AS.C. Visited GHQ	
"	3/11/15	7.45 pm	No 1 left to load AMRE. Took 2 hours.	JSS
		2.0 pm	No 2 Mtly Back 1.50 – 5.0 pm. Picked up various stores at MARRES deft to troops.	
			Visited ABSC.	

A.Fitchdie XO
Forms made Pd/A

R Mitchell Major
OC 3rd Cav Sup Col=

2353 Wt W2544/1454 700,000 5/15 D. D. & L. A.D.S.S./Forms/C. 2118.

Auchinbull ... Appendix XIV Oc 3rd Cavalry Supply Column

Section I   Section II

	15 Miles	No. of Hours on Road		15 Miles	No. of Hours on Road	Remarks
1	12	9	1	18	10	56 lorries
2	20	10	2	12	9	
3	8	10	3	19	11	Rough average
4	12	9	4	7	9	mileage per
5	7	9	5	12	9	gallon of
6	7 1/2	9	6	7	9	petrol
7	7	9	7	12	9	= 5.8.
8	12	9	8	7	9	
9	7	9	9	12	9	
10	12	9	10	7	9	
11	7	9	11	12	9	
12	12	9	12	7	9	
13	7	9	13	12	9	
14	12	9	14	7	9	
15	14	9	15	14	9	6 lorries
16	14	9	16	14	9	
17	14	9	17	15	9	
18	34	11	18	14	9	= 7.8.
19	50/14	10	19	50	14	
20	36	12	20	36	9	
21	19	12	21	50	15	63 lorries
22	50		22	10	11	
23	10	9	23	50	12	
24	50	12	24	12	9	
25	12	9	25	51	12	= 7.8.
26	50	12	26	12	9	
27	12	9	27	50	12	
28	50	12	28	12	9	
29	12	9	29	50	12	
30	50	12	30	12	9	
31	12	9	31	50	12	Av for month
TOTAL	600	304	TOTAL	658	320	= 7.16
DAILY AV.	19.35	9.8	DAILY AV.	21.23	10.3	

3rd Cavalry 15/11/11

D/7639

CONFIDENTIAL

WAR DIARY.

OF.

O.C. 3rd Cavalry Lefffr Column.

From 1st November 1915. to 30th November 1915.

(Volume XII)

Army Form C. 2118.

WAR DIARY
or
INTELLIGENCE SUMMARY. O.C. 3rd Cavalry Supply Column Page 114
(Erase heading not required.)

Instructions regarding War Diaries and Intelligence Summaries are contained in F.S. Regs., Part II. and the Staff Manual respectively. Title pages will be prepared in manuscript.

Place	Date	Hour	Summary of Events and Information	Remarks and references to Appendices
LAMBRES	1/11/15	6 am	No 1 left refill. Back 11·30 AM — 3·15 PM. Early start so as to allow through shipping of packets to take returns with them. Our regiment to-date. Set out of lemons.	
		7.15 am	No 2 took MRE. Took 2 hours. Delayed by bad portion of the Cabo Right brook in yard to keep horse clean.	
			Inspected through Hutchinson in afternoon.	
	2/11/15	8 am	No 2 left refill. Back 1·30 — 5·0 PM	
		8.30 am	No 1 left took MRE. Took 2 hours	
		6.15 pm	Trench Supply series (3) left. Back 5·30 PM. One ton of Strawberries now there from there.	L. 4
	3/11/15	6 am	No 1 left to refill. Back 11·31 AM — 3·0 PM. Early start to return before reinforcements. Mail's	
		8.30 am	No 2 left took MRE. Took 2 hours	
		9 am	No 2 left took MRE. Took 2 hours	corn to ruminate
		7.15 pm	Shipping truly lorries left. Back 5·31 PM.	
			Inspected all detail. North serviceable favorites. Some bad. Require but	
			recom. for 2007 men. Palace will many trucks withers drying means of conclusion	

2353 Wt. W2544/1454 700,000 5/15 D. D. & L. A.D.S.S./Forms/C. 2118.

WAR DIARY or INTELLIGENCE SUMMARY

Army Form C. 2118.

A.C. 3rd Cavalry Supply Column
Page 113

Place	Date	Hour	Summary of Events and Information	Remarks and references to Appendices
LAMBRES	4/11/15	8.0am	No 2 left to refill. Back 1.15 pm – 4.45 pm.	
		9.30am	No 1 to load M.R.E. Took 2 lorries.	
		2.0 pm	T.D. lorries left. Back 5.30 pm.	
			Sent one lorry to D.V.S. ted. G.H.Q. Arrvt. Requested Smith Newm to return keep present guard Renault lorries.	J.R.
	5/11/15	8.0am	No 1 left to refill. Back 1.15 pm – 4.45 pm.	
		9.30am	No 2 to load A.R.E. Took 2 lorries.	
		2.0 pm	T.D. lorry left. Back 5.15 pm. Remainder TD fuel returned to billets.	
			Lieutenant Burg H.O. visited Q branch in reference to emergency party.	J.R.
	6/11/15	8.0am	No 2 left to refill. Back 1.15 pm – 4.30 pm.	
		9.30am	No 1 to lose. Took 2 lorries. Investigated reason for delay last few days. due to breaking of train on rail. R.T.O. requested to alter party to unit apt. of loading. Objected to filling up of cell in troops HQ. Brokenin at railhead in account of whole of timan huts space which could otherwise be usefully employed. Also orders from S.S.O. to receive Cavalry heavy motor rations. Visited H.Q. & S.&.T.	J.R.

2353 Wt. W2544/1454 700,000 5/15 D.D.&L. A.D.S.S./Forms/C. 2118.

Army Form C. 2118.

WAR DIARY
or
INTELLIGENCE SUMMARY.   OC 3rd Cavalry Supply Column
(Erase heading not required.)   Page 117

Instructions regarding War Diaries and Intelligence Summaries are contained in F. S. Regs., Part II. and the Staff Manual respectively. Title pages will be prepared in manuscript.

Place	Date	Hour	Summary of Events and Information	Remarks and references to Appendices
LUMBRES	10/4/15	8 am	No 1 left to refill. Back at 1.15 – 4.45 PM	
		6.30 am	No 2 to load ARE. Took 1.45 mins Hospital & ASC. Paths firm, but not good. Informed probably shall receive 3 ton machine in lieu of 30 cwt.	fair
			Visited O branch and arranged for lorries to collect divisional lorries	
	20/4/15	8 am	No 2 left to refill. Back 1.15 – 4.45 PM	
		9.30 am	No 1 to load ARE. Took 1 hr 40 mins. Men being arranged	
		2.0 am	TD half as before. Lecture down AOD.	
			Met Sanitary Return with column. Several O hours be established to Cavalry Rear HQ. Have to turn out here at midnight to collect returns before fully	fit
	11/4/15	8 am	No 1 left to refill. Back 1.45 – 4.45 PM	
		9.30 am	No 2 load ARE. Took 1 hr 35 mins. Tea in cabin	
		10 am	Sgt 3 lorries TD half SUPEROM. Back 10.15 PM Instructions of transport available used up.	
		2 PM	TD half WALLON CAPPEL as before	
			Sat one hour to make up lost and return regard due & no waves being now carried. Learn lorry talking her to bay. Arrange to 2 lorries fetch mails details	fair
			Roothead 6.30 AM to commence outgoing Beltain	

2353 Wt. W2544/1454 700,000 5/15 D. D. & L.   A.D.S.S./Forms/C. 2118.

WAR DIARY
or
INTELLIGENCE SUMMARY.

Army Form C. 2118.

(Erase heading not required.)

O.C. 34 Cavalry Supply Column
Page 120

Place	Date	Hour	Summary of Events and Information	Remarks and references to Appendices
LAMBRES	10/11/15	8.0 AM	No 2 left. Refill Pack 1.45 P.M — 5.0 P.M	
		9.30 AM	No 1 left to load AIRE. Took 1 hr 40 mins	
		10.30 AM	Detailed 20 Box 1 car 2 lorries & 2 om for food supply party leaving to 5th Corps	
		2.0 PM	WALLON CAPPEL - horse as before.	
			Received notification to stop work on road outlets, including charge of area.	J.K.
	11/11/15	8.0 AM	No 1 left Willy Buck 11.30 AM — 2.30 PM	
		9.30 AM	No 2 left to load AIRE. Took 1 3/4 hours	
		2.0 PM	WALLON CAPPEL party as before.	
			Raid to set two lorries under repair without fuel. Very short of transport. No running	J.K.
			spares. Has to go to G.H.Q.	
	12/11/15	8.0 AM	No 2 left to refill Pack 1.30 PM — 4.30 PM	
		9.30 AM	No 1 to load AIRE. Took 1 hr 40 mins	
		2.0 PM	WALLON CAPPEL party as before	
			Sent Painter over to G.H.Q. for repairs. Received 3 frames issued for G.H.Q. All small bodies are very small, two machine refused entrance, papers to be sent Refused to accept.	J.K.

Army Form C. 2118.

WAR DIARY
or
INTELLIGENCE SUMMARY.
O.C. 3rd Cavalry Supply Column

Page 12/1

(Erase heading not required.)

Instructions regarding War Diaries and Intelligence Summaries are contained in F.S. Regs., Part II. and the Staff Manual respectively. Title pages will be prepared in manuscript.

Hour, Date, Place		Summary of Events and Information	Remarks and references to Appendices
LAMBRES. 13/4/15.	8·0 AM	No 1 left to refill Rauh 1·30 PM – 4·45 PM	
	6·30 PM	No 2 to load AIRE. Took 1 hr. 35 mins	
		Inspected BEAURAINVILLE. Visited Q & AD.S. & T. refuelled Gunsmiths & ADS.t. returning two to G.H.Q. Shentow lorry A.S.D.	fust
—	14/4/15. 8·0 AM	No 2 left to refill. Back 1·15 PM – 4·30 PM	
	9·30 AM	No 1 to load AIRE. Took 1¾ hours	
		Returned 2 lorries to G.H.Q. Received one for 3rd Army yesterday informed	fust
		Visited Q. Informed BEAURAINVILLE not available. Scarcely any cover, no other place offered possible. Wired to find Sup Col=.	
—	15/4/15. 8·0 AM	No 1 left to refill. Back 1·15 PM to 4·15 PM	
	9·30 AM	No 2 to load AIRE. Took 1¾ hours	
		Visited Q & OC ASC. Allowed BEAURAINVILLE visited. Cover enough now	
		Col — Refused to cont lots of refugees on account of extra rations splitting of loads without officers with new narrow hills. So ambulance nights F.H.	
		3 Halfords arrived for G.H.Q.	
—	16/4/15. 8·0 AM	No 2 left to refill 7th Rde in No Inllts. Hot quiet as over.	
	9·30 AM	No 1 to load AIRE. Took 1¾ hours	
	1·30 PM	No 2 Hr. 6th lorries truck located all ashes. Petrol Coy & Staff left 1·30 PM	

Army Form C. 2118.

WAR DIARY
or
INTELLIGENCE SUMMARY.   OC. 3rd Cavalry Supply Column Page/22
(Erase heading not required.)

Hour, Date, Place	Summary of Events and Information	Remarks and references to Appendices
BEAURAINVILLE. 16/11/15. 9 a.m.	No 2 Nos arr at 7.30 a.m. 1½ hours before parked. Ten funny Willerkoml, Porablo very bad. Ice & snow up to 6" deep caused delays & made convoy work unsafe. Arranged RV for 17th	J.A.
LAMBRES. 17/11/15. 8 a.m.	No 1 left for R.V. RIMEUX. Thaw by 11.30 a.m. Roads cut, paths in mess. Were exchanged by S.O. at 1.0 p.m. 7 Rock left 1.30 p.m. Sun through 12.0 Noon. LAD. 2.30 p.m. Roads very bad snow etc. Unsafe to refill to all units.	
BEAURAINVILLE. 8.30 p.m.	No 1 Ret. Ten funny Willerskopf. Workshops when in. Butchers.	
10.30 a.m.	No 2 loaded MARESQUEL. Took 1¾ hours. Moved AD Lorries to MARESQUEL. Called on ASC. O Arranged to communication. Arranged own Lorry to ST OMER.	J.A.
18/11/15. 9 a.m.	R.V. 11 a.m. by 10.15 a.m. train due to rearrangement rations 5th Bde due to difficult billets. No 2 Back 1.30 p.m. & 1.30 p.m. drove lorry to ST OMER	
9.15 a.m.	No 1 left to refill MARESQUEL. Took 1½ hours. Established communication by civil phone. Arranged billets etc. 3 Halfords d'Germain to Base	J.A.

Army Form C. 2118.

WAR DIARY
or
INTELLIGENCE SUMMARY.
(Erase heading not required.)

O.C. 3rd Cavalry Supply Column.
Page 123

Instructions regarding War Diaries and Intelligence Summaries are contained in F.S. Regs., Part II. and the Staff Manual respectively. Title pages will be prepared in manuscript.

Hour, Date, Place	Summary of Events and Information	Remarks and references to Appendices
BEAURAINVILLE 19/11/16 9·0AM	No 1 ready to fall. Started 10·15AM. Back 2·0PM – 6·0PM. Transfer returns for Essex ½ Co @ P.T S. Michel. R & G @ WARONNE X = RH @ COYECQUES. 1st LG @ WICQUINGHEM.	
	Recon. roads to actual regiments. Unfit. Reason left a hill.	
10·30AM	No. 2 loading MARESQUEL took 1¾ hours. Visited Q. requested to dump above rations closer. Cancelled instr. Sect. Officers queried roads unfit at 10·0PM. Sect. as before for same truck for division. Turned 50 butteoff learn Sea.	Sgd
20/11/16 10·0AM	No. 2 unfilled as yesterday. Back 1·30 – 5·30 PM except Essex at EMBRY. No. 1 loading MARESQUEL. Took 1½ hours. Visited Q & inspected roads. Unfit Reported. Found dumps inspected other roads in view to 40 Bde area. Leave lorry for Essex not used. Sect 2 lorries KOS.	Sgd

Army Form C. 2118.

WAR DIARY
or
INTELLIGENCE SUMMARY.

O.C. 3rd Cavalry Supply Column Page 124

(Erase heading not required.)

Instructions regarding War Diaries and Intelligence Summaries are contained in F.S. Regs., Part II. and the Staff Manual respectively. Title pages will be prepared in manuscript.

Hour, Date, Place	Summary of Events and Information	Remarks and references to Appendices
BEAURAINVILLE. 21/11/15. 9·0 A.m.	No.1 to fill. Back 12·30 – 4.15 p.m.	
10·30 A.m.	No.2 loading. MARESQUEL. Took ½ hour.	
	Lost 2 lorries A.S.D. One lorry been sent out to look on Park in Inspected men routes on left Bde area. Visited O.C.A.S.C. + A.D.S.T.	O.S.A.
22/11/15 9·0 A.m.	No.2 to fill. Back 12·30 – 4.15 p.m.	
9·0 A.m.	No.1 to load MARESQUEL. Took 1¾ hrs. Early start road clear	
	yard for coal.	
	Inspected further routes arranged to S.R.T.	J.H.
	Lorries as usual in & out.	
23/11/15 9·0 A.m.	No.1 refilling. Back 12·30 – 4·15 P.m.	
11·15 A.m.	No.2 loading MARESQUEL. Took 1¾ hours. Reinforcements entraining	
	Inspected further roads & bridges	
	Reported CREQUOISE valley road in very bad state. to O.C. A.S.C. Requires immediate repair.	J.H.
24/11/15 9·0 A.m.	No.2 refilling. Back 12·30 – 4·15 P.m.	
10·30 A.m.	No.1 loading MARESQUEL. Took 1¾ hours.	
	Sn Tn road central map to O. 2 R.s+T. Visited by O.C.A.S.C.	
	Rec'd 2 Halfords, 1 Denins from L.A.C.	usual issues lorries	J.H.

Army Form C. 2118.

WAR DIARY
or
INTELLIGENCE SUMMARY.
(Erase heading not required.)

OC 3rd Divn Supply Column
Page 125

Hour, Date, Place	Summary of Events and Information	Remarks and references to Appendices
BEAURAINVILLE 25/4/15		
9.0 AM	Drew 10 tons coal for Col=	
	No 1 left refilling. Back 12.15 PM — 4.30 PM	
10.30 AM	No 3 to load MARESQUEL. Took 1½ hours.	
	Prepared road reports	J.A.
	Sent 2 Hullsails to Paris Plage {?}	
26/4/15 9.0 AM	No 2 left to refill. Back 12.15 PM — 4.30 PM	
10.30 AM	No 1 to load MARESQUEL. Took 1¼ hours	
	Made experiments with manshift for upkt.	
	Sent 1 lorries to GHQ.	
	Sent 4 lorries to 6pm, BOULOGNE. Not yet settled	
	4 tyres falling rear load. Lorries loaded up.	
27/4/15 9.0 AM	No 1 left to refill. Back 12.15 PM — 4.30 PM.	
10.30 AM	No 2 to load MARESQUEL. Took 1¼ hours.	
	Viewed further roads for "C" Bty R.H.A. Referred to S.S.O.	
	of case.	
6.30 PM	Wire received. Behaviour villa by sale end. Asked Q.	
	Inspected North Village. No answer. Absolutely unsuitable. Returned	H.Q.

Army Form C. 2118.

WAR DIARY
or
INTELLIGENCE SUMMARY.

O.C. 3rd Cavalry Supply Column
Page 126.

(Erase heading not required.)

Instructions regarding War Diaries and Intelligence Summaries are contained in F.S. Regs., Part II. and the Staff Manual respectively. Title pages will be prepared in manuscript.

Hour, Date, Place		Summary of Events and Information	Remarks and references to Appendices
BEAUARAINVILLE	9.0 AM	No 2 refilling. Back as usual.	
28/4/16	10.30 PM	No 1 loading MARESQUEL. Took 1½ hours. Visited O.C. ASC at Q. No new funds found yet for Column. Very hard frost during night. 3 Cyl. Hupsons & 1 Hump. Oil no good, nothing will no good worth these in machines.	R.S.
29/4/16	9.0 AM	No 1 refilling as usual except 3rd Regt. Left 9.0 AM for new P.d. ST MICHEL. Back 3.0 PM.	
	10.30 AM	No 2 loading MARESQUEL. Took 1¼ hours.	
		Informed by Q. nothing yet definite never more tomorrow. Searched for possible park in afternoon.	J.X.A.
	10.30 PM	Wire from Q. that we are remain here at present.	
30/4/16	9.0 AM	No 2 refilling. Back 12.15 PM — 3.15 PM.	
	10.30 AM	No 1 loading MARESQUEL. Took 1½ hours.	
	11.30 AM	Informed by Q. that 2 may receive two. Probably 2 days notice to quit. Finally cancelled all new arrangements.	

C.H. Herbert ? Lt.
? ?
J. Ashworth ? Lt Col
OC 3rd Cav Sup Col

Appendix XV
O.C. 3rd Cavalry Supply Column

	Section I			Section II			Remarks
November 15	Miles	No. of Hours on Road	November 15	Miles	No. of Hours on Road		
1	50	12	1	12	9		
2	12	9	2	50	12		Rough average
3	50	12	3	12	9		mileage 65
4	12	9	4	50	12		= 7.6
5	50	12	5	12	9		
6	12	9	6	50	12		
7	50	12	7	12	9		
8	12	9	8	50	12		
9	50	12	9	12	9		
10	12	9	10	50	12		
11	50	12	11	12	9		
12	12	9	12	50	12		= 7.3
13	50	12	13	12	9		
14	12	9	14	50	12		
15	50	12	15	12	9		66
16	12	9	16	60	15		
17	60	14	17	10	11		= 6.01
18	10	10	18	36	12		
19	40	10	19	10	9		
20	10	9	20	42	10		
21	42	10	21	10	9		
22	10	9	22	42	10		
23	42	10	23	10	9		
24	10	9	24	42	10		
25	42	10	25	10	9		
26	10	9	26	42	10		= 6.49
27	42	10	27	10	9		
28	10	9	28	42	10		
29	42	10	29	10	9		
30	10	9	30	40	10		
31			31				
TOTAL	876	306	TOTAL	862	308		
DAILY AV.	29.2	10.2	DAILY AV.	28.7	10.3		6.52

CONFIDENTIAL.

WAR DIARY.

OF

O.C. 3rd Cavalry Supply Column

From 1st December 1915 — 31st Dec '15.

Vol XIII

Army Form C. 2118.

WAR DIARY
or
INTELLIGENCE SUMMARY.

O.C. 3rd Cavalry Supply Column.
Page 1 & 7

(Erase heading not required.)

Instructions regarding War Diaries and Intelligence Summaries are contained in F.S. Regs., Part II. and the Staff Manual respectively. Title pages will be prepared in manuscript.

Hour, Date, Place	Summary of Events and Information	Remarks and references to Appendices
BEAUBRIVILLE. 1/2/15.		
9.0 AM	No.1 Section left Suffolk Bucks 12:45pm — 4:15pm.	
10.30 AM	No.2 — today MARESQUES. Took 1½ hours. P.St. MICHEL rooms empty.	J.H.
	Collected BRIMEUX - AIX - SEMPY. P. St. MICHEL rooms empty.	
	Arranged coal fatigue for Ruthven.	
2/2/15.		
9.0 AM	No.2 refilling Ruck as usual. head MONTREUIL - MANNING # E.M. Road.	
10.30 AM	No.1 loading early: were to clear before coal MARESQUEL	R.M.
	Took 1½ hours	
	Informed by Q arrangements being made to go MONTREUIL.	
	Asked to inspect mulkuls from M.T. Point Q mess.	
	Visited O.C. ASC	
	Coal fatigue to Suffolk man at railhead.	
	Informed lorry broke back axle.	Jn
3/2/15. 9.0 AM	No.1 refilling as usual.	
10.30 AM	No.2 loading MARESQUEL. Took 1½ hours. Visited MONTREUIL	J.H.
	& Ruthven near Reserve park in square refused to move.	
	Could not see O. Gen 10.0 PM	

Army Form C. 2118.

WAR DIARY
or
INTELLIGENCE SUMMARY.
(Erase heading not required.)

OC 3rd Cavalry Supply Colm
Page 128

Hour, Date, Place	Summary of Events and Information	Remarks and references to Appendices
BEAURAINVILLE 4/12/15 9.0 am 10.30 am 11.30 am	No. 2 refilling as usual. No. 1 loaded MARESQUEL. Took 1½ hours. Inspected by ADS&T. OC OC AS&C. Order for new lights. Visited MONTREUIL in afternoon. Billeting officer refused new receipts for awning & car park near station. Saw AQMG ETAPLES. Refilled 9 wagons.	
--- 5/12/15 9.0 am 12.30 pm	Refilled to use whole system. No. 1 refilling returned MONTREUIL 1.0 pm – 4.0 pm. No. 2 loading MARESQUEL. Took 1½ hours. 4 lorries for reinforcements leave etc.	R.A.
MONTREUIL 11.0 pm	Arrived with No. 2 for standard section. Parked in front of main square & small square. Few billets tonight. None for Supply No. 1 who shifted in lorries. Left 1 bivy behind extra do too. Refilled 9.	
--- 6/12/15 9.0 pm 9.0 am	No. 1 loading MARESQUEL. Took 1¾ hours. No. 2 refilling each 1.0 pm – 4.0 pm. Found new billets, arranged offices, telephone etc etc. No place for cookhouse, petrol store, huts, dumping etc. Canteen etc.	arranged with QM for issue fuel &c.

Army Form C. 2118.

WAR DIARY
or
INTELLIGENCE SUMMARY.

(Erase heading not required.)

O.C. 3rd Cavalry Supply Column
Page 129

Instructions regarding War Diaries and Intelligence Summaries are contained in F.S. Regs., Part II. and the Staff Manual respectively. Title pages will be prepared in manuscript.

Hour, Date, Place	Summary of Events and Information	Remarks and references to Appendices
MONTREUIL 7/2/15. 9.0am	No 1 refilling as usual. Road to P⁺ S⁺ MICHEL very bad	
10.30am	No 2 refilling of R.E. Visited O.C. R.E. Col⁻ to arr⁴ Coal for dug-outs firewood fatigue party. No Recon⁻ yet for huts etc etc. MARESQUEL. Took 1½ hours.	J.A.
—— 8/2/15. 9.0am 10.30am	No 2 refilling as usual. No 1 touring MARESQUEL. Took 1½ hours. Arranged winter scheme	J.A.
—— 9/2/15. 9.0am 10.30am	No 1 refilling. R.H.G at AIX. No 2 touring MONTREUIL. Took 1¾ hours Visited O.C. R.E. Arranged more billets	J.A.
—— 10/2/15. 9.0am 10.30am	No 2 refilling as before. Back 12.15pm — 3.30pm No 1 loading MONTREUIL. Took 1¾ hours When winter scheme	J.A.

Army Form C. 2118.

WAR DIARY
or
INTELLIGENCE SUMMARY.
(Erase heading not required.)

O.C. 3rd Cavalry Supply Column
Page 130

Hour, Date, Place	Summary of Events and Information	Remarks and references to Appendices
MONTREUIL 11/12/15 9 am	No 1 refilling rendezvous. 1st Bde date "Embarrassing" Took 1 3/4 hours.	
10:30 am	No 2 (ditto) MONTREUIL minus 5 ffs of Oby Cavalry Luzien.	
— 12/12/15 9 am	Reorganised Column HQ & Sub Pk & and to be evacuated last tery H.O.P. & reorganised that transport (6th Bde lorries returned MARESQUES)	RM
	No 2 refilling as usual. To Bele etc dumps Busk at load 32 tons / load (reserve) (16 lorries at 30 miles)	
5:45 pm	5:45 pm. Justin mileage 460	
10:30 pm	No 1 loading MARESQUES. Took 1 3/4 hours. Arrangement for loading sidelong of coal. Halfsrad Rsry Future lorry A.O.D	Jy
— 13/12/15 9 am	No 1 refilling except 6th Bde at Mosken. On return bother Coal started 5 pm Finished loads 6:30 pm. To Bele etc dumps Back 11 o Pm Justin mileage 900 (30 lorries @ 30 miles)	
10:30 am	No 2 ditto not MRUIL. Took 1 1/2 hours. Arrival (after heavy rain still) Was to come for Bele dumps for these is sufficient stuff. One Consignment has been our front for 3 weeks.	A.M

Forms/C. 2118/10

Army Form C. 2118.

WAR DIARY
or
INTELLIGENCE SUMMARY. OC 3rd Cavalry Supply Column
(Erase heading not required.)

Page 131

Instructions regarding War Diaries and Intelligence Summaries are contained in F.S. Regs., Part II. and the Staff Manual respectively. Title pages will be prepared in manuscript.

Hour, Date, Place		Summary of Events and Information	Remarks and references to Appendices
MONTREUIL 14/12/15	9.0 am	No 2 left to refill. Back as usual. Also sent 10 lorries with Reserve coat. Packed 12 tons to town.	
	10.30 am	No 1 refilling MONTREUIL. Took 1½ hours. Inspected by A.D.M.S. Arranged new cookhouse & new shed to bath. Sent out lorry A.O.D. Gave B G/10 Seconde for Otto office.	R.A.
15/12/15	9.0 am	No 1 refilling. O. B.M. out embussing parties & lunch on tour.	
	10.30 am	No 2 lorries MONTREUIL. Took 1½ hours. Made Xmas & Canteen arrangements. Found lorries to lorries scheme.	J.P.
16/12/15	9.0 am	No 2 refilling as usual.	
	10.30 am	No 1 lorries MONTREUIL. Took 1½ hours. Road Mnt. Lecture by O.C. A.S.C. at FRUGES.	P.A.
17/12/15	9.0 am	No 1 refilling as usual.	
	10.30 am	No 2 lorries MONTREUIL. Took 1½ hours.	
		West Box 100 M.E. Arranged about letting, Canteen for Col — Xmas dinner.	J.R.M.

WAR DIARY or INTELLIGENCE SUMMARY.

Army Form C. 2118.

O.C 3rd Cavalry Supply Column
Page 132

(Erase heading not required.)

Hour, Date, Place	Summary of Events and Information	Remarks and references to Appendices
MONTREUIL 18/9/15 9.0am / 10.30am	No 3 refilling as usual. No 4 loading. MONTREUIL. Took 3/4 hours. Visited O/C a/c & P. Arranged and distributing for "D" units. Also called goods from Sup. Canteen. Opened own canteen.	
19/9/15 9.0am / 10.30am both	No 1 refilling as usual. No 2 ditto. MONTREUIL. Took 1½ hours. Visited OC ASC re question of loads & road to repair. Arranged snow chains to lorry re schools & necessary tackle etc. ED mount horse started.	A.A.
20/9/15. 9.0am / 10.30am	No 2 refilling as usual. No 1 loading. MONTREUIL. Took 1½ hours. Arranged re started bath. Setup a usit/o Cof O. Debatter a day = 1 tub for men for fortnight. Started cord event up in various garage to FRUGES. Letter re communal lands, road, using tenny straw. Visited by A.D.G.S. T.	J.L.R.
21/9/15 9.0am / 10.30am HWV	No 1 refilling as usual. 4th Bde lorries pulled up wood to shelters LOISON. Amounts rather varied little to b/C) use afford former. No 2 loading MONTREVIL. Took 1½ hours. Visited OC A/C, through theatre, xmas church, canteen. Work after dejeuner storing letters.	J.L.R. most use to breads must use for letters, S.A.H.T. invited of "staring" HQ/O, AOST/lts Qn 5, GHQ-AOS/let & AAQm O/lts

Forms/C. 2118/10

Army Form C. 2118.

WAR DIARY
or
INTELLIGENCE SUMMARY.

(Erase heading not required.)

A.E. 31st Div. Sup. Col.

Page - 133.

Instructions regarding War Diaries and Intelligence Summaries are contained in F.S. Regs., Part II. and the Staff Manual respectively. Title pages will be prepared in manuscript.

Hour, Date, Place	Summary of Events and Information	Remarks and references to Appendices
MONTREUIL 22/12/15 9.0 A.M.	No 2 refilling as usual.	
10.30 P.M.	No 1 toiletting MONTREUIL. Took 1¾ hours. Moved for 3rd F/A Sqdn. still insufficient, no nails, no bolts. Rifled AOD lorries and rightful chain on road lying in the ground. Few nails, no newspapers.	J.H.
23/12/15 9.0 A.M.	No 1 refilling as usual.	
10.30 P.M.	No 2. toiletting MONTREUIL. Took ¾ hours. Arranged attitude Xmas dinner. Summary of evidence. Many visits & newspapers.	J.A.
24/12/15 9.0 A.M.	No 2 refilling as usual.	
10.30 P.M.	No 1 toiletting MONTREUIL. Took 1½ hours. Arranged transport of parties. Xmas arrangements. Rations for 100 m. 1, 2 C.S.C.	J.H.
25/12/15 9.0 A.M.	No 1 refilling as usual.	
10.30 P.M.	No 2 toiletting MONTREUIL. Took 1½ hours. Sucked to	J.A.
5.0 P.M.	Inches of Coal. Visited Grease. Men's Xmas dinner etc.	
26/12/15 9.0 A.M.	No 2 refilling as usual. O.B. be a little restriction of rations for 4 parts owing to holiday.	
10.30 P.M.	No 1 toiletting MONTREUIL. Took 1½ hours. Further summary of evidence. Arranged shunting scheme	J.H.

Army Form C. 2118.

WAR DIARY
or
INTELLIGENCE SUMMARY.   OC 3rd Cavalry Supply Column
(Erase heading not required.)   Page 134.

Instructions regarding War Diaries and Intelligence Summaries are contained in F. S. Regs., Part II. and the Staff Manual respectively. Title pages will be prepared in manuscript.

Place	Date	Hour	Summary of Events and Information	Remarks and references to Appendices
MONTREUIL	27/8/15	9.0 am	No 1 refilling. Back no need.	
		10.30 am	No 3 ref touching MONTREUIL. Took 1½ hours.	
		12.15 pm	D.D. to concentrate. Made necessary arrangements.	
			Sent 12 lorries No 1 to ETAPLES for R.S.O. to handle rations for A.D. Arranged start tomorrow 2.0 pm.	P.A.
"	20/8/15	9.0 am	No 2 refilling as usual.	
		12.30 pm	Wire S.S.O. to ask about lorries rations dry 4.0 pm. No numbers yet receivable.	
		2.0 pm	No 2. 20 lorries loaded at MONTREUIL. Left 3.45 pm. At almost by 6.0 pm. Lorries returns	
		2.30 pm	No 1. loading MONTREUIL. Took 1½ hours.	
		11.30 pm	Lorries etc detached at WIZERNE informed lorries to be split up between stations tomorrow	P.A.
"	29/8/15	9.0 am	No 1 refilling as usual.	
		10.30 am	No 2 loading MONTREUIL. Took 1¾ hours.	
		2.0 pm	No 21 loaded 9 lorries with extra men + lorries rations	
			Visited OC A.S.E. Obtained changes in scheme. - No tram rations now to be taken. - R.H.Q. go by road - S.C. to go 1st Jan. etc.	P.A.

2353 Wt. W2514/1454 700,000 5/15 D. D. & L.   A.D.S.S./Forms/C. 2118.

WAR DIARY
or
INTELLIGENCE SUMMARY.

O.C. 3rd Cav. Sup. Col.
Page 135

Army Form C. 2118.

Place	Date	Hour	Summary of Events and Information	Remarks and references to Appendices
MONTREUIL	30/8/15	9.20am	No.2 refilling as usual. Amm⁰ Col⁰ ʀatins returned. Rtn ratn to be drawn for Belges.	
		9.30am	Loaded RHA lorries No.2 with bulk despatched FRUGES via HESDIN. Arrived 1.45 p.m.	
			No.2 lorries BÉOTUN. Took 1¾ hours.	
			Attended F.G.C.M. Capt Preston with Cars 4 & 5. OR left to command D.P.S.S. (detached) ⁄ S.S.	
	31/8/15	9.0am	No.1 refilling as usual less RHA.	
		10.30am	Handed me days rations for D.D. on Rly. gotten lorries of No.1 & No.2.	
		—	No.3 loaded Maucher tin. BÉOTUN in 1½ hours.	
		1.15pm	Start of xD on.T cancelled fr 6-7-8 B⁄n. Rung up A.D.S.&T. O.C. who informed me to send lorries for Batteries & late H.Qrs. — Also 6 who say RHA Start tomorrow. Rations split up /p.20. — to be one such lorries at to unit lorries. Had to send lorries for McG as rations again spanned.	

Alfred [signature]
J.A. Milbury [signature]
O.C. 3rd Cav Sup Col

Appendix XVI.   O.C. 3rd Cav.Sup.Coln.

Section 1.   Section 2.

December 1915	Miles	No. of hours on road.	December 1915	Miles	No. of hours on road.	Remarks.
1	40	10	1	10	9	
2	10	9	2	40	10	Rough average
3	40	10	3	10	9	M.P.G.
4	10	9	4	40	10	= 7.6
5	40	12	5	18	12	
6	24	10	6	40	11	
7	40	11	7	24	10	
8	24	10	8	40	10	
9	35	10	9	6	9	
10	6	9	10	35	10	
11	35	10	11	6	9	= 5
12	6	9	12	43	12	
13	50	15	13	6	9	
14	6	9	14	36	11	
15	35	10	15	6	9	
16	6	9	16	35	10	
17	35	10	17	6	9	
18	6	9	18	35	10	= 5.5
19	35	10	19	6	9	
20	6	9	20	35	10	
21	35	10	21	6	9	
22	6	9	22	35	10	
23	35	10	23	6	9	
24	6	9	24	35	10	
25	35	8	25	6	7	
26	6	8	26	35	9	
27	42	10	27	6	9	5.6
28	6	9	28	48	11	
29	42	10	29	6	9	
30	12	10	30	34	11	
31	35	10	31	12	10	
Total	749	303	Total	706	302	
Daily Average	24.16	9.77	Daily Average	22.77	9.74	

CONFIDENTIAL.

WAR DIARY.

OF

O.C. 3rd Cavalry Supply Column.

From 1st January 1916 to 31st January 1916.

(Volume XIV)

J. Archibald
Major ASC

Appendix XVII. O.C. 3rd Cav. Sup. Coln.

Section 1.   Section 2.

January 1916	Miles	No. of hours on road.	January 1916	Miles	No. of hours on road.	Remarks.
1st	28	12	1st	43	12	
2nd	35	10	2nd	6	9	Rougher
3rd	6	9	3rd	52	11	MPG
4th	28	9	4th	6	9	= 5.2
5th	6	9	5th	28	9	
6th	28	9	6th	6	9	
7th	6	9	7th	28	9	
8th	28	9	8th	6	9	
9th	6	9	9th	28	9	
10th	28	9	10th	6	9	
11th	6	9	11th	28	9	= 5.3
12th	28	9	12th	6	9	
13th	6	9	13th	28	9	
14th	28	9	14th	6	9	
15th	6	9	15th	28	9	
16th	30	10	16th	6	9	
17th	6	9	17th	28	9	
18th	28	9	18th	6	9	
19th	6	9	19th	28	9	= 5.5
20th	28	9	20th	6	9	
21st	6	9	21st	28	9	
22nd	28	9	22nd	9	9	
23rd	8	9	23rd	36	10	
24th	28	9	24th	6	9	
25th	6	9	25th	28	9	
26th	28	9	26th	6	9	= 5.7
27th	6	9	27th	28	9	
28th	28	9	28th	6	9	
29th	6	9	29th	36	9	
30th	30	9	30th	6	9	
31st	6	9	31st	28	9	= 5.44
Total	540	284		596	285	
Daily average	18.38	9.16		19.22	9.19	

WAR DIARY
or
INTELLIGENCE SUMMARY. O.C. 3rd Cavalry Supply Coln.

Page 136

Army Form C. 2118.

Place	Date	Hour	Summary of Events and Information	Remarks and references to Appendices
MONTREUIL	1/1/16	9.0 am	Return of M/c from DD. at B.	
		9.0 am	No 2 filling. Back 11.30 am - 3.30 pm. R4G lorries on wire exhibition.	
		10.30 pm	No 1 loading BEUVIN. Took 12 hours. Had to fetch 2nd lantern. ESCAPE L.& S.W. train fell 7 pm.	
		9.30 am	13 Halford OSD lorries loaded with one days rations to DD from 3CD. All Chevs etc left miles BEUVIN - 35 OR MT 10 SR Supply arrived etc 9.15. 11.15 PM. Handed in later BEUVIN. Arrived etc 9.15. 11.15 PM. Handed	
			One OC DDSC on legend run. 1st Battn returned here.	
			Sacked 30 Amo coal.	
		4.0 pm	News BN entrain 3 Nist & forward supplies to join up same day.	
			Made necessary arrangements.	
			Order for coal for 75 Car Rees to go by road. Supposed rendezvous Ry. exchange.	Non.
	2/11/16	9.0 am	No 1 refilling as normal. Some lorries with 1st lance full 9.30 am cutting up. Put in reserve late.	
		10 am	No 2 loading BEUVIN MONTREUIL took 15 hours. Return to B. loaded in bulk yesterday in flag to fct.	
			Informed No Official news of Change of Railhead. Two lorries took top dress to DD.	
		10 pm	News to wait for road yet. Bn. too late coal travel in lorries sent out, to join DDSC. arrived.	
			DD Advised orders for remainder of column to join DDSC.	/s/

WAR DIARY or INTELLIGENCE SUMMARY

Army Form C. 2118.

O.C. 3 W[estern] Cav[alry] Sup[ply] Col[umn]
Page 137

Place	Date	Hour	Summary of Events and Information	Remarks and references to Appendices
Montreuil	31/1/16	9.0 A.M.	No 2 left to refill as usual except 7th Bde at 8.30am — 1st L & 8 to ROMILLY — empty lorries conveyed men to DESVRES to entrain — return via SAMER.	
		1.30 P.M.	10 Halifords S3 OR left to join DDSC under 2nd Lieut Buchner who returned. Arrived there 5.30 P.M.	
			on Halford broke down cliff about Boulogne & have been left with auxilliary of No 30th B.R.S. & B.S. H.Q. Div	
		10.30 A.M.	No 1 landed MONTREUIL Total 12½ tons / Hopeful material under Captain Stevenson further work arrangies which is being done — Indications by British veterinary M.O.C. Branch into which we urgently required time have an order amendments.	Ass.4
	1/2/16	9.0 A.M.	No 1 left to refill B de Champs 6th Bde as usual — 8 80th MANNINGHEM — 9th Bde FRESSIN & T. (Essex) Ed HESMOND) — Div Tp FROGES. Refill 9.0 am except DTp to 10 am	
		11.0 am — 2.0 P.M.	Sawing weekly estimate £200. Gasoline things in lorries — of regained work single ellts of munitions mules reform available — Saving of one wheel in very very bad a feeling worn night through.	
		10.30 A.M.	No 2 lorry MONTREUIL	
			Lorry for to return DDSC. Received instructions to attend for return convoys DDSC. Arranged canteen commencement. Lorries to go for Re: return to BOULOGNE	

WAR DIARY
or
INTELLIGENCE SUMMARY.

Army Form C. 2118.

OC. 3rd Cavalry Supply Column
Page 188

Hour, Date, Place	Summary of Events and Information	Remarks and references to Appendices
MONTREUIL 5/1/16. 7:0 AM	No. 2 refilling as usual. Followed PC's for Pay to Bar. HQ. Q. lorries sorted stores for DD.S.T. truck while lorry was at Essex Yeo. Supplies at BOUBERS	
10:30 AM	No 1 loading MONTREUIL. Took 1½ hours. Visited B.O.T. office etc. asked about expediting stores. Also exchange of lorries. Also ADS.T.	J.A.
6/1/16. 70 AM	No 1 refilling. 0:30 EO HQ n + moved to HUMBERT	
6:30 AM	No 2 loading MONTREUIL. Took 1½ hours.	
	7 how 4 Pr Can inspected. Condition rather poor particularly steering mechanism — universal joints tight. Not first rate trucks. On steering dangerous. own light full well relaxed. One lorry sent to D.D.S.C.	JR.
7/1/16. 7:0 AM	No 2 refilling. MONTREUIL took 1½ hours.	
10:20 AM	No 1 loading MONTREUIL took 1½ hours. Sgt report on ASC return are South turned W/s stores of arms etc. Still badly hung up for CC spares. Same forms. Received 1 EC Daimler from GTTP to replace 1 IV Tyler seamed to go to HESSEDIN tomorrow	J.A.

Forms/C. 2118/10

WAR DIARY
or
INTELLIGENCE SUMMARY

Army Form C. 2118.

Place: MONTREUIL

Date	Hour	Summary of Events and Information	Remarks and references to Appendices
3/1/16	7am	No 1 refilled as usual. No 2 lorries MONTREUIL took 1½ hours. Only 6 lbs lorries on hand. Worked out scheme for M.T. transport not at all efficient. M.T. available. Refused MONTREUIL - MARQUIN at 10 am on all aircraft & reported to E.S.R. Arm'd to be at HORDBEIGERS. Interesting football match.	
4/1/16	7am / 10:30am	No 2 refilled as usual. Left for 31st Sqdn into Sqk R.A. units at ROLLEZ. No 1 lorry MONTREUIL took 1½ hours. Waited acute. Re Scheme to leave. Nos of lorries & could be served. List very much affected. Nos/In lorry transport. 1st Pn the demand by order. R.T.O. to form section. All vehicles Our F.I.G. overyards No 1. W.D. Turlibrew appr. Petrologue to be drawn, rest 24lbs down & turnishing total. Seems well this trouble. Security of oil wells etc in damp about 30% fuel required was of F.A.	
10/1/16	7am / 10:30am	No 1 refilled as usual. No 2 lorries MONTREUIL took 1½ hours. Little ask gathering of four parts truck starting must at oil authorisations defaulted to us, no trace of grant. Remarks not in order I grant. Rechecked in W/Sh	

Army Form C. 2118.

WAR DIARY
or
INTELLIGENCE SUMMARY.

(Erase heading not required.)

O.C. 3rd Cavalry Supply Column
Page 148

Place	Date	Hour	Summary of Events and Information	Remarks and references to Appendices
MONTREUIL	17/1/16	7 a.m.	No 2 refilling.	
		10.30 am	No 1 Sunday MONTREUIL. Took 1½ hours in TUB Bath only.	
		11 am	Visited by S.A.P.O.T. Inspected billets: good – rifles needs to be more carefully spun thru', men & horses already hardened. Took till 12.30 – horses & wokshops.	
			Refused to listen to chauffeur Road M.T. Depot. He does not agree of urgent purchase except in emergency this morning.	L.S.
	18/1/16	7 a.m.	No 1 refilling. Took out draft (T.T.) too men to each Yeo Ry T.	
		10.30 am	No 2 loading. MONTREUIL. Took 1½ hours. Coal arrived late in afternoon. Arranged for sacks & returned to PROGES by L.O.R. Armourer. Visited Boulogne Hygiene & washed for men use in history on trip. Several crew men attached in road due to freezing by the other crew by truck.	Jo. A.
	19/1/16	7 am	No 2 refilling.	
		10.30 am	No 1 loading MONTREUIL — took 1½ hours. Drew up total 9 mile etc. charts. Respectfully reports all correct.	L.S.

2353 3537 Wt. W2544/1454 700,000 5/15 D.D.&L. A.D.S.S./Forms/C. 2118.

Army Form C. 2118.

WAR DIARY
or
INTELLIGENCE SUMMARY. 3rd Cavalry Supply Column

Page 141

(Erase heading not required.)

Place	Date	Hour	Summary of Events and Information	Remarks and references to Appendices
MONTREUIL	14/1/16	7.0am	No 1 Supply Column	
		10.30am	No 2 Loading. No MONTREUIL. Took 1½ hours.	
			Visited D.S.S.E. Discussed new scheme of Bulk store messing — arrangement to be introduced all motors as a fortnight — 4/16 Cattle — sheep for seven yeo. —:— 9 rations for service. Sgt N Coates to 10 Alb Hosp GHQ.	S.M.
	15/1/16	9.0am	No 1 MONTREUIL. Took 1½ hours.	
		10.30am	90 Sabot types arrived. Reached especially extensive. To be started at BOULOGNE 17th inst. One lorry to Base in visit motor stores. 2 lorries for Div Canters Extra from 31.	
	16/1/16	7.0am	No 1 MONTREUIL. 8n Troops on horse ex/yh 4/3 glans. From PAGES 2 horses each Reb 10 ors with civil.	
		10.30am	No 2 Loading. MONTREUIL. Took 1½ hours.	
			Various armament to Div + Bn enteries. Trept'd Lt Cst kept in with slag/by/chin	S.M.
	17/1/16	7.0am	No 2 refill. 7th Bde M.G. charged to HUPPELLIERS (M ETREE NEUVE).	
		10.30am	No 1 loading MONTREUIL. Took 1½ hours.	
			Cpl Sumrall observed for tuition on narrow gauge with RTO to Etaples likewise.	F.M.

Army Form C. 2118.

WAR DIARY
or
INTELLIGENCE SUMMARY.

O.C. 3rd Cavalry Supply Column Page 142

(Erase heading not required.)

Hour, Date, Place	Summary of Events and Information	Remarks and references to Appendices
MONTREUIL 18/1/16 9.0am	No 1 refilling	
10.30am	No 2 loading MONTREUIL. Took 1½ hours.	
19/1/16 9.0am	No 2 refilling	J.A.
10.30am	No 1 loading MONTREUIL. Took 1½ hours.	
	Received 1 CC Ssundries + 1 CSD Hulford from G.H.Q. Inspected workshops.	
20/1/16 9.0am	No 1 refilling	
10.30am	No 2 loading MONTREUIL Took 1½ hours.	J.A.
	Sent 3 N type Lorries refill supplies to DD T Southern	
21/1/16 9.10am	No 2 refilling	J.A.
10.30am	No 1 loading MONTREUIL. Took 1½ hours.	
22/1/16 7.0am	No 1 refilling. Took reinforcements which arrived 6.30am.	
10.30am	No 2 loading MONTREUIL Took 1½ hours.	J.A.
	Loaded 30 tons of coal for ultering lorries 18 lorries	

Army Form C. 2118.

WAR DIARY
or
INTELLIGENCE SUMMARY.

O.C. 3rd Cavalry Supply Column
Page 143.

(Erase heading not required.)

Instructions regarding War Diaries and Intelligence Summaries are contained in F.S. Regs., Part II. and the Staff Manual respectively. Title pages will be prepared in manuscript.

Hour, Date, Place		Summary of Events and Information	Remarks and references to Appendices
MONTREUIL	23/1/16. 7pm	No. 2 refilling	
	10.30pm	No. 1 loading. MONTREUIL. Took 1½ hours. No. 2 delivered 20 Tons coal. 6.E. 7th & 8th Car Res. No. 1 delivered 10½ Tons stores to B.E.F. Canteen MARONEIUL. Filled Car No. 111 in trailer donated by death train MAIXAUMEN EN	J.A.
—	24/1/16. 7am	No. 1 refilling. No. 2 loading. MONTREUIL. Took 1½ hours. Visited A.D.S.&T at new Establishment. Personnel on particular satisfactory & quite sufficient.	J.A.
—	25/1/16. 7am	No. 2 refilling. No. 1 loading. MONTREUIL. Took 1½ hours. Received 3 C 50 Halfords from D.D.T. Southern. One engine very bad. Requested today what to do with 2 Surplus, and one Ammunition list to S.O.	J.A.
—	26/1/16. 7am	No. 2 refilling. No. 2 loading. MONTREUIL. Took 1½ hours. Saw O.C. A.S.C. re Officers in immobility of units Cars	J.A.

Forms/C. 2118/10

Army Form C. 2118.

WAR DIARY
or
INTELLIGENCE SUMMARY.
(Erase heading not required.)

O.C. 3rd Cavalry Supply Column
Page 144.

Hour, Date, Place		Summary of Events and Information	Remarks and references to Appendices
MONTREUIL 27/1/16	7.0 AM	N⁰ 2 refilling	
	10.30 AM	N⁰ 1 & loading MONTREUIL. Took 1¼ hours. 2 lorries to DESVRES to draw rum rations.	J.A.
—	28/1/16 7.0 AM	N⁰ 1 refilling	
	10.30 AM	N⁰ 2 loading MONTREUIL took 1½ hours.	
		N⁰ 2 lorries to St Hilaire & towed back 2 Sunbeam cars disabled with snow wheel fires. Lieutenant Lovy Indian Hospital	
		Div Troops Lorries brought back heat bread for Col at ease.	J.A.
		2 gd Pack troops with 1 to S.O. D.T.S Cur Bde.	
—	29/1/16 7.0 AM	N⁰ 2 refilling. Took 1 ¼ reinforcements repeat 6.30 am.	
	10.30 AM	N⁰ 1 loading MONTREUIL took 1½ hours.	
		Div Troop lorries brought back lecture of totals	
		See 2 delivered coal to 6th & 7th & 8th Glance	J.A.
		each refilling.	
—	30/1/16 7.0 AM	Sec I refilling. Brought stores of coal back from FRUGES to RUYEN.	
	10.30 AM	N⁰ 2 loading MONTREUIL took 1½ hours.	J.A.

Army Form C. 2118.

WAR DIARY
or
INTELLIGENCE SUMMARY.
(Erase heading not required.)

O.C. 3rd Cavalry Supply Column
Page 145

Hour, Date, Place	Summary of Events and Information	Remarks and references to Appendices
MONTREUIL 31/1/16 7.0 am 7.30 am	No. 2 refilling. Took up lorry load empty petrol tins & 24 gbs. no. 1 loading. MONTREUIL Took 14 hours. New establishment quite inadequate w/ increased output, only 15% spare drivers instead of 25% & that only excluding long old lorry personnel. No allowance of cleaners. Visited & came discussed scheme to my Wheeler others, supplies - inspection of cars &c - new establishment.	See Appendix XVII covering weekly return. J. Archibald Major O.C. 3rd Cav. Sup. Col.

Forms/C. 2118/10

CONFIDENTIAL
───────────

War Diary
of
O.C. 3rd Cavalry Supply Column

From 1st February 1916 to 29th February 1916.

Vol XV

[signature]

Army Form C. 2118.

WAR DIARY
or
INTELLIGENCE SUMMARY.

Be. 3rd Cavalry Supply Column
Page 146

(Erase heading not required.)

Instructions regarding War Diaries and Intelligence Summaries are contained in F.S. Regs., Part II. and the Staff Manual respectively. Title pages will be prepared in manuscript.

Hour, Date, Place	Summary of Events and Information	Remarks and references to Appendices
MONTREUIL 1/2/16 7:00am	No 1 refilling. Back 2.30 p.m. 6th C Rode to Ryf 5-7th C Rode to Hucqueliers via ALETTE. — 8th C Rode at AN-ev-ISSART except Essor yo between HEIMONT JEMBRY - Hopes at HUMBERT - Div Troops FRUGES via HESDIN. - FO Sqdn ROLLEZ.	
10.40am	No 2 refilling MONTREUIL. Took 1¼ hours. Worked scheme to single echelon. No advantage except shorter runs to lorries for S.C. (horse & fines). Fr.	
2/2/16 7.07am	No 2 refilling	
10.25am	No 1 refilling MONTREUIL. Took 13/4 hours. Put Mess tiles 10 tons on wind eaten 3 lbs per horse about ½ cwt per lorry. Some sacked everywhere. Visited ADS&T re 2 surplus lorries. To await instructions re establishment, at moment inferior. News event yet out. Re P.M.L. ration instead 3 lbs a 2 P Q horses, etc this minute. No distribution to hand.	

WAR DIARY
or
INTELLIGENCE SUMMARY

Army Form C. 2118.

OC - 3rd Cavalry Supply Column
Page 14

Hour, Date, Place	Summary of Events and Information	Remarks and references to Appendices
MONTREUIL 3/2/16 7:0am	No 1 refilling	
10:30am	No 2 loading in for 1½ hours. 3 Ukrainian PM in 30 mins. Saw OC ASC, stated who gave distribution of Pars. Decided swift collection of lorries to start at 6 & not too far as possible.	
4/2/16 7:0am 10:30am	No 2 refilling brought back 6 lorries worse from FRUGES. No 1 loading MONTREUIL. Took 1½ hours. SC to dinner. No 2 to MAREUIL, also to Sir Audley. 2 lorries of Capt. Dennis to 2B.T. Southern. Sufford bull fred, complete accident made to Paris I saw Sufford awaiting arrest & decision before I toad. Lorries I saw Sufford.	Saw.
5/2/16 7:0am 10:30am	No 1 refilling. Strong at truck & load of wood from FRUGES. No 2 loading MONTREUIL. Took 1½ hours. Reinforcement arrived & sent up. And from stud here to depot Pr. Arranged with Jesse reinforcements of units Sunday 6th. Orders to say to railhead to observe from 10 & no.	

Forms/C. 2:18/10

Army Form C. 2118.

WAR DIARY
or
INTELLIGENCE SUMMARY.

O.C. 3rd Cavalry Supply Column
Page 148

(Erase heading not required.)

Hour, Date, Place	Summary of Events and Information	Remarks and references to Appendices
MONTREUIL 6/2/16 7.0 AM	No. 2 refilling.	
10.30 AM	No. 1 loading MONTREUIL. Took 1½ hours. Blorries No. 2 cant stove to station. Inspected road MERVILLE to MAMMETZ HEM. Absolutely unfit. Visited O/c and m.e. Arranged cup's exhibition return to new Lorries.	L.A.
7/2/16 7.0 AM	No. 1 refilling.	
10.30 AM	No. 2 loading MONTREUIL. Took 1½ hours. 3 lorries No. 1 coal yard to store. One half Goff to Best Souldan by road.	L.A.
8/2/16 7.0 AM	No. 2 refilling MONTREUIL. Took 1½ hours.	
10.30 AM	No. 1 loading MONTREUIL. Satab was correct. 1 lorry to move by rail servt. 2 lorries lent to carry Y.M.C.A. hutting.	L.A.
9/2/16 7.0 AM	No. 1 refilling.	
6.30 AM	No. 2 loading MONTREUIL. Took 1½ hours. Arranged scheme to supply whole of lorries, return of this with grease scheme for new sheets. Work etc of Sergt.	

Army Form C. 2118

WAR DIARY
or
INTELLIGENCE SUMMARY

O.C. 3rd Cavalry Supply Column Page 149

(Erase heading not required.)

Instructions regarding War Diaries and Intelligence Summaries are contained in F.S. Regs, Part II. and the Staff Manual respectively. Title Pages will be prepared in manuscript.

Place	Date	Hour	Summary of Events and Information	Remarks and references to Appendices
MONTREUIL	10/2/16	7.0 am	No 2 refilling A.G. in Tierdo + 1st R's + 2nd R's to FRUGES via HESDIN – 6th Cav Bde. Also 3rd RD + Leics Yeo to BERMIRAINVILLE – 7th Car Bde to HUCQUELIERS via ALETTE – 8th Car Bde & Pers Roman Yeo to AIX-EN-ISSART. Back at 11.0 am except H at 2.0 pm. C. also RH.G. due which by N°1 took refilling standing. B + H Q.no D.R.a.a + 10th R Hussars by N°2 section. A continuous downside exhibit. Allows of extra 40 lorries for refuses – lorries mileage, great to harvest coat. Mails only to Bely Champs.	
		11.0 am	N°1 in charge of doubling MONTREUIL. Took 1¾ hours. Delay due to party of 1st Canadian today trench greatly. Train. Visited O.C. R.E., C.R.E. D.D.S.S. 9 lorries & 32 O.R. returned from B.D. Arranged for 20 lorries to meet DD detraining tomorrow	A.9

1875 Wt. W593/826 1,000,000 4/15 J.B.C. & A. A.D.S.S./Forms/C. 2118.

Army Form C. 2118

WAR DIARY
or
INTELLIGENCE SUMMARY

OC, 3rd Cavalry Suppl. Column
Page 150

(Erase heading not required.)

Place	Date	Hour	Summary of Events and Information	Remarks and references to Appendices
MONTREUIL	13/2/16	7:15 PM	Lorries refilling.	
		11:10 PM	No. 2 1/2 loading MONTREUIL. Took 1 3/4 hours. 20 lorries to DESVRES & MARESQUEL conveying men from BDs to Regt HQrs. YE Rde lorries reinforcing Lt. Sherford Oxo, Meerstop etc etc. Visited MDBT. G.H.Q. lorries to DESVRES.	fee.
	13/2/16	7 AM	Lorries to refill.	
		11:10 AM	No. 1 1/2 loading MONTREUIL. Took 1 1/2 hours. Visited ET AC. Arranged for wood reconstruction. Wet lorry. Asked ADST to change 2 worn out lorries, & huts, parts of 2 wheels, & 3 fitters in our establishment. Urgently required now. W/t stores in process of being put in order.	fee.
	13/2/16	7 AM	Lorries to refill.	
		10:45 AM	No. 2 1/2 loading MONTREUIL took 1 1/2 hours. 6lb. hey ration afore started loading tyres to Boulinea Service very badly mudd arrived. Solid tyres completed afore for afore into Advanced Scheme for section W/shops to start 14th.	K.A.

1875 Wt. W593/826 1,000,000 4/15 J.B.C. & A. A.D.S.S./Forms/C. 2118.

Army Form C. 2118

WAR DIARY
or
INTELLIGENCE SUMMARY   O.C. 3rd Cavalry Supply Column
(Erase heading not required.)   Regs 1521

Instructions regarding War Diaries and Intelligence Summaries are contained in F.S. Regs., Part II. and the Staff Manual respectively. Title Pages will be prepared in manuscript.

Place	Date	Hour	Summary of Events and Information	Remarks and references to Appendices
MONTREUIL	14/2/16	7.0am 10.30am	Lorries off to refill. No. 1 in charge loading MONTREUIL. Took 1½ hours. Whole of store staminants detailed to each section. Started on making shelestays for repair work. Visited O.C.R.E. re question of attaching FMWD to Sup Col.	J.A.
	15/2/16	7.0am 11.0am	Lorries to refill. No. 2 i/c loading MONTREUIL. Took 1½ hours. Workshops nearly complete to start work. Inspected same	J.A.
	16/2/16	7.0am 10.45am	Lorries to refill. No. 3 i/c loading MONTREUIL. Took 1½ hour. Workshops at work. Very satisfactory. 3 lorries 1 car – Capt. Hut B. Preston rejoined from D.O.S.C.	J.A.
	17/2/16	7.0am 10.45am	Lorries to refill. No. 2 i/c loading MONTREUIL. Took 1½ hours. Visited O. Inspected store inters.	J.A.

WAR DIARY
or
INTELLIGENCE SUMMARY

O.C. 3rd Cavalry Supply Column
Page 152

Army Form C. 2118

(Erase heading not required.)

Instructions regarding War Diaries and Intelligence Summaries are contained in F.S. Regs., Part II. and the Staff Manual respectively. Title Pages will be prepared in manuscript.

Place	Date	Hour	Summary of Events and Information	Remarks and references to Appendices
MONTREUIL	18/7/16	7 am	Lorries to refill. No.1 lorry MONTREUIL. Took 1½ hours.	
		10:45 am	Coal arrived, double guards detailed to PRUGES & MCQUELIERS by Lt. Roy. Provisions loaded M.T. except some unloaded. Start of subs away to divl amounts.	See
			Visited ADSOT LUCAS.	
	19/7/16	7 am	Lorries to refill. No.2 ½ lorry MONTREUIL. Took 1½ hours. Visited by Major T & O/C ASC. Inspected shops. Decided them to be arranged into group place. Found necessary instns.	
			Coal lorries to AIX & ROYON.	
	20/7/16	9 am	Lorries to refill. No.1 ½ lorry MONTREUIL. Took 1½ hours.	
		10:45 am	Inspected shops & made new arrangements. Report to O/C who said more could not be made for one week.	

WAR DIARY / INTELLIGENCE SUMMARY

Army Form C. 2118

O.C. 3rd Cavalry Supply Column Page 15-3

Place	Date	Hour	Summary of Events and Information	Remarks and references to Appendices
MONTREUIL	21/9/15	7.0am	Lorries to refill.	
		10.0am	See 2 i/c lorries. MONTREUIL. Took 1½ hours.	2 lorries evacuated from workshop. Appeared.
			Visited O.C. A.S.C. at A.D.S.T. Referred workshop arrangements to Reference D to E both R.H.A. Notified troops concerned.	
			Received instructions re supply.	
	22/9/15	7.0am	Lorries to refill.	
		10.45am	See i/c lorries MONTREUIL. Took 1½ hours. Issued for R.H.H. Bde.	
		10.45am	Visited Q re work on instructional gun. Received instructions re turnover on reliefs.	
		10.25pm	Visited workshops. A Wks Snow + Frost. Remaining lorries + personnel engaged from D.D.S.C. & W.D. Risley.	
			Lorries refilled. Not delivered owing to Battalion in billets to	
	23/9/15	7.0am	See 2 i/c lorries MONTREUIL. Took 1½ hours.	
		11.0am	Arrangements for but reinforcements. Hunters. Issue of reinforcement cancelled, arranged to store Boxing tournament in theatre.	
			as to be drawn in one from Berguin. Very heavy frost a wilted Snow. Roads frozen.	
	24/9/15	6.0am	30 lorries left for WARDRECQUES via FRUGES when Sir Douglas Haig's command R.H.H. at FRUGES.	
		7.0am	Lorries to refill.	
		10.45am	Running totals: MONTREUIL. Took Storage. 1st Both lorries bathing for wailor.	
			See i/c lorries. Very heavy frost. 1 Radiator, 1 Cyl head, 1 Pump gove.	
			A Sec. on roads so two lorries to 2 CC. Trainless. See Q. 2CC. Trainless left from G.H.Q. to complete establ.	

Army Form C. 2118

WAR DIARY
or
INTELLIGENCE SUMMARY

(Erase heading not required.)

O.C. 3rd Cavalry Supply Column
Reg: 1847

Place	Date	Hour	Summary of Events and Information	Remarks and references to Appendices
MONTREUIL	29/8/16	20th	Lorries back from WARDREQUES. O/C reported delay due to hostility bombing storms late, other drivers not trained (?) Supplies all at station. 1 large (3) only issue. Infact spite of orders, remainder had to be marched. 850 ½ class difficult work when night fell on account of the a flimsy roadway work too dangerous. Lorries to refill.	
		7.30am 10:45am	No. 2 ½ Freddy MONTREUIL. Took 2½ hours lorries left auto state of roads. Smith sick a hungry fast. 3 Bat hosts gone. 20 at crush. Inspected settling arrangements against frost salute to NCO's. 2 Lt WA. Steel joined as WS Sp. (Tempor.) No 2 in cov flakes. Lorries to refill. No 1 fit doubly MONTREUIL. Took 2½ hours. 7.E. Batteries late due to state of road, more ice. Need moreshods very good serviceable. Cannot yet to Chauvenes lorries like Mulforts. Rains about 10:00am. Head for A.B.S.T. late from MN. P.B. Ry. Corps. Divisional Arrives forward for Con. 2 E.6 off to Wales.	

Army Form C. 2118.

WAR DIARY
or
INTELLIGENCE SUMMARY.

(Erase heading not required.)

O.C. 3rd Cavalry Supply Column
Page 133.

Instructions regarding War Diaries and Intelligence Summaries are contained in F. S. Regs., Part II, and the Staff Manual respectively. Title pages will be prepared in manuscript.

Place	Date	Hour	Summary of Events and Information	Remarks and references to Appendices
MONTREUIL	21/9/16	7am	Lorries to refill. Also Set out cart for No 2 Section in afternoon. No 2 lorry Montreuil took 2½ hours to refill. Weather warm. No casualties from first but over 2600 speed. Petrol consumption was on target, day owing to heavy route. Lorries engines run to prevent freezing. Also field workshop doing. Sgt W.R. STEED the fitter, w.s.o.to column. Notified two parties in local scheme to start tomorrow Sept 10 Re Path to arrive 10 am W.E. to assist.	JM
"	30/9/16	6am	Lorries to refill & Troops E1st R.D. at FRUGES — 6th CSG — 1st RoD at BERMINVILLERS — 7th CSG to BERMIEULLES — 8th CSG to ARMEUX. No trace of WF Res. Pk. troops at BERMIEULLES. Troop sent to Officer to try to pick up supplies taken to HUCQUELLERS at 3.30pm. Res Park. No 91 ½ Horse — MONTREUIL took 2 hours. Slow a little snow. Roads still have Snow Slush very soft Surface. Reserve filled and.	J.M.

2353 Wt. W2544/1454 700,000 5/15 D. D. & L. A.D.S.S./Forms/C. 2118.

Army Form C. 2118.

WAR DIARY
or
INTELLIGENCE SUMMARY.
(Erase heading not required.)

O.C. 3rd Auxy Supply Column
Page 156

Place	Date	Hour	Summary of Events and Information	Remarks and references to Appendices
MONTREUIL	24/9/16	7.0am	Lorries to fulfill Arras scheme. Took 2½ hours shift. Loads at Boisleux arrived late. Saw O/C 6th Res Pk & arranged return from future trips am orders fatigue party.	
		10.15pm	3rd S.C. Lorries Montreuil took 2 hours. Visited Q + O.C. Res. Inkerman Car Coy to be attached to Lorries etc. Arranged for more petrol from dump reserve. T Capt G. Farran left 2.15 before NE2 at T/Kent	Appendix XVIII

Rates from mileage etc.
J Archibald Major ASC
O.C. 3 Car Sup Col=

Appendix XVIII   O.C. 3rd Cav.Sup.Coln.

February 1916	Section 1. Miles	No. of hours on road		Section 2. Miles	No. of hours on road	Remarks
1st	28	9		6	9	5L. 52.
2nd	6	9		28	9	
3rd	25	9		6	9	Rough
4th	6	9		30	9	av. M.P.G.
5th	25	9		7	9	
6th	6	9		30	9	= 5.9
7th	30	9		6	9	
8th	7	9		28	9	
9th	30	9		6	9	
10th	6	9		32	9	
11th	50	15		38	15	25
12th	32	9		28	9	= 5.4
13th	32	9		28	9	
14th	32	9		28	9	
15th	32	9		28	9	
16th	32	9		28	9	
17th	32	9		28	9	= 4.8
18th	34	9		30	9	
19th	36	9		30	9	
20th	32	9		32	9	
21st	32	9		32	9	
22nd	32	9		28	9	
23rd	34	9		28	9	34
24th	38	9		44	9	4.2
25th	32	9		38	9	
26th	32	9		33	10	
27th	32	9		33	9	
28th	36	10		32	10	
29th	25	9		26	9	
Total	815	268		771	269	
Daily av.	28.06	9.24		26.58	9.27	5.0

Confidential.

War Diary

O.C. 3rd Cavalry Supply Column.

From 1st March 1916 to 31st March 1916.

Pages 157 — 167.

Vol XVI

WAR DIARY
or
INTELLIGENCE SUMMARY.

(Erase heading not required.)

Army Form C. 2118.

O.C. 3rd Cavalry Supply Column
Page 157.

Place	Date	Hour	Summary of Events and Information	Remarks and references to Appendices
MONTREUIL	1/3/16	7.0 pm	No 1 F/c loading at MONTREUIL took 2 hours.	
		10.45 pm	Inspected automobiles, arranged to get at lorries can road during a move. Message from OC ASC that we have to move only Resources by FA. Lorries to refill	F.A.
	2/3/16	8.0 am	No 2 F/c loading at MONTREUIL took 2 hours.	
		10.45 pm	Visited OC FAC re question of interchange of food in FA Dumps etc. Also told we had to move to SOMMER on 6th – 7th & that billets ? ? C & S.	F.A.
	3/2/16	4.0 pm	Lorries to refill. Barriers on roads removed.	
		10 a.m.	No 1 F/c loading MONTREUIL took 2 hours. Visited STOMER Rumour more than 7h. 7.30 pm confirmed by 30 HQE. Seen Major Hutchison re question of booking OC Divn lorries Back wheels. He himself to assist in fitting special nuts to blades.	F.A.
	4/3/16	4.0 pm	No 2 F/c loading MONTREUIL took 2 hours.	
		10.45 pm	Informed by G that Column would shortly have to vacate MONTREUIL. Visited villages suggested west between here & HESDIN in the further direction except MONTREUIL – HESDIN & FRUGES	F.A.

Army Form C. 2118.

WAR DIARY
or
INTELLIGENCE SUMMARY.

(Erase heading not required.)

O.C. 3rd Cavalry Fifth Column
Feb 1/15

Place	Date	Hour	Summary of Events and Information	Remarks and references to Appendices
MONTREUIL	5/3/15	7.0am	Rode to refill. Brought back Smith's car. 10 tons from FROSSY to PETBOL B.F. Pack of S.E.	
		10.45am	11/2 ½ London MONTREUIL took 3 hours. Met Q at BEAURAINVILLE. Handed over my report. Further instructions	
			reconnaissance. Date of move not known. Mother ceased. Gave him copy of above letter	Ans
			Leave to refill.	
	6/3/15	7.0am	M.9½ hours MONTREUIL took 2 hours.	
		11.0am	Manage that villages between here & HESDIN not available for S.C. Then onwards visited CAVRON & WAMBER COURT W/cost	
			refusal. Same to Q of CE ASC. Then W of HESDIN inspected very	
			suitable without going to town. Between W towards MARCONELLE	
			Sugar refinery possible for workshop.	
			To Q at Staff late Pg ASC into Cy/ Left to join 5th Advan B.S.	gone
			Wrote requesting news why 207 L.B. Barlace are not permitted also	
			letter regards such supply of new lorries up to CC Donald Backslee	
			As per note U 7268. Though OC ASC hearing close copies	
			to Major Hutchinson CMP	

Army Form C. 2118.

WAR DIARY
or
INTELLIGENCE SUMMARY. C. 3"9 Cavalry Supply Column
Page 159
(Erase heading not required.)

Instructions regarding War Diaries and Intelligence Summaries are contained in F. S. Regs., Part II and the Staff Manual respectively. Title pages will be prepared in manuscript.

Place	Date	Hour	Summary of Events and Information	Remarks and references to Appendices
MONTREUIL	7/3/16	9.0am	Lorries to refill.	
		10.45am	No 1 7c lorry MONTREUIL took 1¾ hours. Inspected return vehicles. All run first class + looked after.	Ja.
	8/3/16	7am	Lorries to refill. Y 1800 truck late owing to heavy snow in night.	
		10.45am	No 2 7c lorry MONTREUIL. Took 1¾ hours. Inspected all roads to HQ 9 ELLIERS. Only one through BEUSSENT ENQUIN now but should want few days extra. Referred to be HQ. Suggested using H.T. ones with own scheme. Inspected workshops. Work good.	Jb.
	9/3/16	7am	Lorries to refill.	
		10.45am	No 1 7c lorry MONTREUIL. Took 1¾ hours. Inspected vehicle workshops as usual. 6 tankers 30 Pounders took tyres but lacking at three wheels, needed chromic grenades. Visited O.C. ASC. he went to HQ QUEZ 15/3. Re Commles. & Hellinod & Band stores.]	Jc.

2353 Wt W2544/1454 700,000 5/15 D. D. & L. A.D.S.S./Forms/C. 2118.

Army Form C. 2118.

WAR DIARY
or
INTELLIGENCE SUMMARY. 3rd Cavalry Bde HQ Column Page 160
(Erase heading not required.)

Instructions regarding War Diaries and Intelligence Summaries are contained in F. S. Regs., Part II and the Staff Manual respectively. Title pages will be prepared in manuscript.

Place	Date	Hour	Summary of Events and Information	Remarks and references to Appendices
MONTREUIL	9/3/16	7.0 am 10.15 PM	Lorries to refill. No 2 to took MONTREUIL Took 1 3/4 hours. Accident between Souverain Bray & 7301 of Crossley Car M.19451 21st Sqdn A Flight RFC. Enquiry held. Subbeam totally to blame. 9 lots of coal arrived. One let dry hail to Rimper Riembeley Sunfected. This "Scheme of MT" to 9th Can Bde rations distant 12E	
	11/3/16	7.0 am 10.45 am	Lorries to refill. No 1 1/6. Lorries MONTREUIL Took 1 3/4 hours. Sended to 10th Res Bde Show "So 7th Can Bde, arranged delivery of rations to Can Bde in usual 12 E No 2 took Coal to Royon & HOMBERT.	Z.O
	12/3/16	7.0 am 10.45 am	Lorries to refill. No 2 1/6 Lorries MONTREUIL Took 2 hours. Found 10th Res Bde & arranged to start scheme tomorrow. M.T. at BERNIEULLES at 7.30 am dut by A.T. X once to HOCQUELLERS 12.30 PM Football match br R.H.Guards lost 1-2.	Z.O

2353 Wt. W2544/1454 700,000 5/15 D. D. & L.   A.D.S.S./Forms/C. 2118.

WAR DIARY or INTELLIGENCE SUMMARY

Army Form C. 2118.

O.C. 3rd Artry Supply Column
Pg 161.

Place	Date	Hour	Summary of Events and Information	Remarks and references to Appendices
MONTREUIL	13/3/16	7.0 am	Lorries to refill. 7th Car Coy BERNEVILLE.	
		10.45 am	No 1/4 Monday MONTREUIL. Took 1¾ hours. 2 Sitn lorries along required per Rte for 2 IC for squadrons = 5 fm sctn = 12 fm Col = 13 = 25⅙ Those only now possible with single echelon. C in C to TRUE. Sp rail. Arranged with R.T.O. emergency of wortly Rail/ket. Visited HQ. Will later subst 3 requisition lorries. Lorries to refill.	/ko
	14/3/16	7.0 am	No 2 to South MONTREUIL. Took 1¾ hours	
		10.40 am	Detachment GHQ different. Officers lorries noted with their output. Lorries to refill.	/ko
	15/3/16	7.0 am	No 1 1/c South MONTREUIL. Took 1¾ hours.	
		10.30 am	Inspected No 1 section. Lorries very clean, well looked after. Trouble with timers/Carbre Nos No. of hubs & backwheels CC Daimlers petrol loose. Tightened up, at out & will now set Screw steel + places.	/ko

2353 Wt. W2514/1454 700,000 5/15 D.D.&L. A.D.S.S./Forms/C. 2118.

WAR DIARY
or
INTELLIGENCE SUMMARY

Army Form C. 2118.

of 3rd Cavalry Bde/M. Column

Place	Date	Hour	Summary of Events and Information	Remarks and references to Appendices
MONTREUIL	16/3/16	7am	Loose to refill	
		10:45am	No 2 1/2 touring MONTREUIL. Took 1 3/4 hours. Inter section football match. Notified to carry rations for Labour Bns to FRUGES. Only possible on present supply echelon basis 2 lorries daily. Not allowed effective due to 2 Sqn Lorries attached & no extra return of her.	Sqr
	17/3/16	7am	Loose to refill.	
		10:45am	No 1 1/2 touring MONTREUIL. Took 1 3/4 hours.	
			3 Lorries (3 tons) arrived from G.H.Q.	
	18/3/16	7am	Loose to refill.	
		10:45am	No 2 1/2 touring MONTREUIL. Took 1 3/4 hours. Letter from D.A.D.S.T. G.H.Q. stating change of 6.3 Tn for 6 3.ton lorries was to carry rations for McGill squadron. Replied as established minimum is 12 echelon lorries & 1/3 3 tn in reserve, of which 1st 3ton is at present further out of these to all Reserve of petrol. No/o further requirements.	S/A

WAR DIARY
or
INTELLIGENCE SUMMARY

Army Form C. 2118.

HQ 2nd Cavalry Supply Column

Place	Date	Hour	Summary of Events and Information	Remarks and references to Appendices
MONTREUIL	19/3/16	7am	Lorries to refill.	
		10.30am	Went back to MONTREUIL. Took 1 3/4 hours. Visited the A.D.Q. & told him it would be more shortly to BEAURAINVILLE. Asked H.E.S. Div afterwards. Said to refuel with 3 C.H.S.E. & Br. Meur is rather BEAURAINVILLE impossible.	Sig.
	20/3/16	7am	Lorries to refill.	
		10.30am	No 2 1/2 Lorries MONTREUIL Took 1 3/4 hours.	
		12.30pm	Order to move to BEAURAINVILLE immediately. Possibly found motor lorries. Sent off lorries overload. Asked G.H.Q. for more horses to take over remnants to No 2 2nd Corps at Guay, Noellepen unto they strengthen & pass in them.	
			(Signed) E.F.G.	Sig
	21/3/16	7am	Lorries to refill. Old Forges lorries travelled north & onwards to 1st F.B. Bde. Took 3 1/2 hours.	
		10.45am	No 1 1/2 Lorries MONTREUIL.	
			Visited BEAURAINVILLE during the day. Days delayed & permission arranged to leave officer on sick leave and more Rochester & Hallford on repair.	Sig.

Army Form C. 2118.

WAR DIARY
or
INTELLIGENCE SUMMARY.
(Erase heading not required.)

Place	Date	Hour	Summary of Events and Information	Remarks and references to Appendices
MONTREUIL	22/3/16	7am	[illegible handwritten entries]	
BEAURAINVILLE		9am		
		4pm		
	23/3/16			
		10am		
		10.30am		
	24/3/16	7am		
		11am		

Army Form C. 2118.

WAR DIARY
or
INTELLIGENCE SUMMARY. Of 8grd Cavalry Field Column
(Erase heading not required.) Page 105.

Instructions regarding War Diaries and Intelligence Summaries are contained in F. S. Regs., Part II and the Staff Manual respectively. Title pages will be prepared in manuscript.

Place	Date	Hour	Summary of Events and Information	Remarks and references to Appendices
BERGAINVILLE	25/3/16	7.0am	James to M.M.	
		12 noon	No. 1 & 2 bombing M.M. CREUIL. Took 1½ hours. Duty the horses. Visited case of GB. Informed men levels of transport ready for front squadrons. Explained dispensably of cases on a doubt Sister sent. S.D. of kind of kit to man. at now TREUIL at present. Explained G.M. Officer 3603 Loveth to be exercised now. Today if no sickness to disturb. Staff of 1st Inspection.	
			6.30 pm S.M.M. call W. Workshops up? morning. detached GD FB FB to all defects. Smoke Kmt. changed if present 4 country vehicle. Smithain Centry. Stanleton	
	26/3/16	7.00am	M.2/C. kind MONTREUIL took 1½ hours. Delayed by hires. Snow to up-fall.	
			Cold & exceedingly wind. Pass to cross running 2 Regt & down the stables. Arrived P.M.O.'s letter - on lay off one section for inspection.	
			Our 3 ton Lan. arrived R.H.E. our 30.4t no men off. Riders in yet.	

Army Form C. 2118.

WAR DIARY
or
INTELLIGENCE SUMMARY. O.C. 3 W. Army, S.W. Column
(Erase heading not required.)

Page 16.

Instructions regarding War Diaries and Intelligence Summaries are contained in F. S. Regs., Part II. and the Staff Manual respectively. Title pages will be prepared in manuscript.

Place	Date	Hour	Summary of Events and Information	Remarks and references to Appendices
BETHUNEVILLE	29/3/16	7.30am	Forms & refill. N° 1 ½ lorry MONTREUIL. Took 1 Jockeuno.	
		10.45am	Sent 2 lorries S.H.Q. Various Coys arrangements. Established MONTREUIL Lorries tonight.	
	28/3/16	7am	N° 2 ½ loading MONTREUIL. Took 1½ hours. Sent 2 lorries S.H.Q. Various Coys arrangements.	
		10.45am	11 Lorries from Base. Testing rigs for tents. Army HQ in place. Vacated from HQ Jn. New Checkerboard pad. statf generally.	
	24/3/16	7.30am	Lorries tonight. N° 1 ½ lorry MONTREUIL. Took 1 Jockeuno.	
		10.45am	Vested at 11.30. About to now are attachen. Arrangeth on ordering.	
			Refilling by sections. Lorries tonight. Brought back bread & Pay of A.S.C. to HQ.	
	2/4/16	7.30am	N° 2 ½ loading MONTREUIL. Took 1½ hours. Established refilled next day.	
			Worked out horse rates to current requirements. New troublesome	

2353 Wt. W2544/1454 700,000 5/15 D. D. & L. A.D.S.S./Forms/C. 2118.

Army Form C. 2118.

WAR DIARY
or
INTELLIGENCE SUMMARY.   Og. 2nd Cavalry Supply Column
(Erase heading not required.)   Aug 1917

Place	Date	Hour	Summary of Events and Information	Remarks and references to Appendices
SERAINVILLE	31/8/17	noon	From Forces tonight. No 11 K loading MONTFORT. Took 1 3/4 hrs. S.1 to ROSIN + JUMSERT. Rules now required such at 30 cwt = 78 animals (eg ½ what 300 cf include gives) no motor transport is supposed fed supplies to DIVNS. Visited all billets, horses transport turnouts all satisfactory.	

J Mitchell Major
O.C. 2nd Cav Sup Col

Appendix XIX

Section 1.

Section 2.

O.C., 3rd Cav. Sup. Coln.

March 1916	Miles	No. of hours on road.		Miles	No. of hours on road.	Remarks
1	28	9		28	9	
2	28	9		26	9	
3	32	9		28	9	Rather
4	32	9		28	9	MRG
5	32	9		30	9	= 4.7
6	32	9		28	9	
7	32	9		28	9	
8	32	9		28	9	
9	33	9		28	9	
10	33	9		28	9	
11	33	9		31	9	= 5.5
12	34	9		31	9	
13	26	9		28	9	
14	26	9		28	9	
15	26	9		28	9	
16	26	9		28	9	
17	26	9		28	9	
18	26	9		28	9	= 5.7
19	26	9		30	9	
20	28	9		30	9	
21	28	9		46	11	
22	39	11		42	11	
23	34	10		40	10	
24	36	9		35	9	
25	38	9		35	9	= 5.9
26	36	9		32	9	
27	38	9		33	9	
28	38	9		33	9	
29	38	9		33	9	
30	38	9		33	9	
31	40	10		35	10	
TOTAL	984	283		969	285	
Daily Av.	31.74	9.1		31.25	9.19	5.6

Army Form C. 2118

WAR DIARY
or
INTELLIGENCE SUMMARY

Headqrt: 3rd Can. Div. Ad.

(Erase heading not required.)

Place	Date	Hour	Summary of Events and Information	Remarks and references to Appendices
FRUGES	1.4.16		Rendezvous, Refilling Points, Railhead and Billets as before.	M1
Fruges	2.4.16		R. R. Railhead & Billets as for 1st. Directed by "Q" to take steps to abolish 1st Aux: Personnel & vehicles (less 1 car 1 lorry & drivers) is to be absorbed by Supply Column.	M1
Fruges	3.4.16		R. R. Railhead & Billets as for 2nd. "Q" Directed Supply Column to send an Officer each week to Railhead to meet reinforcements.	M1
Fruges	4.4.16		R. R. Railhead & Billets as for 3rd.	M1

WAR DIARY or INTELLIGENCE SUMMARY

Army Form C. 2118

Hazebr., 3rd Cav. Div. A.S.C.

Place	Date	Hour	Summary of Events and Information	Remarks and references to Appendices
Steugse	5.4.16		R., R.E. Billets + Railhead as for 4th.	R.1
Bruges	6.4.16		R., R.E. Billets + Railhead as for 5th. Motor car & 30 cwt lorry of A.H.Q. evacuated to G.H.Q.	R.1
Bruges	7.4.16		R., R.E. Billets + Railhead as for 6th. Item issue to 3rd Cav. Div. ceases. Dumps of 7th Cavalry Brigade changed to MANNINGHEM. This will release horse transport of 10th Reserve Park since take effect from 11th instant.	R.1
Bruges	8.4.16		R., R.E. Billets + Railhead as for 7th.	R.1

WAR DIARY or **INTELLIGENCE SUMMARY**

Army Form C. 2118

3rd Cav. Div. H.Q.

Place	Date	Hour	Summary of Events and Information	Remarks and references to Appendices
Fruges	9.4.16		R. R. Billets & Railhead as for 8th. Canadian Cavalry Brigade to arrive CRECY EN PONTHIEU on 9th rationed to 10th inst. Hon. Lieut. S.F.S. JOHNSTON to 35th Div. Train noted to be relieved by Temp. Lieut. A. BAYLY.	
Fruges	10.4.16		R. R.R. Billets & Railhead as for 9th. 3 days supply of coal, wood & potatoes delivered to Canadian Cavalry.	
Fruges	11.4.16		R. R.R. Billets & Railhead as for 10th except T.C. Temp. Lieut. A. BAYLY reported for duty & sent to Supply Column for instruction in M.T. work. Supplies for 7th Cav. Bde. taken by S.T. direct to MANNINGHEM.	

WAR DIARY or INTELLIGENCE SUMMARY

Army Form C. 2118

Ad Ds
2nd Can Divl Ale

Place	Date	Hour	Summary of Events and Information	Remarks and references to Appendices
Bruges	12.4.16		R. R.E. Billets + Railhead as for 11th. Received instructions from D.A.D. of S.+ T. that 2nd Ale 2nd Cav. Div. is to administer Canadian Cavalry Brigade as regards Ale duties. On the authority of D. of T. 9598/4 of P.m.16, the following mo. vehicles were sent to D. D.T. (Northern), St Omer, on reduction of establishment. From H.Q. 2nd Car. Div:— Daimler Car M 9016, De Dion Lorry 7211, Wolseley Car M 1795, Wolseley Car M 575, From H.Q. Divl. Ale. Sunbeam Car M 755, From 2nd C. Supply Col. Wolseley Car M 559. One other car M 1796 Wolseley, also to be sent to D.D.T.(N) is now in shops will not be transferred for a few days.	M

WAR DIARY
or
INTELLIGENCE SUMMARY

H.Qrs. 3rd Can Divl Adm

Army Form C. 2118

Place	Date	Hour	Summary of Events and Information	Remarks and references to Appendices
Bruges	13.4.16		R., R.E., Billets, Railhead as for 12th.	
Bruges	14.4.16		R., R.E., Billets, Railhead as for 13th. Submitted to A.A.&Q.M.G. a scheme whereby, with a railhead at MARESQUEL, supplies could be delivered to units by a single echelon of supply column. A. Cav. Can. Cav. Bde. called.	

Army Form C. 2118

WAR DIARY
or
INTELLIGENCE SUMMARY

Hd.Qrs. 3rd Cav. Div. A.C.

(Erase heading not required.)

Instructions regarding War Diaries and Intelligence Summaries are contained in F.S. Regs., Part II. and the Staff Manual respectively. Title Pages will be prepared in manuscript.

Place	Date	Hour	Summary of Events and Information	Remarks and references to Appendices
FRUGES.	15.4.16		R. A. F. Billets & Railhead as for 14th. Court of Enquiry convened to 11a.m. 16.4.16. Anx Parc Office to investigate circumstances of collision between Lorries known as Ant. A.9393 of 6th Car. B. Anti. Supply Column Lorry 52185 near LEBIEZ on 10th inst.	Nil
Fruges.	16.4.16.		R. A. F. Billets & Railhead as for 15th. Received authority from D.A.D.S.T., G.H.Q. (336.14/3) to continue purchasing potatoes. Cramped lorries at C.U.C.Q. Training Camp to be opened at ETAPLES.	Nil
Fruges.	17.4.16		R. A. F. Billets & Railhead as for 16th. Authority received for Supply Column to draw 10,000 rounds S.A.A. for practice purposes to open range at BEURAINVILLE. W.3333 to S.A.D.S.T. covering loss of 14,400 lbs of oats through faulty tracing of sacks.	Nil

Army Form C. 2118

WAR DIARY
or
INTELLIGENCE SUMMARY

(Erase heading not required.)

H.Q. of Bre Cavalry Loire all

Place	Date	Hour	Summary of Events and Information	Remarks and references to Appendices
FRUGES.	18.4.16		R.R. Billets Railhead as for 17th. 3rd Field Sqn. reported men suffering with boils caused by an insufficiency of green vegetables. Replied that green vegetable are practically impossible to obtain & that these are exorbitant. Received from A.Q.M.G. details of arrangements to be made in case of a forward move. Supply Officer of Canadian Cavalry Brigade reports about 60 tons of straw at BLANGY have authority to draw. This was referred to G.H.Q.	MU
Surpel	19.4.16		R. R.R. Billets Railhead as for 18th. Orders received yesterday for Major G.R. Archibald, 3rd Cavalry Supply Column to proceed to England report to Deverets Transport, War Office.	SW
FRUGES	20.4.16		R. R.R. Billets Railhead as for 19th. Major G.R. Archibald left for England. Lieut. S.P. Johnston left to join 35th Divisional Train. Capt. H.G. Lane took over duties of Supply Officer 4th Cav. Bde. & 2 Lt. B.A. Emby those of Requisitioning Officer.	MU

Army Form C. 2118

WAR DIARY
or
INTELLIGENCE SUMMARY

W. Dro.
3rd Cav. Div. C. Ack.

(Erase heading not required.)

Instructions regarding War Diaries and Intelligence Summaries are contained in F. S. Regs., Part II. and the Staff Manual respectively. Title Pages will be prepared in manuscript.

Place	Date	Hour	Summary of Events and Information	Remarks and references to Appendices
Fruges	21-4-16		R., R.P., Billets. Railhead as for 20th. Cav. Sqn. & Cyclist Coy. of 19th Divn to be attached to 3rd Cav. Div. for training - Ration for consumption on 23rd arranged.	WM
Fruges	22-4-16		R., R.P., Billets. Railhead as for 21st. Orders received for Capt. R.H. Dewkey to proceed to the W.T. Mullen School of Instruction at Oun. Dump for "C" Battery, R.H.A., changed to FRESSIN, with effect from tomorrow. Lieut. F.S.H. Stuart Ale. reported from Boulogne, vice Capt Heather.	WM
Fruges	23-4-16		R., R.P., Billets. Railhead as for 22nd. Capt. (T. Major) L.O.R. DUNPHY, Ale. posted from 6th Divisional Supply Column to 3rd Cavalry Divisional Supply Column, vice Major Archibald.	WM

1875 Wt. W593/826 1,000,000 4/15 J.B.C. & A. A.D.S.S./Forms/C. 2118.

Army Form C. 2118

WAR DIARY
or
INTELLIGENCE SUMMARY
Head Qrs. 3rd Cav. Divl. Arty.

(Erase heading not required.)

Instructions regarding War Diaries and Intelligence Summaries are contained in F.S. Regs., Part II. and the Staff Manual respectively. Title Pages will be prepared in manuscript.

Place	Date	Hour	Summary of Events and Information	Remarks and references to Appendices
Fruges	24.4.16		R. R.C. Billets + Railhead as for 23rd. Railhead to be changed to BEURAINVILLE — first drawing on Thursday, 27th inst.	AH
Fruges	25.4.16		R. R.C. Billets + Railhead as for 24th. Capt. H. Huntley, S.O. 6" Cd. yesterday left for L'Amer. New supply dump arranged near evacuation to S.O.s + Moves. New dump to come into force with change of Railhead. Major Dunphy reported for duty as O.C. Supply Col.	HP
Fruges	26.4.16		R. R.C. Billets + Railhead as for 25th.	HP
Fruges	27.4.16		R. R.C. Billets as for 26th. Railhead Beurainville.	HP

Army Form C. 2118

WAR DIARY
or
INTELLIGENCE SUMMARY

HQrs 2nd Can Div Arty

(Erase heading not required.)

Instructions regarding War Diaries and Intelligence Summaries are contained in F.S. Regs., Part II. and the Staff Manual respectively. Title Pages will be prepared in manuscript.

Place	Date	Hour	Summary of Events and Information	Remarks and references to Appendices
Bruges	28.4.16		R.F.C.; Billets & Railhead as for 27th	HP
Bruges	29.4.16		R.F.C.; Billets & Railhead as for 28th	HP
Bruges	30.4.16		R.F.C.; Billets & Railhead as for 29th. Issued instructions re supply arrangements for impending move of Divn. to ST RIQUIER area. Forwarded to A.A. & Q.M.G. the report of Supply Column Workshop Offr on neglected state of cars Nr 142 & 7 (HQrs. 8th Can Bn).	HP

H. Robbs
Major A/C
for OC A/C 2nd Can. Div.

May - 1916.

Army Form C. 2118.

WAR DIARY
or
INTELLIGENCE SUMMARY.
(Erase heading not required.)

Instructions regarding War Diaries and Intelligence Summaries are contained in F. S. Regs., Part II. and the Staff Manual respectively. Title pages will be prepared in manuscript.

Place	Date	Hour	Summary of Events and Information	Remarks and references to Appendices
Beaurainville	1-5-16	—	Column in rare billets. Railhead at Beaurainville. Loading and delivery of supplies by rail; echelon of lorries to Lumeron in billets in FRUGES area except one Brigade in training on the coast). Remainder of Column laid off for repairs - painting etc.	
	6-5-16	—	Lt B.S. Cumberlege and H/M R.O. Steel proceeded to England on leave. Meet S. Sgt Wood. B.S. sent to Flying Corps on being granted commission on the General List.	
	9-5-16	—	Published stringest orders to Column re danger of espionage. 2 Lorries and 5 men, attached from 19th Divisional Supply Column with 19th Divisional Cavalry, returned to own unit.	
	12-5-16	—	Lieut M.A. Looney granted leave to England.	
	13-5-16	—	One Lorry (for repair) and two men evacuated to No 1 A.S.C. Repair Shop. One Lorry (for repair) and 1056 men evacuated to No 2 A.S.C. Repair Shop.	
	14-5-16	—	One reinforcement (Supply) received from Base. Arrangements made for dumping surplus stores in case of move.	
	18-5-16	—	Lieut B.S. Cumberlege promoted Captain - Lieut L.O. Rustace promoted Lieut.	
	20-5-16	—	Lieut N. Coales granted leave to England.	

Army Form C.-2118.

Instructions regarding War Diaries and Intelligence
Summaries are contained in F. S. Regs., Part II.
and the Staff Manual respectively. Title pages
will be prepared in manuscript.

WAR DIARY
or
INTELLIGENCE SUMMARY.

(Erase heading not required.)

Place	Date	Hour	Summary of Events and Information	Remarks and references to Appendices
	28-5-16	—	Two Lorries (one 3 ton and one 30 cwt) received from G.H.Q. Troops Sup Column in replacement of those evacuated to Base.	
	29-5-16	—	Lieut A Bagly granted leave to England. One NCO and 9 men sent to G.H.Q. railhead for unloading supplies for our Brigade on to narrow gauge railway. Lorries for this Brigade taken off.	
	30-5-16	—	Medical Officer (Capt J Bigger) to 7 C.C.S. on being relieved by Capt W Halliman R.A.M.C.	
	31-5-16	—	During the month the workshops were hurried up - one complete shop being allotted to each section and also to Hd Qrs, the latter for repair of Divisional Cars and Ambulances, in addition to certain small jobs on Reserve Corps Signal wheels. Very useful work was carried out but was hindered somewhat owing to difficulty in obtaining spares from A.M.T.s, such as Color rings, gudgeon pins etc. During the month practically all the autumn personnel was re-inoculated against Typhoid.	

1577 Wt.W10791/1773 500,000 1/15 D. D. & L.   A.D.S.S./Forms/C. 2118.

Army Form C. 2118.

WAR DIARY
or
INTELLIGENCE SUMMARY.
(Erase heading not required.)

June 1916 3rd Cav.^y D. Supply [?] No 21

Instructions regarding War Diaries and Intelligence Summaries are contained in F.S. Regs, Part II. and the Staff Manual respectively. Title pages will be prepared in manuscript.

Place	Date	Hour	Summary of Events and Information	Remarks and references to Appendices
Beauvainville	1-6-16	–	Major H.A.C. Gartner. A.S.C. arrived from 6th Army Sup. Park to assume command.	
	2-6-16	–	Major H.A.C. Gartner took over the command of 3rd Cavalry Supply Column from Capt A.E. Bowes Dean A.S.C.	
	3-6-16	–	Column was at this time working on single echelon; half the horses being laid off for re-painting and overhaul. Railhead was at Beauvainville, and the Division was round about Auxi-le-Chateau with the equivalent of a Brigade near Berck Plage.	
	4-6-16	–	An "Orderly Officer" was instituted in the Column.	
	5-6-16	–	The "Guards" from each section well mounted centrally by the Orderly Officer.	
	6-6-16	–	One Officer from time allowed on leave – average of men – 1 per week.	
	7-6-16	–	The Supply of wood to the Division was not economical - wood being brought near Etaples and carried to Berck etc by lorry.	
	9-6-16	–	The return of Officers from leave etc to their units present difficulties, all Officers arriving requiring either conveyance to their unit or to spend the night – a suggestion put forward that a Box-Car be provided for this purpose	
	15-6-16	–	On account of men authority obtained for the evacuation of our Leveris Lorry (engines out-standing) and 2 (30 cwt) Halfords to below and out of date to keep up with the Column	

Army Form C. 2118.

WAR DIARY
or
INTELLIGENCE SUMMARY.
(Erase heading not required.)

Instructions regarding War Diaries and Intelligence Summaries are contained in F.S. Regs., Part II. and the Staff Manual respectively. Title pages will be prepared in manuscript.

Place	Date	Hour	Summary of Events and Information	Remarks and references to Appendices
Beauvainville	24-6-16	—	New SSO, Major E.T. Carver, arrived & took over from Major Welch. O.g.e. Lieut L.O. Luther evacuated to Hospital.	
	25-6-16	—	No 2 Section L/P Beauvainville — dumped at Domart and proceeded to Cardas. No I Section Loaded at Cardas.	
	26-6-16	—	Workshops and HQ 8/s moved to La Neuville. No I Section dumped at La Neuville. No 2 Loaded at Cardas and proceeded to La Neuville. Rain. Road on which lorries were camped (between La Neuville and Domay) impassable except for one lorry at a time, hence the entire column had to move to extricate one lorry.	
	27-6-16	—	No 2 dumped at La Neuville — Domay, and the column, except Workshops, moved to La Neuville — Port Noyelle road — No I Loaded at Mericourt 5.30 a.m.	
	28-6-16	—	No I dumped at Domay. No 2 Loaded at Mericourt.	
	29-6-16	—	No 2 dumped at Domay. No 1 Loaded at Mericourt.	
	30-6-16	—	No 1 dumped at Domay. No 2 Loaded at Mericourt.	
			Note:— It would be preferable for the Staff to take an MT officer when prospecting sites for an MT Company.	
			I. Great resistance is required to erase ranks of New Army to bring necessary arrangements for fuel, water and provision of Latrines	

J. Murray, Major.
OC 3rd (Cavalry Supply Column)

Army Form C. 2118

3 C D Supply Col

VOL 20

WAR DIARY or INTELLIGENCE SUMMARY

(Erase heading not required.)

Place	Date	Hour	Summary of Events and Information	Remarks and references to Appendices
Road from Corby to Pont-Noyelles	1/7/16		One lorry sent to 19th Div. Supply Col in command – as one Squad. was temp: transferred to this div:	
	2/7/16		This lorry returned to the Supply Col.	
	3/7/16		The lorry recq from 4th army T.P.C. was sent to R.E. Dump at Meaulte to await orders	
	4/7/16	7.30 P.M	Orders recq to move to Longpré. 1 lorry was sent to Forges for intrenching tools. – The attached lorry reported from Meaulte	
Longpré	5/7/16		Column moved to Longpré – moving in rear of the Division. This scheme did not succeed as certain Brigades not halting where ordered a lot of passing was necessary. Railhead was Longpré.	
Airaines	6/7/16		Column moved to AIRAINES which was not available for M. Oising to have Pictures.	
"	8/7/16	Noon	Recq orders to return to Corby – Pr Noyelles Road.	
	9/7/16	9 A.M	Workshops arrived from Airaines – arrived 6 P.m.	

Army Form C. 2118

WAR DIARY
or
INTELLIGENCE SUMMARY
(Erase heading not required.)

Instructions regarding War Diaries and Intelligence Summaries are contained in F.S. Regs., Part II. and the Staff Manual respectively. Title Pages will be prepared in manuscript.

Place	Date	Hour	Summary of Events and Information	Remarks and references to Appendices
Corby - Mr Voyelles	10/7/16		Railhead Mericourt. 3.30am - train arrived 8am	
	11/7/16		Today turn again.	
	12/7/16		Train always 3 or 4 hours late - it was deemed however that train must be cleared at once. Hence no time for crews to wait train 9 upform.	
	13/7/16		Blumm - Efforts to get steamer driver to R.H. ineffective as no Room	
	16/7/16		Steamer broke out in column owing to bad water. Water supply changed and arrangements for water 9 time 9. investigated	
	19/7/16		Every fifth dance is two bodies at R.T. Column did not arrive R.H. until 6am but always in front of train	
	20/7/16		A few bottles out in no 1 Loco: no serious damage; fire caused by patrol being mis - taken for water - All cans for water again passed back with "W' on them.	
	23/7/16		Lorry no 3870 de ??? was evacuated to Paris	
	24/7/16		Rations delivered to Fricourt for working parties - this is the nearest pt to line reached by 3. C. D in this report.	

WAR DIARY or INTELLIGENCE SUMMARY

Army Form C. 2118

(Erase heading not required.)

Instructions regarding War Diaries and Intelligence Summaries are contained in F.S. Regs., Part II. and the Staff Manual respectively. Title Pages will be prepared in manuscript.

Place	Date	Hour	Summary of Events and Information	Remarks and references to Appendices
Beauxanville	21/7/16		New D.D.O. Major E.T. Carver arrived to take over from Major Peebles. A.S.C.	
	24/7/16		Lt. Durbar evacuated to H. No.1 sec dumped near C.R.C.S. & proceeded to Candas	
	25/7/16		No.2 Sec left Beauxanville – dumped at Dernart and proceeded to Candas. No.1 Sec loaded at Candas	
	26/7/16		Workshops & HQ moved to la Neuville. No.1 Dumped at Neuville – No.2 loaded at Candas and proceeded to La Neuville. Rain – Road on which lorries were dumped (between La Neuville & Bonnay) impossible except for 1 lorry at a time. Since the whole column had to move to extract 1 lorry.	
	27/7/16		No.2 dumped at Neuville – Bonnay & the column except for Workshops moved to the la Neuville – Pont Noyrup R.R. – No.1. loaded Mericourt 5:30am	
	28/9/16		No.1. dumped Bonnay – No.2 loaded Mericourt	
	29.		No.2 dumped Bonnay No.1 loaded Mericourt	
	30/7/16		No.1 dumped Bonnay. No.2 loaded Mericourt	

Notes: I Member to Infantry for the Staff to take an M.T. officer in properly the sign of an M.T. Convoy. Great moreover is required to ensure ranks of New Army taking necessary arrangement for pure water & provision of Latrines.

Lt. 3 Car left of Corps

WAR DIARY
or
INTELLIGENCE SUMMARY
(Erase heading not required.)

Army Form C. 2118

Place	Date	Hour	Summary of Events and Information	Remarks and references to Appendices
Beauval	1/6/16		Major H.A.C. Gardner A.D.C. arrived from 6th Aux. Pub. Park to assume command	
	2/6/16		Major H.A.C. Gardner took over command of 3 Aux. Supply Col. from Capt. C. Preston.	
	3/7/16		Column was at this time working on Single Eschelon - Half the lorries being familes & overloaded. Rouxheads was Rouxauville - and the Division was in and of Fringes - into the equivalent of a Brigade near Berk Plage.	
	4/7/16		An orderly officer was installed in the column.	
	6/7/16		The Supply Section were mounted centrally by the Brit. Officer	
	8/7/16		One officer per lorry allowed on leave - average of men 4 per week. Wood very bought	
	7/7/16		The Supply of Wood to the division was not economical -	
			Near Fringes a convoy to Berk go by lorry.	
	9/7/16		The delivery of officers to their units from leave to present difficulties - all officers arriving either requiring conveyance, to wait in the lodges up for the Majors -	
	9/7/16		A suggestion put forward that a box car should be forwarded for the purpose	
	9/7/16		The a/c of orders & move authority attached for evacuation of 1 Demme (Engine outstanding). 42 3/Lieut. Hallfords - One flour 9 out of date to keep up with column.	

Army Form C. 2118

WAR DIARY
or
INTELLIGENCE SUMMARY
(Erase heading not required.)

Instructions regarding War Diaries and Intelligence Summaries are contained in F.S. Regs., Part II. and the Staff Manual respectively. Title Pages will be prepared in manuscript.

Place	Date	Hour	Summary of Events and Information	Remarks and references to Appendices
Pt Noyelles R.	26/7/16		Considerable trouble caused by Can: Corps female drivers allocated to Column without any lorries to ration them. 3DS&T. ruled that they should be on "attached strength" however. Also Postal Services Car	
	28/7/16		Inspected kits of Sec II	
	29/7/16		Efforts made to start a Canteen — been most difficult to obtain in Amiens. Inspected kits to 4 workshops. 3 sacks of flour bought in Amiens from Canteen funds to make puddings. News rec: late that Column would deliver near Hangest on 31st	
	31/7/16		No 1 Sec. moved loaded to Pisquigny on 31st	

Crawford
Maj.
O.C. 3rd Can. Supple Col.

WAR DIARY.

August.

1st. Division moved back from position of waiting behind the line. 1st. Section refilled units at Picquiny, 2nd. Section moved loaded to St. Riequier.

2nd. 2nd. Section refilled units around St. Riquier, 1st. Section loaded at St. Riquier.

3rd. 1st. Section refilled units around St. Riquier, 2nd. Section loaded.

4th. 2nd. Section refilled units around St. Riquier, 1st. loaded.

5th. 1st. Section delivered to units in Crècy area and proceeded to Beaurainville. Section 2 proceeded to Beaurainville.

6th. Section 2 loaded in Beaurainville and the old billets etc were resumed.

7th. It was decided that considerable waste was entailed to supply 8th. Brigade which reached from Hesdin to Anvin, and a scheme was put forward that the Column should move to Hesdin, and supply units by the Reserve Park and horse transport.

14th. Column moved to Hesdin - Workshops accomodated in Sugar Factory.

15th. Division now supplied their Divnl. Troops and 7th. Bde. by light railway from Montreuil to Ergny. 8th Bde. by the Reserve Park to Blingel and thence by H.T. to units towards Anvin. 6th. Bde. by Reserve Park to Wamin or Beaurainville and thence by H.T. to Units - the H.T. of units being increased by two or more waggons from the Reserve Park.

16th. The Column began to thoroughly clean, look over and repair all lorries.

20th. Company paraded 400 strong for Church Parade.

21st. Most minor repairs to lorries being completed, drills and route marches were undertaken in afternoon.

24th. Digging Party of 150 conveyed by lorry to Bouzincourt.

30th. All reinforcements were sent direct to units - also fuel. These lorries and those for taking digging parties etc to Reserve Army were the only ones used, and consequently lorries by the end of the month became in very good condition.

31st. Lorries for 6th & 8th Brigades took dismounted party to Bouzincourt.

MAJOR, A.S.C.,
3rd CAVALRY SUPPLY COLUMN.

War diary. - Continued.

September.

1st. to 4th. Company Training.

5th. 3 lorries to Arras and 1 to Aveluy. Arras lorries staying 3 days.

7th. 67 lorries to Aveluy to collect dismounted men and convey to billets in Hesdin area, also 3 lorries to Arras for return of snipers. 1800 gallons of petrol used. The 3 lorries which left on 5th. returned.

9th. Sent 20 lorries to 6th & 7th Brigades also R.H.G. to take men to General Sports, waited, and took men back.

10th. Section 1 left Hesdin, refilled Authie area and proceeded to St. Riquier. Section 2 loaded at Hesdin and Montreuil and parked in Hesdin.

11th. Section 1 loaded at St. Riquier and parked there the night. Section 2 left Hesdin 12 noon refilled St. Riquier area and proceeded to Vignacourt

12th. Headquarters left Hesdin and proceeded to Vignacourt. Section 2 loaded at Vignacourt and parked there for night. Section 1 left St. Riquier, refilled in Belloy to Argoeuvres area and proceeded to Vignacourt to park.

13th. Section 2 refilled in Belloy to ARGOEUVRES area and proceeded to park at La Motte. Section 1 loaded at Vignacourt and stayed there.

14th. Section 2 went to load at Corbie at 5 a.m. Loading finished at 10 p.m. having to draw hay & oats short on train from barges. Section 1 left Vignacourt and refilled in Daours area at 10.30 a.m. and afterwards collected oats & iron rations from barges also about 20,000 iron rations from Reserve Park at St. Gratien and delivered to units - finishing at 10 p.m. Headquarters & Workshops from Vignacourt to La Motte.

15th. Section 1 left La Motte for Park on Millencourt-Albert road at 7 a.m. to load at Albert, Lieut. Bewley left with S.Sgt. Herberts Shop at 2 p.m. to report to Lieut. Borton. Rations loaded for Aux. H.T., Reserve Park and A.S.C. limbers joining Division.(no extra transport allowed) 65 lorries loaded. Formed B Echelon at Daours. Section 2 left La Motte to refill 4 p.m. to new Park on Albert - Millencourt road on completion. Section 1 loaded at Albert - 3 other Divs. also loaded there.

16th. Section 1 left to refill at 1 p.m. Section 2 loaded at Albert at 10 p.m. Loaded in bulk - reloaded following morning.

17th. Section 2 left park to refill 4 p.m. and then to park at La Motte. Section 1 loaded at Albert - train arrived at 1 p.m. congestion at railhead as before. Orders received railhead for 18th will be Frechincourt.

18th. Wire from Q 3rd. Cav.Div. 8 a.m. serious derailment loading will be at Vecquemont train not in till 4.30 p.m. 1 lorry to Frechincourt for petrol loading completed 7 p.m. Section 1 left Albert 10 a.m. to refill - to park at La Motte on completion.

19th. Section 1 loaded at Frechincourt waited there from

War Diary - Continued.

September; continued.

19th.   From 10 a.m. till about 7 p.m. loading completed 9 p.m. Reported by Police for using wrong road. Section 2 delivered at Daours at 3 p.m.

20th.   Another breakdown on rail. Section 2 loaded at Vecquemont 5 p.m. Section 1 deliver at Daours 2 p.m.

21st.   Section 1 loaded at Frechincourt 12 noon. Section 2 delivered at Daours 2 p.m. Orders received that Division would go back next day. Collected Column B. Echelon 8 p.m.

22nd.   Column delivered to units in Hangest area and spent night at Hangest. Section 2 moved loaded from Frechencourt and spent night with Headquarters near Picquigny.

23rd.   Section 2 rendezvous - noon at Auxi-le-Chateau and delivered to units in that area. Moved to Hesdin. Section 1 loaded at Auxi-le-Chateau and remained the night.

24th.   Section 1 delivered to units in Crécy and moved to Hesdin. Headquarters moved to Hesdin. Section 2 loaded at Hesdin.

25th.   Division arrived in Rest area reaching from Hesdin to sea.
7th. Bde. N. of Ancre as far as Aix-en-Issart.
8th. Bde. South of Ancre to Brimeux and Bois Jean
6th. Bde. South of 7th. Divl.H.Q. at Cappelle.

27th.   7th & 8th. Brigades supplied by single echelon Section 1.

30th.   6th Brigade moved to the Merlimont - Rang - Verton area.

F. A. Gardner

MAJOR, A.S.C.,
3rd CAVALRY SUPPLY COLUMN.

WAR DIARY or INTELLIGENCE SUMMARY

Army Form C. 2118.

3 Can Sup Col

Vol 25

Place	Date	Hour	Summary of Events and Information	Remarks and references to Appendices
Hesdin	1/8/16	-	Division supplied by lorry from Hesdin - 6th Brig. in Merlimont Area. 7th, 8th, 9th, S of R Conche respectively.	
	2		On the 1st Det. of 20 lorries sent to Wailly to feed 65 Brig. 8 Puppy all of Sec 4 Sent to Montreuil. Total 2 Off. B.O.A.R. Cpl. T.R. Blakeman ordered 20 lorries loaded at Montreuil.	
	3		20 lorries delivered 6th Brig. Merlimont area & reloaded Montreuil	
	4		Funeral of Cpl T Blakeman, 8 lorries attached to 3rd Field S9 In anticipation of a move to Somme area 5 lorries of reserve rat tots was transported to Daours. to Aug. 1st T. Coy.	
	5		O. to H.Q. Capt. Thorpe in command.	
	11		A.D.M.S. Inspected camp - all correct	
	13		A.D.S.&T. (on Pops) visits Workshops (7.00 o'clock hours)	
	16		15 lorries from Sec II sent for night to Wailly to move 6th Brig	
	19		Dismounted party to Aubigny	
	20		These 15 lorries proceeded to Aubigny with party of 3. D.G.R 2 returned with party of men relieved - another charges 3rd D.G.R. investigated	

Army Form C. 2118.

WAR DIARY
or
INTELLIGENCE SUMMARY.
(Erase heading not required.)

Place	Date	Hour	Summary of Events and Information	Remarks and references to Appendices
Hesdin	21		H. Bailton & 6.O.R & 18 lorries attached to 1st Cav Div. for feeding 4th Brig. R.H.A.	
	22		15 lorries from 8th Brig area to Avesluy with relief for digging party — returned with relieved party each way.	
	24th		14 lorries Peel moved diggings party of 7th Bn from 9th B. area to Bouzincourt. Returned with relieved party.	
	25		11 lorries Peel moved stores for 8th Brig from old to new area.	
	26		16 lorries Peel " " " " "	
			16 lorries proceeded to Rue to move stores for Cav Corps — not required	
	27		9 lorries for R.H.Gds. to move reg'l stores from B'ville to A'x-Bu. 10 Appai	
	Monthly		During the single echelon ye only half the lorries were in use at at time, overhauls were undertaken freely on workshops — there were considerable traces of wear in the lorries returned from the Baltips, the roads being very bad. Coy football started in the Monder & preparations to spend the winter at Hesdin	

Ja formed
Mijon
MAJOR, A.S.C.,
3rd CAVALRY SUPPLY COLUMN.

Army Form C. 2118.

WAR DIARY
or
INTELLIGENCE SUMMARY.
(Erase heading not required.)

3 Cav Sup Col Vol 26

Place	Date	Hour	Summary of Events and Information	Remarks and references to Appendices
HESDIN	1/11/16		Unit in same place, and utilized in the same way as in the previous month, i.e; Main Body and Workshops at HESDIN. The Supply Personel of Section I at BEAURAIN-VILLE to supply 7th & 8th Brigade from that Railhead, total 54 & 3 lorries. The Supply Personel of Section II at MONTREUIL to supply 6th Brigade & Division-al Troops by means of a Detachment of 26 lorries from Section II at WAILLY. With the exception of these the lorries were for the most part laid off.	
	7/11/16		Captain N.D. Riley, S.O. Section I to 50th Railhead.	
	13/11/16		F.G.C.M. on Pte. Brown, G.	
	20/11/16		Two lorries & 5 A.R. to 5th Corps with 8th Pioneer Bn. Section II. Two lorries & 5 A.R. to 2nd Corps with 7th Division Mn. Pioneer Bn. Section I.	
	25/11/16		One lorry returns from 5th Corps.	
	27/11/16		Detachment with R.H.A. rejoined from Nr. Bouzincourt. Two Officers & 59 O.Rs. 14 lorries, one car, one Motor Cycle. Roads in area in shocking state - Column under shell fire infrequently - no battle casualties. Lieut. F. R. Hodgson joined from 12th Div. Sup. Coln. One lorry returned from 5th Corps.	
	28/11/16		Lieut. A.H.Borton to No.5 G.H.Q.Amn.Pk. 10 men to 7th Brigade to work under S.O. 7th. Up to the present, the least eventful month we have had.	

H.C. Gurney

Major.

Commanding 3rd Cavalry Supply Column.

WAR DIARY
or
INTELLIGENCE SUMMARY. 3rd D. Supply Col
Vol ΣΣ

Army Form C. 2118.

Place	Date	Hour	Summary of Events and Information	Remarks and references to Appendices
HESDIN	1/12/16		Unit in same place, and utilized in the same way as last month. Its Main Body and Workshops at HESDIN. The Supply Personnel of Section I at BEAURAINVILLE.	
	2/12/16		To supply 7 & 8 Brigades from MARESQUEL Railhead. The Supply Personnel of Section II at MONTREUIL to supply 6 Brigade and Divisional Troops by means of a detachment of 26 lorries from Section II.	
	5/12/16		Sergt COXETER to Cadet School, England for commission. Sentence on Private Brown G. quashed on the grounds of insufficient evidence by order of D.J.A.G.	
	6/12/16		6 men to 7th Brigade for mat making. 6 men to Post Office for Xmas postal work.	
	7/12/16		Establishment of Officers reduced. 1 M.S.S + 9 Officers to Base.	
	9/12/16		1 N.C.O. to ROUEN for cookery class.	
	12/12/16		Captain Thorpe assumes command temporarily during absence of C.O. on leave	
	13/12/16		11 lorries from 4th Pioneer Batt. to HESDIN	
	14/12/16		14 lorries moving huts from HESDIN to MONTREUIL. 5 reinforcements (Supply) from Base.	
	15/12/16		16 lorries to 4th Pioneer Batt. from HESDIN to AMIENS.	
	16/12/16		6 lorries lent to Div. H.Q. to move from WAILLY to TRÉPIED.	

Army Form C. 2118.

WAR DIARY
or
INTELLIGENCE SUMMARY.
(Erase heading not required.)

Instructions regarding War Diaries and Intelligence Summaries are contained in F. S. Regs., Part II. and the Staff Manual respectively. Title pages will be prepared in manuscript.

Place	Date	Hour	Summary of Events and Information	Remarks and references to Appendices
HESDIN.	19/12/15		4 lorries with K Batt R.H.A. 3 lorries with C Batt R.H.A.	
	20/12/15		43 lorries to bring 6" Pioneer Batt to MARESQUEL	
	21/12/15		24 lorries sent to 8" Brigade to load baggage & stoves.	
	22/12/15		6" Brigade change area with 8" Brigade. The 24 lorries sent on 21st to the 8" Brigade return loaded with 6" Brigade. Commence supplying 6" Brigade with rations from	
MARESQUEL	25/12/15		Major Gardner resumes command on return from leave vice Capt Thorpe	
	29/12/15		The M.O. Lt Clarke relieved by Capt Wilmot from 8" C.F.A.	

H. O. Gardner

10/4/17

MAJOR, A.S.C.,
3rd CAVALRY SUPPLY COLUMN.

WAR DIARY or INTELLIGENCE SUMMARY

Army Form C. 2118.

3 Can Sup Col

Vol 28

Place	Date	Hour	Summary of Events and Information	Remarks and references to Appendices
HESDIN	1/1/17		Unit in same place and utilized in the same way as last month. i.e. Main body and Workshops at HESDIN. The Supply personnel of Section I at BEAURAINVILLE to supply 6th and 9th Brigades from MARESQUEL Railhead. The Supply personnel of Section II at MONTREUIL to supply 8th Brigade and Divisional Troops by means of a detachment of 26 lorries from Section II	
	2/1/17		2 lorries to Section I from 8th Brigade detachment	
	4/1/17		1 lorry to Workshops " " " for overhaul	
			1 lorry to 8th Brigade detachment to replace from Section II	
	6/1/17		9 lorries to convey men of 4th Pioneer Batt. to DOULLENS	
	7/1/17		1 N.C.O. to Divisional Anti-Gas School.	
			2 lorries for H.Q. 4th Pioneer Batt. to DOULLENS	
	8/1/17		9 lorries for men of 4th Pioneer Batt. to DOULLENS to remain the night	
	9/1/17		9 lorries return from DOULLENS with men of 6th Pioneer Batt.	
	10/1/17		Capt B.L. Thorp having joined Heavy Section M.G.C. is struck off the strength. Lieut P.G. Clarke assumes command of Section I vice Capt B.L. Thorp	

WAR DIARY
or
INTELLIGENCE SUMMARY.
(Erase heading not required.)

Army Form C. 2118.

Place	Date	Hour	Summary of Events and Information	Remarks and references to Appendices
HESDIN	10/7		Transfer of 1 "C.B" Type Daimler lorry to 1st Cavalry Supply Column	
	"		" " 1 " " " " 1st Cavalry Corps Troops Supply Col.	
	12/7		Receipt of 4 "Y" Type Daimler lorries from 1st Cavalry Supply Column.	
	"		Transfer of 6 "B" Type Daimler lorries to 4th Cavalry Supply Column.	
	"		Receipt of 2. 30 cwt Dennis lorries from Cavalry Corps Troops Supply Col.	
	"		" " 4 "Y" Type Daimler lorries " " " " "	
	13/7		1 N.C.O from cookery class ROUEN.	
	"		4 lorries to M.M.G.S to DIXON	
	"		Section I railhead changed from MARESQUEL to BEAURAINVILLE.	
	14/7		8 lorries to DOULLENS for duty with Wm Pioneer Batt. to remain until relieved	
	16/7		2/Lieut F.C. Burne to 8th Brigade detachment.	
	19/7		8 lorries of Section I to DOULLENS to relieve 8 sent on 14/7/17.	
	20/7		2 lorries from 8th Brigade detachment.	
	21/7		"	
	22/7		1 N.C.O to Divisional Anti-Gas school	
	"		Sections I and II move from HESDIN to BEAURAINVILLE.	

WAR DIARY
or
INTELLIGENCE SUMMARY.

(Erase heading not required.)

Army Form C. 2118.

Place	Date	Hour	Summary of Events and Information	Remarks and references to Appendices
BEAURAINVILLE	23/1/17		Headquarters move from HESDIN to BEAURAINVILLE. Workshops	
	25/1/17		" " " "	
	26/1/17		Capt. M Toomey assumes command during absence of Major H.A Gardner on leave	
	27/1/17		Commencement of exchange of area between 7th and 8th Brigades.	
			1 lorry to ETAPLES	
			5 lorries to FRESSIN	
			2 lorries to DOULLENS for duty with 7th Pioneer Battn	
	29/1/17		18 lorries to DOULLENS with 8th Pioneer Battn to relieve 7th Pioneer Battn. lorries return same day with 7th Pioneer Battn.	
			Major H.A Gardner assumes command on his return from leave.	
	30/1/17		8 lorries to VILLERS AU BOIS with 6th M.G.S.	
	31/1/17		18 lorries to DOULLENS with 8th Pioneer Battn returning with 7th Pioneer Battn	
			Exchange of area between 7th and 8th Brigades - 24 lorries for conveyance of surplus kits	

H.A Gardner
MAJOR, A.S.C.
3RD CAVALRY SUPPLY COLUMN.

10/2/17

Army Form C. 2118

Vol 2a

WAR DIARY or INTELLIGENCE SUMMARY

Supply Column
3rd Cavalry Division

Place	Date	Hour	Summary of Events and Information	Remarks and references to Appendices
Beaurainville	1/2/17		Severe Frost. Unit at BEAURAINVILLE E.E. Train Body Motorlorries & supply personnel. Sec I. Supply personnel at BEAURAINVILLE Railhead to supply 6th & 8th Brigades. Sec II Supply personnel at MONTREUIL Railhead. Lorries detraining the Units at CAVRON & ROYON, for 8th Bde. 11 lorries off road on a/c of frost casualties. 1 Car 4 lorries.	
	2/2/17		3½ Lorries utilized to move Tractor Kits of Brigades changing area. 1F 6 Merlimont area, 8F Fruges area.	
	3/2/17		11 Lorries to convey troops from ROYON to DOULLENS & St JOSSE & MERLIMONT. 10 " " " " " FRUGES & MERLIMONT.	
	4/2/17		Represented A.S.C. at G.O.C. Brigades changing of men's clothing & one no conveyed to new area (6F 17F 8th).	
	13/2/17		Captain B.S. Burbidge & Lieut Q.R.R. Clark inspected lorries detailed for fetching Co. G. Batteries & 7th M.G.	
	14/2/17		7 Lorries to convey troops of F&n Machine Guns from CREUY & CAMBLAIN L'ABBE	

WAR DIARY or INTELLIGENCE SUMMARY

Army Form C. 2118

(Erase heading not required.)

Instructions regarding War Diaries and Intelligence Summaries are contained in F.S. Regs., Part II. and the Staff Manual respectively. Title Pages will be prepared in manuscript.

Place	Date	Hour	Summary of Events and Information	Remarks and references to Appendices
	19/2/17		One N.C.O. to Divisional Anti-Gas School.	
	22/2/17		Motor Busses - addition of number waiting for Lorry Traffic - Motor Transports drawn from Railhead. 6" & 8" from B'ville. 7" & D.T. from Zuoin in rear of Rang de Flers posted troops as usual except for day of 19/2/17 only.	
	23/2/17		2/Lieut. G.V. Campbell reports for duty as Supply Officer - proceeds to No 2 Section at MONTREUIL. Lieut. F.R. Thompson assumes duties of acting Town Major of BEAURAINVILLE. on departure for the day of Dr R. Gardner.	
	25/2/17		2/Lieut L.C. Barlow + 2/Lt F.O. Bennett inspect lorries detailed for feeding C+ G Batteries + 7th M.G.G.	
	27/2/17		2/Lieut G.L. Taylor - Supply Officer die I hours to H.Q. Royal Flying Corps to report for duty under R.T.O. Duties of G.O.O. due I taken over by 2/Lt F.O. Bennett. Classes of Instruction instituted for N.C.O.s + M.T. Drivers. 2/Lieut L.C. Barlow to Divisional Anti-Gas School for Course of Instruction.	

1875 Wt. W593/826 1,000,000 4/15 J.B.C. & A. A.D.S.S./Forms/C. 2118.

Army Form C. 2118

WAR DIARY
or
INTELLIGENCE SUMMARY
(Erase heading not required.)

Place	Date	Hour	Summary of Events and Information	Remarks and references to Appendices
	28/2/17		Captain B.S. Cautley attached to H.Q. 3rd Cavalry Ammunition Park as member of F.G.C.M.	
			Various hours off for road making of front transline. (Working horses)	
			There has been a little stern during the afternoon front. In spite of much, a certain amount of trouble with Daimler lorries — otherwise casualties practically Nil.	
			By aid of a syringe one is able to extract most of the water from the "Daimler" leads but no experient for this syringe was refused in store so that off "Y" type lorries was not sufficient to meet the bottom of the leads; had to continue to break into the leads with axes, one type lead has been plugged & syringe adapted to work to bottom of leads causalties all nil.	

Signature: *[signed]* 9/3/17

3rd CAVALRY SUPPLY COLUMN

Army Form C. 2118.

WAR DIARY
or
INTELLIGENCE SUMMARY.

3 Cav Sept (?)

Vol 30

Place	Date	Hour	Summary of Events and Information	Remarks and references to Appendices
BEAURAINVILLE	1/3/17		Unit at BEAURAINVILLE with train Body & Workshops & Supply Personnel of Sec I	
	2/3/17		Sec I personnel at BEAURAINVILLE Relieved to supply 6th & 8th Brigades.	
	8/3/17		Sec II personnel at MONTREUIL Relieved.	
	11/3/17		Lieut. E.T.W. Stewart to M.T. School of Instruction (N)	
			15 Lorries to VILLERS-AU-BOIS to carry 6th & 8th Brigades from Canadians to MARESQUEL & CREQUY.	
			Captain Pinlock from from General H.Q. A.S.C. attached as S.O. Sec I.	
			2/Lt. B.G. Bowers from M.T. School of Instruction (N) - posted Sec I (Road Officer).	
			Captain Pinlock - from General as S.O. Sec I - 2/Lt F.G.Bowes taking over.	
	15/3/17		81 Lorries to AUXI-LE-CHATEAU to convey 6th & 8th Junior Batts. to their Brigade Area.	
	17/3/17		Lorry No 7281 proceeded to PARIS	
	19/3/17		4 Lorries to AUXI-LE-CHATEAU to convey Batt - to 6th Brigade H.Q.	
	20/3/17		Double Echelon for units of 8th Brigade landing at BEAURAINVILLE in 10th Hussars & Canadian	
			from dumping @ ROYON - Essex Yeomanry & 8th Brigade H.Q. @ CAVRON.	

Army Form C. 2118.

WAR DIARY
or
INTELLIGENCE SUMMARY.
(Erase heading not required.)

Instructions regarding War Diaries and Intelligence Summaries are contained in F. S. Regs., Part II. and the Staff Manual respectively. Title pages will be prepared in manuscript.

Place	Date	Hour	Summary of Events and Information	Remarks and references to Appendices
	20/3/17		6 Lorries to CALAIS to load Ordnance stores & convoy same to Ordnance dump @ MONTREUIL	
	21/3/17		Lorry 5741 evacuated to Rouen.	
	22/3/17		2 Lorries to Abbeville for two water trailers for Column.	
			2/R.C.R. Stragglers joined from H.T.&S. Depôt HAVRE & posted to Sec I as A.O.	
			Detachment of 20 Lorries + 20 Supply men to ARRAS area	
	23/3/17		1 Lorry to convoy parts of 3rd Field Amcultn R.- Lorry returning with parts in replacement of ARRAS.	
	25/3/17		18 Lorries to WOINCOURT to load Huts + convoy same to OUISANS.	
			6 Lorries to convoy parts of 6th Brigade to ARRAS.	
			7 " " 8 " " " "	
			1 " " " ARRAS.- one to remain for duty with C.A.E. Cas. Corps.	
	27/3/17		Lorries 6418 + 6974 evacuated to ROUEN.	
			9 Lorries to convoy parts of 6th Brigade to ARRAS.	
	31/3/17		Lorry 3067 evacuated to PARIS.	

J.O. Copeland
Lt
O.C. No 9
Canadian Supply Column

26/4/17

Army Form C. 2118.

Supply Column
3rd Cav Divn

Vol 31

WAR DIARY
or
INTELLIGENCE SUMMARY.
(Erase heading not required.)

Place	Date	Hour	Summary of Events and Information	Remarks and references to Appendices
Beaurainville	1-4-17	-	Divison supplied as follows :- 4th Cav Bde in MERLIMONT area supplied from MONTREUIL Railhead by Light Railway to St JOSSE and thence by H.T. to until a Divi Troops from MONTREUIL by Light to TREPIED = 6th Cav Bde by H.T. from Beaurainville (rough echelon) : 8th Cav Bde by Lorry to CARRON and BARLES (lump) except R.H.A. who were fed by light railway from MONTREUIL to FRUGES (rough echelon)	
"	2-4-17		Demonitized roads near BOURQUEMAISON with S.S.D. roads near GOUY in a cheering OGO	
"	3-4-17		Lorries went on returning R.E. and A.D.S. stores to Railhead	
"	3-4-17		Sect II loaded for Divison at BEAURAINVILLE dumps for delivery on 4th 1 Lorry (30 cwt) 2 Ambulances and 3 other ranks evacuated to Depôts Ships by rail.	
"	4-4-17		Section I loaded for all Divi Troops less Supply Column and Divi #7 C3 and 10th Hussar Bde at MONTREUIL and for 6th and 8th Bdes at BEAURAINVILLE. Sect II delivered to units in original areas and brought back 50 men per Bde for details by rail to FREVENT.	

Army Form C. 2118.

WAR DIARY
or
INTELLIGENCE SUMMARY.
(Erase heading not required.)

Instructions regarding War Diaries and Intelligence Summaries are contained in F.S. Regs., Part II and the Staff Manual respectively. Title pages will be prepared in manuscript.

Place	Date	Hour	Summary of Events and Information	Remarks and references to Appendices
Beaurainville	4-4-17		One lorry accompanied this party to carry P.O.L or otherwise. 108 dismounted men of C.H.A joined the Column for transport to VERCHOEQ for R.H.A base. 4 lorries sent to BOUQUEMAISON. All returning supply lorries used by 8th Cav Bde to return surplus B.L.S to BEAURAINVILLE except also a further 9 lorries which returned about midnight. All detachment, including 20 lorries from ARRAS and Supply detachment from MONTREUIL rejoined the Column. Note - 6th Div disposed of their surplus Lot AT to HQ on 4th = 4th Cav Bde returned their surplus ACS stores by Amm Park lorries.	
	5-4-17		Division moves into concentration area "PLUMOISON - FRESSIN - CAVRON - MARENLA - DOULLENS area" I deliver rations in this area and then proceed to new park en route REVENT - DOULLENS road. 2nd Ech & 1st Ech at BEAURAINVILLE and proceed to MARCONNE to park. H.L. Coy and advanced workshops move to MARCONNE. Div. Railhead Coy (3157) evacuated 6 days train from BEAURAINVILLE. Field Cashier joined the unit under Div I instructions. Div Railhead Coy (6022) joined park Bde Cav Bde HQ Column.	
		6 P.M.	Orders received that men of Divisional postponed 24 hours. Note: The Column loaded at BEAURAINVILLE on the morning of 5th and evacuated the village the same morning, which made it difficult to clear the place clear in view of the fact that the Div. 7th Cav Bde	

Army Form C. 2118.

WAR DIARY
or
INTELLIGENCE SUMMARY.
(Erase heading not required)

Instructions regarding War Diaries and Intelligence Summaries are contained in F.S. Regs., Part II. and the Staff Manual respectively. Title pages will be prepared in manuscript.

Place	Date	Hour	Summary of Events and Information	Remarks and references to Appendices
Beauxville	5-11-17		Entered the village before the column had left. There difficulties were particularly experienced in the Officers' Mess.	
	6-11-17		Section II returned to unit in same order as 5th and the proceeded to fresh at BOUQUEMAISON. Section I loaded at BOUQUEMAISON.	
	7-11-17		H.Q. Div. and Divisional Workshops moved to BOUQUEMAISON. Section II loaded at BOUQUEMAISON (early on 8th inst) Train 26 hours late. Sect. I returned to Brigades at 10 am as follows:- 7th Bde = BOUBERS = 8th Bde = FREVENT = 6th Bde = VACQUERIE. Div. Troops = CONCHY	
	8-11-17		Division moved to GOUY. Section II loaded at BOUQUEMAISON = 4:000 The Ray station was drawn from LIGNY ST. FLOCHEL and FREVENT. Sect-II rendezvous 2 PM at GOUY and FOSSEUX, except for "B" section, which was relieved at BOUBERS at 4 PM. Note:- The road between AVESNES LE COMTE and HAUTEVILLE is closed to lorries without special permission. great inconvenience caused through this fact not being published, and unmetalled roads had to be used in consequence with bad results. 6 Lorries delivered Hay to PAVINCOURT Railhead for A.D.S.T	

1577 Wt.W10791/1773 500,000 1/15 D.D.&L. A.D.S.S./Forms/C. 2118.

Army Form C. 2118.

WAR DIARY
or
INTELLIGENCE SUMMARY.
(Erase heading not required.)

Instructions regarding War Diaries and Intelligence Summaries are contained in F. S. Regs., Part II. and the Staff Manual respectively. Title pages will be prepared in manuscript.

Place	Date	Hour	Summary of Events and Information	Remarks and references to Appendices
Bouquemaison	8-4-17		Car Corps :- ex BOUQUEMAISON. Lorry 538ft (Halford) returned from C.R.E. Car Corps and evacuated same night to Paris by road.	
"	9-4-17		Division moved to beyond ARRAS. Amm Colums left the fighting strength of the Division. Rations only delivered (by Sector I) to "B" echelon and following units at Gov'ts Heavy section of C.P.A.S = 25 S.M.V.S. = Sanitary Section = Heavy Section Amm Colum = Detatchment 10th Reserve Park at BARLY. Sect I loaded BOUQUEMAISON = 7 Lorry loads hay also on train drawn from H.P.C. 2 new Ambulances received from Car Corps to B Ech. One for 6th and one for 8th F.A.C.s	
"	10-4-17		Sect I unloaded train at BOUQUEMAISON on to P.S.O.'s dump in station yard. Sect II delivered Hay and moved to the Division in the evening, also Plum, or St P.C.- ARRAS road - "B"echelon rations by Lt.	
"	11-4-17		Sect II again loaded at BOUQUEMAISON and dumped on Ranh, returned to Rivillard and debarked from P.S.O. dump, returned to tank and again dumped, thus elevated original load. Supplies for "B" echelon sent by lorry to ETREE WAMIN.	
		1.30 p.m	Orders received from D.A.P.M.G. Car Corps. to send up 20 hay lorries to dumps now on DOULLENS - ARRAS Road.	

WAR DIARY or INTELLIGENCE SUMMARY

Army Form C. 2118.

Place	Date	Hour	Summary of Events and Information	Remarks and references to Appendices
BOUQUEMAISON	11-4-17		near ARRAS :- Note :- This order was sent by D.A.D.O.S. 3rd Cav. Div. who took the lorries and attack on a field for 2 or 3 hours. Consequently then orders were received about 3 hours later than if sent by special D.R. attached to Cav Corps Signals for this purpose, or by Lieut Clark, who was waiting for orders at Cav Corps. 1st Column reported to Cav Corps about 3 P.M. and received orders to rendezvous three hay lorries one mile from ARRAS on ST POL - ARRAS road. Reconnoitred the road from BERNEVILLE to WARLUS and DUISSANS with Lieut Clark, several changes appear not shown on traffic map. Met hay lorries, under Lieut Betchett, near BERNEVILLE at about 6 P.M. and Lieut Clark conveyed them to rendezvous, near WARLUS, however, they were held up by an A.P.M. who said they must have a special pass to proceed as the road half mile. No previous intimation had been received, and lorries had to be diverted to HABARCQ, causing 3 hours delay as the road was in a bad state. Lorries arrived at rendezvous about 11 P.M. road packed with traffic, and a special order was obtained by D.A.P.M.G. Cav Corps for lorries to halt on the side of the road. Hay was then off loaded, and on lorry was sent to ARRAS dump for them. Units were too tired to make use of the hay. Lorries returned to park via ARRAS and DOULLENS.	
		6.30 P.M	Orders received to send out on section complete, not of Section I sent out - 3 3 lorries. at about 7.30 P.M. it seeming hopeless that these lorries could deliver that night. D.A.D.O.S. was	

WAR DIARY or INTELLIGENCE SUMMARY.

Army Form C. 2118.

Place	Date	Hour	Summary of Events and Information	Remarks and references to Appendices
BOUQUEMAISON			was detailed to stop them if possible. This he failed to do. Sect I then arrived at DUISSANS about 1 P.M. and on verbal instructions received from D.A.Q.M.G. Res Corps about 1.30 p.m. they were sent back to park, no petrol on the 5TH POL — ARRAS road being allowed. Sect I drove through a blizzard and reached camp at 9 A.M. following morning – 10 ⅔	
	12-4-17		Section II delivered at BERNEVILLE — SIMENCOURT and GOUY, intelligence HPM at LA HERLIERE. Sect I loaded at BOUQUEMAISON, after dumping previous days load on Park. 8 Lorries sent to ARRAS under Lieut BAILLON to take rations to, and bring in stragglers of X & 2nd Divisions – etc	
			forwarded to Section II loaded at BOUQUEMAISON (no train till following morning) Sect I delivered in GOUY area.	
	13-4-17			
	14-4-17		Section I loaded from dump in park. Section II delivered in GOUY area.	
	15-4-17		Short train arrived. Section I loaded partly from train and partly from their own dump. Sect I delivered in GOUY area. 8 Amm Park lorries journey for transport of fuel etc to Division. 1 lorry joined from Res Corps Troops Sup Column	

WAR DIARY
or
INTELLIGENCE SUMMARY.
(Erase heading not required.)

Army Form C. 2118.

Place	Date	Hour	Summary of Events and Information	Remarks and references to Appendices
BOUQUEMAISON	16-4-17		Division moved to AUXI-LE-CHATEAU area except 8th Cav Bde. Section II took @ BOUQUEMAISON. Section II relieved 1st F.S. Bn at GOUY at FAM. Rendezvous for sui troops. DOULLENS = 11 A.M. for 4th Bde. OUTREBOIS noon = 6th Bde. AUXI. noon. The 9th Bde Train now Claude to and dismounted men from GOUY to new area for the rest of Division. 10th Reserve Park being horse rugs & 2nd Gear and 6 Lt Bde to BOUQUEMAISON. Dumps and parks for the night. Bags taken to Division by return lorries. Section I took 48 tons of oats at BOUQUEMAISON and dumps on farm.	
	17-4-17		Section II delivers to Division in AUXI area. Section II took at BOUQUEMAISON. 8 Amm Park Lorries report to 6th Bde H.Q. to move dismounted men etc to new area. 8th Bde moves to AUXI area. Rations dumped at OUTREBOIS Church at 2 P.M.	
	18-4-17		Section II delivers. Section I took at BOUQUEMAISON. 3 Amm Park Lorries fetch oats from GOUY to new area for 8th Bde and sui troops, and H.Q.s moved to the Division. Section I delivery 90000 "cob" oats and 20000 "gaf" iron rations at BOUQUEMAISON. Lieut D.C. Bowley promoted Capt. to date 1-4-17.	

WAR DIARY
or
INTELLIGENCE SUMMARY.

(Erase heading not required.)

Army Form C. 2118.

Instructions regarding War Diaries and Intelligence Summaries are contained in F. S. Regs., Part II. and the Staff Manual respectively. Title pages will be prepared in manuscript.

Place	Date	Hour	Summary of Events and Information	Remarks and references to Appendices
BOUQUEMAISON	19-4-17		Division moves to LIBESCOURT area. Section I trots at BOUQUEMAISON at 12 noon. Section I leaves park at 10 a.m. to deliver to Divisions in new area rendezvous = 6th Bde - MAINTENAY = 3 Pm = ½ Bde. Near LAGROYE = 3 Pm = 3rd Bde = PLUMOISON. noon. Sui. troops LIBESCOURT. 3 P.m. Section I then proceeded to BEAURAINVILLE. Lieut Clerk to England on special leave.	
"	20-4-17		Section I back at BEAURAINVILLE = Section II leaves park 9.30 a.m to deliver in new area = Hd Qrs Dump 10,000 lbs oats to No. 10 Rec Park. Field Cashier saw column. Hd Qrs and half M/T Workshops now to BEAURAINVILLE.	
"	21-4-17		Section I deliver = Section II back at BEAURAINVILLE = 8th Bde drawn in bulk and dumped in BEAURAINVILLE.	
"	22-4-17		8th Bde back by H.T. (800 horse Yeomanry and 6th M.G.S. Cy. Corps) i.e. = Brig.G.echelon. Sec II deliver to all units except 8th Bde. = Section I back for Divisions Hdq 8th Bdes = Section II on return to park pick up rations for 7th Bde and Sui. troops. 12 lorries proceed to TANGRY - RECQUES and MONT CAYREL with rations for 450 men and 900 horses coming from BOULOGNE.	
"	23-4-17		Rations for Sui. troops delivered by Section II at LIBESCOURT at 11 a.m. and trucked for by Section I at 10 a.m. - i.e.	

2353 Wt. W3544/1454 700,000 5/15 L. D. D. & L. A.D.S.S./Form/C. 2118.

WAR DIARY or INTELLIGENCE SUMMARY

Army Form C. 2118.

Place	Date	Hour	Summary of Events and Information	Remarks and references to Appendices
BEAURAINVILLE	23-4-17		Double echelon days and double echelon lorries. 1st Echelon lorries delivered by Section II at BOUBIEZ at 9am and loaded for by com. lorries at 11AM. i.e. double echelon days on rough echelon lorries. 1st Echelon rations delivered by Section II to MAINTENAY area. 9-30am and loaded again by com. lorries at 11AM. n - e. double echelon days - rough echelon lorries. 2 lorries W2/82 troops of 1st Echelon to ETCHINGHEM for lorry reinforcements. 9 lorries sent to ABBEVILLE for lorry - 2 days on job. Halford lorry 6022 collides with wall at BRIMEAU through being misled in. Hill by a light car.	
"	24-4-17		Normal loading and delivery	
"	25-4-17		Normal loading and delivery. 9 lorries 2 ABBEVILLE for lorry. 8 lorries 6 ETCHINGHEM for reinforcement. Court of Inquiry held onto Capt. Ainslopp - on accident to lorry 6022.	
"	26-4-17		Normal. Frost precautions discontinued.	
"	27-4-17		Normal. 9 lorries 1 ABBEVILLE for lorry. 8 lorries 6 ETCHINGHEM for reinforcements	

Army Form C. 2118.

WAR DIARY
or
INTELLIGENCE SUMMARY.
(Erase heading not required.)

Instructions regarding War Diaries and Intelligence Summaries are contained in F. S. Regs., Part II. and the Staff Manual respectively. Title pages will be prepared in manuscript.

Place	Date	Hour	Summary of Events and Information	Remarks and references to Appendices
BEAURAINVILLE	28-4-17	Normal =	6 Lorries went(?) down at LA-BOISSE Church at 4 PM to take troops to ABBEVILLE.	
	29-4-17	Normal.		
	30-4-17	Normal.	9 lorries to ABBEVILLE for train. 9 lorries to DOUQUEMAISON to bring remainder of 500 reinforcement (dismounted) arrive at Railhead 10 AM for Division sent 6 units by Lorry (18) also 3 from Amm Park.	

G. A. Forshall(?)
Major.
Commdg 3rd Cavalry Supply Column

Army Form C. 2118.

WAR DIARY
or
INTELLIGENCE SUMMARY.

(Erase heading not required.)

May 1919

Place	Date	Hour	Summary of Events and Information	Remarks and references to Appendices
Beauvenille	1st		Usual tending & Watering. 9 Horses Section II to Allonville for train dumping Dies Corps Returns	
	2nd		At Chayes. 132 Reinforcements for 6th, 7th, 8th M.G. Squadrons. 6th & 8th M.G. Squadrons to trucks by lorries (1st 8th) whilst the reinforcement halted for the night [illegible] to turn. Remaining time devoted to employing our [illegible]	
	3rd		Normal. 9 horses sent to [illegible] for train	
	4th		Leading & Watering as usual. 7 horses Section II to Allonville for train. Vet being officer for Corps Hd.	
	5th		Usual. Pony Sec I to Augusmecourt (as total). 9 horses Section I to Allonville for train.	
	6th		Tending & Watering as usual. 50 reinforcements for Div. arrived & had 5:30 am to trucks by lorry (1)	
	7th		Tending & Watering as usual. 9 horses Section I to Allonville for train. Vet being out to [illegible] to entire sick.	
	8th		Normal. Not very attended to pay.	

WAR DIARY
or
INTELLIGENCE SUMMARY

Army Form C. 2118.

(Erase heading not required.)

Aug - 1918 (Continued)

Place	Date	Hour	Summary of Events and Information	Remarks and references to Appendices
Beauvainville		9 A.	Channel boating & returning. Lieut Begg (2nd Lieut) sent to yards Sr. Sec. Adj. Lieut Bigg evacuated to Base by Col. G. Unis. Section 2 to assemble for Mass.	
		10 A.	Personnel. Section I bade & returned with one ton car to Bn. Hqrs. J.K. S.V.K. Alex. Bn. Hqrs. Section II horses after bringing returns tied with one pair Mk. Rec. Pk. & convoy to S.O. Vehicles Section I and II lorries from Beauvainville for another load.	
	11 A.	Section I replied by Bn. Adj. and I good yeomanry Hers. tied at Beauvainville for whole Division (Pk. A.S.C. form Conv. at Beauvainville) Section II supplied 4th Bn. I Bn. Hqrs. Section I - 12 lorries. Section II 4 lorries to Gatesa-St-Amey for ms from Bus Park to Beauvainville 22 horse of Section II returning from 4th I Bn. Hqrs. cross-country remounted men to Beauvainville	
	12 M.	Section I supplied Bouzan - 5K. A.M. DOURIEZ, J.A. LE BUISLE, 9 K. RUBIN-ST-YAAST. Bn. Hqrs. DUISBOURG Returning lorries bring pack ammunition from Lottery I wait for division at Beauvainville I Lieut wait for orders from Rear Welcome Farm WT. Schof of Instruction	

WAR DIARY
or
INTELLIGENCE SUMMARY.

Army Form C. 2118.

Place	Date	Hour	Summary of Events and Information	Remarks and references to Appendices
Rouxmesnil	13th		Section I load at Rouxmesnil. Section II replied Division - 6th Bde in res - 1st Echelon area - 4th Divisional area - S.K.T - 29 Boxes ea - H.Q. proceeding to Envermeu - & Park Hqrs temp to work FSB.	
	14th		Section II load at Envermeu. 10am I park at Envermeu and Section I to Rouxmesnil. Echelon Division - DW Hqrs at Envermeu - 6th Bde - Staff - 9th - Corps - 8th Bde - 20 boxes ea. Proceed to am park at Lwsette Batterie. At 20. 1 half Workshop left Rouxmesnil 11am for 9th Bde Lwsette Batterie arriving 4.30pm to 2wagons of amm. DK joined Echelon to Rouxmesnil it in 5th and moved with Echelon (16 with Att 2a and Rouxmesnil with Section I)	
Lorettes Batterie	15th		Section I lies at Lorettes and Section II relieves to Division. Pm Envermeu. Division = 6th Bde - Envoy Hrs - H.R. Loretts area - 8th Bde - Echelon area - 4 proceeds to pm Echelon at Lorettes Batterie.	
	16th		All Ammn Park arrive Lorette to reserve arrt. Section I lord pm loretts & return to Park. Section II replied Division. Div Hqrs at Envermeu, 6th Bde - 20 Boxes area 4th Bde - Lorette area 6th Bde. Alhorville.	

WAR DIARY
or
INTELLIGENCE SUMMARY

Army Form C. 2118.

Place	Date	Hour	Summary of Events and Information	Remarks and references to Appendices
	17th		Section I. lent at Anvil? Where to park. Section I. split Division. Dw. Troops at Anvilliers — Ambers = 64 Hds. Daysvilles, 7th Bn. at Couroy, 8th Bn. at Atane, and the personnel to La Targe. 2 3ton & 3-3 cwt lorries. Section I. & 2cwt Van, the lot to fed Battalion. Phillips armed with one lorry of Bn.	
	18th		Section II. lent at 24 Hdqs R.E. Auxonville at 2am to haul park at Stenay & Section I. which is Dronilleurs in bringing lorry into and reserve of M.A. park. At 10:30 Y cylinders received to rail park of Stenigny. Section II. Find of 4th Rifle Bde. Sedan? When to Verdun. Dw. Vets at Inville & Hauxmont? & Villerrand 64 Bn. Rear ard Hcopent 7th Bn. 8th Bn. at Precourt? 8th Bn. Gravelle. Orders published warning men not to touch explosives.	
Stengeny	19th			
	20th		Section I. supplied Division in one area. Div. Troops & 7th Bn. has lorry returned to Rethel, returned & returned to Park. Section I. lorries for 6th 11th Bns. Y returned to Park. Exploring lead about B.3. and boy in Sec.I park. I found to be a lad sig. explosive and seriously wounded two men. Pte. SMITH & Lieutenant Wick Taken to hospital Bn (6.6.)	

WAR DIARY
or
INTELLIGENCE SUMMARY.

(Erase heading not required.)

Army Form C. 2118.

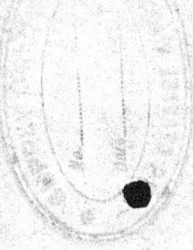

Place	Date	Hour	Summary of Events and Information	Remarks and references to Appendices
Rouen	21st		Section I arrived Rouen transport & 4th Res. with Army no. Section II O.R. & O.R. Res. Cars brought up in cars & Rem. men used at L. Hop. Wri. All lorries went to our park near Gare de Regis. M.T. Res. & Pickup went to same park. Report made from 21.375. 8 & L & O. Officers Res. C. 3 men.	
	22nd		During the morning the Light Lorries proceeded on their run etc. during which up wounded loads at H.Q.T.D. etc. Lunch etc. on to Sommerville to bring mattress covers etc. Capt. Somerville A.D.M.S. arrived 2pm 3 to lorries sent on volunteered trip carrying stores to C.C.S. at Rouen.	
	23rd		During the morning an unusual trip for Pte. who was used as Section I en-(?) M. Lunch Party (A) Have Parts Amm. lorries to Rouencourt to pick up 10 tons Shrapnel in lorry to Rouen troops and big & 3 lorries took troops from us later to Yellow Lancers.	
	24th		During morning arrival of Section I had four trucks taken up from unit for carrying troops under O.C. T. Instructions.	

Army Form C. 2118.

WAR DIARY
or
INTELLIGENCE SUMMARY.
(Erase heading not required.)

Nov 1914 (Continued)

Place	Date	Hour	Summary of Events and Information	Remarks and references to Appendices
	25th		[illegible handwriting]	
	26th		[illegible handwriting]	
	27th		[illegible handwriting]	
	28th		[illegible handwriting]	
	29th		[illegible handwriting]	

Army Form C. 2118.

WAR DIARY
or
INTELLIGENCE SUMMARY.

(Erase heading not required.)

Instructions regarding War Diaries and Intelligence Summaries are contained in F. S. Regs., Part II. and the Staff Manual respectively. Title pages will be prepared in manuscript.

Place	Date	Hour	Summary of Events and Information	Remarks and references to Appendices
	3rd		Arrived at [illegible]	
	31st		Arrived. 31 Annuals used by [illegible]. [illegible] II [illegible] of [illegible] 4 a.m. 1 Am. 2 M.E. cycles to [illegible] 1 [illegible] bay [illegible] temporary [illegible]	

Army Form C. 2118.

Vol 55

3rd Cavalry Supply Column

WAR DIARY
or
INTELLIGENCE SUMMARY.
(Erase heading not required.)

Instructions regarding War Diaries and Intelligence Summaries are contained in F. S. Regs., Part II. and the Staff Manual respectively. Title pages will be prepared in manuscript.

Place	Date	Hour	Summary of Events and Information	Remarks and references to Appendices
PETRONNE J.19.Central Sheet 62 c	1-6-17	—	Section II at Cartier. Division feeding by Horse Trans: part was supp. French troops in double echelon of lorries. Railhead at Guiscard.	
	2-6-17	2.2	Lorries on extraneous duty.	
	3-6-17	2.3	Lorries on extraneous duty	
	4-6-17	3.0	Lorries on extraneous duty. Pte White died by A.D.C.M. a/c at Cas. Rec. Stn. 55 for self inflicted injury — i.e. tampering with German fuzy caps — inquest — Court of Inquiry held by Supply Division on Pte Cleghan's accidental wounds when Lyre Pz S Clark.	3. D. R.'s Cas. Supplies to establishment.
	5-6-17	2.3	Lorries on extraneous duty — Major Gardner represent from Lance — Lyre Pz S Clark. and Lieut N Coates to be Captains — date London Gazette 7/4-6-17	
	6-6-17	3.5	Lorries on extraneous duty.	
	7-6-17	2.5	Lorries on extraneous duty — Court of Inquiry held on Corpl Lucas No 84453 — struck by train at Excurine station as Senior Lorry trans conductor — Result: no blame. driver	
	8-6-17	3.2	Lorries on ex. Sp. to Gsd	
	9-6-17	2.0	Lorries on extr. spa. duty — 7 additional lorries used for carrying Horse rations up to Ruech Troops.	

2353 Wt. W2514/1454 700,000 5/15 L.D. & L. A.D.S.S./Forms/C. 2118.

Army Form C. 2118.

WAR DIARY
or
INTELLIGENCE SUMMARY.
(Erase heading not required.)

Instructions regarding War Diaries and Intelligence Summaries are contained in F.S. Regs., Part II. and the Staff Manual respectively. Title pages will be prepared in manuscript.

Place	Date	Hour	Summary of Events and Information	Remarks and references to Appendices
Abbeville	10-6-17		23 Lorries on Cav Corps Detail - 2 Lorries to AIRAINES - to be attached to 4th Cavy Div. Purchasing Officer.	
Tincourt	11-6-17 to 14-6-17		20 Lorries on Cav Corps detail daily.	
Querrieu	15-6-17		25 Lorries on extraneous duties. Section II move to AMIENS for work under Town Commdt, on completion of duty at Candas.	
	16-6-17 to 22-6-17		20 Lorries on extraneous duties daily.	
	22-6-17		23 Lorries on extraneous duty - 2 Lorries returned from Candas on completion of work with 4th Army	
	23-6-17 to 26-6-17		23 Lorries daily on Cav Corps detail.	
	27-6-17		34 Lorries on extraneous duties - One Halford Lorry (7159) evacuated to Paris.	
	28-6-17		30 Lorries on Cav Corps detail	
	29-6-17		30 Lorries on extraneous duties - Dennis lorry (7189) evacuated to Rouen.	
	30-6-17		29 Lorries on extraneous duty - Section II Refrain Column from AMIENS on completion of duty.	

H. A. Sanders
O.C. 3rd Cavalry Supply Column.

Army Form C. 2118.

WAR DIARY
or
INTELLIGENCE SUMMARY

3rd Cavalry Divisional Supply Column

July 1917.

Place	Date	Hour	Summary of Events and Information	Remarks and references to Appendices
PERONNE (T.19 Central) Sheet 62 c	1-7-17	—	Column at T.19 Central - Sheet 62 c - Railhead at Tincourt - Reinf. troops in single echelon of lorries - Section I - Section I. loads for Division from Depôt on front - 3 lorries on wait with reserve regime rations - also Supply Train from Peronne 2 three ton lorries (1 Leyland 1 Halford) joined Column from Car Corps Sup Column to replace casualties evacuated.	
	4th		Section II 3rd Cav. Div. Loaded at Tincourt and delivered to 6 & 8 Cav. Bdes. also C.D. Ammn in BRAY-SUZANNE area and returned to Column - 18 lorries (3 per section) also 2 lorries attached from 59th Division attached to 2nd Cav. Sup. Column for feeding Batteries left behind.	
	5th		Section I. left park by Brigades to repls Division in area no. 6th Cav. Bdes. - Suzanne - midday - 9th Bde - Suffgame - midday. ★ 8th Bde - Moricourt - 8 am - Ski Troops - Suzanne - midday. Also proceed to LA FLAQUE after decamping - Section II. loads at Tincourt for whole Division less Batteries. E Son Horse overseas munitions Drers marked with Lorries Go ye 16 4/2-6-17.	
	6		Section I. load at LA FLAQUE 6.30 a.m. - Section II. delivers to Division as follows:- area ? 6th Bde - TREUX - 9th - SUZANNE - 8th AMPLIER - Ski Troops - SUZANNE	

1577 Wt. W10791/1773 500,000 1/15 D. D. & L. A.D.S.S./Forms/C. 2118.

WAR DIARY or INTELLIGENCE SUMMARY

Army Form C. 2118.

(Erase heading not required.)

July 1917 Contd.

Place	Date	Hour	Summary of Events and Information	Remarks and references to Appendices
	4th		and proceed to new park at Regel. Hd Qrs and Workshops leave park 1-30 pm for new park (via Pernes and Olhain) at BOUQUEMAISON.	
	5th		Section I deliver to Division in area 6. 6th Bn at DR IVILLE - 7th HOILLY - 8th Bn ESTREE YAMIN - Div Troops - TREUX - and park, after dumping, at Bouquemaison.	
	6th		Section II load at ROSEL at 7 AM. Section II deliver - 6th Bn - ESTREE YAMIN - 7th AMPLIER - 8th VAUCHOUX - Div Troops - FRAMECOURT. and proceed to new park at BRUAY.	
	7th		Section II load at BRUAY - 2 PM. Section II deliver - 6th Bn - MARLES-LES-MINES - 7th Bn - ESTREE YAMIN - 8th Release Div Troops - PERNES. and proceed to new park at BRUAY. Hd Qrs and Workshops move to new park at BRUAY.	
	8th		Section II deliver to Division in area 6 - Div Troops - PERNES - 6th Bn - MARLES - 7th Bn - SAVY - 8th Bn - DIEVAL - Sect. I loads at BRUAY 2 PM. H reinforcements (artificers) from Base.	
	9th		Section I deliver in area 6, as previous day. Section II load at Bruay at 2.15 PM.	

WAR DIARY or INTELLIGENCE SUMMARY.

Army Form C. 2118.

(Erase heading not required.)

Instructions regarding War Diaries and Intelligence Summaries are contained in F.S. Regs., Part II and the Staff Manual respectively. Title pages will be prepared in manuscript.

Place	Date	Hour	Summary of Events and Information	Remarks and references to Appendices
Breny	10/17	—	Section II delivers in area, as preceding day and returned at Breny (cringt rehule) or 3 P.M.	
			Section I sent 30 lorries to Breno station to convey dismounted Battalion to unit, these	
			lorries with permission of section (Gen. 9 lorries left in Fd Pro and Battery lorries detached) proceed	
			to Masseoure for work under Hay Purchasing Board.	
	11/7/7	—	Section II delivers in morning and parked at Breny 2 P.M. Section I lorries detached on	
			parties — Fd Pro — Fd Pro or motorcars — 20 at Beauvais — 6 at Carbos — One workshop and one	
			Stores Lorry under Lieut Dasley joins Section I. Sect working under Central Purchase Board	
	12			
	13		Section II delivers and work as usual	
	14		Loading and delivery normal. Lorries detached with Batteries rejoin column.	
	15		Normal. One Halford 30 cwt lorry irrepairable.	
	16		Normal.	
	17		Section II leave park 7.15 A.M. to refill Fd s etc — Lui Loops — Buenos — 6th Bn —	
			Havrincourt — 7th Bn — Guarlus — 8th Bn — Thiennes — and proceed to Arce to unload.	
			Fd Pro and workshops move to Arce arriving 3 P.M.	

1577 Wt. W10791/1773 500,000 1/15 D. D. & L. A.D.S.S./Forms/C. 2118.

Army Form C. 2118.

WAR DIARY
or
INTELLIGENCE SUMMARY.

(Erase heading not required.)

Instructions regarding War Diaries and Intelligence Summaries are contained in F. S. Regs., Part II. and the Staff Manual respectively. Title pages will be prepared in manuscript.

Place	Date	Hour	Summary of Events and Information	Remarks and references to Appendices
Aire	18/2/17		Section II Lorries on same area and reload at Aire - 3 Lorries HQ Co ~~on Ry Stn~~ Railhead to Div troops at Quernes. 9 HQ Co Lorries on coal from Estrury and Fouquy to Divisions.	
	19		Section II Lorries and train as usual - 9 Section I Lorries sent from HQ Co to Repair Section II Lorries carrying reinforcements + lt. trucks in/between - (7 p.m. daily).	
	20		Normal - 5 reinforcements (MT drivers) received from base.	
	21		Normal - Lieut Stafford Earg (30 out) received from Cav Bgde troops Sup Col to Replace casualty.	
	22		Normal -	
	23		Normal - 4 Lieut Stafford transferred to MT Inspection Branch - G.H.Q. - Lieut Osbohurst appointed Workshops Officer - E Sgt Herbert to England for Cadet School (Tanks) Workshop School attached to Column. Nothing of for return.	
	24		Normal - 4 Lorries Section II Load client at Burquest and return to Div troops.	
	25		Normal -	
	26		Normal - Section I Supplied Columns from Aladin, picking up H4 Billy Cosno Sup Section a Bethune en route 5 and Salt battn - 1 Lorry Section II to Caestre to Sup Field Squadron.	
	27		Normal.	
	28		Normal - 10 reinforcements (MT drivers) received from base.	

1577 Wt.W10791/1773 500,000 1/15 D. D. & L. A.D.S.S./Forms/C. 2118.

Army Form C. 2118.

WAR DIARY
or
INTELLIGENCE SUMMARY.
(Erase heading not required.)

Instructions regarding War Diaries and Intelligence Summaries are contained in F. S. Regs., Part II. and the Staff Manual respectively. Title pages will be prepared in manuscript.

Place	Date	Hour	Summary of Events and Information	Remarks and references to Appendices
Aire	29/7		Normal.	
	30 "		Normal – Six reinforcements (M.T. drivers) from Rouen.	
	31 "		Normal.	

[signature]
Major
Commg 3rd Cavalry Supply Column

Army Form C. 2118.

WAR DIARY
or
INTELLIGENCE SUMMARY

(Erase heading not required.)

3rd Cavalry Supply Column

Place	Date	Hour	Summary of Events and Information	Remarks and references to Appendices
AIRE	1-8-17	—	Column and Railhead at AIRE: Division in BUSNES area — feeding by supply echelon 6th and 7th Brigades and Div Troops = Section II = 8th G.R. by H.T. = 42 Lorries Gap Ration proceeded to CROIX-DE-POPERINGHE and SCHAXKER to dump and returned to tank. — 12 Lorries Sect II and Pk Co to BRUAY for coal — delivered same to respective journey	
	2-8-17	—	Section II deliver as usual. — 6 Lorries Section I carry troops HAVERSKERQUE & LUTZ HEM Bruises 4 Lorries Section on short from BERGUETTE to ST FLORIS =	
	3-8-17	—	Section II load and deliver = 5 Lorries Section I to BETHUNE for wood — delivered to P. Res. and seven loads out at AIRE for Gap Ration dumps = 12 D.P.O (A.M.T and S.Supply) to Bhos and his Establishment.	
	4-8-17	—	Section II as usual — 15 Lorries Section I load wood at THIENNES and dump at Bhoir Est Bo.	
	5-8-17	—	Section II as usual — Section I mt/r from BOESEGHEM to AIRE	
	6-8-17	—	Section II normal — 5 Lorries Section I to CALLON-RICQUART for Baverie area & to BRUAY for Wheat earth at build dumage dump for R.S.D. AIRE.	
	7-8-17	—	Section II normal. 10 Lorries Section I to BRUAY for mine earth for dumpership of Railhead. 4 Lorries Section I load and deliver rations to R.H.G at BOESEGHEM.	
	8-8-17	—	Section II normal = 11 Lorries Section I to BRUAY and FERFAY for coal — delivering & ration to 12 later Journey — 2 Lorries Pk Co to work with following learn parties.	

Army Form C. 2118.

WAR DIARY
or
INTELLIGENCE SUMMARY.
(Erase heading not required.)

Instructions regarding War Diaries and Intelligence Summaries are contained in F. S. Regs. Part II. and the Staff Manual respectively. Title pages will be prepared in manuscript.

Place	Date	Hour	Summary of Events and Information	Remarks and references to Appendices
AIRE	9.8.17	—	Normal.	
	10.8.17	—	Section I normal. Section II load and deliver to 2 & 4 Bde on Rde Charging area to H.Q.M.F.W.-- ARTOIS - 10 Lorries Section I to BPUAY for rum cwt. for Rentiers, the remainder on 3 Fd Co. Lorries N. o. & Bu. for moving field etc.	
	11.8.17	—	Normal. At 3 a.m. an enemy plane anti-aircraft shell dropped in convoy at Lorry 7359 on Section II. Tears during air raid. Slight damage to lorry but no serious hits.	
	12.8.17	—	Normal delivery etc. 10 Lorries Section I to LILLERS for wood - dumped in Column Stores Park.	
	13.8.17	—	Normal - 10 Lorries Section I Bad wood at Fd Cos. and deliver at Brps water works.	
	14.8.17	—	Normal. Capt. Cumberledge to 2nd Anzac Corps on Argoubers to S.M.T.O. - 14 men attached for B.S. duties.	
			Railwar with R with local farmers - 1F lorries on Supply have demanded at Hesdigneul Fd Co Lorries on Supply train dumped at Blanre Fd Co by Sec'n I	
	15.8.17	—	Normal - 11 Lorries Section I to BPUAY for coal - delivered to events who govern. - 10 tons in all on Supply train dumped at Blanre Fd Co by Sec'n I	
	16.8.17	—	Normal.	
	17.8.17	—	Normal.	
	18.8.17	—	Normal - 9 cuts wood on Supply Train dumped at Col. Fd Co. by Sec'n I at Fd Co.	
	19.8.17	—	Normal - 18 bis wood on Supply Train dumped by Section I at Fd Co. 8 "	

Army Form C. 2118.

WAR DIARY
or
INTELLIGENCE SUMMARY.

(Erase heading not required.)

Instructions regarding War Diaries and Intelligence Summaries are contained in F. S. Regs., Part II. and the Staff Manual respectively. Title pages will be prepared in manuscript.

Place	Date	Hour	Summary of Events and Information	Remarks and references to Appendices
AIRE	20.8.17	-	Normal - 6 lorries Section I got wood from Supply train and delivered to 7th Dr Posts - 3rd Dn Col - Union D.A.O.B detachment under distinct instruction of the A.S.C - in exchange for 3 - (30 cwt) lorries	
	21.8.17	-	Normal - 20 lorries Section I proceeded to SCHAKKEN and issued one G.S Pattern decauville to another ham (reinforcement - Sheet 29. X. 5 - A. Central.) 1 Halford lorry received from Cemetery section in lieu of Establishment - no small lorries to Car Coys. Trops Supply Column as supplies.	
	22.8.17	-	Normal - 15 lorries Section I to BRUAY for coal - delivered to units in relation Journey -	
	23.8.17	-	Normal - 5 lorries Section I to BRUAY for ammunition for reinforced drainage dumps.	
	24.8.17	-	Normal - 10 lorries Section I to BRUAY for small arms ammunition for reinforced drainage dumps - 9 lorries Section I to CAMERTINGHE and 10 relief for division Col Coy - 8th Dn Rel.	
	25.8.17	-	Normal - 10 lorries to ELVERDINGHE with relief for ammunition Coy of 9th Rel.	
	26.8.17	-	Normal. 10 lorries to VLAMERTINGHE with relief for ammunition Coy of 9th Rel	
	27.8.17	-	Normal - Order received to dispatch 53 "Category A" men to 1st Base m-Sycbn. Establishment of above drivers reduced to 15% - numbers to be completed by 31st - Also Laclet (Drivers journeyoff (Reserve for Infantry Brigade a/c)	
	28.8.17	-	Normal - 2nd Regt (30 men) to B-m-T Sycbn	
	29.8.17	-	Normal - 3rd Regt (3 men) to B-m-T Sycbn	

Army Form C. 2118.

WAR DIARY
or
INTELLIGENCE SUMMARY.
(Erase heading not required.)

Instructions regarding War Diaries and Intelligence Summaries are contained in F. S. Regs, Part II. and the Staff Manual respectively. Title pages will be prepared in manuscript.

Place	Date	Hour	Summary of Events and Information	Remarks and references to Appendices
AIRE	30-8-17	–	Normal – Remaining coys of 6 men to D.M.T. Depot	
	31-8-17	–	Normal –	
			During the month – frequent air raids took place – mostly on Dock and Station. Several bombs fell in the town.	

A. Ford A.S.C.
A/Comm. A.S.C.
Comdg. 3rd Cavalry Supply Column

1577 Wt. W10791/1773 500,000 1/15 D. D. & L. A.D.S.S./Forms/C. 2118.

Army Form C. 2118.

WAR DIARY
INTELLIGENCE SUMMARY.

(Erase heading not required.)

3rd Cavalry Supply Column September 1917

Place	Date	Hour	Summary of Events and Information	Remarks and references to Appendices
	1/9/17		Column Y billeted at AIRE. To warm feeding as under. YR Bde - Civile echelon. 8th Bde. 4 H.T. direct from Railhead. 2 3-ton Civilin detached to 5th Bde. Supa Supply Column to Ypd. C. & T.G. Batteries.	
	2/9/17		Normal feeding arrangements. 5 Lorries Sec. I to CRUISETTE to bring back troops from shoe them.	
	3/9/17		Normal. 9 Lorries Sec. I to BRUAY for coal, delivered to Bdes. on return.	
	4/9/17		Normal. Farriery detachment (11 men) rejoined column.	
	5/9/17		Normal. 10 Lorries Sec. I to BERGUETTE for straw - delivered to YR Bde.	
	6/9/17		Normal.	
	7/9/17		Normal.	
	8/9/17		Normal. 9 Lorries Sec. I to BRUAY for coal, delivered to units on return. Y Lorries Section I take wood to YR Bde.	
	9/9/17		Normal.	
	10/9/17		Normal.	
	11/9/17		Normal. 5 Lorries Section I to BRUAY for coal, delivered to units on return.	
	12/9/17		Normal.	
	13/9/17		Normal.	

Army Form C. 2118.

WAR DIARY
INTELLIGENCE SUMMARY
(Erase heading not required.)

3rd Cavalry Supply Column   September 1917

Place	Date	Hour	Summary of Events and Information	Remarks and references to Appendices
	16/9/17		Normal. Establishment reduced (under authy. Q.M.G. letter no 6699, 24/9/17) by 1 car & 2 motor cycle. One motor cycle to Res. Vehicle Park, ST. OMER, one returned to replace casualty. One to U.K. Army Troops Supply Coln.	
	15/9/17		Normal. 4 lorries to BRUAY for coal. 2 lorries to WESTOUTRE to work under Field Sqn. (to super'de 10/k to U.K. Cav. Sup. Coln) for work under 4th Cav. Field Sqn.	
	16/9/17		Normal. 16 lorries to U.K. Cav. Sup. Coln. at MONS-EN-CHAUSSÉE for work under 4th Cav. Fd. Sqn. Major Luithlen & Capt. Black to England on leave. Command resumed by Capt. R.C. Bentley.	
	17/9/17		Normal. 4 reinforcements (M.T. Drivers) received from Base.	
	18/9/17		Normal.	
	19/9/17		Normal. Capt. R.C. Bentley to England on leave. Command resumed by Capt. W. Coate.	
	20/9/17		Normal.	
	21/9/17		Normal.	
	22/9/17		Normal. 10 lorries to BRUAY for coal.	
	23/9/17		Normal.	
	24/9/17		Normal.	
	25/9/17		Normal.	

Army Form C. 2118.

WAR DIARY
INTELLIGENCE SUMMARY

(Erase heading not required.)

3rd Cavalry Supply Column September 1917

Place	Date	Hour	Summary of Events and Information	Remarks and references to Appendices
	26/9/17	Normal	1st Fld Amm to detachment at 4th Cav. Fld. Bak. from 5 hours at field Ruilled	
	27/9/17	Normal	Major Gordon assumed Command on Majoring from leave.	
	28/9/17	Normal		
	29/9/17	Normal		
	30/9/17	Normal		

MAJOR, A.S.C.,
3rd CAVALRY SUPPLY COLUMN.

Army Form C. 2118

3rd Cavalry Supply Column

Page 1.

October 1917

WAR DIARY
or
INTELLIGENCE SUMMARY

(Erase heading not required.)

Instructions regarding War Diaries and Intelligence Summaries are contained in F. S. Regs., Part II. and the Staff Manual respectively. Title Pages will be prepared in manuscript.

WO 95 / 37

Place	Date	Hour	Summary of Events and Information	Remarks and references to Appendices
AIRE	1. Oct.		Column detrained at AIRE. Division in BUSNES area. Loading & delivery of rations as follows:- 6th Brigade single echelon; 7th Brigade - Double echelon; 8th Brigade three transport drawing direct from Railhead; Divisional Troops rail & echelon. 26 Lorries used for Coal most issues to Division.	
	3rd Oct.		20 Supply Lorries transferred to "O" Corps Troops Supply Column on reduction of establishment under authority Q.M.G letter (Q.A.I.) 1/27:4:17.	
	5th		21 Lorries with one Officer and 6 O.R.s rejoined from detachment with 4th Cavalry Supply Column. 11 Lorries load Coal at AIRE & convey to HAUTE VISSÉE (S. 20; 9 cwts.)	
	6th		10 Lorries load wood at AIRE convey to 5th Ration Dump at SCHAKKEN and proceed to DICKEBUSCH for two days duty with 3rd Field Squadron	
	7th		4 Lorries load wood at AIRE & deliver to S.O. Divisional Troops at BUSNES.	

Army Form C. 2118

Page 2
October 1917

WAR DIARY
or
INTELLIGENCE SUMMARY
(Erase heading not required.)

Place	Date	Hour	Summary of Events and Information	Remarks and references to Appendices
AIRE	Oct 8th		20 Lorries detailed for work under Camp Commandant - Cavalry Corps (also to POPERINGHE)	
	9th		5 Lorries after dumping 7th Brigade rations load coal at BRUAY + deliver to 6th + 7th Brigades	
			8th Brigade supplies load + deliver by lorry (simple return)	
			10 Lorries detailed for duty into Cavalry Corps	
	10th		7th Brigade moved to MERVILLE area - Rations delivered to new area 4.0 p.m.	
			11 Lorries load coal at BRUAY + deliver to 8th Brigade.	
	12th		10 Lorries to SCHAKKEN to work for Jambe to CROIX-DE-POPERINGHE + lorries load work at AIRE + deliver to 6th Brigade.	
	14th		43 Lorries moved to fetch Ration Jambe at CROIX-DE-POPERINGHE load all Rations + return to AIRE	
	15th		Wolseley Car 14857 (S.O.C. 8th Brigade) evacuated replaced by Wolseley 9041	
			7 Lorries load coal at BRUAY + deliver on Colenso Park.	

Army Form C. 2118

Page 3.
October 1917

WAR DIARY
or
INTELLIGENCE SUMMARY
(Erase heading not required.)

Place	Date	Hour	Summary of Events and Information	Remarks and references to Appendices
AIRE	16th		10 Lorries to BRUAY for CorC & dumps on Column Park	
	17th		7 Lorries detailed for Cavalry Corps for work at POPERINGHE & PERONNE areas	
	18th		Supplies of 6th Brigade delivered in PERNES area.	
	19th		Two lorries return from Cavalry Corps.	
	20th		Fifteen lorries report from Cavalry Corps — Loading 7th & 8th Brigades double echelon — 6th Brigade Divisional Troops single echelon. 6th Brigade & Divisional Troops in PERNES area — 7th Brigade MERVILLE area. 8th Brigade - ROBECQ area.	
	21st		Supplies delivered to Brigades in following area - 6th & 6th TREVENT - 7th MERVILLE Divisional Troops - PERNES area.	
	22nd		Railhead at TREVENT - 6th Brigade Divisional Troops on single echelon - 7th & 8th Brigades double echelon - 6th & 8th Brigades Divisional Troops in CANAPLES area - 7th Brigade in PERNES area. Column Head Quarters Workshops move to BERNAVILLE.	

Army Form C. 2118.

Page 4.
October 1917

WAR DIARY
or
INTELLIGENCE SUMMARY
(Erase heading not required.)

Place	Date	Hour	Summary of Events and Information	Remarks and references to Appendices
BERNAVILLE	Oct 22nd		Reviewed at CANDAS. — 3rd Cavalry Divisional Ammunition Park (less Headquarters) consisting of 2 cars — 5 cycles — 26 - 3 Ton Albion Lorries with 2 Officers — 96 ORs join Column under authority Cavalry Corps "Q" Letter No. Q/2888 d/28-9-7. Section III after dumping, park at BERNAVILLE — See I remain parked at FREVENT.	
	23rd		7th & 8th Brigades in double echelon. — 6th Brigade & Divisional Troops on 24th echelon. Supplies delivered as follows:- 6th Brigade in RIBEAUCOURT area, 7th & 8th Brigades in FREVENT area & Divisional Troops at DOMART. LCAMPS unpacked. See I joined rest of Column at BERNAVILLE	
	24th		Loading at CANDAS & supplies delivered as follows:- 6th Brigade at LONGPRE area 7th Brigade - RIBEAUCOURT area — 8th Brigade VIGNACOURT area — Divisional Troops - DOMART.	
	25th		Supplies delivered as on the 24th — 50 Lorries to RiouLLuent to load 100 tons of Coal — 30 tons delivered to each Brigade — remainder dumped in Column park	

Army Form C. 2118.

Page 5
October 1916

WAR DIARY
or
INTELLIGENCE SUMMARY.

(Erase heading not required.)

Place	Date	Hour	Summary of Events and Information	Remarks and references to Appendices
BERNAVILLE	Oct 27th		See II wire 68 lorries, one Workshop and 2 Gastong unit 2 Officers and 91 O.Rs to LE MESNIL to prepare & carry out tasks. Took up 1,000 men at Brigade H.Q. & convey same to DOINGT.	
	29th		6th Brigade took on double echelon — 7th Brigade took by Motor transport from Railhead Lor 'K' Battery and trailers from 6th Brigade also loaned by Motor transport less R.H.G. Maxims from Brigade H.Q. 5 reinforcements (London) arrived from Base (H.T.) depot.	
	30th		Loading & delivery as before	
	31st		Hartford Lorry (30 cwt) No. 100449 evacuated to 1st A.S.C. Repair Shop, Paris	

MAJOR, A.S.C.,
3rd CAVALRY SUPPLY COLUMN.

WAR DIARY
of
INTELLIGENCE SUMMARY

Army Form C. 2118

Diary for month of NOVEMBER 1917

3rd CAV. SUPPLY COL.

PAGE 1.

WO 38

Place	Date	Hour	Summary of Events and Information	Remarks and references to Appendices
BERNAVILLE	Nov. 1.		Headquarters of Column, Section I & motor lorries at BERNAVILLE. Nos. II at LE MESNIL. Reached CANDAS. 6th Arrived for an chaser relation - DUNC & LONGPRÉ each. 7 & 8 Arrived for an single relation - 20 Lorries took fuel at Railhead and dumps on Colunin Park.	
	2.		Loaded & Refuen as on 1st - Mametz - 5 lorries with fuel to DOMART.	
	3.		Four 3 Ton lorries detailed for work with O.R.E. Cavalry Corps.	
	5.		9 Lorries to R.E. Dump BRAY. 15 tons of tents & country camps to Infantry, returned - CADOURS.	
	7		Loaded & Refuen as on 1st inst; 20 Lorries loaded coal at HAUTEVILLE - country dumps to DOMART.	
	8		12 Lorries loaded Coal & country to Brigade Units.	
	10		One Officer & 73 O.R. with 26 lorries with 30 tons Coal & 20 tons Wood to LA FLAQUE. Lorries returned to division at LA FLAQUE for work under direction of R.S.O.	
	12		Battens went out test in following places MQ {VIGNACOURT K {FLESSELLES. Lorries returned Army CAS A.D.S.S./Forms/C. 2118. G. Boat. BOURDON ÷} for fitting under A/C Campbell.	

WAR DIARY
INTELLIGENCE SUMMARY

(Erase heading not required.)

Army Form C. 2118

NOVEMBER 1917   PAGE 2.   3rd Cav. Supply Col.

Place	Date	Hour	Summary of Events and Information	Remarks and references to Appendices
BERNAVILLE	Nov. 13		2/13 Completed attachment for feeding 6 & 7th Brigade R.H.A. / owed by around relation from LA PLAQUE detachment at CORBIE. Detachments troops at CORBIE from 1st Cav. Div., feed and returns in CORBIE area.	
	14		Left for R.H.A. Brigade at LA CHAPELETTE from 5th Cav. Div.; feed and delivered to them in ALLAINESSON.	
	15		25 Lorries, Section II, carrying Divn. of Pioneer Battalion to their billets in DOMART area from LE MESNIL and returned to BERNAVILLE. Section II returned from LE MESNIL to BERNAVILLE.	
	16		6th Brigade lorries refueled — transport & refreshen for 7th Brigade. 6 lorries carried up Ketmark from 6th & 7th Brigade to VIGNACOURT. (chainmail) Sec II met to CORBIE.	
	17.		Division took in the following areas:— 6th & 7th Brigade in new area CONTAY. 8th Brigade & Divisional troops — DOMART area. Section II Ammy. marched into supplementing area — 6th Brigade — SUZANNE. 7th Brigade TROYART. 8th Brigade BRAY. Section I trains at CORBIE. Section II park at HARBONNIERE. Ammunition Park at ETINEHEM to carry out a special programme.	

WAR DIARY
INTELLIGENCE SUMMARY
(Erase heading not required.)

NOVEMBER 1917   Army Form C. 2118
PAGE 3.   3rd Cav. Supply Col.

Place	Date	Hour	Summary of Events and Information	Remarks and references to Appendices
HARBONNIERES	Nov 18.		Relieved LA FLAQUE – Division fell in reserve.	
	19.		Headquarters workshops went to HARBONNIERES. Ammunition section to QUINCONCE forest. Ammunition returned to ETINEHEM. O/C W. Turner Cran to be attached troops to 6th Cavalry Brigade.	
RANCOURT	20th		Division fell in concentrated area – Column marched to RANCOURT on the LE TRANSLOY BOUCHAVESNES Road. (Forward area)	
	21.		Division located at west Railhead ROCQUINY.	
ACHEUX	23		Action III after fording, Division in the following order proceeded to the Park at ACHEUX. Division. BEAUQUESNE – 6th Brigade TALMAS and 7th Brigade BEAUCOURT – 8th Brigade VILLERS BOCAGE area.	
	24		Lorries at west Railhead "BELLE EGLISE" – Action I after opening proceeded to ACHEUX. Horses out of Column.	
			Column at ACHEUX for new 24 hours & then moved – landing at our Railhead to pick up Brigades in 3 and areas.	
	30.		Lorries sent to ROISEL on detachment detachment unit I unwounded until returned army supply – orders received being cancelled.	

J. Jacoby
O.C. 3 Cav. Sup. Col.

Army Form C. 2118.

3rd Cavalry Supply Col:

WAR DIARY
or
INTELLIGENCE SUMMARY. December 1917.

(Erase heading not required.)

9/R/39

Place	Date	Hour	Summary of Events and Information	Remarks and references to Appendices
ACHEUX	Dec 1.		Column at ACHEUX - Railhead BELLE EGLISE. Brigade fed in following areas:- 6th Brigade. TALMAS - 7th Brigade. BEAUCOURT - 8th Brigade - VILLERS BOCAGE. At 3.15 a.m. 6 lorries loaded 4,800 Iron Rations issued (two to each Brigade) to join other lorries taking Divisional Troops to forward area at 5.30 a.m. Lorries remain on detachment in forward area.	
	2.		Landed a refilled Division - 8th Brigade in new area - BELLOY & PICQUIGNY. Divisional Troops - CORBIE.	
	3 & 5.		Landed & refilled Division. One N.C.O. & 3 O.R. (supply) to SALEUX Corps dump (3rd) 7 lorries & 3rd Cav. Div. Divisional Brigade Detachment. (3rd)	
	6th.		Sec. I & II to new Park at LANEUVILLE - Railhead CORBIE - Headquarters & others remain at ACHEUX until 8th instant.	
CORBIE	9.		6th Brigade landed in bulk - except 10th Hussars & 8th machine gun - 6th Brigade landed - 7th Brigade by Iron Knockout with the exception of 2nd Life Guards [illegible]	

1577 Wt. W10791/1773 500,000 1/15 D.D.&L. A.D.S.S./Forms/C. 2118.

WAR DIARY
or
INTELLIGENCE SUMMARY
(Erase heading not required.)

Army Form C. 2118

December 1917

Place	Date	Hour	Summary of Events and Information	Remarks and references to Appendices
CORBIE	Dec 10.		Loading & refitting as on 9th.	
	11		7 O.R.(supply) to 4th Brigade R.H.A. Detachment.	
	12		Two Lorries to LIGNY-ST-FLOCHEL - took up Corps thresh wastage & driven to ROISEL.	
	14		6 Lorries from 4th Brigade R.H.A. Detachment return to Column.	
	17		9 Animal Lorries - 6th Brigade & 6th Brigade Loaded - 6th Brigade in Park & 6th Brigade by Regimental.	
			Lorries of 8th Brigade proceeded to dump at mid-hort in the morning but were unable to proceed far on the road owing to snow drifts. These lorries were held up all night and were unable to deliver supplies accordingly. 2 Lorries with supplies for 2nd Lt from 3s met with a similar experience but continued put through to the Regiment by the early morning of the 18th.	
	18		Supplies loaded by Dec I on 17th remain in Park with the exception of Divl. Motor delivered in Lorries wastage and conditions making this imperative.	
	19		Lorries with 6th Brigade Rations which left Park on 17th evening put through + the supper supplies in the afternoon. Dec I Lorries loaded for 8th Brigade on 18th also dumped.	

Army Form C. 2118

WAR DIARY
or
INTELLIGENCE SUMMARY
(Erase heading not required.)

December 1917

Place	Date	Hour	Summary of Events and Information	Remarks and references to Appendices
CORBIE	Dec. 20		Loaded & dumped for 6th Brigade & Divisional Troops mg.	
	21		Loaded dumped 8th Brigade Supplies & loaded for 6th, 7th & Div. Troops. See 1-II to refuel at CANAPLES-HALLOY-PERNOIS.	
HALLOY	22		Statcenlier moves to join 1st of Column, leaving workshops at CORBIE. Brigades for in following sub areas 6th Brigade AILLY-L-HAUT.; 7th Brigade-RIBEAUCOURT & 8th Brigade-VIGNACOURT. Divisional Troops-DOMART. New Railhead CANDAS.	
	23		Formed 6th Brigade in bulk - 7th & 8th by units.	
	24		5 lorries to DOULLENS for Coal-remainder to units. 3 lorries to BRUSLE for stores.	
	25		6th, 7th & 8th Brigades loaded & refueled.	
	26		Same loading & dumping as on 25th.	
	27		6th Brigade & 2nd Lift Grats on night station. 4 lorries to Divisional School to meet same from DAOURS-to BERNAVILLE.	

Army Form C. 2118

WAR DIARY
or
INTELLIGENCE SUMMARY
(Erase heading not required.)

December 1917

Instructions regarding War Diaries and Intelligence Summaries are contained in F. S. Regs., Part II. and the Staff Manual respectively. Title Pages will be prepared in manuscript.

Place	Date	Hour	Summary of Events and Information	Remarks and references to Appendices
HALLOY	Dec 28		Loading & delivering as on 27th. 14 lorries loaned today in addition to 7th Brigade lorries at RIBEAUCOURT in connection with Plans Scheme. All lorries experience great difficulty on the roads owing to drifting snow.	
	29th		Same loading & delivering as on 28th & also for the rest of the month. The month was estimable for the extreme winter conditions. The difficulties resulting from the same for mechanical transport work in several occasions during the month. Lorries were held up by snow drifts for many hours. Frost precautions have been rigidly adhered to, with from recent there being no frost casualties during the month to cylinder heads, blocks etc. The extra work dispatch with the hardships experienced in the snow was cheerfully borne by the men & C.O. heart, on several occasions shown marked initiative in the work.	

Army Form C. 2118

WAR DIARY
or
INTELLIGENCE SUMMARY
(Erase heading not required.)

Page 1. 3rd Cavalry Supply Column.
January 1918.

Place	Date	Hour	Summary of Events and Information	Remarks and references to Appendices
HALLOY.	1918. Jan 1.		Headquarters & Section 2. of Column at HALLOY, Section 1. at PERNOIS, workshops at CANAPLES. 6th Brigade fed on single echelon — other Brigades being fed by Home transport. 9 Lorries to CORBIE to move R.S.O's dump to CANONS Railhead.	
	2.		Loaded & refilled 6th Brigade — 50 Tons of Coal from BELLE EGLISE. The remainder of R.S.O's dump at CORBIE moved to CANDAS.	
	3		6th Brigade fed as on 1st & 2nd instant — 6 Lorries to move dismounted men of 2nd Life Guards from SIGRATIEN to RISEAUCOURT.	
	4		Normal — 3 Lorries to 2nd Life Guards for the same purpose as on 3rd instant. 2/Lieut Bardon promoted Lieutenant (vending of London Gazette)	
	5		Normal as far as feeding Division i.e. 6th Brigade only.	— 3 Lorries with bread to 6th Brigade.
	6		Normal.	" " " " 7 lorries with food to 7th Spare Sqn Transport
	7		Normal.	
	8		14 Lorries with food to 6th, 7th & 8th Brigade.	
	9		Normal — fed 6th Brigade + 3 lorries with bread to 7th Brigade	
	10		Normal " " " " "	— 3 Lorries with bread to 6th Brigade. 7 Lorries with food to 7th Spare Div Troops.
			2/Lt T. O. Bone promoted Lieutenant. (vending of London Gazette)	— 3 Lorries with food to DOMART.

J.C. McAuley Major,
for 3rd CAVALRY SUPPLY COLUMN.
on duty

MAJOR, A.S.C.,
3rd CAVALRY SUPPLY COLUMN.

Army Form C. 2118

JANUARY 1916

Page 2.

3rd Cavalry Supply Column.

WAR DIARY
or
INTELLIGENCE SUMMARY
(Erase heading not required.)

Place	Date	Hour	Summary of Events and Information	Remarks and references to Appendices
HALLOY	JAN. 11.		Thaw precautions Cant. into operation at 6.0. p.m. All lorries off road in consequence. Supply details to CANDAS	
	12 13		Thaw precautions remain in operation.	
	14.		Thaw precautions relaxed — 6th Brigade loaded & refilled — Lorries deliver one days hay rants to replenish Train dump of Brigades. 35 Lorries to VIGNACOURT to pick up Officers men arriving by train from Grannulier Division, and take them to billets.	
	15.		50 Lorries to LONGPRE for same service as on 14th 6th Brigade fed — One days hay rants to 6th Brigade in addition to replenish Train dumps.	
	16		Thaw precautions again in operation	
	17 18		Thaw precautions remain in operation.	
	19.		Thaw precautions relaxed — 6th Brigade loaded & refilled. 6th Brigade also one days hay rants, the whole to be dumped at LA FOLIE cross rds. Captain [?]ithout [?] ceased to be attached as transpt. to C.F.A.	

A.B. [signature]
Major, A.S.C.
3rd CAVALRY SUPPLY COLUMN.

Army Form C. 2118

Page 3.
3rd Cavalry Supply Column
January 1915.

WAR DIARY
or
INTELLIGENCE SUMMARY
(Erase heading not required.)

Place	Date	Hour	Summary of Events and Information	Remarks and references to Appendices
HALLOY.	JAN. 20.		No change in Column.	
	21.		Loaded & despatched 6th Brigade – Two lorries detached to find Australian Corps Cavalry attached to 6th Brigade – 28 lorries with food to Brigade.	
	22.		Turned in 6th Brigade Fm.	
	23.		ditto ditto. 3 lorries for work with Army Commandant VIGNACOURT. Lorries from 4th Brigade R.H.A. return to Column.	
	24.		Loaded – 5 lorries with food to 6th & 8th Brigades – 15 lorries to move coal truck from Rachel to Column Park.	
	25.		6th & 8th Brigade Divisional Trains on double echelon.	
	26.		Refilled 6th & 8th Brigades in present area – Divisional Trains – Lorries for Royal Horse Guards – and 6th & 8th Bgds – Div. Trains.	
	27.		Refilled 8th Brigade in PROYART area – also Reserve Park – Refilled 6th Brigade in present area, also Divisional Train. Lorries returned for Royal Horse Guards – lorries for 6th & 8th Bgde Div. Train. ½ C.S.C. Cav. Joins as Supply Officer from H.Qrs. A.S.C.	
	28.		Refilled 6th Brigade in MERCOURT area – also 6th Brigade Div. Train – also lorries for Div. Train.	

J. R. Newton
for MAJOR A.S.C.
3rd CAVALRY SUPPLY COLUMN

Army Form C. 2118

WAR DIARY or INTELLIGENCE SUMMARY
(Erase heading not required.)

Cav. 4.
3rd Cavalry Supply Column.
January 1915.

Place	Date	Hour	Summary of Events and Information	Remarks and references to Appendices
HALLOY.	Jan 29		Refilled 6th Brigade in TROYART area - also 6th Brigade in reserve. Lorries & Reserve Royal transports. Lorries for 6th & 7th Brigade divisional trains. 6th Brigade Lorries after refilling at TROYART area, picked up 12 Tons of Coal & 12 Tons of Wood from 5th Cav: Div: dump at LA CHAPELLETTE & delivered same to 8th Brigade Section 1 & 2. to no back at ESTREES-EN-CHAUSSEE.	
ESTREES-EN-CHAUSSEE.	30.		Movements of Column - 6th Brigade refilled at TETRY - Divi: trmsps at MONCHY LEGACHE. 7th Brigade at VIGNACOURT - 10 Lorries refilled 7th Brigade trmsps & RIBEAUCOURT/which took it 2 W.ks firewood & tarpaulin dumps to TREFCON. Lorries at work Railhead LA CHAPELLETTE for 6th Brigade Divi: trmsps & it in 8th Brigade.	
	31.		Refilled 6th Brigade in TETRY area - 7th Brigade in TROYART area - 7th Brigade Lorries drew 12 Tons of Coal & 12 Tons of Wood from 5th Cav: Div: dump. LA CHAPELLETTE & delivered to 6th Brigade TETRY area - also 10 Tons of fuel to S.O. Divi: trmsps at MONCHY LEGACHE.	

N.R. Ilmsley Capt.
for
MAJOR, A.S.C.,
3rd CAVALRY SUPPLY COLUMN.
On duty.

WAR DIARY or INTELLIGENCE SUMMARY

Army Form C. 2118

PAGE. 1.
3rd Cavalry Supply Column
February 1918.

Place	Date	Hour	Summary of Events and Information	Remarks and references to Appendices
ESTREES-EN-CHAUSSÉE	Feb 1.		The Column at ESTREES-EN-CHAUSSÉE – RAILHEAD LA CHAPPELLETTE – Loaded and fed 6th & 8th Brigade Divisional Troops. Loaded 7th Brigade in bulk. The following units attached for feeding purposes – 3rd Labour Company, 311th Brigade R.F.A., 313th Road Construction Company, 48th Ottawa Tabular Workshop, 17th Brigade R.H.A. Ammunition Column & Canadian Ammunition Column and most details. 6 lorries took fuel to Hdqrs. to MONCHY. LAGACHE.	
	2		Repeat 7th Brigade traded on 1st instant – Brigade Divisional Troops on 2nd instant. Loaded 24 tons of feed at Railhead & delivered to 7th Brigade. Lorry No. T7296 evacuated. 4 lorries after refilling 7th Brigade picked up R.E. stores at TERTRY and sent to FOURQUES delivered to BRIG.	
	3		Loading & delivering – normal. 5 lorries to BERNAVILLE to move turnouts of Divisional school 16 DAOURS. Lorry T 7296 evacuated.	
	4		Normal – Captain R.P. Clark struck off strength of Column on assuming command 3rd Cavalry Corps Troops Supply Column.	
	5			
	6		Normal – Lt. C.S. Crockard to be attached on being evacuated to Hospital. Lorry T5111 sent as a refusement.	W.

Army Form C. 2118

WAR DIARY
or
INTELLIGENCE SUMMARY
(Erase heading not required.)

Cap. 2.

3rd Cavalry Supply Column.
February 1916.

Place	Date	Hour	Summary of Events and Information	Remarks and references to Appendices
ESTREÉS-EN-CHAUSSÉE	Feb 7.		Supplies for Division loaded as usual & despatched at usual hour by Barsimer at usual point east of ESTREÉS-EN-CHAUSSÉE. Coal dump at Roiglise to be moved to Column Park - all available lorries to Roisel to move same. Daimler Lorry No. T2180, sent as replacement.	
	8.		Division fed as on 7th - 5 lorries sent from Roiglise to Column Park	
	9.		Corbie - 20 lorries for Corps to Railhead & to dump same on Column Park.	
	10.		Corbie - Six lorries to AMIENS for Bran & Forage for Horses. The following lorries evacuated T7114, 5658, 3084, 6558, 6581, 6640, 3461, 6583. Lorry T13025 (Daimler) sent as replacement.	
	11.		Corbie.	
	12.		Corbie - Lorry T9902 evacuated. N.	

Instructions regarding War Diaries and Intelligence Summaries are contained in F.S. Regs., Part II. and the Staff Manual respectively. Title Pages will be prepared in manuscript.

Army Form C. 2118

WAR DIARY of INTELLIGENCE SUMMARY

(Erase heading not required.)

Page 3.
3rd Cavalry Supply Column.
February 1918.

Place	Date	Hour	Summary of Events and Information	Remarks and references to Appendices
ESTRÉES-EN-CHAUSSÉE	Feb. 13		Division fed as usual with exception of 6th Brigade. - The Brigade remained at Thoix & Athies. 4 Athies lorries with G.O.R's transferred from Ammunition Section to 1st Cavalry Ammunition Park.	
	14		Normal - First lorries load at Railhead for 6th Brigade delivered on 15th. Lorry No. T.35631 evacuated. & the following lorries sent as replacements T.4356, 4255, 7155 (Athies) 3 Lorries to carry out Cavalry Corps detail. 1 Albion lorry from Amm. Sec. to 1st Cav. Amm. Park.	
	15		Normal - 3 lorries on Cavalry Corps detail.	
	16		Normal. Laundry service started for Division - one lorry to Athies for picking up soiled clothes from Brigades & returning with clean the next day. One lorry to rail & unit.	
	17		Normal - 4 lorries on Cavalry Corps detail. One Daimler T.7306 evacuated.	
	18		Car loading & delivery of supplies taken over by Reserve Park except supply column & local units. 20 lorries to Railhead for Coal. 15 Column duty. Two Reservists from detachment into Dismounted Division.	
	19		3rd Lorries on Cavalry Corps detail - 2/C R.W.F. Saddler/driver from M.T. School of Instruction posted to Ammunition Section. N.	

Army Form C. 2118

WAR DIARY
or
INTELLIGENCE SUMMARY
(Erase heading not required.)

Army Page 4.

3rd Cavalry Supply Column
February 1918

Place	Date	Hour	Summary of Events and Information	Remarks and references to Appendices
ESTREÉS-EN-CHAUSSÉE	Feb. 20		17 Lorries on Cavalry Corps detail.	
	21		Two Columns in operation – no lorries on the road.	
	22		10 Lorries with Meat &c to ATHIES – unit spares proceeding to Chaulnes Station.	
	23.		Three Columns in operation – 7 lorries with Meat to G. FLEZ.	
	24.		15 Lorries to Railhead for Coal for Column Supply.	
	25.		The following Albion Lorries sent as replacements T.44424, 41425, 41427, 30517, 30521, 30525. 17 lorries on Cavalry Corps detail.	
	26} 27} 28}		Three – Lorries detailed each day for Cavalry Corps.	

Monro Capt.
O.C. 3rd Cavalry Supply Column

Army Form C. 2118.

3RD CAVALRY M.T. COMPANY.

WAR DIARY
INTELLIGENCE SUMMARY

March 1918

(Erase heading not required.)

Instructions regarding War Diaries and Intelligence Summaries are contained in F. S. Regs., Part II. and the Staff Manual respectively. Title pages will be prepared in manuscript.

Place	Date	Hour	Summary of Events and Information	Remarks and references to Appendices
ESTREES-EN-CHAUSSÉE	1 to 11		Column at ESTREES-EN-CHAUSSÉE. Division fed by H.T. Column coming direct under Cav. Corps. for detail.	
	2 to 11		Normal. Cavalry Corps detail on an average 30 – 40 lorries each day. Column came under 19th Corps for detail	
	12		Reorganization of Company takes place, personnel not up to establishment Arrangements made to evacuate surplus lorries and personnel.	
	15		The following lorries and personnel evacuated to 33rd. Auxiliary M.T. Company. 33 – 30 cwt lorries 1 Workshop 1 Store 44 Drivers and 10 Artificers	
	16		33 – 30 cwt lorries 1 Workshop 1 Store lorry 3 Cars 5 Motor-Cycles 47 Drivers 10 Artificers Evacuated to 33rd. Auxiliary M.T. Company.	
	17		Company moved to MONS-EN-CHAUSSÉE.	

Army Form C. 2118.

WAR DIARY
of
INTELLIGENCE SUMMARY

3RD CAVALRY M.T. COMPANY.

March 1918

Page 2

Instructions regarding War Diaries and Intelligence Summaries are contained in F.S. Regs., Part II. and the Staff Manual respectively. Title pages will be prepared in manuscript.

(Erase heading not required.)

Place	Date	Hour	Summary of Events and Information	Remarks and references to Appendices
18.3.18. MONS-EN-CHAUSSÉE			O.C. returns from leave.	
	19th 20th 21st.	4.30 am.	Terrific drum fire heard all along front. MONS & ESTREES shelled intermittently during day. Most of the shells fell on the Flying ground between these two villages.	
		4.30 pm.	Instructions received from O.C. A.S.C. to be ready to move that night at instant notice.	
		4.35 pm.	Instructions received from O.C. A.S.C. that Column would not move until 23rd. Stragglers from VERMAND begin to arrive at the Camp. Arrange with Divisional Headquarters to move to VILLERS CARBONNEL for the night. Column reach there by 8 pm. 1 immobile lorry and a few workshop stores only are left at MONS also 50 tons coal. 100 tons coal are left with two men at ESTREES-EN-CHAUSSÉE. 20 lorries sent to Divisional Headquarters. These take dismounted men to CHAULNES and return on 22nd.	
22nd. VILLERS CARBONNEL.		6 am.	Railhead-LA CHAPELLETTE. Rendez vous GUISCARD. 1 pm. Train very late. Lorries deliver to brigades S.E. of NOYON, and 1 lorry per brigade takes rations to Dismounted men near CHAUNES AND Lorries passing through HAM, en route for Rendez vous come under shell fire and a dozen Supply men, in obeying what appears to have been a general order to take cover, become missing. Pte Thacker wounded by shell burst. Under instructions from O.C. A.S.C. 2 lorries from 6th Brigade return to ATHIES for wheelers' shop but whole village was deserted on account of proximity of enemy. Column park for the night at LARBROYE. Bombs are dropped in the neighbourhood.	
23rd. LARBROYE.			Railhead. ARPILLY. Rations were delivered for 6th, 7th, and Canadian Brigades to VARESNES by H.T. from Railhead. HARMAN. General ~~BAUMSECKER~~ having collected a mounted party, moved same up to near	

Army Form C. 2118.

WAR DIARY

INTELLIGENCE SUMMARY.

March 1918

Cal 3

3RD CAVALRY M.T. COMPANY.

Place	Date	Hour	Summary of Events and Information	Remarks and references to Appendices
LARBROYE.	24th		HARMAN. Rations are collected from 3rd Brigade dumps and taken up to General Harmond. 3 crippled lorries left on Park on 22nd leave on account of hostile activity and move towards NOYON, where they are met by the first aid.	
		11 am.	ARRILLY- Railhead. Supplies drawn by lorry for advanced parties. HARMANS Instructions received from S.M.T.O. 3rd Corps that General Harmons party of 900 would be rationed etc, under Corps arrangements. Lieut Bowers detached with 6 lorries for this service. Attached to 3rd Corps M.T. Company.	
		2 pm.	9 lorries sent to 3rd Corps M.T. Company to help with ammunition. 9 wheels for re-tyring go to ABBEVILLE leaving 4 lorries out of action.	
		6 pm.	S.M.T.O. 3rd Corps wires to evacuate Workshops etc, to RESSON. This is done.	
		10.30 pm.	a 3rd Corps lorry half breaks through the NOYON-LA-BROYE bridge. As traffic is much impeded the first aid is sent to lift this out. Bridge all clear 11.30 pm.	
		11.35 pm.	Confused messages come through from Divisional Headquarters and S.M.T.O. 3rd Corps that Column should move to REMY. Column moved off in parties of 6 lorries.	
	25th		Column continues to evacuate LARBROYE, last mobile lorry moves off 5.30 am. Staff Sergeant Halsall remains with 4 immobile lorries, to await wheels from Workshops at RESSONS these arrive about 9.am. Column reach REMY. HARMANS Lieut Bowers under Corps arrangements, delivers rations to General Harmond party at MURANCOURT. Self and Lieut Baillon take up rations to 6th, 7th, and Canadian dismounted, at CARLEPONT (2 am on 26th.) and to rest of Division at OLLENCOURT. Railhead - ESTREES.	

Army Form C. 2118.

3RD CAVALRY M.T. COMPANY.

WAR DIARY
or
INTELLIGENCE SUMMARY.

March 1918

(Erase heading not required.)

Instructions regarding War Diaries and Intelligence Summaries are contained in F. S. Regs., Part II. and the Staff Manual respectively. Title pages will be prepared in manuscript.

Place	Date	Hour	Summary of Events and Information	Remarks and references to Appendices
	26th		Railhead – COMPEIGNE. Rendez-vous JONQUIERES. Lieut Bune takes rations to division near (CHOISY – LE – BAC Lieut Campbell delivers to General Portal's party near CLOYES. Lieut Bowers to Generals HARMAN's party near ELLENCOURT. COMPEIGNE heavily bombed by aeroplanes.	
	27th		RAILHEAD- COMPEIGNE. Now deserted. Rendez-vous BAILLY. Division start to reform as Cavalry. Lieut Hodgson with 12 lorries goes to IInd Cav. M.T. Company at VEDETTE to ration Canadian Brigade. Column move to La CROIX ST OUEN and deliver rations near BAILLY. NOTE to date one (borrowed) map is all that exists among the 400 odd Officers and men of the unit.	
	28th		RAILHEAD- ESTREES. Column start to load 8.am. 7 lorries detached to 19th Corps to ration and munition 2nd Division R.H.A. Batteries and heavy Section Ammunition Column. Detached 1 lorry sent to aid the 6th Cav. Field Ambulance.	
	29th	1 am. 5 am.	Wire received from "Q" "Be ready to move at instant notice". Wire received from "Q" "Lorries to load at COMPEIGNE and proceed FOURNIVAL" Lorries complete loading by noon. Headquarters, Workshop, and Ammn. Sec. move off 11 am. via ESTREES ST DENIS. Rendez-vous ERQUINVILLERS. Divisional Headquarters BULLES-LE-MESNIL. 6th Brigade deliver at AIRION. 7th Brigade deliver at AUREONY. B Echelon LES CARIGNONS. Lorries all back on park 8 pm.	
	30th		Railhead – LOEUILLY. Loading completed 4 pm. B Echelon to WAILLY. Remainder of Division to SAINS SUR AMIENOIS. Between Column park on the LOEUILLY, NAMPTY Road. Lorries return to park, deliver 2 am and 4 am.	

Army Form C. 2118.

3RD CAVALRY M.T. COMPANY

WAR DIARY or INTELLIGENCE SUMMARY.

(Erase heading not required.)

March 1918.

Instructions regarding War Diaries and Intelligence Summaries are contained in F.S. Regs., Part II. and the Staff Manual respectively. Title pages will be prepared in manuscript.

Place	Date	Hour	Summary of Events and Information	Remarks and references to Appendices
	31st.		Railhead - ST ROCHE. (AMIENS) Column load in afternoon? B Echelon deliver to WAILLY. Column park on the POIX-AMIENS Road 1½ miles South West of AMIENS. Rations for Division delivered to SAINS EN AMIENOIS. Lorries return to park about 2 pm.	

REMARKS.

During the month the Column lose one Echelon. This causes considerable confusion during the operation at end of month, not only on account of one Echelon not being sufficient, but also it was difficult to organize the Column to best advantage at the short notice.

Apart from A.O.D. services and Post, 9 lorries were attached to the Divisional Headquarters for various purposes (other than Ammunition and Supply) which made the task of rationing etc the Division very difficult indeed.

On average the ration lorries did not return to park, during operations, until after 2 am.

The Road discipline on the moves from LABROYE to REMY and to FOURNIVAL was very bad. On the former move no traffic men at all apparent and lorry drivers and H.T. were double banking frequently.

A French Heavy Battery halted for the night near LABROYE without clearing the road, and various Batteries R.G.A. did the same thing at LASSIGNY.

K.O. [signature] Major,
Commanding 3rd Cavalry M.T. Company.

Army Form C. 2118.

3RD CAVALRY M.T. COMPANY.

April 1918 - Page 1.

WAR DIARY
INTELLIGENCE SUMMARY.
(Erase heading not required.)

Instructions regarding War Diaries and Intelligence Summaries are contained in F. S. Regs., Part II. and the Staff Manual respectively. Title pages will be prepared in manuscript.

Place	Date	Hour	Summary of Events and Information	Remarks and references to Appendices
April	1.	1918	Headquarters and Column at SAISUEL near AMIENS. Railhead ST ROCHE (AMIENS). Division fed around SAINS-LES-A MIENOIS.	
"	3.		LOADED FOR Division at AMIENS. Rendez-vous Boulevard near Circus, AMIENS, and fed Division around BLANGE TRONVILLE.	
"	4.		Normal. Division fed in same areas.	
"	5.		Division fed in same areas. 10 lorries arrived from the 4th Cavalry Supply Column to help temporarily with supplies.	
"	6.		8 Daimler "C.C." lorries and 16 M.T. personnel evacuated to 4th Army Troops M.T. Company, to comply with new War Establishment. 25 lorries, 1 car, and 50 O.Rs. arrived as a foundation for a second Echelon, from 4th Army Convoy. 8 lorries to Cavalry Corps.	
"	7.		Column move to RIVERY (AMIENS). Railhead AMIENS. Division fed in following areas. Headquarters RIVERY. 6th Brigade+Canadians in CAMON area, 7th Brigade LA MOTTE BREBIERE.	
"	8.		Division loaded and fed in same place. 41 Supply Details to H.T.&S. Base, HAVRE in accordance with new War Establmt.	
"	9.		Railhead. AILLY-SUR-SOMME. The 10 lorries and 20 O.RS. from 4th Cav. Supply Column cease to be attached, also 25 lorries, 50 O.RS. and 1 car, they being returned to their respective units. 1 officer 83 O.Rs with 37 lorries join the Company from No. 2 Reserve M.T. Coy. Division fed in areas just East of AMIENS.	

Army Form C. 2118.

WAR DIARY
INTELLIGENCE SUMMARY.
(Erase heading not required.)

Instructions regarding War Diaries and Intelligence Summaries are contained in F.S. Regs., Part II. and the Staff Manual respectively. Title pages will be prepared in manuscript.

3rd CAVALRY M.T. COMPANY.

April 1918 - Page 2.

Place	Date	Hour	Summary of Events and Information	Remarks and references to Appendices
April.	11.		Division moves to new area. Column loaded for Division at AILLY-SUR-SOMME, and fed it in BOYAVAL-EPS-CONTEVILLE areas. 6 lorries to ABBEVILLE with men for Remounts. 30 lorries to take dismounted men of 6th and 7th Brigades from CAMON to LONG. These lorries after delivering the men proceeded back to Railhead to load. The Column moved to new Park at AUXI-LE-CHATEAU.	
"	12.		Railhead ST LEGER, DOMART. Division fed in same area as on 11th.	
"	13.		Division move to new area around PERNES. Column load at PERNES Railhead and move to new Park at SAINS-LES-PERNES. Division fed in following new areas:- 6th Brigade FEREAY. 7th Brigade FLORINGHEM. Canadian Brigade COUTEVILLE. Div. Troops PERNES.	
"	14.		Normal.	
"	15.		Normal, with exception that Brigades move their areas to the following places. D.T. Units PESSY-LES-PERNES. 4th Brigade R.H.A. PERNES. Field Squadron SAINS-LES-PERNES. 6th Brigade remain in FERFAY. 7th Brigade in new area around EAM-EN-ARTOIS and MOLINGHEM. 3 lorries from 7th G.H.Q. Reserve M.T. Company join, viz, Daimler 30783 & 23306, Commer 30180.	
"	16.		Normal.	
"	17.		Railhead changed to CALONNE RICOUART. Division fed in same area.	
"	18.		Railhead PERNES.	
"	20.		Normal. Company moved to BOURS on ST POL road.	

Army Form C. 2118.

3RD CAVALRY M.T. COMPANY

WAR DIARY or INTELLIGENCE SUMMARY.

(Erase heading not required.)

April 1915. Page 2.

Place	Date	Hour	Summary of Events and Information	Remarks and references to Appendices
April.	22.	1918	Normal. Railhead PERNES. Saurer lorry 43745 arrived. The following lorries evacuated. Albion 10695. Peerless. 2790, 2791, & 2699.	
"	23.		Normal.- The following lorries arrived. Peerless 56336. Daimler 7624, and Thornycroft 5457. from 7th G.H.Q. Reserve M.T. Coy.	
"	24. 25.		Normal. Albion lorry 40007 arrived, and posted to F. Sec.	
"	26.		Railhead BRYAS. Division fed in same area.	
"	27.		Company Inspected by Colonel A.E. Cuming, O.C. A.S.C. Division fed in following areas. Canadian Brigade. LISBOURG. VERCHIN- area. 6th Brigade FONTAINE-LES-VIERMENS area. 7th Brigade FIEFS-BOYAVAL area.	
"	28.		Railhead BRYAS. Otherwise normal.	
"	29.		Railhead DIEVAL. Division fed around area as on 27th. Lieut. Cockshutt left Company and proceeded to 179 A.F.A. Brigade Park Section	
"	30.		Railhead DIEVAL.	

Army Form C. 211

May 1916.

3rd Cavalry Div: M.T. Company.

Page 1.

WAR DIARY
or
INTELLIGENCE SUMMARY.
(Erase heading not required.)

Instructions regarding War Diaries and Intelligence Summaries are contained in F.S. Regs., Part II. and the Staff Manual respectively. Title pages will be prepared in manuscript.

Place	Date	Hour	Summary of Events and Information	Remarks and references to Appendices
	MAY.			
PERNES.	1.		The Company was parked on the PERNES – St POL Road, 2 miles south of PERNES. Railhead for the day was DIEVAL. The Division was fed in the following areas:- Divisional Troops – PERNES. 6th Bde. – FONTAINE-LES-HERMANS. 7th Bde. – FIEFFES – BOYAVAL. Canadian Brigade LISBOURG & VERCHIN. The following lorries were evacuated T.30525 (Albion) T.7231 (Daimler)	
	2.		Normal – Railhead changed to PERNES.	
	3.		Normal.	
	4.		Major G.K. Shafford assumed Command of the Company, in relaxation of Major H.A.E. Gardner to the 12th F.H.Q. Reserve M.T. Company. Division moved from PERNES area, and was fed in the following new areas:— Div: HQ. WAIL, Brigades in TROHEN – LE GRAND & St GEORGES areas.	
DOMART-EN-PONTHIEU.	5.		The Company then Waterloho moved to DOMART-EN-PONTHIEU, on the DOMART–CONDÉ Road	

Army Form C. 2118.

WAR DIARY
or
INTELLIGENCE SUMMARY.
(Erase heading not required.)

May 1915.
3rd Cavalry Divn. M.T. Company.
Page 2.

Place	Date	Hour	Summary of Events and Information	Remarks and references to Appendices
DOMART-EN-PONTHIEU	MAY 5. contd		Railhead for the day - PERNES, and the Division was fed in the following areas:- Divl. Troops. YRENCH, 6th Brigade. VACQUERIE area, 7th Brigade. GRIMONVILLERS, Canadian Brigade - LE PLUOY area.	
	6		Division moved to forward area - CONTAY. Company remained on DOMART-CONDÉ Road, and Railroad at ST. LEGER-LES-DOMART.	
	7		Division fed in CONTAY area. 10 lorries to Railhead. Cast Roots. Shell + debris to Brigades. 1st Hotchkiss + 2/Life Guards proceeded over 16 lorries of Ammunition Section in detachment to VIGNACOURT for work under III Corps.	
	8		Division fed in same area as on 7th instant. Ammunition Section, in detachment, dumped their established ammunition at MOLLIENS-au-BOIS. The lorries returned to VIGNACOURT Railhead in the evening to unload Ammunition Train, and conveyed the following ammunition to III Corps Dump at MOLLIENS au BOIS:- "A" 5,260 rounds, "AX" 1,200 rounds, "BX" 900 rounds.	

Army Form C. 2118.

May 1916.
3rd Cavalry Div. M.T. Company.
Page 3.

WAR DIARY
or
INTELLIGENCE SUMMARY.
(Erase heading not required.)

Place	Date	Hour	Summary of Events and Information	Remarks and references to Appendices
DOMART-EN-PONTHIEU	MAY. 9.		Division fed in same forward area. — III Corps detail 30 lorries to the dumping of the 2nd Echelon of supplies in Column Park after loading. The 30 lorries thus released proceeded to POULAINVILLE for work under III Corps R.E. Officer, returning to Park between 6.0. & 10.0. pm. Ammunition Section on detachment, carry on with the unloading of ammunition train as on previous day, & convey the following of ammunition to III Corps Dump, completing the duty at 2.0. a.m. & 10.55:- "A" 3,762 rounds, "AX" 1,236 rounds, "N" 1230 rounds, "NX" 145 rounds.	
	10		Division carry on to supply Echelon J supplies as the Column came under S.M.T.O. III Corps for detail. — Loading at 6.30 am. the supply lorries R.V. MUILLERS-BOCAGE and released to Brigades in CONTAY area. 26 lorries are detached under 2/Lt Gordon Clark to 16th Divisional M.T. Company for supply duty with that Div. Column Watership joined up with remains of J. Column. The Ammunition Section at VIGNACOURT conveyed the following of ammunition from	F.5

Army Form C. 2118.

May 1918.
3rd Cavalry Div. M.T. Company
Page 4.

WAR DIARY
or
INTELLIGENCE SUMMARY.
(Erase heading not required.)

Instructions regarding War Diaries and Intelligence Summaries are contained in F. S. Regs., Part II. and the Staff Manual respectively. Title pages will be prepared in manuscript.

Place	Date	Hour	Summary of Events and Information	Remarks and references to Appendices
DOMART-EN-PONTHIEU.	MAY. 10 Contd		Railhead to III Corps Dump:- "A" 2,400 rounds; "AX" 1,660 rounds.	
	11		Loading & delivery of supplies as on 10th instant. Arrangements made with the Division for 3 lorries at present attached to Field Ambulances to be at Railhead each day and to be available for loading the Division.	
			(6.0) the lorries of Ammunition Section working under III Corps for Ammunition detail, are detailed to carry supplies for 5th Division. (Authority, D.A. & Q.M.G - III Corps.)	
	12		Division transferred & supplied as on 11th instant. Six lorries loaded fuel marked & delivered to Brigades.	
			Eighteen lorries in Attachment with Cavalry Corps H.Q. are attached & replaced with other attached to the Company from 1st S. H.Q. Reserve M.T. Company.	
			Ammunition Section in Attachment loaded & drew the following :- T.M.G. 360 rounds, "A" 1,920 rounds; "AX" 460 rounds; T.M.C. 1,800 rounds, S.A.A. 60,000 rounds.	
	13		Normal - 26 lorries cease to be attached with 18th Division M.T. Company and return to Park.	

2353 Wt. W2314/1454 700,000 5/15 D. D. & L. A.D.S.S./Forms/C. 2118.

Army Form C. 2118.

3rd Cavalry Div M.T. Company.

Page 5.

WAR DIARY
or
INTELLIGENCE SUMMARY.
(Erase heading not required.)

Instructions regarding War Diaries and Intelligence Summaries are contained in F.S. Regs., Part II. and the Staff Manual respectively. Title pages will be prepared in manuscript.

Place	Date	Hour	Summary of Events and Information	Remarks and references to Appendices
DOMART-EN PONTHIEU	MAY. 13 Cont.		Lorry T4007 reported taken on strength of Company.	
	14		Normal - Second echelon of lorries ceases to come under III Corps for Petrol, and 39 lorries are ear-marked for work under S. Transport Officer IV Army. 16 lorries of Ammunition Section on detachment return to Company after picking up establishment ammunition.	
	15 } 16 }		Normal.	
	17		The Division, less one Brigade (Canadian), was back from forward area, and are at the following new areas:- Div. Troops YZEUX, 6th Brigade BELLOY-SUR-SOMME, 1st Brigade - ST OUEN - Canadian Brigade - CONTAY (1 Lancer). 7 lorries to PERNES to clean S.S.O: lorry left the when Division was in that area. Two sections of the 16 F.H.Q. Reserve M.T. Company, with 2 motor cycles and two Officers (Lt W.B. Whitehead and 2/Lt S.J.R. Neasley) reported to relieve 2nd Echelon supplies by the Reserve Army Troops M.T. Company. The two sections arrived about less 3 lorries	

Army Form C. 2118.

WAR DIARY
or
INTELLIGENCE SUMMARY.

(Erase heading not required.)

3rd Cavalry Div. M.T. Company
Page 6.

Place	Date	Hour	Summary of Events and Information	Remarks and references to Appendices
DOMART EN PONTHIEU	MAY 17 contd		which was telegraphed for.	
	18		The second notice from Reserve Army Corps M.T. Company cease to be attached owing to this unit with 2/Lt Gordon Clark i/c. Division handed in expected as on 17th instant — Road & Kindred Corps was delivered to Brigades.	
	19		Normal. Three lorries which had been attached with Divisional H.Q. "Q" are returned on the understanding that they are earmarked for the same duty in the event of a sudden move.	
	20		Arrangements are made for 7th Brigade reclaim Unit of Divisional Troops to be fed by Horse Transport. The remainder of the Division being fed by the Column. 3 lorries to TERVES to clean stores damped six lorries to Railhead to bring up work to Column dumps.	

WAR DIARY or INTELLIGENCE SUMMARY.

Army Form C. 2118.

3rd Cavalry Div: M.T. Company
Q.a.f.c. 7

Place	Date	Hour	Summary of Events and Information	Remarks and references to Appendices
DOMART-EN-PONTHIEU	MAY 21		In view of the fact that the feeding of the Division by Mechanical Transport is retained, efforts are made to keep two sections of the Company off the roads. This Course is impossible so drivers have had little or no time to attend to their vehicles. 5 lorries had load moved & delivered to Brigades – 4 lorries are detailed by IVth Army for duty with Ordnance Officer at FRESSELLES, and to remain attached for 3 days. Two lorries sent from 16th F.H.Q. Reserve M.T. Company – these together with one from Workshops at ABBEVILLE complete the two sections attached from the time.	
	22		Feeding arrangements for Division same as on the previous day. Army T 20053 (Division C.B.) granted from 7th Siege Reserve M.T. Company in accordance with A.D.S.T.'s instruction.	
	23		From 23rd May the Company was re-organized on the following lines. The system already then existed 2 sections were sub divided creating & was replaced by 8 sections of roughly 16 lorries each, each under a Subaltern. Captain Conti, Senior R.T.O. Officer, assumed the	

2353 Wt. W3514/4454 700,000 5/15 D.D.&L. A.D.S.S./Form/C. 2118.

WAR DIARY
INTELLIGENCE SUMMARY

Army Form C. 2118.

3rd Cavalry Divl. M.T. Company
Page 5.

Place	Date	Hour	Summary of Events and Information	Remarks and references to Appendices
DOMART-EN-PONTHIEU	MAY 23 Cont'd		Duties of O/C Convoy, and men in future concern himself solely with the loading and delivery of supplies leaving work from 2nd Baggage assumed the duties of Transport Officer dealing solely with the detailing of Transport. Lorries Nos. T16199 (Thornycroft) T5301 (Thornycroft) from 7th J.M.S. Reserve M.T. Company reported, making 2nd Section up to 36 lorries. 4th Army to army that from lorries detached for 3 days from 21st instant will remain detached for another two days.	
	24		7th Brigade church service into Canadian Brigade unit to make that the 3 Battalion en Fête by lorries for the day.	
	25		Division Ordered to afield on an 21st instant. Two lorries apart from 7th J.M.S. Reserve M.T. Company making the total attached up to 38.	
	26		Canadian Brigade lorries & afield by Motor Transport. 6th Brigade in BELLOY and 7th in [?] area by Column.	B

Army Form C. 2118.

3rd Cavalry Div. M.T. Company

WAR DIARY
or
INTELLIGENCE SUMMARY.
(Erase heading not required.)

Page 9.

Place	Date	Hour	Summary of Events and Information	Remarks and references to Appendices
DOMART EN PONTHIEU	MAY. 27.		Division Festival on 26th instant. One workshop & one 3 ton lorry with one M.S.S. & 12 O.R. sent from 16th STHQ Reserve M.T. Company	
	28 / 29 / 30		Normal.	
	31.		6th Division changed over with 7th Division – 6th going forward	
			In view of the work of the work of the Company was (1) an extremely arduous nature. The Division being in a forward area & Railhead some 25 miles in its rear, drives were at the wheel for 12-13 hours a day for a fortnight on end. This meant that vehicles could only be over-hauled at extremely limited periods for lubrication oil & refilling of spare mechanical defects. Difficulties were reverted owing to the 2nd echelon of lorries carried at Rail-Line under the S.M.T.O. III Corps for details. Later on in the month when the Company was relieved to a extent [illegible] by [illegible]	R

Army Form C. 2118.

WAR DIARY
or
INTELLIGENCE SUMMARY.
(Erase heading not required.)

3rd Cavalry Div. M.T. Company.

Page 90.

Place	Date	Hour	Summary of Events and Information	Remarks and references to Appendices
	MAY		Transport Tubing return of the Brigades, 39 lorries were earmarked for work with the army.	
	25/5/15		Captain B.C. Bentley O/C workshops was mentioned in dispatches (London Gazette 5/5/15). 2/Cpl. C. Slaughter was awarded the Military Medal for conspicuous work during the Hanover function at the end of March last.	
			Mileage & Petrol Return for the month. Lorries Hours. 36,233. " Empty 36,512. 72,745 miles 12,757 gallons Total Case issued Assault tires for lorries ? 5.93. Above figures are exclusive of 14 lorries overseas.	Crimes & Punishments for the month F.G.C.M. - Nil. Field Punishments No. 1. - Nil. No. 2. - Nil.

A. Spratt? Lieut
M.T. Co.
O/C 3rd Cav. Div. M.T. Coy.

AMMUNITION ISSUED

MAY 1918

3RD CAVALRY M.T. COMPANY.

No. ....
Date ....

DESCRIPTION	NUMBERS ISSUED	REMARKS
"N"	1,525	
"N.X"	1,164	
S.A.A. .303 ORD.	631,000	
" M.G.	31,584	
" TRACER	648	
" ARM. PIER.	14,976	
" PRACTICE	90,000	
PISTOL WEBLEY	4,744	
" COLT	1,000	
GRENADE HAND No 5	144	
GRENADES RIFLE No 23	Nil	
CARTRIDGES ILLUM D.I. 1½"	Nil	
CARTRIDGES ILLUM D.I. 1"	1,218	
CARTRIDGES SIGNAL PARACHUTE 1½"	1,788	

G.L. Sill
MAJOR
3RD Cav Div M.T. Coy

3/6/18

<u>Précis of work carried out
in workshops during month of May.</u>

(A.) <u>Number of vehicles</u> which have
undergone a thorough overhaul.
5 lorries. 3 cars. 3 Motor Ambulances.
3 Motor cycles.

(B) <u>General condition</u> of vehicles as found
after dismantling engines etc.
2 C.C Daimlers required a new crankshaft
each & about 50% new sleeves, pistons &
rings. All parts worn.
1."Y". Daimler required new crankshaft &
gear box overhaul etc.
1. Albion. Valves & seatings very burnt.
Generally worn.

1 20 H.P Daimler car required new crankshaft.
General wear & tear condition of other
cars was normal.

The Motor Ambulances were in better
condition than the cars. & merely required
overhauls.
<u>Motor cycles</u> chief wear found in ball &
roller races. Other parts very little worn.

(C) <u>Large demands for spares.</u>
244 Tarpaulins for recovering lorries
11 cwt various paint for painting
vehicles.

(6) Cont'd: Various spanners etc to complete equipment of attached Peerless lorries.

(D) <u>Long working hours of Artificers</u>
Average per diem 8½ to 9.
½ working day on 2 Sundays.

(E) <u>Fortnightly Inspections.</u> 24 hours
27 out of 42 car inspections carried out.
17 out of 27 Ambulances.
N.B. The programme only really came into practical effect about 10th May.

(F) <u>Alteration to establishment.</u> Nil.
4th workshop attached during last week for maintenance of attached lorries.

(G) <u>W.D. Nos. of evacuated Vehicles.</u>

<u>Lorries.</u>	<u>Cars.</u>	<u>Ambulances.</u>
Y231.	M55.	
30525.	M.24989.	Nil.
23059.		
Y217*	<u>2 Motor cycles.</u>	

* Authority to evacuate obtained in May. Lorry still on park.

(H) <u>Spares difficult to obtain</u>
Cardan shaft for 3 ton Hallford.
Type E.1.D.100.
Cylinders, set of gudgeon pins for 32 H.P. Albion.

General remarks. The C.C. Daimler lorries are in most cases not worth repairing. The lengthy overhauls which they require impair the general efficiency of the other vehicles. These lorries have done hard work with the Unit in France since October 1914.

3RD CAVALRY M.T. COMPANY.
No. 51/175/127
Date.......

No 4

June 1915.

War Diary.

3rd Cavalry Division. M.T. Coy.

PAGE 1.
Army Form C. 2118.

3RD CAVALRY M.T. COMPANY.

WAR DIARY
INTELLIGENCE SUMMARY.
(Erase heading not required.)

June 1916.

Instructions regarding War Diaries and Intelligence Summaries are contained in F.S. Regs., Part II and the Staff Manual respectively. Title pages will be prepared in manuscript.

Place	Date	Hour	Summary of Events and Information	Remarks and references to Appendices
DOMART-en-PONTHIEU.	JUNE 1.		The Company was parked on the DOMART–CONDE Road, with Railhead at ST LEGER-LES DOMART. The whole of the Division, with the exception of a few Divisional Troops Units was fed by the Company in the following areas:— 6th Brigade – MONTIGNY (forward area) 7th Brigade – BELLOY–SUR–SOMME. Canadian Brigade – ST OUEN. Divisional Troops – YZEUX.	
"	2.		Loaded and refilled for 6th and 7th Brigades, and Divisional Headquarters. Canadian Brigade going on to HORSE TRANSPORT. IV Army Transport Officer asked for the help of 25 lorries in addition to normal detail, to off load Supply Trains at ST RIQUIER for 2 or 3 days. This detail was cancelled however for the day.	
"	3.		Division loaded and refilled as on 2nd instant. The 25 lorries promised for IV Army Transport Officer are detailed to be at ST RIQUIER railhead at 10.0 am. After waiting all day the lorries return no Supply Train having arrived.	
"	4.		Division fed as on 3rd instant. The 25 lorries for IV Army stand by and cyclist sent to ST RIQUIER but reports no train in.	
"	5.		Division fed as on 4th instant. O1/c Workshops of 16th G.H.Q. Reserve M.T. Company inspects attached lorries "G" & "H" Sections. He expressed himself very satisfied with their mechanical condition.	
"	6.		Division fed as on 5th instant. 20 lorries are detailed by IV Army to proceed to WOINCOURT for duty for 3 days to carry rifles under directions of a Staff Officer. The Detachment proceeded at 1.0 pm with Lieut. Whitehead as Officer in Charge. Lorry No. † 3381 G.B. Daimler, reported as a replacement.	

PAGE 2.
Army Form C. 2118.

3RD CAVALRY M.T. COMPANY.

WAR DIARY
INTELLIGENCE SUMMARY.
(Erase heading not required.)

JUNE 1918.

Place	Date	Hour	Summary of Events and Information	Remarks and references to Appendices
DOMART-en-PONTHIEU.	JUNE. 7		Division fed as on 6th instant. 18 lorries to ST RIQUIER to unload Supply Train and deliver to IV Army Dump at GORENFLOS. a/M.S.M. Rowland, L.O. reported for duty from 40th Auxiliary Petrol Company. To ensure an increased return of Empty Petrol Tins to Railhead from Units, a more effective system is instituted. In future no petrol will be issued unless the equivalent number of empty tins are returned.	
"	8.		Normal loading and delivering of rations to Division as on 7th instant. The 20 lorries detailed by IV Army on 6th instant to collect rifles at WOINCOURT, return. O/c reported that after waiting for 2 days the detail had been cancelled. The unnecessary mileage done by these lorries, waste of time and inconvenience caused was reported to "Q" IV Army. 20 lorries proceeded to ST RIQUIER to off load Supply Train as on 7th instant. Lieut. L.C. Baillon and 3 O.Rs detailed for short Hotchkiss Rifle course.	
"	9.		Division fed as on 8th instant. 20 lorries again to ST RIQUIER (IV Army) detail, as on 8th instant. Arrangements made for the Ford Box Car, attached to Sanitary Section, to be retained by Company, for the purpose of carrying small quantities of Ammunition &c, thus saving lorry transport.	
"	10.		Normal. 20 lorries to ST RIQUIER as on 9th instant.	
"	11.) 12.) 13.)		Normal.	
"	14.		7th Brigade changes area with 6th Brigade which returns from MONTIGNY (Forward area) to BELLOY-SUR-SOMME area. The Brigades are fed by the Company in their respective new areas.	

PAGE 3.

Army Form C. 2118.

3RD CAVALRY M.T. COMPANY.

JUNE. 1918.

WAR DIARY
or
INTELLIGENCE SUMMARY.
(Erase heading not required.)

Instructions regarding War Diaries and Intelligence Summaries are contained in F.S. Regs., Part II and the Staff Manual respectively. Title pages will be prepared in manuscript.

Place	Date	Hour	Summary of Events and Information	Remarks and references to Appendices
DOMART -en- PONTHIEU.	JUNE 15.		6th and 7th Brigades loaded and refilled as on 14th instant. 2/Lieut. B.A. Bowers rejoined from leave.	
"	16 - 21.		Normal.	
"	22.		Canadian Brigade changed areas with 7th Brigade in forward area.(MONTIGNY). The 3 Brigades are loaded and refilled by the Company in the following areas 6th Brigade - BELLOY-SUR-SOMME. 7th Brigade - ST OUEN- Canadian Brigade - (MONTIGNY) Divisional Troops - YZEUX.	
"	23.		6th, 7th and Canadian Brigades all fed by the Company in their respective areas.	
"	24.		Normal. O.C. A.S.C. (Lieut. Colonel Cuming) inspected the Company Park, Workshops, Cookhouse, and Billets. 2/Lieut. R.W. Courtney joined the Company from 12th G.H.Q. Reserve M.T. Company and is posted as O1/c "B" Section.	
"	25.		6th Brigade moved from the BELLOY-SUR-SOMME area (less the G.F.A.)to an area around LE MESGE. The three Brigades of the Division are fed by the Company for the day.	
"	26.		The Company was inspected by the G.O.C. of the Division at 10.0am. Two Companies consisting for the most part of the original members of the Company, who came overseas in 1914, were drawn up on the Company Parade Ground. After inspection the G.O.C. addressed the Parade and congratulated Officers and men on their work during the strenuous operations at the end of March and beginning of April. The Companies then marched past, after which the G.O.C. proceeded to inspect Workshops, Lorry Park, Cookhouse, etc. On his departure he congratulated the Commanding Officer (Major.P.L. Spafford) on everything he had seen and desired him to convey to Officers and men his appreciation of the "turn out" on parade, and general cleanliness of lorry park and Billets. All ranks very much appreciated the G.O.C's remarks on Parade which will	

PAGE 4.
Army Form C. 2118.

3RD CAVALRY M.T. COMPANY.

WAR DIARY
INTELLIGENCE SUMMARY.
(Erase heading not required.)

JUNE 1918.

Instructions regarding War Diaries and Intelligence Summaries are contained in F. S. Regs., Part II. and the Staff Manual respectively. Title pages will be prepared in manuscript.

Place	Date	Hour	Summary of Events and Information	Remarks and references to Appendices
DOMART-en-PONTHIEU.	JUNE 26.		undoubtedly incite them to make even greater efforts to give satisfaction to the Division in future. The Brigades were fed by the Company in the following areas:- Canadian Brigade - (MONTIGNY) 6th Brigade --- (LE MESGE) and Divisional Troops - (YZEUX)	
"	27) 28)		NORMAL.	
"	29.		Loaded and refilled for 6th Brigade and Canadian Brigade as on the previous day. The 4th Brigade R.H.A. with Royal Canadian Horse Artillery Brigade attached (less S.A.A. Sub Section of the Ammunition Column) moved into Australian Corps area. The Gun Section of the Ammunition Section, (12 lorries) together with 8 lorries to feed the Brigades are detached under Lieut. F. R. Hodgson. The detachment coming under 3rd Australian Division M.T. Company for orders Location COISY. The Brigade being fed on single echelon with Railhead at POULAINVILLE.	
"	30.		Normal. The work of the Company for the month was of an ordinary nature. For the greater part of the month 2 Brigades of the Division have been fed by the Company. As in the previous month 39 lorries were earmarked for work by the IV Army, and the daily average detailed by the Transport Officer of the Army was 25.	

PAGE 5.

Army Form C. 2118.

3RD CAVALRY M.T. COMPANY.

JUNE, 1918.

WAR DIARY
or
INTELLIGENCE SUMMARY.
(Erase heading not required.)

Instructions regarding War Diaries and Intelligence Summaries are contained in F.S. Regs., Part II. and the Staff Manual respectively. Title pages will be prepared in manuscript.

Place	Date	Hour	Summary of Events and Information	Remarks and references to Appendices
DOMART -en- PONTHIEU.	JUNE.		CRIMES AND PUNISHMENT FOR THE MONTH OF JUNE. F.G.C.M. F.P. No.1. F.P. No.2. N I L. STATEMENT OF AMMUNITION ISSUED. JUNE 1918. Description. Rounds. "N" S.A.A. ord Service. 327. S.A.A. (M.G.) 216,000. S.A.A. "Practice" 31,584. Pistol Webley. 146,000. Pistol Colt .45. 11,184. Grenades Hand No.5. 403. " Rifle No.23. 108. 48 - Returned to Railhead. MONTHLY MILEAGE RETURN. May 29th - June 25th. LORRIES Loaded. Empty. Total. 36101. 48489. 84590. Petrol Drawn. Gallons. 15253. Miles per Gallon. 5.54.	

2353 Wt.W2544/1454 700,000 5/15 D.D.&L./Forms/C.2118.

PAGE 6.
Army Form C. 2118.

3RD CAVALRY M.T. COMPANY.

WAR DIARY
or
INTELLIGENCE SUMMARY.
(Erase heading not required.)

Place: DOMART-en-PONTHIEU
Date: JUNE 1918.

Summary of Events and Information

ECONOMY.

PERCENTAGES OF RATIONS UNDERDRAWN FOR JUNE 1918.

Week-ending.	P.M.	Biscuits	Jam.	Cheese.	Sugar.	Tea.	Candles.
8.6.18.	11%	7%	—	13%	12½%	—	100%
15.6.18.	9½%	16½%	22%	14%	—	—	100%
22.6.18.	4%	2½%	12%	13%	5%	7%	100%
29.6.18.	7½%	6%	12¼%	—	5½%	6¼%	100%

WAR LOAN.

Five Hundred and Twenty £1 War Saving Certificates bought by the N.C.O's & Men through the Coy Office during June.

PAGE 7

Army Form C. 2118.

WAR DIARY
or
INTELLIGENCE SUMMARY.
(Erase heading not required.)

3RD CAVALRY M.T. COMPANY.

JUNE 1918.

Instructions regarding War Diaries and Intelligence Summaries are contained in F. S. Regs., Part II. and the Staff Manual respectively. Title pages will be prepared in manuscript.

Place	Date	Hour	Summary of Events and Information	Remarks and references to Appendices
DOMART -en- PONTHIEU.	JUNE.		PRECIS OF WORK CARRIED OUT DURING MONTH OF JUNE.	
			(a) Number of vehicles which have undergone a thorough overhaul.	
			LORRIES. 12 4 of which did not have complete engine overhauls.	
			CARS. 4 a 5th car in process of overhaul.	
			AMBULANCES. 1 a 2nd in process of overhaul.	
			MOTOR CYCLES. 5 N.B. Signal unit carry out a quantity of minor repairs themselves.	
			(b) General condition of engines.	
			About 90% "Y" and "C.C." type Daimlers overhauled during the month have required new crankshafts, the old ones being reckoned as repairable for regrinding.	
			(c) Large demands for spares.	
			(d) N I L.	
			Working Hours of Artificers. About 63 hours a week. 3 half days given and 1 special after inspection by G.O.C.	
			(e) Inspections.	
			Cars, ambulances and lorries are being sent in very regularly for periodical inspection (24 hours)	

PAGE 6

Army Form C. 2118.

3RD CAVALRY M.T. COMPANY.

WAR DIARY
or
INTELLIGENCE SUMMARY.
(Erase heading not required.)

JUNE 1915.

Instructions regarding War Diaries and Intelligence Summaries are contained in F. S. Regs., Part II. and the Staff Manual respectively. Title pages will be prepared in manuscript.

Place	Date	Hour	Summary of Events and Information	Remarks and references to Appendices
DOMART -en- PONTHIEU.	JUNE.			

(f) Alteration in Establishment, NIL.
   2 fitters taken by A.D.S.&T. for temporary duty with Cav. Corps M.T. Company, a serious handicap to my Workshops.

(g) Vehicles evacuated to Base.

   Cars. M↑ 1802 Sunbeam. Engine completely worn out. (8508e~).

   Ambulances NIL.

   Lorries. F.217. and F 248 "G.C." Daimlers completely worn out. Frame of cycle past repair, required rebuilding.

   Sidecar Combinations.
      1 Douglas frame of cycle past repair, required rebuilding.
   Motor cycles.
      1 Triumph worn out.

(h) No special delay in obtaining stores from Base.

REMARKS. The "J" type THORNYCROFT lorries have given an undue amount of trouble.

1. Every oil sump has had to be taken down and moulders sand cleaned out.
2. Hand brake lever arms too weak and have frequently to be re-set.
3. Steering lock unequal, necessitating taking out steering box to set drop arm.
4. Gudgeon pins very soft, very rapid wear takes place.
5. One faulty worm housing casting replaced.

Army Form C. 2118.

WAR DIARY
INTELLIGENCE SUMMARY

(Erase heading not required.)

3RD CAVALRY M.T. COMPANY.

Instructions regarding War Diaries and Intelligence Summaries are contained in F.S. Regs., Part II and the Staff Manual respectively. Title pages will be prepared in manuscript.

Place	Date	Hour	Summary of Events and Information	Remarks and references to Appendices
JULY	1st 1918		The Company was parked on the DOMART-CONDE ROAD with Railhead at ST LEGER-LES-DOMART. The 5th Brigade was fed by the Company in the LE MESGE Area, and the Canadian Brigade in the Montigny Area. Divisional Headquarters at YZEUX. The remainder of the Division was fed by Horse Transport.	
	2nd		Division fed as on the 1st instant. The following Officers reported for duty in accordance with A.D.S.T., Cavalry Corps No.P.1150/245/6/7/8 to complete establishment. 2/Lieut. M.Morgan from the 4th Army Troops M.T.Coy. 2/Lieut. F.Barker from the M.T.School of Instruction. 2/Lieut. R.Collis from M.T.School of Instruction.	
	3rd		Normal. 11 Lorries of the 4th Bde. R.H.A. Detachment proceeded to SALEUX at mid-night - drew 650 rounds "N", 2,250 rounds "NX", and delivered the same to 4th Australian Division Artillery at QUERRIEU. 1,120 rounds "N" were also drawn, and dumped on Detachment Park.	
	4th		Normal. 2Lieut. J.P. Jones reported from A.S.C.Base Depot, Havre, as Supply Officer to complete establishment in accordance with A.D.S.T.Cav. Corps No.P.1150/245/6/7/8. 2/Lieut. F.Barker proceeded to join 4th Bde. R.H.A. Detachment.	
	5th		The Canadian Brigade moves to BOURDON Area. 6th Brigade fed in same Area. -- LE MESGE. Arrangements are made whereby the lorries delivering supplies to Divisional Hd.Qrs. & 6th C.F.A. are available each day for picking up discharged P.U.O. patients, and conveying them to the various Brigades.	
	9th		Normal. Feeding of the Division as on the previous days of the month. 4th BDE. R.H.A. DETACHMENT. 12 lorries loaded with Establishment ammunition & proceeded to 3rd Corps Reserve Dump to off load, & proceeded to a new park at RAINNEVILLE. Units of 3rd Cav.Bde. refilled in new area around BEAUCOURT.	

2353 Wt. W2544/1454 700,000 5/15 D.

Army Form C. 2118.

WAR DIARY
INTELLIGENCE SUMMARY
(Erase heading not required.)

Instructions regarding War Diaries and Intelligence Summaries are contained in F.S. Regs., Part II and the Staff Manual respectively. Title pages will be prepared in manuscript.

3RD CAVALRY M.T. COMPANY.

Page 2

Place	Date	Hour	Summary of Events and Information	Remarks and references to Appendices
JULY	10th 1918		Normal. Major P. L. Spafford - O.C. - proceeded to England on Leave.	
	11th		Normal. Captain N. Coates assumed Command of the Company, loco Captain B.C. Bewley, who proceeded on Special Leave.	
			The 4th Bde. R.H.A. Detachment. O.i/c. Lieut. F.R. Hodgson ceases to be attached to the Australian Corps, and came under the orders of the III Corps.	
	12th) 13th) 14th		Normal.	
			Normal. Daimler Lorry W.D.No.3832 evacuated.	
	15th, 16th, 17th		Normal.	
	18th		Normal. 2/Lieut. R.H. Sadler proceeded on Special Leave to England.	
	21st		The Divisional Railhead is changed to HANGEST, and the whole of the Division less the 3rd Field Sqdn., and M.T.Company is fed by Horse Transport. The Supply Personnel with Lieut. A.V. Campbell O.i/c. proceed to new Railhead. Ten lorries are detached with 2/Lieut. F. Barker O.i/c. to help with various extraneous details. Ten lorries of 4th Bde. R.H.A. Detachment proceeded to FLESSELLES to load ammunition, and off load same at ST.GRATIEN.	
b	24th		Lieut. L.C. Baillon granted special leave to England to 24/8/18.	
	25th		Major P.L. Spafford assumes Command of the Company on return from leave	

Army Form C. 2118.

Page 3

3RD CAVALRY M.T. COMPANY.

WAR DIARY

INTELLIGENCE SUMMARY.

(Erase heading not required.)

Place	Date	Hour	Summary of Events and Information	Remarks and references to Appendices
JULY	25th 1918		Leyland Lorry W.D.No.23551 despatched to 8th G.H.Q.Reserve M.T.Co. Vide ADST. Cav.Corps. T/594/25/3, d/23/7/18. Albion Lorry WD.No.50234 arrived in replacement.	
	28th		Lieut. A.V. Campbell proceeds from Railhead HANGEST to take over duties of Supply Officer of the 4th Bde. R.H.A. 2/Lieut.J.P. Jones taking over the duties of Supply Officer at Divisional Railhead.	
			Small Box Respirators of all available personnel tested in GAS.	
	30th		Nothing of an exceptional nature has occurred during the month. The work has been consistently normal and opportunity has been taken to so divide the work amongst the various sections to enable time to be spent on thorough mechanical examination.	
			The two brigades of the Division were fed by the Company for the first half of the month. The Ammunition Section has been detached for the whole of the month, whilst the 4th Army has detailed about 22 lorries per day.	

AMMUNITION ISSUED.

```
S.A.A.   Ord.        119,000 rds.     Pistol Webley .45    4,368
         M.G.         16,920  "       Pistol Auto Colt .380  200
         Tracer          369  "              "      "   "     36
         Practice     56,000  "       Cartridges Sig.Para.   594
                                      S.A.A. Black. /303   7,020

         "N"   1594 rds.  )  Dumped at "C"
         "NX"  1208  "    )  Corps Res.Dump.
```

Army Form C. 2118.

WAR DIARY
or
INTELLIGENCE SUMMARY.
(Erase heading not required.)

[Stamp: 3RD CAVALRY M.T. COMPANY.]

Instructions regarding War Diaries and Intelligence Summaries are contained in F.S. Regs., Part II. and the Staff Manual respectively. Title pages will be prepared in manuscript.

Place	Date	Hour	Summary of Events and Information	Remarks and references to Appendices
July 1918			Number of N.C.Os. admitted to Cadet Units with a view to Commission during the month — S E V E N	
			Crime and punishment for month of July :-	
			F.G.C.M. Nil.	
			F.P.No.1. One (7 days).	
			2. Two (5 days).	
			PRECIS OF WORK CARRIED OUT IN WORKSHOPS DURING MONTH OF JULY.	
			A. Vehicles which have undergone a thorough overhaul. Lorries - 8 (9 more in process). Cars - 1 (1 more in process) Motor Ambulances - 1 (1 more in process). Motor Cycles - 5 (24 partial overhauls carried out).	
			B. Condition of vehicles after dismantling engine. About 90 % of Daimler lorry overhauls required new crankshafts. The sleeves & pistons were also excessively worn. Chassis of Daimler "Y" type & Albion lorries overhauled in excellent condition - considering mileage and work.	
			C. Large demands for spares. NIL.	
			D. Working hours of artificers - 8¼ to 9 hours average per day. Half day Sundays.	
			E. Alteration in Establishment. NIL.	

Army Form C. 2118.

WAR DIARY
or
INTELLIGENCE SUMMARY.

(Erase heading not required.)

3rd CAVALRY M.T. COMPANY.

Page 5

Place	Date	Hour	Summary of Events and Information	Remarks and references to Appendices
July 1918			WORKSHOPS -(Continued)	

F. Cars & ambulances are being sent in regularly for 24 hours fortnightly inspections.

G. Vehicles evacuated to Base Heavy Repair Shops :-
   Lorries :-
   W.D.No.3832 & 7289 - "CC" Daimlers. Both completely worn out.
   Cars :-
   M.15966 - 16/20 HP Open Wolseley. Smashed differential, also in very worn condition.
   Ambulances :- Nil.
   Motor Cycles :-
   One Triumph Clutch frame also required various other repair.

H. No delay in detaining stores.

REMARKS. Work considerably handicapped through rain storms this month.

W A R   L O A N.

Number of War Saving Certificates purchased by the Unit for month of July 405

Total purchased since June 1st 925

The above figures include only certificates purchased by N.C.Os. & men through the Company Office. Large amounts have been purchased privately through sending money home to England.

Army Form C. 2118.

WAR DIARY
~~INTELLIGENCE SUMMARY~~

(Erase heading not required.)

3RD CAVALRY M.T. COMPANY.

Page 6

Place: July 1918.

Summary of Events and Information

ECONOMY ACCOUNT FOR THE MONTH.

Percentage of Rations Underdrawn :-

Week Ending.	P.M.	Bis.	Jam.	Cheese	Sugar	Tea.	Candles.
July 5th	8⅞%	13¼%	12⅜%	7%	10½%	7⅞%	50%
12th	10%	15%	—	—	—	—	33⅜%
19th	11%	15⅝%	—	—	14%	13¾%	50%
26th	6⅜%	10⅝%	—	—	—	—	25%

****

MILEAGE & PETROL RETURNS FOR THE MONTH. (June 26/30 July)

```
Mileage Loaded    35,705      Petrol Drawn  14,137 gals.
"      Empty     44,427      Average miles per gallon = 5.67.
       Total.    80,132
```

[signature]
Major
O.O. 3rd Cavalry Divisional M.T. Coy.

PAGE 1.

Army Form C. 2118.

3rd CAV. DIVL. M.T. COY

WAR DIARY
or
INTELLIGENCE SUMMARY.
(Erase heading not required.)

Place	Date	Hour	Summary of Events and Information	Remarks and references to Appendices
DOMART-EN-PONTHIEU. August.	1.		The Company was parked on the DOMART-CONDE Road with Railhead at ST LEGER-LES-DOMART. The Division was being fed by Horse-Transport. Instructions received to the effect that no further detail would be received from 4th Army until further notice.	3RD CAVALRY M.T. COMPANY.
"	2.		3 Box Cars (Crossley) were drawn from the M.T. Reserve Vehicle Park to complete new Establishment.	
"	3.		4th Army "Q" detailed 16 lorries to report at 4-0am on 4th inst., to 4th Australian Division at sheet 62 D.S.17.a. lorries left at 8.30.pm (Oi/c 2/Lieut. J.R. Marley) Lieut F.C. Bune granted special leave to England to 17th inst.,	
"	4.		4th Army "Q" detailed 14 lorries to report at 7.30.am at X-Roads sheet 62D.N.27.a.5.4. to 5th Australian Brigade. A further 10 were detailed for R.E. work by the Army with various other details the total detailed amounted to 40. The following ammunition was drawn from FLESSELLES Railhead. N. 1780. N.X. 1120. S.A.A. 324.000. This ammunition was delivered to the Auxiliary H.T. Company. The following ammunition was also drawn from FLESSELLES Railhead. N. 3360. N.X. 2240. S.A.A. (O) 100-000. S.A.A. (M.G.) 100,000. The lorries after drawing R.V. at Hospice near RIVERIE (AMIENS) and dumped on the BOVES-GLISSY Road. The Brigades were completed to Establishment in S.A.A. Pistol Webley, Cartirdges Illuminating, all practice S.A.A. being exchanged for S.A.A. ordinary.	

PAGE 2.

Army Form C. 2118.

3rd CAV. DIVL. M.T. COY

WAR DIARY
INTELLIGENCE SUMMARY.
(Erase heading not required.)

August 1914.

Place	Date	Hour	Summary of Events and Information	Remarks and references to Appendices
DOMART-EN-PONTHIEU. August.	5.		Divisional Troops, 6th and 7th Brigades were fed by the Company, drawing at HANGEST Railhead and delivering to Units in the following areas:- Divisional Troops. YZEUX. 6th Brigade. LE MESGE area. 7th Brigade. ST OUEN. Lieut. A.V. Campbell Supply Officer returned from 4th Brigade R.H.A. Detachment being relieved by 2/Lieut.J.P. Jones. 2/Lieut. F. Barker, rejoined Company with the Railhead Detachment from HANGEST. 30 lorries detailed by 4th Army "Q" to transport Ammunition from HANGEST Railhead to dump at SOUES, also 8 lorries to SALEUX for the same purpose.	
	6.		The Company, less workshops, moved to SALEUX. Loading for the day at HANGEST, supplies were delivered to Units in PONT DE METZ area. Lieut. F.R. Hodgson with 4th Brigade R.H.A. detachment rejoined the Company, together with 2/Lieut. J.P. Jones. (Supply Officer)	
	7.		Loading at new Railhead (SALEUX) the Brigades were fed in the same areas as yesterday at mid-day. Railhead SALEUX. Supplies were loaded for A.and A2 echelons (half hay rations) with a view to active operations. Ration lorries together with the Ammunition Sec, left Park at 4.pm. and Rendez-vous at the West end of DOMART SUR-LA-LUCE. Rations and Ammunition dumped at Sheet 62D.V.19.d. Owing to great congestion of traffic the lorries remained at the dump for the night and returned to Park during the early morning.	
	8.		Four lorries were left at Dump to assist S.S.O. in delivering of rations.	

Army Form C. 2118.

PAGE 3.
August 1918.

3rd CAV. DIVL. M.T. COY

WAR DIARY
INTELLIGENCE SUMMARY.
(Erase heading not required.)

Place	Date	Hour	Summary of Events and Information	Remarks and references to Appendices
August.	9.		No Pack Train arrived at Railhead, supplies loaded in consequence from 2nd Echelon dump at AMIENS.	
			Convoy under Captain N. Coates proceeded to V.23.a. Sheet 62D. via Villers Bretonneux, Lamotte, Marcelcave.	
			Road shelled but no casualties occurred.	
			It was only possible to reach V.23.a. by means of tracks which were in a terrible condition, and on my making a reconnaissance it was considered almost impossible feat to get the lorries over the shell holes which in places were of sufficient dimensions to drop a car into. To make matters worse it was dark by the time the lorries had to travel over these tracks. It is to the credit of the Officer Commanding the Convoy and the N.C.Os and men that the supplies reached their destination. Every lorry in turn had to be towed out of one place on the road, the difficulties were still more increased by a tank and ammunition waggons blocking the road. It was found necessary to make the road up from timber found in German dug-outs.	
			While this was being done, the Convoy was subjected to most severe bombing by Enemy Aircraft, and the vicinity was being fired at by Machine Guns. There were nine casualties to personnel of the Ammunition waggons.	
			As it would have been impossible to get the lorries back over the same road that night, it was decided to remain at the dump until dawn.	
			Railhead at LONGNEAU.	
	10.		2.700 Iron Rations collected from LA FOLIE during the night and sent to MAISON BLANCHE at 8.0.am on the 11/8/18.	
	11.		Railhead LONGNEAU, Rendez-vous at MAISON BLANCHE 12.B.noon. Rations delivered to Units in BEAUFORT & CAIX areas.	
			Owing to the Division receiving instructions to return to BOVES for the night, rations are left on the lorries and issued at night in new area South of BOVES.	

Page 4.
Army Form C. 2118.
August 1918.

3rd CAV. DWL. M.T. COY.

WAR DIARY
INTELLIGENCE SUMMARY.
(Erase heading not required.)

Place	Date	Hour	Summary of Events and Information	Remarks and references to Appendices
August.	11.		Great delay is caused by the lorries travelling behind the Division. Lorries return to Park about 6.0.am. Dismounted men brought back in lorries remain with the M.T. Company.	
"	12.		Railhead as on the 11th. Lorries loaded in detail. 6 lorries to forward area to bring back 179 Dismounted men. 6 lorries also to forward area for hay.	
"	13.		Railhead as on 12th. Brigades fed in the following areas:- Divisional Troops. REMIENCOURT. BOVES. 6th Brigade. FOUENCAMPS. 7th Brigade. GUYENCOURT & JUMEL. Canadian Brigade. LE PAQCLET.	
"	14.		Railhead as on the 13th inst., Loading and delivering the same as yesterday with the exception of rations for Divisional Troops which were split up at the Rendez-vous. 40 lorries detailed to report to SOUES Ammunition Dump at 4.0. am. Lieut W.E. Whitehead proceeded with same and after loading ammunition proceeded to forked roads under "G" in LONGUEAU and there received instructions from Staff Officer to dump at BOUCHOIR. Lorries returned via BOVES and arrived back on Park by 6.0.pm. A.A.&.Q.M.G. Cavalry Corps notified by priority message of completion of detail. 40 lorries were detailed to report at BLANGY Railhead by 8.0.pm to assist in clearing trains of the following ammunition. A.X. 6.400. B.X. 5.850. The lorries reported to Lieut Donaldson of the 2nd Canadian Division M.T. Company at the Railhead and the ammunition was duly delivered to the 4th Canadian Dismounted A.R.P.	

Army Form C. 2118.

WAR DIARY
INTELLIGENCE SUMMARY

3rd CAV. DIVL. M.T. COY.

(Erase heading not required.)

Place	Date	Hour	Summary of Events and Information	Remarks and references to Appendices
August.	15.		Railhead changed to AMIENS. The Brigades moved from BOVES to SOUES and ST OUEN areas and rations were delivered to the units in their new areas. The 40 lorries detailed by the S.M.T.O. Canadian Corps yesterday return at 6.0.pm. The drivers of these lorries were 40 hours on end at the wheel with one break of two hours.	
"	16.		Railhead at AMIENS, and Division fed in same areas as yesterday. Supply Dumps of old areas are moved to DOMART. 12 lorries proceed to AMIENS Dump on GLISSY-BOVES Road, picked up ammunition and proceeded to SALEUX and off loaded. The Company moved to the old Park on the DOMART-CONDE Road.	

"	17.		Railhead at ST LEGER-LES-DOMART.
			Brigades fed in the following areas:-
			
			    Divisional Troops. YZEUX.
			    6th Brigade. LE MESGE.
			    7th Brigade. ST OUEN.
			    Canadian Brigade. HANGEST.	

"	18.		Railhead as yesterday. The Division (less one Brigade fed by Horse Transport) was fed by the Company in the same areas.	
"	19.		Railhead as yesterday. Canadian Brigade (alone) fed by the Company, the remainder of the Division by Horse Transport.	
"	20.		Railhead changed to HANGEST-SUR-SOMME, the whole of the Division being fed by Horse Transport.	

Page 7.

Army Form C. 2118.

August 1918

3rd CAV. DIV. I.T. COY

WAR DIARY

INTELLIGENCE SUMMARY.

(Erase heading not required.)

Instructions regarding War Diaries and Intelligence Summaries are contained in F. S. Regs., Part II. and the Staff Manual respectively. Title pages will be prepared in manuscript.

Place	Date	Hour	Summary of Events and Information	Remarks and references to Appendices
August.	27.		Railhead FREVENT. Division fed in same areas as yesterday. The M.T. Company moving to AVENDOIGHT in the afternoon (S.of TINQUES on the ST POL-ARRAS Road.)	
"	28.		Railhead TINQUES. After loading lorries Rendezvous at Park. Rations were eventually delivered to Brigades in the same areas as yesterday about 7.0.pm. 7 lorries sent to HANGEST to remove forage dump to LA FOLIE.	
"	29.		Railhead TINQUES. After loading, rations were ordered to the following areas:- Divisional Troops. ETRUN. 8th Brigade. WAILLY. } West of ARRAS. 7th Brigade. LOUEL. Canadians. ST AUBIN. The Order was cancelled in the late afternoon and the lorries recalled. Delivery was eventually made at night in the same areas as yesterday. Workshops joined the rest of the Company at AVEN DOIGNT.	
"	30.		Railhead TINQUES. Division fed in same areas as yesterday with the exception of the 10th HUSSARS and one third of men and animals of the 6th Machine Gun Squadron, who had gone forward to WAILLY near ARRAS.	
"	31.		Railhead TINQUES. Loading and delivering same as yesterday.	

Army Form C. 2118.

page 5.
August 1918.

3rd CAV. DIVL.
M.T. COY

WAR DIARY
or
INTELLIGENCE SUMMARY.
(Erase heading not required.)

Place	Date	Hour	Summary of Events and Information	Remarks and references to Appendices
			SUMMARY OF WORK CARRIED OUT IN WORKSHOPS DURING AUGUST.	
			(a) VEHICLES WHICH HAVE UNDERGONE A THOROUGH OVERHAUL.	
			LORRIES. 8 completed, 9 more in process.	
			CARS. 2.	
			MOTOR AMBULANCES. 1	
			MOTOR CYCLES. 3. (22 partial overhauls carried out.)	
			(b) CONDITION OF VEHICLES AFTER DISMANTLING.	
			In practically every case Daimler lorry engines had to be fitted with new or Base repaired crankshafts. The old being returned to Base for regrinding.	
			(c) LARGE DEMANDS FOR SPARES.	
			N I L.	
			(d) WORKING HOURS OF ARTIFICERS.	
			2 Sunday afternoons off. Between 70 and 75 working hours per week, practically from Daybreak to Sunset during one week.	
			(e) FORTNIGHTLY INSPECTION OF CARS AND AMBULANCES.	
			Attendance extremely erratic this month owing to moves etc., As a result cars and ambulances will in the majority of cases require to remain in for over 24 hours when they do report.	

Page 9.

Army Form C. 2118.

August 1918

3rd CAV. DIVL.

WAR DIARY
INTELLIGENCE SUMMARY.
(Erase heading not required.)

Summary of Events and Information

SUMMARY OF WORK CARRIED OUT BY WORKSHOPS DURING AUGUST.
(continued 2)

(f) ALTERATIONS IN ESTABLISHMENT.

1 Coppersmith in lieu of 1 Wheeler. Exchange not yet carried out.

(g) VEHICLES EVACUATED TO HEAVY REPAIR SHOPS.

LORRIES. 1 "C.C." Daimler No. 7243. Completely worn out.

CARS. N I L.

MOTOR AMBULANCES. 1 F.I.A.T. A1063. Completely worn out.

MOTOR CYCLES. 2 Triumphs. Smashed frames beyond repair.
2 Douglas 2¾ H.P. (one worn out, one smashed frame beyond repair.)

(h) STORES FOR WHICH THERE IS A GREAT DELAY IN OBTAINING FROM BASE.

TANK PETROL. For 16/20 H.P. Wolseley car ¾ elliptic rear springing ordered on 2/6/18 and subsequently hastened not yet received. Urgently required.

PISTONS. Engine for "Y" and "C.C." type Daimlers lorry engines. Earliest outstanding indent 19/7/18 has been hastened together with other subsequent indents for similar parts.
A Daimler lorry has been delayed 2 weeks for lack of pistons. Many other workshops are suffering in a similar way.

Cap 10.

Army Form C. 2118.

August 1918.

3rd CAV. DIVL. M.T. COY

WAR DIARY
or
INTELLIGENCE SUMMARY.
(Erase heading not required.)

Instructions regarding War Diaries and Intelligence Summaries are contained in F. S. Regs., Part II. and the Staff Manual respectively. Title pages will be prepared in manuscript.

Place	Date	Hour	Summary of Events and Information	Remarks and references to Appendices
			SUMMARY OF WORK CARRIED OUT BY WORKSHOPS DURING AUGUST.	
			GENERAL REMARKS. All parts for following makes of cars evacuated according to Director of Transport's instructions.	
			SUNBEAM. 12/16 H.P. Car.	
			VAUXHALL. Cars.	
			FORD. "	
			ALBION. ⎫	
			Thornycroft.J.Type. ⎬ Lorries.	
			PEERLESS. ⎭	
			Am already experiencing difficulty and great inconvenience owing to no stock of parts for these makes.	

Army Form C. 2118.

3rd CAV. DIVL.

WAR DIARY
INTELLIGENCE SUMMARY.

(Erase heading not required.)

STATEMENT OF AMMUNITION ISSUED FOR MONTH OF AUGUST 1918.

Description.	Rounds.
N.X.	9,136.
N.X. ord Service.	6,008.
S.A.A. M.G.	1,266,000.
S.A.A. Tracer.	264,280.
S.A.A. A.P.	2,052.
S.A.A. Practice.	384.
Pistol. Webley.	26,400.
Pistol. Colt .45.	4,656.
Auto Colt .380.	250.
Mills hand grenades No. 5.	100.
Cartirdges Illum. D.l. 1"	1,800.
" " 1½"	1,650.
Ground flares, Red.	156.
	1,330.

FIELD PUNISHMENT.

1 14 days F.P. No.1.   1 28 days F.P. No.2.

2 Men sent home for Commissions R.A.F.

Page 12.

Army Form C. 2118.

August 1918

3rd CAV. DIVL.

WAR DIARY
or
INTELLIGENCE SUMMARY.
(Erase heading not required.)

Place	Date	Hour	Summary of Events and Information	Remarks and references to Appendices
			ECONOMY AUGUST 1918.	
			Percentage of Rations underdrawn.	
			for Week-ending. P.M. Biscuits. Tea. Cheese.	
			August. 2. 12¼% 10⅛% 5¼% —	
			" 9. — 8% — 5%	
			" 16. — — — —	
			" 23. 3⅔% 4⅛% — —	
			" 30. 4% 7¾% — —	
			AMOUNT OF WAR SAVINGS CERTIFICATES PURCHASED TO END OF AUGUST 1918.	
			CERTIFICATES. 928 @ 15/6 = £719"4"0.	
			FOR AUGUST ONLY.	
			CERTIFICATES. 47 @ 15/6 = £36"8"6.	

Instructions regarding War Diaries and Intelligence Summaries are contained in F. S. Regs., Part II. and the Staff Manual respectively. Title pages will be prepared in manuscript.

Page 13.
Army Form C. 2118.
August 1918.

WAR DIARY
INTELLIGENCE SUMMARY.
(Erase heading not required.)

3rd CAV. DIV.

Instructions regarding War Diaries and Intelligence Summaries are contained in F. S. Regs., Part II. and the Staff Manual respectively. Title pages will be prepared in manuscript.

Summary of Events and Information

MILEAGE AND PETROL.

Lorries on Detachment during Month ending 30-7-18.

Mileage.			Petrol.	
Loaded.	Empty.	Total.	Gallons.	Average. M.P.G.
13,411.	12,351.	25,762.	4,781.	5.39.

Monthly Mileage Return 31/7/18 to 27/8/18 inclusive, including mileage of lorries on Detachment.

Mileage.			Petrol.	
Loaded.	Empty.	Total.	Gallons.	Average. M.P.G.
47,266.	39,738.	87,004.	16,896.	5.15.

Place	Date	Hour		Remarks and references to Appendices

WAR DIARY
or
INTELLIGENCE SUMMARY.
(Erase heading not required.)

Army Form C. 2118.

GENERAL NOTES ON THE ~~AUGUST~~ October QUESTIONS FROM A MECHANICAL TRANSPORT POINT OF VIEW.

with

(a) Pack arrived daily shortage of 700 rations. This necessitated much waste of time in an officer of the M.T. Company going round the country endeavouring to borrow rations from other Railheads.

It would be a help to the M.T. Company if the S.S.O. was at Railhead each morning during operations.

(b) Too many lorries detached from the M.T. Company. There were as many as 24 detached with the Division, besides 40 that were lent to Canadian Corps to move Ammunition Dump for 48 hours.

During active operations the following lorries only should be detached.

To C.F.A. for walking wounded.	3.
Sanitary Section.	1.
A.O.D.	3.
A.S.C. Headquarters.	1.
Signals.	1.
Postal Service.	1.
"A" Mess.	1.
Canteen.	1.
	12.

24 lorries are almost sufficient to feed two Brigades of Cavalry.

WAR DIARY
or
INTELLIGENCE SUMMARY.
(Erase heading not required.)

Army Form C. 2118.

-2-

6

Of the remaining, 12 lorries did no mileage whatsoever and were used as a store for extra kits. This is a great wastage of transport.
Four lorries were employed in moving advanced dumps of forage. This should be avoided see (c) below.

(c) Full rations of hay should not be taken forward with the rations. During the recent operations we had 4 forage dumps, one for each night supplies were delivered. Four lorries were used for moving these dumps forward and in the end the whole quantity had to be brought back to the M.T. Company.

This could be avoided if only half rations of hay were loaded and the Brigade Supply Officer would say daily at Rendez-vous whether they would accept the hay. If it could not be accepted, then they hay would not be off loaded but brought back to the M.T. Company and dumped. If accepted by Brigades then it is not to be dumped and moved forward daily. In other words the custom of making forage dumps at every refilling point must cease.

(d) Fuel. A small quantity of fuel should be loaded on supply lorries daily. In recent operations fuel dumps were formed, not used at all, and had to be brought back.

(e) A.O.D. Lorries. D.A.D.O.S. to be allotted 3 instead of six lorries. These lorries are sufficient to clear Railhead etc. As units are unable to accept full horse rations, it stands to reason that they will not accept Ordnance Stores.
In the event of extra lorries being required the M.T. would supply transport on demand from D.A.D.O.S.

(f) In choosing Refilling Points the conditions of the roads or tracks should be considered, as the lorries will have to travel at night without lights.

Army Form C. 2118.

WAR DIARY
or
INTELLIGENCE SUMMARY.
(Erase heading not required.)

PAGE 1.

September 1918

8th CAVALRY M.G. COMPANY

Place	Date	Hour	Summary of Events and Information	Remarks and references to Appendices
AVERDOIGNT. September.	1st.		The Company was at AVERDOIGNT. Railhead at TINQUES. The Division was loaded and refilled in the following areas:- Divisional Troops WAIL. 6th Brigade. NUNCQ. 7th Brigade. CONCHY. Canadian Brigade. MONCHEL. The 10th Hussars and about one third of the 6th Machine Gun Squadron at WAILLY, South of ARRAS.	
"	2nd.		Railhead TINQUES. Loading and refilling same as yesterday.	
"	3rd, 4th,} 5th. }		Normal. Captain B.C. Bewley granted leave to England to 17/9/18.	
"	6th.		The Company less Workshops moved from AVERDOIGNT to VACQUERIE le BOUCQ. Railhead for the day TINQUES. Rations delivered to Brigades in the same areas as yesterday with the exception of the 6th Brigade which moved from the NUNCQ area. to an area between WAIL and HESDIN. Divisional Headquarters moved to FONTAINE L'ETALON. Advised that Railhead for the 7th would be FREVENT. This was altered late during the night to TINQUES. Lieut A.V. Campbell proceeded on leave to England for 14 days.	
VACQUERIE.	7th.		Railhead FREVENT. Brigades fed in the same areas as on 6th inst., Workshops joined the Company from AVERDOIGNT.	
"	8th.		Normal	
"	9th.		Railhead FREVENT. The Company refilled 6th Brigade and Divisional Troops, and certain units of the 7th Brigade. The remainder of the Division was fed by Horse Transport.	

Army Form C. 2118.

WAR DIARY
or
INTELLIGENCE SUMMARY.

PAGE 2. September 1918

(Erase heading not required.)

Place	Date	Hour	Summary of Events and Information	Remarks and references to Appendices
VACQUERIE. September.	10th.		Railhead as on 9th inst., Loading and refilling also as yesterday except that the Reserve Park drew by their own transport. 7th Brigade was fed by the Company in new area around WILLEMAN.	
"	11th - 15th		Normal.	
"	16th.		Railhead.FREVENT. The Division in conjunction with other forces took part in manoeuvres, consequently the Company loaded for the whole Division. Rendez-vous for the day ST POL - HESDIN Road with head of Column at LE BOUT HAUT Cross Roads at 1.0pm. Brigade Supply Officers guided the lorries for their respective Brigades to the following areas:-	

			6th Brigade. GRIGNY & HESDIN.
			    7th Brigade. ROLLENCOURT.
			    Canadian Brigade. BLANGY.
			    Divisional Troops. ESTRAVAILE.	

"	17th.		Railhead as on the 16th inst., Lorries after loading returned to Park to await orders from the Senior Supply Officer. Brigades were refilled in the following areas during the afternoon.	

			6th Brigade. AUTHEUX.
			    7th Brigade. WAVANS.
			    Canadian Brigade. OUTREBOIS.
			    Divisional Troops. WAVANS.	

			Two sections of lorries with Workshop and Store lorry attached from the 16th G.H.Q. Reserve M.T. Company with Lieut, W.E. Whitehead and 2/Lieut, S.R.J. Marley returned to their unit in accordance with Cavalry Corps Q/4340/4. The 6 lorries attached from 7th G.H.Q. Reserve M.T. Company also returned to their unit.	

Army Form C. 2118.

WAR DIARY
or
INTELLIGENCE SUMMARY.

(Erase heading not required.)

PAGE 3.   September 1918

8th C.M.T. COMPANY

Instructions regarding War Diaries and Intelligence Summaries are contained in F. S. Regs., Part II. and the Staff Manual respectively. Title pages will be prepared in manuscript.

Place	Date	Hour	Summary of Events and Information	Remarks and references to Appendices
VACQUERIE. September.	18th.		Brigades return to their old areas at the close of manoeuvres and are fed there. 3 Sections of 16 Albion lorries each arrived from ROUEN in relief of 2 Sections of the 16th G.H.Q. Reserve M.T. Company to complete new War Establishment and as a second echelon. The following two officers report with the lorries Lieut, H.B. Davis, and 2/Lieut, H.J. Bleach.	

"	19th		The Brigades re-adjust areas as follows, and are refilled there:-
			
			     6th Brigade. REBREUVE.
			     7th Brigade. WILLEMAN.
			     Canadian Brigade. BOUBERS-SUR-CANCHE.
			     Divisional Headquarters remain at FONTAINE L'ETALON.
			
			 Colonel Cuming, O.C.A.S.C. inspected Company, i.e. Lorry Park, Cook-house, Billets, etc.	

"	19th, 21st.		Loading and refilling as on 19th.	
"	22nd.		Normal. Lieut. W.L. Biard reported for duty to complete establishment of Officers. 1 Sgt. and 19 O.Rs. reported to complete establishment of Supply Details. Two lorries (Albion) also reported to complete new War Establishment.	
"	23rd, 24th.		Normal.	
"	25th.		Division loaded in detail at FREVENT and Brigades are fed in the following new areas:-	

Army Form C. 2118.

WAR DIARY or INTELLIGENCE SUMMARY.

PAGE 4.

September 1916

(Erase heading not required.)

Place	Date	Hour	Summary of Events and Information	Remarks and references to Appendices

VACQUERIE. September.	25th.		Continued.
			
			   Divisional Troops. MARIEUX.
			   Canadian Brigade. THIEVRES.
			   6th Brigade. MARIEUX.
			   7th Brigade. AMPLIER.
			
			  In view of the Division moving to a forward area, the Ammunition Section was sent forward to Dump Establishment Ammunition. A dump was made at MOISLANS and lorries returned to VACQUERIE on the 26th inst., Notified at 4.8pm. that Railhead for the morrow would be TRONES WOOD. During the evening Section "B" together with Lieut, A.V. Campbell and Supply personnel, proceeded to the neighbourhood of the new Railhead. Lieut, B.A. Bowers proceeded to England.	

MOISLANS.	26th.		The Division was loaded for in detail at FREVENT, the information that TRONES WOOD would be the Railhead for the day being cancelled. The Company excluding Workshops moved to MOISLANS and after delivering rations to the units in the following areas, the dumping lorries returned to new Park.
			
			   Divisional Troops. ALBERT.
			   Canadian Brigade. (MARTINSAART.
			   6th Brigade. (MEAULT.
			   7th Brigade. AVELUY.	

"	27th.		Railhead for the day MOISLANS.
			Loading at Mid-day the units were fed in the following areas:-
			
			   Divisional Headquarters.
			   Canadian Brigade. CURLU.
			   6th Brigade. HEM.
			   7th Brigade. CURLU.	

Army Form C. 2118.

WAR DIARY
or
INTELLIGENCE SUMMARY.

(Erase heading not required.)

PAGE 5. September 1918

Place	Date	Hour	Summary of Events and Information	Remarks and references to Appendices
MOISLANS. September.	27th.		Continued. Lieut. F.R. Hodgson, O/c Ammunition Section arrived with Section to new Park. 9 lorries load tents etc, at LA CHAPELLETTE and deliver to Division at CLERY.	
"	28th.		Division loaded at LE PLATEAU and refilled the units in the following areas:- Divisional Troops.) CLERY. Canadian Brigade.) CURLU. 6th Brigade.) 7th Brigade.) HEM.	
"	29th.		Railhead LE PLATEAU. Supplies were dumped in same area as yesterday by mid-day. Orders were received that the Division was at 3 hours notice to move, later that Brigades were moving immediately to a forward area. Supplies were re-loaded and taken to forward area. Rendez-vous HACOURT Cross Roads. Brigades were refilled late at night in area around VERMAND. 30 lorries to CHIGNOLLES loaded ammunition and dumped at QUINCONCE. The Company moved to new Park at FEUILLERES. 10 lorries pick up tents and great coats at CURLU and dump same at LA CHAPELLETTE.	
"	30th.		Railhead LE PLATEAU. Rations dumped to units in same areas as yesterday i.e. VERMAND area. Divisional Headquarters POEUILLY. Workshops joined Company from VACQUERIE. 16 lorries load great coats and tents at LA CHAPELLETTE & LE PLATEAU, and deliver the same to units in the forward area.	

Army Form C. 2118.

WAR DIARY
or
INTELLIGENCE SUMMARY.

(Erase heading not required.)

PAGE 6. September 1918

Summary of Events and Information

The first part of the month the work of the company was normal. The arrival of new sections of lorries from England to complete the new War Establishment occurred just prior to the Division taking part in Active Operations. The personnel of the 3 sections was composed in the main, of men with extremely short experience in Mechanical Transport work, and with practically no overseas experience.

In view of strenuous work which was inevitable, it was thought advisable to re-arrange the personnel of the whole Company. This was done and men with experience were put on lorries with the new men.

This arrangement worked extremely well, and the efficient working of the Company was well maintained during the strenuous days at the end of the month.

Army Form C. 2118.

WAR DIARY
or
INTELLIGENCE SUMMARY.

(Erase heading not required.)

PAGE 7.

September 1918

Summary of Events and Information

SUMMARY OF WORK CARRIED OUT DURING SEPTEMBER 1918.

(a) VEHICLES THOROUGHLY OVERHAULED.

    Lorries.   6.   and 3 still undergoing overhaul.

    Cars.   3.   and 18 minor repairs.

    Motor cycles.   3.

    Ambulances.   1.

(b) CONDITION OF VEHICLES AFTER DISMANTLING.

Taking into consideration the age of some of the vehicles overhauled, the amount of wear is fairly light. Daimler "C.C." lorries are now showing signs of extreme wear.

(c) LARGE DEMANDS FOR SPARES.

    N I L.

(d) WORKING HOURS.

The working hours during the month have been normal. 7.30am to 5.0pm. with 1 hour for dinner.

Army Form C. 2118.

WAR DIARY
or
INTELLIGENCE SUMMARY.

(Erase heading not required.)

PAGE 8. September 1918

Summary of Events and Information

(e) FORTNIGHTLY INSPECTION OF CARS AND AMBULANCES.

This was very irregular during the 1st half of the month owing to the Military Situation.
During the 2nd half of the month the attendance of cars etc for inspection was quite regular.

(f) ALTERATIONS IN ESTABLISHMENT.

Workshop and Store lorry with personnel attached from 16th G.H.Q. Reserve M.T. Company rejoined their unit on 17/9/18. These have been replaced by 1 Albion Store and 1 Workshop lorry on the 25th to complete establishment. This shop is complete with personnel but no N.C.Os.

(g) VEHICLES EVACUATED TO HEAVY REPAIR SHOP.

2 Daimler "C.C." lorries Nos. 7288 and 7252 worn out.

Cars.   NIL.

Motor cycles.   2 Triumphs - smashed frames.
                1 Douglas - worn out.

(h) PISTONS FOR DAIMLER "Y" TYPE LORRY.

The petrol tank for Wolseley 16 - 20 H.P. car, mentioned in last month's report, has not yet been received.

These were advised on the 19th inst., but have not yet been received and means delay in this lorry being returned for duty.

Army Form C. 2118.

WAR DIARY
or
INTELLIGENCE SUMMARY.

PAGE 9. September 1918

(Erase heading not required.)

Place	Date	Hour	Summary of Events and Information	Remarks and references to Appendices
			(i) Daimler "C.C." lorries are gradually crocking up. A.D.S.&T. Cavalry Corps has been informed it is desired to evacuate up to 7 of these. To date 2 have been evacuated and authority has been asked for the evacuation of the third.	

AMMUNITION ISSUED FOR MONTH OF SEPTEMBER 1918.

Description.	Rounds.
N.	Nil.
NX.	Nil.
S.A.A. Ord.	118,000.
S.A.A. M.G.	58,824.
S.A.A. Tracer.	372.
S.A.A. A.P.	11,232.
S.A.A. Practice.	45,000.
Pistol Webley.	8,640.
Cartridges Ill. 1"	600.
Signal Par. 1½"	185.
Ground Flares, Red.	992.

Instructions regarding War Diaries and Intelligence Summaries are contained in F. S. Regs., Part II. and the Staff Manual respectively. Title pages will be prepared in manuscript.

Army Form C. 2118.

WAR DIARY
or
INTELLIGENCE SUMMARY.
(Erase heading not required.)

PAGE 10. September 1918

O.O. 3rd Cavalry Divisional M.T. Coy.

Major.

ECONOMY   SEPTEMBER 1918.

Percentage of Rations underdrawn.

Week-ending.	P.M.	Biscuits.
September 6.	-	14½%
" 13.	4%	18%
" 20.	-	7½%
" 27.	-	-

FIELD PUNISHMENTS.

1 28 days Field Punishment No.2.

WAR SAVINGS.

Total purchased to end of September 1918.
935 Certificates = £724-12-6.
Amount purchased in September 1918 only.
7 Certificates = £5-8-6.

Army Form C. 2118.

WAR DIARY
or
INTELLIGENCE SUMMARY.
(Erase heading not required).

3RD CAVALRY M.T. COMPANY.

PAGE 1. October 1918.

Place	Date	Hour	Summary of Events and Information	Remarks and references to Appendices
FEUILLERES. October	1st.		Railhead LA PLATEAU. Column remains at FEUILLERES. Brigades fed in same area as on 30th. ultimo. Divisional Troops CAULINCOURT POEUILLY 6th. Brigade BEHICOURT 7th. Brigade VERMAND Canadian Brigade CAULINCOURT	
"	2nd.		Loading and refilling as yesterday. Ammunition Section despatched to load Ammunition (Establishment) which had been dumped at MOISLANS in view of a forward move. Two lorries join Company loaded with 4.5 Detail of the 4th. Guards Brigade are attached to the Company with 9 lorries. 2nd. Echelon of supplies loaded from dump on Park.	
"	3rd.		Railhead FLAMMICOURT. Company on double Echelon. Section loaded 3-10-18. Section refilled Brigades in following area :- Divisional Troops VERMAND. 6th. Brigade BELLE EGLISE. 7th. Brigade BEHICOURT. Canadian Brigade VERMAND.	
"	4th.		Railhead FLAMMICOURT. Section loaded 2-10-18 refilled Brigades :- Divisional Troops BEHICOURT 6th. Brigade " 7th. Brigade " Canadian Brigade VERMAND.	

Army Form C. 2118.

3RD CAVALRY M.T. COMPANY.

WAR DIARY
or
INTELLIGENCE SUMMARY.

(Erase heading not required.)

PAGE 2   October 1918.

Instructions regarding War Diaries and Intelligence Summaries are contained in F. S. Regs., Part II. and the Staff Manual respectively. Title pages will be prepared in manuscript.

Place	Date	Hour	Summary of Events and Information	Remarks and references to Appendices
FEUILLERES October	5th.		Railhead FLAMMICOURT. Supplies were delivered to Units in following area :- Divisional Troops BEHICOURT 6th. Brigade TREFCON 7th. Brigade VERMAND Canadian Brigade VERMAND Workshops moved from FEUILLERES to PERONNE.	
"	6th.		Railhead FLAMMICOURT. Supplies were delivered to Units in following area :- Divisional Troops POEUILLY - BEHICOURT 6th. Brigade TERTRY - TREFCON 1 Squadron at) BELLE EGLISE.) 7th. Brigade BEHICOURT Canadian Brigade VERMAND. 2/Lieut. W.S. Jones. R.F.A. rejoined from leave to England	
"	7th.		Railhead FLAMMICOURT. Supplies were dumped in same area as yesterday.	
"	8th.		Railhead FLAMMICOURT. Rendez-vous BELLENGLISE, and lorries dumped later in the forward area. Great congestion of traffic was experienced on the road and Column was considerably delayed at the bridge of BELLENGLISE. Lorries after dumping parked at ROISEL for the night.	

Army Form C. 2118.

3RD CAVALRY M.T. COMPANY.

WAR DIARY
or
INTELLIGENCE SUMMARY.

PAGE 3.   October, 1918.

(Erase heading not required.)

Instructions regarding War Diaries and Intelligence Summaries are contained in F. S. Regs., Part II. and the Staff Manual respectively. Title pages will be prepared in manuscript.

Place	Date	Hour	Summary of Events and Information	Remarks and references to Appendices
HAMELET-BERNES ROAD October	9th.		Railhead ROISEL. The Company moved to the road HAMELET - BERNES. Refilling Section rendez-vous East of ESTREES on ESTREES - MARETZ road, and later dumped in forward area.	
"	10th.		Railhead ROISEL. Refilling Section left Park at 7 a.m. rendez-vous at cross roads South of SEQUAIN, dumped later in forward area and returned to Park at 2.a.m. on 11th. instant. Lieut. F.R. Hodgson and 2/Lieut. W.S. Jones. R.F.A. proceeded with the Ammunition Section to forward area and there, was joined by the Ammunition Section of the 1st Cavalry Division, and formed a Cavalry Corps Ammunition Park. Lieut. F.R. Hodgson became Officer in charge. 2/Lieut. C.H. Wyatt joined the Company from the Central M.T. School of Instruction.	
"	11th.		Railhead ROISEL. Brigades refilled in the following area :- Divisional Troops CLAIRY - MONTIGNY 6th. Brigade ELINCOURT 7th. Brigade BERTRY Canadian Brigade MONTIGNY.	
"	12th.		Railhead ROISEL. Brigades were fed in the following area :- Divisional Troops ELLINCOURT - MONTIGNY 6th. Brigade ELLINCOURT 7th. Brigade BERTRY Canadian Brigade MONTIGNY	

Army Form C. 2118.

WAR DIARY
or
INTELLIGENCE SUMMARY.
(Erase heading not required.)

3RD CAVALRY M.T. COMPANY.

PAGE 4. October 1918

Place	Date	Hour	Summary of Events and Information	Remarks and references to Appendices
HAMELET-BERNES ROAD. October.	12th.		Five lorries left with Ordnance from PERONNE for the Divisional area, and did not return until the following morning.	
"	13th.		Railhead ROISEL. Brigades moved back and were fed in the following areas :- BANTOUZELLE & HONNECOURT.	
"	14th.		Railhead ROISEL. Division was fed on Single Echelon. Lorries loaded and delivered to Brigades in following area :- Divisional Hd. Qrs. HENNOIS WOOD 6th Brigade HENNOIS WOOD 7th Brigade BERTINCOURT Canadian Brigade YTRES The lorries which loaded rations on 13th. instant remained loaded. 2/Lieut. W.S. Jones. R.F.A. rejoined the Company with some lorries of the Ammunition Section from forward area. Lieut. F.R. Hodgson. remained in the forward area, awaiting return of lorries which had been detailed by the Division to convey Tents etc. to the Brigades.	

Army Form C. 2118.

WAR DIARY
or
INTELLIGENCE SUMMARY.

3RD CAVALRY M.T. COMPANY.

PAGE 5. October 1918.

(Erase heading not required.)

Place	Date	Hour	Summary of Events and Information	Remarks and references to Appendices
BARASTRE October	15th.		Railhead LE TRANSLOY. Company moved to BARASTRE Supplies for the Division were loaded in bulk. Rations loaded on the 15th. instant were delivered to Brigades in same area as on 14th. instant. Lieut. F.R. Hodgson rejoined the Company from forward area with the remaining Ammunition Section lorries.	
"	16th		Loading and refilling as on 15th. instant.	
"	17th to 19th.		Normal	
"	20th.		70 lorries were detailed to VERMAND 6.30 a.m. to move the 6th Division. This necessitated the use of H.T. for loading and refilling Division. Troops were conveyed to ST. SOUPLET, two journeys were necessary. Lorries parked for the night at EPEHY. Lieut. L.C. Baillon left the Company for Tour of Duty in England.	
"	21st.		Railhead LE TRANSLOY. 70 lorries returned from detail of previous day. Division refilled by lorries with exception of Divisional Troops. 12 Albion lorries joined Company to replace 12 lorries being transferred to Base, under authority A.D.S.&T. Cav. Corps No. T 515/12.	
"	22nd.		Railhead LE TRANSLOY Divisional Troops refilled by H.T. remainder of Division by lorries. 3 cases of P.U.O. were discovered in the Company.	
"	23rd.		Railhead LE TRANSLOY. Loading and refilling same as on 22nd. instant. Under authority A.D.S.&T. Cav. Corps. No. T 515/12, 2 Dennis, 2 Halfords, 1 Leyland, 2 Peerless and 6 Saurer Lorries were despatched to Base. 2 more cases of P.U.O. in the Company.	

Army Form C. 2118.

3RD CAVALRY M.T. COMPANY.

WAR DIARY or INTELLIGENCE SUMMARY.

(Erase heading not required.)

PAGE 6.   October 1918

Place	Date	Hour	Summary of Events and Information	Remarks and references to Appendices

BARASTRE. October	24th.		Normal
			51 lorries were detailed to move H.A.C. and 4th. Guard's Brigade
			as follows :-
			    H.A.C. from PRUY FARM to BAPAUME
			    4th. Guard's Brigade from COMBLES to BAPAUME
			The detail was completed and lorries returned to the Park.
			One more case of P.U.O.	

"	25th.		Normal. Three more cases of P.U.O.	
"	26th.		Normal. Six more cases of P.U.O.	
"	27th.		Normal. Five more cases of P.U.O.	
"	28th.		Normal. 2/Lieut. R.H.F.P. Sadler was evacuated to Hospital suffering from P.U.O.	
"	29th.		Normal. Six more cases of P.U.O. Captain N. Coates was evacuated to Hospital suffering from P.U.O.	
"	30th.		Normal. Eight more cases of P.U.O. 2/Lieut. J.H. Whiteley joined the Company to complete Establishment of officers.	

Army Form C. 2118.

WAR DIARY
or
INTELLIGENCE SUMMARY.

3RD CAVALRY M.T. COMPANY.

PAGE 7   October 1918.

(Erase heading not required.)

Instructions regarding War Diaries and Intelligence Summaries are contained in F. S. Regs., Part II. and the Staff Manual respectively. Title pages will be prepared in manuscript.

Place	Date	Hour	Summary of Events and Information	Remarks and references to Appendices
BARASTRE. October.	31st.		Normal. Three more cases of P.U.O. Altogether during the month there has been 5 officers and 37 O.R.s of the Company taken sick with P.U.O.	

[signature]
Major,
O.C. 3rd Cavalry Divisional M.T. Coy.

Army Form C. 2118.

3rd
CAVALRY
M.T. COMPANY.

WAR DIARY
or
INTELLIGENCE SUMMARY.

(Erase heading not required.)

October 1918.

Place	Date	Hour	Summary of Events and Information	Remarks and references to Appendices

AMMUNITION ISSUED FOR MONTH OF OCTOBER 1918.

Description.	Rounds.
N.	2148
N.X.	1504
S.A.A. Ord.	100000
S.A.A. Tracer.	966
S.A.A. Practice.	2000
S.A.A. A.P.	6192
Pistol Webley.	7406
Auto. Colt. .45	250
Cartridges. Ill. 1"	156
Signal Para. 1½"	236
Auto. Colt. .380	30
Ground Flares Red.	1722

Major.
O.C. 3rd Cavalry Divisional M.T. Coy.

Army Form C. 2118.

WAR DIARY
or
INTELLIGENCE SUMMARY.

(Erase heading not required.)

3rd CAVALRY M.T. COMPANY.

October 1918.

Place	Date	Hour	Summary of Events and Information	Remarks and references to Appendices
			SALVAGE DURING THE MONTH:-	
			18 pdr. Ammunition. 3652	
			do. Cases 7300	
			4.5 Ammunition 478	
			4.5 Charges 267	
			6" How. 466	
			6" Shells 55	
			6" Cartridges 3 Cases	
			6" Fuzes 18 Boxes	
			60 pdr. Ammunition 483	
			60 pdr. Cartridges 14 Cases	
			60 pdr. Fuzes 16	
			5.9 Cases 60	
			9" Cases 400	
			Misc. Shell Cases 4043	
			S.A.A. 55495	
			S.A.A. M.G. 24982	
			S.A.A. Boxes only 700	
			Drums for Lewis Gun) 5 Drums.	
			Loaded S.A.A.)	
			Telephone Wire 1 Coil.	
			(approx. 220 yards)	
			15 cm. German Shells 230	
			S.A.A. German 270	
			Rifles 48	
			Shell Clips 18 Bags	
			M.T. Oil. 1 Barrel	
			Steel Helmets 21	
			Petrol Tins 8	
			Scrap Brass 2 cwt.	
			Brass Hub Caps 5	
			Dray Washers 1	
			Ammunition Pouches 1	
			M.G. Belt. 1	
			Riding Pants 25 Pairs	
			Saddles 189	
			Boots Ankle 8 Pairs	
			Swords 108	
			Bandoliers 82	
			Pack Saddles 3	
			Pack Saddle Tools 2	
			Signallers Flags 4	
			Signallers Rolls 4	

Army Form C. 2118.

3RD CAVALRY M.T. COMPANY.

WAR DIARY or INTELLIGENCE SUMMARY.

(Erase heading not required.)

November 1918

page 1.

Place	Date	Hour	Summary of Events and Information	Remarks and references to Appendices
BARRASTRE. November.	1		RAILHEAD - LE TRANSLOY. Normal.	
"	2		Normal.	
"	3		Normal.	
"	4		Normal. Lieut. F.C. Bune proceeded on Special Leave.	
"	5		Normal.	
"	6		RAILHEAD - LE TRANSLOY. Supplies delivered to Division and parked for the night at CAMBRAI.	
"	7		RAILHEAD - MARCOING. Supply Train arrived 5.pm. Column left BARRASTRE and parked S.E. of DOUAI on main DOUAI - ARRAS Road.	
"	8		RAILHEAD - DON. Supply Convoy left park for EON and fed Division. Column left park near DOUAI for new destination PHALEMPIN.	
"	9		RAILHEAD - DON. Double Echelon of lorries and Lieut. W.L. Biard attached to 2nd Army for feeding VII Brigade.	
"	10		RAILHEAD - DON. Supply Echelon rendez-vous SAINGHIEN then proceeded to Brigades and returned to park at PHALEMPIN.	
"	11		RAILHEAD - FIVES Nr. LILLE. Column moved from PHALEMPIN to FIVES and parked. 2nd Echelon proceeded to rendez-vous at TOURNAI and from thence to ANTOING TO dump and returned to park at FIVES.	

Army Form C. 2118.

WAR DIARY
or
INTELLIGENCE SUMMARY.
(Erase heading not required.)

NOVEMBER 1918 Page 2.

Instructions regarding War Diaries and Intelligence Summaries are contained in F. S. Regs., Part II. and the Staff Manual respectively. Title pages will be prepared in manuscript.

Place	Date	Hour	Summary of Events and Information	Remarks and references to Appendices
FIVES. November.	12.		RAILHEAD - FIVES. Supply lorries left park for rendez-vous TOURNAI from thence to Dumps and returned to FIVES on completion of duty.	
"	13		RAILHEAD - FIVES. Ammunition Section proceeded to CALAIS to collect Ordnance Stores for the Division. Division fed by M.T.	
"	14.		RAILHEAD - FIVES. Ammunition Section returned from CALAIS. Normal. Trains greatly delayed.	
"	15		RAILHEAD - FIVES. Lorries returned from CALAIS delivered Ordnance Stores to Dumps. 25 lorries unloaded train of Hay - 2 days - and dumped at park. No Supply Train.	
"	16		RAILHEAD - ASCQ. Ammunition collected from dump at PHALEMPIN and evacuated to Ammunition Railhead ASCQ. 1 days Hay collected from park and Division fed on hard rations.	
"	17		RAILHEAD - ASCQ. Division fed on hard rations. Supply lorries loaded at Railhead and returned to park loaded.	

Army Form C. 2118.

Page 3

NOVEMBER 1918.

3RD CAVALRY M.T. COMPANY.

WAR DIARY
or
INTELLIGENCE SUMMARY.
(Erase heading not required.)

Instructions regarding War Diaries and Intelligence Summaries are contained in F. S. Regs., Part II. and the Staff Manual respectively. Title pages will be prepared in manuscript.

Place	Date	Hour	Summary of Events and Information	Remarks and references to Appendices

ENGHIEN. November	18		RAILHEAD – SWEVEGHEM.
			Column left Fives and parked at ENGHIEN.
			Division fed by loaded section at following dumps:-
			    Divisional Troops. — ENGHIEN.
			    3rd Field Squadron. — STEENKUP.
			    Div'l Ammn. Coln. — COQUAINE.
			    Aux. Horse Transport — ENGHIEN.
			    VI Brigade. — SAINTES.
			    VII Brigade. — CASTRE.
			    Canadians. — HERINNES.	

"	19		RAILHEAD – SWEVEGHEM. System of treble Echelon commenced. Division fed by Mechanical Transport at dumps as November 18th.	
"	20		Railhead moves from SWEVEGHEM to AUDENARDE. Normal. Dumps same as 19th. Five busses reported for duty from Cavalry Corps Troops M.T. Company. 2 kept for duty at Company Headquarters, 3 despatched to Railhead for duty at Leave Rest Camp.	

"	21		RAILHEAD – AUDENARDE.
			Division fed in Brigade bulk.
			    Div. Troops and VII Bde. — WATERLOO.
			    Canadians — LA HUPPE.
			    VI Brigade. — OTTIGNIES.	

Army Form C. 2118.

Page 4
NOVEMBER 1918

WAR DIARY
or
INTELLIGENCE SUMMARY

(Erase heading not required.)

3RD CAVALRY M.T. COMPANY.

Place	Date	Hour	Summary of Events and Information	Remarks and references to Appendices
ENGHIEN. November.	22		RAILHEAD – AUDENARDE. Division fed in bulk dumping at Divisional Headquarters at THORRENBRAIS. 40 kilometres South East of BRUSSELS.	
"	23		RAILHEAD – AUDENARDE. Divisional Troops – PERWEZ. VI Brigade. – ECHEZES. VII Brigade. – TODOIGNE – THORREMBRAIS. Canadians. – on LOUVAIN – ECHEZE Road. Division fed in Brigade Bulk.	
"	24		RAILHEAD – AUDENARDE. Division fed in Brigade bulk. Divisional Troops – ST. MARIE – WASTIGNES. VI Brigade. – DHUY. VII Brigade. – INGOURT. Canadians. – PERWEZ. Train unloaded in Bulk at Railhead and dumped.	
"	25.		RAILHEAD – AUDENARDE. Division fed on Hard Rations from dump accumulated at M.T. Company ENGHIEN. Dumped in Brigade Bulk. Dumps same as 24th.	
"	26		RAILHEAD – AUDENARDE. Division fed and rations dumped in Divisional Bulk at WAVRE.	

Army Form C. 2118.

pages 5
NOVEMBER 1918

3RD CAVALRY M.T. COMPANY

WAR DIARY
or
INTELLIGENCE SUMMARY.
(Erase heading not required.)

Instructions regarding War Diaries and Intelligence Summaries are contained in F. S. Regs., Part II. and the Staff Manual respectively. Title pages will be prepared in manuscript.

Place	Date	Hour	Summary of Events and Information	Remarks and references to Appendices
ENGHIEN. November	27.		RAILHEAD - AUDENARDE. Division fed at Brigade Dumps. Dumps same as 24th. Railhead moves from AUDENARDE to AUVELAIS map ref NAMUR H.1.	
GEMBLOUX. November	28.		Column moves from ENGHIEN to GEMBLOUX. Railhead cancelled at AUVELAIS to AUDENARDE. 1 Echelon immediately despatched from GEMBLOUX to AUDENARDE to off load train on 29th. Detachment of 35 lorries provided by 2nd Army off loaded train 28th - 29th. Division fed and supplies dumped at Brigade Dumps same as 27th.	
"	29.		RAILHEAD - AUDENARDE. 19 of 2nd Army Detachment arrived with supplies. 14 of 2nd Army Detachment arrived with supplies. 1 days iron rations consumed from Reserve Park. Railhead moves from AUDENARDE to NAMUR.	
"	30.		RAILHEAD - NAMUR. No Supply train arrives owing to serious congestion of the railway.	

Army Form C. 2118.

page 6.
NOVEMBER 1918

3RD
CAVALRY
M.T. COMPANY

WAR DIARY
or
INTELLIGENCE SUMMARY.
(Erase heading not required.)

Summary of Events and Information

It is possible that the last fortnight of the month has been the most strenuous time of the War for the Mechanical Transport Company.

Had the roads been better, trains arrived to time, and not such congestion on the roads it would have been quite a simple operation to feed the Division on Treble Echelon.

The greatest difficulty was the narrow pave roads encountered on the GRAMMONT - AUDENARDE Road which was a single route going East to West for British Troops, and a single route going West to East for the French and American Transport.

Convoys completing the 4 hours journey from ENGHIEN to Railhead within 12 hours considered themselves fortunate.

The casualties to lorries in Springs and Tyres were abnormal.

As many as 29 lorries at a time were off the road, and as the unit was a few lorries short of the Treble Echelon to start with it necessitated trying to work on Double Echelon at times.

Every possible assistance was given the Mechanical Transport Company from the Divisional Headquarters and from the Brigades who fully realized the difficulties that we were up against, and were most sympathetic and helpful.

I have never seen men more weary and exhausted than were the drivers of the Supply Lorries towards the end of the month.

It is solely due to the untiring energy of every individual in the Company that supplies never failed to be delivered to units.

Army Form C. 2118.

page. 7.
November 1915

3rd CAVALRY M.T. COMPANY.

WAR DIARY
or
INTELLIGENCE SUMMARY.
(Erase heading not required.)

Summary of Events and Information

WORKSHOPS REPORT FOR NOVEMBER.

(a) THOROUGH OVERHAULS.

    Lorries   11   (chiefly engines)
    Cars   5
    Ambulances   4
    Motor Cycles   12

(b) General condition on dismantling slightly better than preceeding months.
    Owing to evacuations, lorries etc. taken for overhauls not quite so deteriorated.

(c) Large demand for spares, general stock largely increased by order for providing spares during occupation of Germany.

(d) Artificers have worked exceedingly long hours, about 70 hours a week recently.

(e) Vehicles have not been sent in regularly for inspection.

(f) Alterations in Establishment. NIL.

(g) EVACUATIONS. (LORRIES)
    Daimler C.C. Type. W.D. Nos:- 7239 7254 7215 7221 7299
    Daimler Y Type. W.D. Nos:-   30289
    Albion 3 Ton W.D. Nos:-   2166 7155
        All for complete overhaul.

    In addition Daimler Lorries C.C. Type W.D. Nos:- 7213 7328 7282
    7292 7723 6968 were transferred to Reserve Vehicle Park L of C (N)
    only fit for Base Duties and were replaced by 6 New Albions.

Army Form C. 2118.
Page. 9.
NOVEMBER 1915.

3RD CAVALRY M.T. COMPANY.

WAR DIARY
or
INTELLIGENCE SUMMARY.
(Erase heading not required.)

Place	Date	Hour	Summary of Events and Information	Remarks and references to Appendices
			(g) EVACUATIONS. (CARS)	

			Wolseley Car M 14826 alloted to Divisional Headquarters.) For general
			    Ford Box Car M 45733 " 3rd. Signal Squadron) overhaul.
			    Sunbeam Car M 59105 " S.S.O.3rd. Cav. Div. with smashed rear axle and caseing	

			EVACUATIONS (CYCLES)	
			1 Triumph completely worn out 2 Douglas with cracked steering heads.	
			(h) Delay in obtaining following spares from base :- Crossley Gear Box parts	
			(k) Frost casualties :- Reported to Workshops NIL.	

Major.
O.C. 3rd Cavalry Divisional M.T.Coy.

Instructions regarding War Diaries and Intelligence Summaries are contained in F. S. Regs., Part II. and the Staff Manual respectively. Title pages will be prepared in manuscript.

WAR DIARY No. 1. Sheet No. 1.

INTELLIGENCE SUMMARY.

Army Form C. 2118.

3RD CAVALRY M.T. COMPANY.

Place	Date	Hour	Summary of Events and Information	Remarks and references to Appendices

GEMBLOUX.	December 1.		Railhead NAMUR. Train due November 30th not yet arrived. No train for this day. Division fed in Brigade Dumps.
			
			  Divisional Troops — ST MARIE - WASTINES.
			  VI Brigade — DHUY.
			  VII " — INCOURT.
			  Canadian Brigade — PERWEZ.	

"	2.		Railhead NAMUR. Train due November 30th arrived 8.am. Division fed in Brigade Dumps as 1.2.1918.	
"	3.		Railhead NAMUR. Train due 1st and 2nd arrived. Division fed in Brigade Dumps. No change.	
"	4.		Railhead NAMUR. Train due December 3rd arrived. Normal.	
"	5.		Railhead NAMUR. Train due 4th inst., loaded, Normal. 20 lorries of 10th G.H.Q. detachment ordered to 2nd Cavalry Division M.T. Coy for Temporary Duty.	

3RD
CAVALRY
M.T. COMPANY.
No. 8/45/31
Date 10/1/19

Army Form C. 2118.

WAR DIARY Nº 1. Sheet No. 2.

INTELLIGENCE SUMMARY.

(Erase heading not required.)

Instructions regarding War Diaries and Intelligence Summaries are contained in F. S. Regs., Part II. and the Staff Manual respectively. Title pages will be prepared in manuscript.

Place	Date	Hour	Summary of Events and Information	Remarks and references to Appendices
GEMBLOUX.	December. 6.		Railhead NAMUR. Train due 5th inst, arrived, Normal.	
"	7.		Railhead NAMUR. Train for 6th and for this day arrived. Loaded.	
"	8.		Railhead NAMUR. Position normal.	
"	9.		Railhead NAMUR. Position normal.	
"	10.		Railhead NAMUR. Position normal. VI Brigade rations dumped at WANZE North of HUY in NAMUR-LIEGE Road. 15 Lorries of 10th G.H.Q. detachment returned from duty with 2nd Cavalry Division M.T. Company.	
"	11.		Railhead NAMUR. Position normal. 5 Lorries of 10th G.H.Q. Detachment returned from 2nd Cavalry Division M.T. Company.	
"	12.		Railhead NAMUR. Position normal. VI Brigade supplies dumped at YERNWE 7th Kilometre stone on road running N.N.E. from AIUAY 6 Kilometres beyond HUY on LIEGE Road.	

Army Form C. 2118.

WAR DIARY N°1. Sheet No. 3.
or
INTELLIGENCE SUMMARY.
(Erase heading not required.)

Instructions regarding War Diaries and Intelligence Summaries are contained in F. S. Regs., Part II. and the Staff Manual respectively. Title pages will be prepared in manuscript.

3RD CAVALRY M.T. COMPANY
No. S/4.S/31
Date 10/1/19

Place	Date	Hour	Summary of Events and Information	Remarks and references to Appendices
GEMBLOUX.	December. 13.		Railhead NAMUR. Normal. Railhead moves from NAMUR to HUY. Refilling lorries parked for night at HUY for loading 14th.	
"	14.		Railhead HUY. Position normal. Railhead moves from HUY to SERAING. Lieut. WYATT and 9 lorries proceeded on duty to PARIS.	
SERAING.	15.		Railhead SERAING. Division re-filled at following dumps. VI Brigade — WARFUSEE. VII " — EHEIN. Canadian Brigade — EHEIN. Divisional Troops. — TINLOT.	
"	16.		Railhead SERAING. No train. 1 lorry proceeded to LILLE on duty.	
"	17.		Railhead SERAING. Train due 16th loaded and train due this day. 34 lorries proceeded to LILLE Concentration Camp to convey re-inforcements for the Division.	
"	18.		Railhead SERAING. Position normal. 2 lorries proceeded to LILLE re-inforcement Camp.	

Army Form C. 2118.

3RD CAVALRY M.T. COMPANY.
No. 81/M.S./31
No. 1/1/19

WAR DIARY No 1. Sheet No. 4.
or
INTELLIGENCE SUMMARY.
(Erase heading not required.)

Instructions regarding War Diaries and Intelligence Summaries are contained in F. S. Regs., Part II. and the Staff Manual respectively. Title pages will be prepared in manuscript.

Place	Date	Hour	Summary of Events and Information	Remarks and references to Appendices
SERAING.	December. 19.		Railhead SERAING. Normal. Railhead moves from SERAING to ENGIS.	
ENGIS.	20.		Railhead ENGIS. Normal. Column moves from SERAING to ENGIS. 20 Lorries Specially detailed to HUY to off load Casualty Clearing Station. Casualty Clearing Station did not arrive.	
"	21.		Railhead ENGIS. Normal.	
"	22.		Railhead ENGIS. 20 Lorries sent to HUY to clear Casualty Clearing Station train.	
"	23.		Railhead ENGIS. Normal.	
"	24.		Railhead ENGIS. Position normal. Double delivery of rations made on this day.	
"	25.		Railhead ENGIS. Position normal.	

3RD CAVALRY
M.T. COMPANY.

No. S/AS/31
Date 10/1/16

WAR DIARY N°1.

INTELLIGENCE SUMMARY.

Army Form C. 2118.
Sheet No. 5.

(Erase heading not required.)

Instructions regarding War Diaries and Intelligence Summaries are contained in F. S. Regs., Part II and the Staff Manual respectively. Title pages will be prepared in manuscript.

Place	Date	Hour	Summary of Events and Information	Remarks and references to Appendices
ENGIS.	December. 26.		Railhead ENGIS. Lorries attached from 10th G.H.Q. left the Column, their tour of duty having finished.	
"	27.		Railhead ENGIS. Position normal.	
"	28.		Railhead ENGIS. Position normal.	
"	29.		Railhead ENGIS. Position normal.	
"	30.		Railhead ENGIS. Position normal.	
"	31.		Railhead ENGIS. Position normal.	

WAR DIARY N°1

INTELLIGENCE SUMMARY.

Sheet No. 6.

3rd CAVALRY
M.T. COMPANY
No. 9/4.S/31
Date 10/1/19

Army Form C. 2118.

WORKSHOP REPORT FOR DECEMBER 1918.

(a) THOROUGH OVERHAULS.

    Lorries.   9.
    Cars.   8.
    Ambulances (motor) 2.
    Motor cycles.   16.

(b) GENERAL CONDITION ON DISMANTLING.

Big ends of Albion engines very slack. Oil in many cases too thick and does not seem to have circulated quickly enough after starting engine.
Sunbeam crankshafts badly scored.
Sleeves on 20 H.P. Daimler cars cracked, rapid wear in their gear boxes.

(c) LARGE DEMANDS FOR SPARES.

    NIL.

(d) Artificers have worked very long hours under very exposed conditions. Xmas and New Year's day as whole holidays.

(e) Vehicles sent in rather more regularly than preceeding month, for fortnightly inspection.

(f) ALTERATIONS IN ESTABLISHMENT.

New G.1098 for December only just to hand. Not yet checked.

WAR DIARY N° 1.

or INTELLIGENCE SUMMARY

Army Form C. 2118.

3RD CAVALRY M.T. COMPANY

Sheet No. 7.

No. 8145/31
Date 10/1/19

Summary of Events and Information

WORKSHOP REPORT FOR DECEMBER 1918 (contd)

(g) W.D. NOS. OF VEHICLES EVACUATED.

    Ford open car No. M.54572.   To 3rd Heavy Repair Shop for general overhaul.

    2 Douglas Motor cycles.   To 2nd Heavy Repair Shop for general overhaul.

    3 Triumph Motor cycles.   To 2nd Heavy Repair Shop for general overhaul. (Triumphs all with fractured frames)

(h) DELAY IN OBTAINING SPARES FROM A.M.T.D.

    Great delay in transit. Spares with issue vouchers dated 31st November, not yet to hand.

(k) FROST CASUALTIES.

    NIL.

WAR DIARY
or
INTELLIGENCE SUMMARY

(Erase heading not required.)

Army Form C. 2118.

Sheet No. 8.

Place	Date	Hour	Summary of Events and Information	Remarks and references to Appendices
			During the whole of the period the Company has been working under extreme difficulties owing to the serious dis-organization of the railways.	
			The Supply Trains being greatly overdue, in some cases the delay amounted to days.	
			A great shortage of personnel has also had to be met owing to leave details returning late due to the general transport dis-organization.	
			Generally the extraneous detail during the month has been abnormal.	
			------*****------	
			O.C. 3rd Cavalry Divisional M.T. Coy.	

Instructions regarding War Diaries and Intelligence Summaries are contained in F.S. Regs., Part II and the Staff Manual respectively. Title pages will be prepared in manuscript.

Sheet No. 1.

Army Form C. 2118.

WAR DIARY No. 2.
or
INTELLIGENCE SUMMARY.
(Erase heading not required.)

Instructions regarding War Diaries and Intelligence Summaries are contained in F. S. Regs., Part II. and the Staff Manual respectively. Title pages will be prepared in manuscript.

Place	Date	Hour	Summary of Events and Information	Remarks and references to Appendices

ENGIS.	January. 1.		Railhead ENGIS.
			VI Brigade fed by Narrow Guage railway direct from Railhead.
			Canadian Brigade fed partly by Horse Transport and partly by Mechanical Transport.
			VII Brigade and Divisional Troops fed by Mechanical Transport.
			
			Dumps as follows:-
			
			    Divisional Troops. TINLOT.
			    3rd Field Squadron. TILLEUR.
			    Canadian Brigade VIERSET-BARSE.
			    Fort Garry Horse St. SEVERIN.
			    L.S.H. HODY.
			    Canadian Machine Gun. EHAIN.
			    Headquarters. CLERMONT.
			    "A" Battery. OMBERT RANCA.) Horse
			    "B" HUY.) Transport.
			    R.C.H.A. Headquarters. "
			    Ammunition Column. :
			    Cavalry Field Ambulance.
			
			    VII Brigade Headquarters. XHOS.
			    7th Dragoon Guards. SENY.
			    17th Lancers. OUFFET.
			    Inniskillings. DURBUY.
			    "K" Battery. TOHOGNE.
			    7th Machine Gun Squadron. MEAN.
			    7th Cavalry Field Ambulance. VERVOX.	

Sheet No. 2.

Army Form C. 2118.

WAR DIARY No. 2.
or
INTELLIGENCE SUMMARY.
(Erase heading not required.)

Instructions regarding War Diaries and Intelligence Summaries are contained in F. S. Regs., Part II. and the Staff Manual respectively. Title pages will be prepared in manuscript.

2ND CAVALRY M.G. COMPANY.

Place	Date	Hour	Summary of Events and Information	Remarks and references to Appendices
ENGIS.	January 2/18.		Railhead ENGIS. Normal.	
"	January 19.		Railhead ENGIS. Position Normal. Major P.L. SPAFFORD returns from leave and assumes command.	
"	January 20/31.		Railhead ENGIS. Position Normal.	

Army Form C. 2118.

WAR DIARY No. 2.
or
INTELLIGENCE SUMMARY.
(Erase heading not required.)

Sheet. No. 3.

3RD CAVALRY M.T. COMPANY

Place	Date	Hour	Summary of Events and Information	Remarks and references to Appendices
ENGIS.			Owing to shortage of personnel, there was only one driver per lorry, and very few men for Railhead and Company duties. Lorries have suffered in consequence. Demobilization, Salvage, Courses of Instruction in Driving and Artificers Courses for N.C.Os and men of the Division, Collection and distribution of Daily Papers have made the personnel question even more difficult, so it was necessary to almost stop leave towards the end of the month.	
			The under mentioned Officer Casualties occurred:-	
			Lieut. A.V. Campbell. Demobilized.	
			2/Lieut. F.N. Van-der-Pant. "	
			Captain. D. Pocock. Evacuated Sick.	
			Lieut. F.R. Hodgson. "	
			The following numbers have been demobilized:-	
			Officers. O.Rs.	
			2 17	
			MILEAGE & PETROL RETURN FOR JANY. 1919.	
			Miles loaded 53,693 Miles empty 29,021 Petrol Consumption 14,452	

Army Form C. 2118.

Sheet. No. 5.

WAR DIARY No. 2.
or
INTELLIGENCE SUMMARY.

(Erase heading not required.)

[Stamp: 3RD CAVALRY M.T. COMPANY]

Place	Date	Hour	Summary of Events and Information	Remarks and references to Appendices
ENG13.			WORKSHOP REPORT FOR JANUARY 1919.	
			(a) THOROUGH OVERHAULS.	
			Lorries — 11.	
			Cars. — 4.	
			Ambulances — 3.	
			Motor cycles — 12.	
			(b) GENERAL CONDITION ON DISMANTLING.	
			Nothing abnormal to note.	
			(c) LARGE DEMANDS FOR SPARES.	
			N I L.	
			(d) Artificers working under very exposed conditions.	
			(e) Vehicles are reporting regularly for inspection, but the cars are apt to come in on wrong dates	
			(f) ALTERATIONS IN ESTABLISHMENT.	
			New G.1098. not yet to hand.	
			(g)	

Instructions regarding War Diaries and Intelligence Summaries are contained in F. S. Regs., Part II. and the Staff Manual respectively. Title pages will be prepared in manuscript.

(19375) Wt W2358/P1562 600,000 12/7. J.D. & L. Sch 52a. Forms/C2118/15

Army Form C. 2118.

WAR DIARY
or
INTELLIGENCE SUMMARY.

(Erase heading not required.)

Summary of Events and Information

Sheet. No. 4.

Place	Date	Hour	Summary of Events and Information	Remarks and references to Appendices
ENG.13.			WORKSHOP REPORT FOR JANUARY 1919.	
			(g) W.D. NUMBERS OF VEHICLES EVACUATED.	
			LORRIES. CARS. AMBULANCES. M/CYCLES.	
			Frame Nos.	
			6899.) 15373. A. 144268. 276267.	
			3rd Fld. Sqdn.) 1872. 281922.	
			20056.) 144268. 6675.	
			No.5.Telegraph Co. R.E.) No.5. Telegraph Co.)	
			7234.	
			7206.	
			7321.	
			REPLACEMENTS.	
			January.	
			LORRIES. CARS. M/CYCLES.	
			Frame Nos.	
			61442. M. 53594. 39356.	
			61432. M. 63249.)	
			52482. No.5. Telegraph Co.)	
			(h) Great delay in obtaining spares from A.M.T.D. on account of the bad working of the Railways. This is becoming a very serious matter.	
			(j) FROST CASUALTIES.	
			N I L .	

F. T. Spafford.
Major,
O.C. 3rd Cavalry Divisional M. T. Coy.

SHEET 1.

Army Form C. 2118.

WAR DIARY
or
INTELLIGENCE SUMMARY.

(Erase heading not required.)

3RD CAVALRY M.T. COMPANY

Vol 12

Instructions regarding War Diaries and Intelligence Summaries are contained in F. S. Regs., Part II. and the Staff Manual respectively. Title pages will be prepared in manuscript.

Place	Date	Hour	Summary of Events and Information	Remarks and references to Appendices
ENGIS	Feburary		RAILHEAD ENGIS.	
			The position was normal through the month.	
			The Division was fed in the following Areas.	
			VII. Brigade XHOS	
			Canadian Brigade EHEIN	
			Divisional Troops TINLOT	
			VI. Brigade WARFUSEE.	
			The following numbers have been Demobilized.	
			Officers. 1.	
			Other Ranks.	
			M.T. 18.)	
			Artificers. 3.) 28.	
			Supply. 7.)	
			MILEAGE & PETROL RETURN FOR FEB. 1919.	
			Miles loaded, 30,073. Miles empty 29,423. Petrol consumption 12,166.	

SHEET 2.

Army Form C. 2118.

WAR DIARY
or
INTELLIGENCE SUMMARY.
(*Erase heading not required.*)

3RD CAVALRY M.T. COMPANY.

Place	Date	Hour	Summary of Events and Information	Remarks and references to Appendices
ENGIS	FEBRUARY		**WORKSHOPS REPORT FOR FEBRUARY**	
			(A) General Overhauls	
			Lorries 5.	
			Cars 3.	
			Ambulances 2.	
			Motor Cycles 15.	
			Minor Repairs.	
			To all types of vehicles on charge 30. or maintenance	
			(B) General condition on dismantling nothing abnormal to note.	
			(C) Large demands for spares -Nil-	
			(D) Artificers working hours - Normal Conditions under which working and exposed position of workshops have somewhat restricted output of work during the month.	
			(E) Vehicles are reporting regularly for inspection with the exception of Divisional Cars which continue to report on the wrong dates.	
			(F) Alterations in Establishment. -Nil-	
			(G) W.L. Nos. of Vehicles evacuated	
			DAIMLER C.C. 6916 - 30 cwt. lorry	
			Motor cycles 11.	
			All the above were sent to Heavy Repair Shops for Complete Overhaul	O.C. 3rd Cavalry Divisional M.T. Coy.

SHEET 3

Army Form C. 2118.

3RD CAVALRY M.T. COMPANY.

WAR DIARY or INTELLIGENCE SUMMARY.
(Erase heading not required.)

Place	Date	Hour	Summary of Events and Information	Remarks and references to Appendices
ENGTS	FEBRUARY		WORKSHOPS REPORT FOR FEBRUARY (Cont.)	
			(H) Considerable delay is still expirienced in the receipt of Stores from A.M.T.D. - due principally to railway congestion	
			(J) FROST CASUALTIES	
			Only one serious casualty occurred - namely the bursting of the Water jacket of an Albion Lorry Cylinders.	
			Court of Enquiry held and Driver in fault and ordered to pay part cost.	
			A large number of Albion Radiators were also dealt with for burst tubes. This can only be attributed to the small bore of the tubes of the Albion Radiator	
			The top and bottom ends of these tubes become furred up and it is then not possible to completely drain the Radiator	

A.L. Grafton
Major,
O.C. 3rd Cavalry Divisional M.T. Coy.

Army Form C. 2118.

Sheet 1

WAR DIARY 5.
INTELLIGENCE—SUMMARY.
(Erase heading not required.)

Place	Date	Hour	Summary of Events and Information	Remarks and references to Appendices
ENGIS	MARCH		RAILHEAD ENGIS	
			The position was normal throughout the month.	
			The Division was fed in the following Areas:-	
			VII. Brigade. XHOS	
			Canadian Brigade EHEIN	
			Divisional Troops TINLOT	
			VI. Brigade WARFUSSE	
			A detachment of 2 Officers, 41 O.Rs, 26 Lorries and 2 M/Cycles proceeded to ANDENNE to feed the Canadian Bde. from 2/3/19 to 13/3/19	
			The following numbers have been Demobilized during the Month of March	
			Officers M.T. 1	
			" Supply 1	
			O.Rs M.T. Drivers 24	
			O.Rs M.T. Artificers 5	
			O.Rs Supply 13	
			O.Rs Supply Attached 1	
			O.Rs 773 Employ. Coy. 5	
			TOTAL 50	

Army Form C. 2118

WAR DIARY

INTELLIGENCE SUMMARY.

(Erase heading not required.)

SHEET 2.

3rd C.V. DVL. M.T. Coy.

Place	Date	Hour	Summary of Events and Information	Remarks and references to Appendices
ENGTS	MARCH		WORKSHOPS REPORT FOR MARCH	
			(A) General Overhauls	
			Lorries 6	
			Cars 2	
			Ambulances Nil	
			Motor Cycles 10	
			(B) General condition on dismantling	
			We have had several Albion lorries in Workshops with Big Ends run out, No. 4 Cylinder always being the faulty one	
			(C) Large demand for spares Nil.	
			(D) Artificers are working full hours under better weather conditions than previously.	
			(E) Vechicles are reporting regularly for inspection, Divisional Cars being erratic.	
			(F) Alteration in establishment	
			7 Fitters have been sent to 1st Cav. Div. M.T. Company and have been replaced by 7 Fitters from that Unit.	
			(G) Vechicles evacuated during March	
			M. 53557 Ford Open Car	
			M. 1584 Daimler Closed Car.	
			57169 Albion 3 Ton Lorry	
			2180 Daimler C.C. 30 cwt. Lorry	
			13024 "	

Instructions regarding War Diaries and Intelligence Summaries are contained in F. S. Regs., Part II. and the Staff Manual respectively. Title pages will be prepared in manuscript.

Army Form C. 2118

WAR DIARY
or
INTELLIGENCE SUMMARY

(Erase heading not required.)

SHEET 5.

Instructions regarding War Diaries and Intelligence Summaries are contained in F. S. Regs., Part II. and the Staff Manual respectively. Title pages will be prepared in manuscript.

Place	Date	Hour	Summary of Events and Information	Remarks and references to Appendices
ENGIS	MARCH		Workshop report for March (continued)	
			(G) Continued.	
			M. 55446 Crossley Box Car All to No. 8. Vechicle Reception Park ATH. on 20/3/19 for General Overhaul.	
			Motor Cycles Nil.	
			(H) The bad working of Railways make for delay in obtaining spares from A.M.T.D.	
			(J) Frost casualties Nil.	

H.B.Davis L.

O.C. 3rd CAVALRY M.T. Co.

3rd Cavalry Divl. M.T. Coy.

War Diary of your Unit is not required by me,
and is returned herewith.

This should be dealt with as heretofore.

[signature]
A.D.S.T., No. 4 Area.

15. 5. 1919.

H.

2.

D.A.G.,
No. 7 Sub. Section, (Records)
Wimereux.

Passed to you for disposal, please.

[signature] Wyatt Lt for Capt
O.C. 3rd Cavalry Divisional M.T. Coy.

Spa 18.5.19.

D.D.S.T.
No 4 Area.

Herewith War Diary
No.6 for this Coy for last month.
Please acknowledge.

C. Williams Capt
O.C. 3RD CAVALRY M.T. Co.

Army Form C. 2118.

WAR DIARY No. 6.

~~INTELLIGENCE~~ SUMMARY

(Erase heading not required.)

Sheet = 1.

3RD CAVALRY M.T. COMPANY

Place	Date	Hour	Summary of Events and Information	Remarks and references to Appendices
APRIL 1919. ENGIS			RAILHEAD = ENGIS The position being normal throughout the month. Cadre's Brigades were fed in the ENGIS AREA. During April 1919 the following exchange of vehicles was effected between this Unit and 1st Cavalry Division M.T.Co. 1st Cav. Div.M.T.Coy. 57173, 57171, 57167, 57165, 57170, 57161, 52005, 57159, 57164, 57158, 57162, 57166, 57151, 57157, 57143, 57142, 57146, 57153, 57150, 57149, 57148, 57145, 57147, 57152, 51299, 52010, 52333, 51997, 52201, 40007, 52505, 52209, 51996, 52911, 51724, 52218, 52482, 52508, 60119, 57155, 41427, 41425, 52411, 52004, 52007, 52518, 60163, 60141, 52217, 57244, 52409, 52489, 60128, 41424, 57144, 52219, 60396, 52516, 52408, 50001, 32002, 52009, 52008, 50234, 57156, 52003, 60137, 52407, 52406, 57154, 52410, 51998. These were replaced from 1st Cavalry Div.M.T.Co. by :- Halford 3 ton lorries:- 10591, 20330, 21254, 21529, 27193, 26385, 28250, 28252, 32878, 33739, 33744, 33750, 32861, 23196, 26439, 32860, 28251, 21528, 21253, Daimler 3 ton lorries :- 2735, 3195, 3193, 4160, 2830, 2712, 7680, 6956, 5680, 11824, L.G.O.C. 30 cwt. lorries :- 2635, Continued.	O.C. 3RD CAVALRY M.T. CO.

Army Form C. 2118.

WAR DIARY No. 6.
~~INTELLIGENCE SUMMARY~~

Sheet = 3.

3RD CAVALRY M.T. COMPANY.

(Erase heading not required.)

Instructions regarding War Diaries and Intelligence Summaries are contained in F. S. Regs. Part II. and the Staff Manual respectively. Title pages will be prepared in manuscript.

Place	Date	Hour	Summary of Events and Information	Remarks and references to Appendices
ENGIS	2/4/19		2/Lieut. W.L. DuPreez, R.A.S.C. left with 19 O.Rs. and 16 lorries for Pepinster to assist in rationing Units of 2nd Cav.Div.M.T.Coy. ~~withdrawn~~ owing to the withdrawal of 2nd Cavalry Div.M.T.Co.	
	4.4.19		19 M.T.drivers 2 Supply Details and 43 lorries were despatched to the 1st Cav.M.T.Co. and 12 M.T.Drivers and 12 lorries received from the 1st Cav.M. T.Co. These are further exchanges under the exchange scheme.	
	7/4/19		A further batch of 31 lorries arrived from the 1st Cav.M.T.Co. 12 M.T. drivers, and 1 Supply Detail.	
	9/4/19		Captain H.C. WILLIAMS, R.A.S.C. joined from 21st Div.M.T.Co. and assumes Command of the Company. Lieut. H.B. DAVIS, R.A.S.C. relinquishes the Command of Company and assumes duty as Transport Officer.	
	12/4/19		Under authority of QMG 4440 QP/23C/2264g/1296 4.19. 2/Lieut. E. Dawson, R.A.S.C. is struck off the strength as from 6.4.19 A further detachment of 45 O.Rs. with 33 lorries and 1 M/Cycle with 2/Lt. W.L. DuPreez i/c and left for Pepinster and are attached to Cav.Corps H.Q. for salvage and general duties.	

Army Form C. 2118.

WAR DIARY No. 6.

Sheet = 2.

INTELLIGENCE SUMMARY.

3RD CAVALRY M.T. COMPANY.

Place	Date	Hour	Summary of Events and Information	Remarks and references to Appendices
ENGIS			Pierce Arrow 3 ton lorries :-	
			12151, 42619, 42621, 42625, 42627, 42628, 42652, 42656, 42653, 57311, 57317, 57320, 57323, 57319.	
			Daimler 30 cwt. lorries :-	
			10522, 8806, 10504, 10501, 10533, 6306, 20745, 10348, 10529, 10362, 10350, 10326, 10325, 10360, 5165, 10508, 3357, 10345, 6003, 10309, 5182, 5822, 2852, 10370, 10337, 10507, 6304, 10509.	
			The Company Car Wolseley No.M.1180 was exchanged for Vauxhall Car M.25824	
			No lorries or cars were evacuated to Heavy Repair Shops during this month.	
			Cycles evacuated = NIL.	
			Detachment at Pepinster increased by 45 O.Rs., 33 lorries and one M/Cycle for the purpose of feeding Units of the 2nd Cav.Div. Arrival of 30 O.Rs. M.T. Drivers, 1915 class, from No.1 Water Tank M.T.Co. and 20 M.T.Drivers from 75 Aux. Petrol Co. 1915 class, to relive the same number of 1914 class men for demobilization. 50 N.C.O.s. and men 1914 class left for dispersal to Cav.Corps Con. Camp. Stelles on 23rd instant.	
SPA.	30/4/19		Hd.Qrs. M.T.Co, plus Workshops and remainder of Section moved to SPA, Cadre Bde. fed by detachment left at ENGIS, from the R.S.O. Detail Stores.	
			The following number having been demobilized during month of April :- Officers = NIL. M.T.Drivers = 58. Artificers = 3. Supply = NIL. 34 M.T. Drivers, 9 Artificers & 6 Supply details arrived from 1st Cav.M.T. CO. with 30 lorries, this was the 1st draft of the exchange of the demob- ilizable and retainable men, between the two Companies.	Continued.

Army Form C. 2118.

Sheet 2.

WAR DIARY
or
INTELLIGENCE SUMMARY.
No. 7.

(Erase heading not required.)

Instructions regarding War Diaries and Intelligence Summaries are contained in F. S. Regs., Part II. and the Staff Manual respectively. Title pages will be prepared in manuscript.

Place	Date	Hour	Summary of Events and Information	Remarks and references to Appendices
MAY	1919			
	29/5/19.		~~Foden Disinfector~~ Transferred to 4th. Army Troops M.T. Coy	
	29/5/19		2 Foden Disinfector 3 .37 Transferred to 4th. Army Troops M.T. Coy	
	31/5/19		16 3 Ton Lorries sent to HUY Liege Sub-Area for temporary duty.	
			Evacuations during month. Albion Lorry 4235 to 22nd Vehicle Reception Park CALAIS.	
			Cars. NIL.	
			TRIUMPH Motor Cycles 2.	
			Transfer	
			T2/Lieut. R. Coilis. Proceeded on one months leave to U.K. on 12th inst	
			Instructions for move of u/m Officers were received.	
			T2/Lieut. W.L. DuPreez. to No.5 G.H.Q. Res. M.T. Coy. No.3 Area.	
			T2/Lieut. R. Coilis. to No. 6. G.H.Q. Res M.T. Coy. L.of C.	
			Lieut. W.L. Baird. to No.20 G.H.Q. Res. M.T. Coy. THEUX.	
			Auth. QP/A30/23104 d/22/5/19	
			T2/Lieut. J.P. Jones to Base Supply Depot. CALAIS.	
			Auth. QP/A30/23062 d/27/5/19.	
			T/Lieut. S.E. Bold.(Q.W.) Form 13th .G.H.Q. Res. M.T. Coy.	
			T/Lieut. J.D. Hanan. From 66th. Div. Train.	

WAR DIARY No. 7.
or
INTELLIGENCE SUMMARY.

(Erase heading not required.)

Army Form C. 2118

Sheet. 1.

3RD CAVALRY M.T. COMPANY.

Place	Date	Hour	Summary of Events and Information	Remarks and references to Appendices
MAY	1919		RAILHEAD PEPINSTER LOCATION SPA. DEMOBILIZATION FOR MAY. Officers.............2 M.T. Drivers........90 Artificers..........7 Supply Details......18 R.H.A...............1 On the 19th inst. 11 Belgian Artificers were engaged for work from VERVIERS, rate of pay Frs.1-75 per hour for fitters and Frs.2-00 per hour for foremen. Auth. No. 74 civilian Labour Bureau. Letter A/113 d/15/5/19. 20/5/19. Packard Workshop Lorry No. 10400 and Packard Store Lorry 10525 Transferred to 4th. Army Troops M.T. Coy. on withdrawal of all Lorries of that make from service. 21/5/19. Albion Lorries Nos. 40070 57172 58220 60131 39742 52488 57168 60139 52221 Transferred to 4th. Army Troops M.T. Coy. in exchange for 9 Lorries of a non standard type. 23/5/19. Instructions received from Luxemburg Sub-Area. C. to move Unit to WAVRE. Brabant Sub-Area. 24/5/19. Move to Brabant Sub-Area. Cancelled, owing to orders being received for the Unit to be broken up. 24/5/19. All Lorries on detachment, with the exception of 3 with British Armistice Commission Spa. and 1 with 2nd. Kings Own. MALMEDY rejoined 28/5/19 Albion Lorries Nos. 57163 33645 39717 51727 39736 37219 57241 60129 34605 34080 Transferred to 4th. Army Troops M.T. Coy. in exchange for 10 Lorries of a non standard type.	

Army Form C. 2118.

No. 38. **No 3. Cav D M T Coy**

WAR DIARY
or
INTELLIGENCE SUMMARY.

(Erase heading not required.)

Sheet 1.

Instructions regarding War Diaries and Intelligence Summaries are contained in F. S. Regs., Part II. and the Staff Manual respectively. Title pages will be prepared in manuscript.

Place	Date	Hour	Summary of Events and Information	Remarks and references to Appendices
JUNE.	1919			

JUNE.

June 1st.
Location. SPA.
Railhead. PEPINSTER.

Unit awaiting Orders for move to No. 23 V.R.P. ABBEVILLE for breaking up.

June 3rd.
Lieut. a/Capt. H.C.Williams. R.A.S.C Granted O.B.E. Auth. London Gazette 3/6/19

June 4th.
Lieut. W.L. Biard. R.S.C. Transferred to 20th. G.H.Q. Res. M.T. Coy.
w/Lieut. J.P. Jones, " On leave to U.K. 4/6/19 to 18/6/19.

June 5th.
Company ordered to move to 23rd. V.R.P. ABBEVILLE. Move to start by 7th. inst. 25 O.Rs. Received from 4th. Army Troops M.T. Coy. to assist in taking Lorries to Base. 40 Lorries off the road for lack of personnel

June 7th.
Move from SPA to ENGIS

June 8th.
Move from ENGIS to CHARLEROI. Hallford W.D. 2825 broken down at HUY. Wired to No.4 Area to collect and evacuate as it was not possible to tow Lorry.

June 9th.
Moved from CHARLEROI to BAVAI 30cwt. Daimler Lorry broke front axle at BINGE. Handed Lorry over to No.4. V.R.P. at MORS [MONS] for evacuation on 10th inst. W.D.10508

June 10th.
Move from BAVAI to CAMBRAI.

June 11th.
Move from CAMBRAI to ALBERT.

June 12th.
Move from ALBERT to AMIENS.

June 13th.
Reported to O.C. 23rd. V.R.P. who ordered the Column to Park at St. RIQUIER. Sir J.C.&S. Move from AMIENS to St. RIQUIER.

3rd CAV. DIVL. M.T. COY.

Army Form C. 2118.

WAR DIARY No. 8.

Sheet 2.

or

INTELLIGENCE SUMMARY.

(*Erase heading not required.*)

Instructions regarding War Diaries and Intelligence Summaries are contained in F. S. Regs., Part II. and the Staff Manual respectively. Title pages will be prepared in manuscript.

Place	Date	Hour	Summary of Events and Information	Remarks and references to Appendices
JUNE	1919			
			June 15th. Break up of Unit temporally cancelled by D. of T. Instructions however were received to carry on with all preparations for breaking up.	
			June 16th. Classification of Units Vehicles begun By D. of T. Inspector	
			June 19th. T2/Lieut. R. Collis. R.A.S.C. Transferred to 6th. G.H.Q. M.T. Coy. T/Lieut. J.D. Hannan " Reported for duty from 66th Div. Train. Cadre.	
			June 27th. Commenced sending in vehicles to 23rd V.R.P.	
			June 30th. All vehicles and personnel transferred to 23rd V.R.P. UNIT BROKEN UP.	

3rd CAN. DIVL. M.T. COY.